Rockville Rips, Charles River,
Central Coastal Watersheds
Photo: Philip Preston

AMC RIVER GUIDE
Central/Southern New England
Volume 2

Appalachian Mountain Club

Comments and corrections should be addressed to:

AMC River Guide Committee
5 Joy Street
Boston, MA 02108

AMC New England Canoeing Guide

> *First Edition* 1965
> *Second Edition* 1968
> *Third Edition* 1971

AMC River Guide,

Volume I, Northeastern New England, 1976
Volume II, Central/Southern New England, 1978

> *Copyright* 1978
> Appalachian Mountain Club

cover photo: **Philip Preston**

> Pemigewasset River near Bristol
> (Merrimack Watershed) at 500 cfs.

> *The* **AMC River Guide** *was designed by*
> Intramedia, Boston, Massachusetts.

Publisher's Preface
AMC RIVER GUIDE Volume 2

The Appalachian Mountain Club — what does America's oldest mountaineering club have to do with river running?

The Club's 2,400 or more avid canoeists would resent that question, and would point out that the AMC's name is not nearly broad enough to cover the scope of its present day activities.

In the first place, take "Appalachian." In 1876 Edward Pickering, the Club's first president, glossed this first word of its name as follows: "By Appalachian . . . we should include everything east of the Mississippi, while by 'adjacent regions' some insist that the Himalayas and even the lunar mountains should be included." The Club's purview now extends far beyond the eastern United States, and its voice is heard nationally and even internationally — though it has yet to sponsor an expedition to the moon!

Nor is the AMC solely a mountain club these days, even though its original charter called its prime purpose the exploration of the mountains of New England and adjacent regions. Today Club activities have shifted from exploration and scientific measurement to outdoor recreation, management and conservation. Canoeing and kayaking, the sports pertinent to this guidebook, are an important part of the wide spectrum of outdoor activities Club members engage in.

With over 22,000 members, it would be hard to claim that the AMC was not a "club." It is, in fact, the largest hiking club in the country, with its members totaling almost half the hikers who belong to trail organizations. However, the conventional notion of a club is too narrow to define the AMC.

A case in point is this book. It was produced by a committee of canoeing enthusiasts chaired by Philip Preston. Preston personally checked almost 500 miles of river in the three years prior to publication. This kind of dedication and involvement, rarely associated with unpaid volunteers, is the common currency of the AMC. It allows an organization with a very small full-time staff to accomplish things far beyond the scope of groups with quiescent memberships. All in all, it is a place where old-fashioned words such as "leadership" and "service" do not sound out of place.

So, the Appalachian Mountain Club, its avid canoeists, its River Guide Committee, its staff and volunteers are justified in wishing you "whitewater" and good boating.

Arlyn S. Powell, Jr.
Director of Publications

Preface

The first guidebook on New England rivers, **Quickwater and Smooth** by John C. Phillips and Thomas D. Cabot, was published in 1935, but it went out-of-print and it was unavailable for many years. In 1965, the Appalachian Mountain Club published its **New England Canoeing Guide**, a book which evolved, with many additions and corrections, from the one by Phillips and Cabot. There were subsequent editions in 1968 and 1971.

The two-volume **AMC River Guide** is, in fact, an updated edition of the AMC's earlier guidebook. The name has been changed because lake and tidewater descriptions have been largely eliminated. Travel on lakes and oceans are enjoyable pastimes in their own right, but in both cases maps are more helpful than paragraphs, and so the scope of these books has been confined to rivers, with only brief comments on the lakes through which they flow. A very limited number of salt-water rivers has been included, and for these, tidetables are recommended.

Paddling, like hiking, has achieved a popularity that threatens the environment which the sport utilizes. There are no new rivers, just as there are no new mountains. The impact that paddlers have on river areas, while relatively small, can be reduced by the dispersion of boaters. For this reason, the *AMC River Guide* attempts to be comprehensive and to supply the curious paddler with enough information to safely approach unfamiliar rivers. Other books give greater detail on the most popular runs — the *AMC River Guide* prepares you for a trip on almost any river in New England.

The compiling and updating of material for this guidebook was a considerable task. This volume embodies the work of the following contributors and committee members:

James B. Adelson	Northern Vermont Canoe
Frank Bowles	Cruisers
Jeffrey Davis	Roioli F. Schweiker
Stephen W. Hitchcock	Roy R. Schweiker
Anton T. Moehrke	David P. Sinish

Rivers have always been a symbol of change, and some of the descriptions may no longer be accurate by the time this book is published. When you go boating, take a few minutes to check the descriptions. Then send us your comments, for you are both the input and the benefactor of a useful guidebook.

Philip Preston
Editor
April, 1978

"I beg your pardon," said the Mole . . . *"but all this is so new to me. So — this — is — a — River!"*

"The River," corrected the [Water] Rat.

"And you really live by the river? What a jolly life!"

"By it and with it and on it and in it," said the Rat. *"It's brother and sister to me, and aunts, and company, and food and drink . . . It's my world, and I don't want any other. What it hasn't got is not worth having, and what it doesn't know is not worth knowing. Lord! the times we've had together! Whether in winter or summer, spring or autumn, it's always got its fun and its excitements."*

Kenneth Grahame, **The Wind in the Willows**

CENTRAL/SOUTHERN
NEW ENGLAND WATERSHEDS

Vol. I

MEMPHREMAGOG

CHAMPLAIN

UPPER CONNECTICUT

SACO

CENTRAL COASTAL

MERRIMACK

PISCATAQUA

CENTRAL COASTAL

HUDSON

LOWER CONNECTICUT

CENTRAL COASTAL

THAMES

SOUTHEASTERN

HOUSATONIC

SOUTH COASTAL

SOUTH COASTAL

Contents

Introduction 12
Chapter 1   Memphremagog Watershed 31
Chapter 2   Champlain Watershed 37
Chapter 3   Hudson Watershed 67
Chapter 4   Upper Connecticut Watershed . . 73
Chapter 5   Lower Connecticut Watershed . 129
Chapter 6   Housatonic Watershed 175
Chapter 7   South Coastal Watersheds . . . 187
Chapter 8   Thames Watershed 191
Chapter 9   Southeastern Watersheds . . . 207
Chapter 10 Central Coastal Watersheds . . 231
Chapter 11 Merrimack Watershed 251
Chapter 12 Piscataqua Watershed 311
Chapter 13 Saco Watershed 331
Appendix 355
Bibliography 359
Index 360

Introduction

Guidebook Organization

The descriptions in this book are grouped by watersheds and coastal regions. Each chapter begins with a map that identifies and locates the rivers covered in the text. Within the chapter the rivers are described in alphabetical order with two exceptions: (1) chapters that are named for a large fresh-water river begin with the description of that river; (2) rivers in chapters that have the word "coastal" in the title are arranged in order from south to north or west to east.

Format for New River Descriptions

New descriptions of many rivers have been written for this book, and they appear in a format where general comments, important information, and details are treated separately. The text you are now reading is an example of the typeface used for this new material.

      General comments about the river and the country through which it flows follow the headings and subheadings. Much of this information is intended to help you select a river and decide which parts of it to run.

1978   Format for New River Descriptions
              Difficulty of the river
              Recommended water levels
              Description of the scenery
                 USGS: maps
               Portages:
             Campsites:

      The detailed write-up appears next. This is the section to which you will most often refer once you are on the river.

Format for Old River Descriptions

USGS: maps

The write-ups that have not been recently checked appear
in this typeface, one which more closely resembles that
used in the *AMC New England Canoeing Guide*. However, many descriptions have been slightly modified with
the help of suggestions and corrections received during the
past seven years.

Explanation of Terms
Date
The date in the margin refers to the year when the person
who supplied the information last ran that section of the
river. The symbol "XXXX" indicates slightly less reliable
information due to the fact that some parts of a section
have not been run recently or that dependable information
has been obtained second-hand. Italicized statements
either mention exceptions to the date or alert you to the
possibility of errors or omissions in the text.

Difficulty of the River
A river is rated by one or more of the following four terms.
If two or more are used, one of the terms may describe a
significantly larger portion of the river. When it does, it
appears in **bold type**.

Lake . . . is used only when the river in a particular section
flows through a lake, or when it is necessary to paddle
across one to the beginning of a river.

Flatwater . . . applies to the river only, not to lakes.

Quickwater . . . is fast-moving water. The surface of the
river is nearly smooth in high water, apt to be choppy in
medium water, and usually shallow in low water.

Class . . . refers to the general classification of the rapids
(I, II, III, or IV) on the river. There may be one or two more
difficult ones noted in the text.

Recommended Water Levels
These water levels represent the stages at which the river
can be navigated. The terms — subject to wide interpreta-
tion — refer to the river's yearly range and not merely to its
lesser fluctuations within a normal spring run-off. Likely
dates for these water levels are also given.

A river for which high water is recommended may be travelled in medium water, but it is likely to be scratchy with some sections that may have to be waded down.

High water . . . occurs when the river is full, with the bases of bushes and trees, especially alders and swamp maples, standing in water.

Medium water . . . occurs when the river extends up to the vegetation on the banks, but few woody plants are underwater. Marshy areas may be wet. This level is good for gradients of ten to twenty feet per mile, but less than enough for good passage on small rivers with a gradient of over twenty feet per mile.

Low water . . . is acceptable for flatwater paddling and for some rapids on large rivers.

Description of the Scenery

Wild . . . implies long sections of semi-wilderness, with no more than a few isolated camps and only occasional road access. Dirt roads may parallel the river within sight or sound, but they do so only for short distances, and they do not noticeably alter the semi-wilderness character of the trip as a whole. They may, in fact, be closed to the public or impassable altogether.

Forested . . . banks on both sides of the river appear to be densely wooded; but there are good dirt and tar roads which follow along the river or not far from it, or which frequently approach or cross it. There may be farms and houses nearby, but not many of them are visible from the river.

Rural . . . sections have farms that are visible from the river, and some fields may extend down to the water.

Towns . . . along the river are small and isolated. They are quickly passed, with their presence, other than their effect upon the quality of the water, felt for only a short distance.

Settled . . . areas contain many houses or small buildings within sight or sound of the river.

Urban . . . areas contain multi-storied buildings. The shorelines are frequently unattractive.

USGS Maps

The most practical maps to use with this book are the official highway maps for each state. They are more detailed than oil company maps.

For reference purposes, topographic maps are listed; and they are in either the 7½ minute or the 15 minute series. Titles of the latter are followed by the number "15." The name of a map is in italics if it covers only a very small portion of a route. Topographic maps may be ordered from the Branch of Distribution, Eastern Region, U.S. Geological Survey, 1200 South Eads Street, Arlington, VA 22202. They cost $1.25 apiece.

Portages

The portages listed include all unavoidable carries (such as dams and waterfalls) and difficult sections where there is usually insufficient water to make them runnable. In addition, some rapids are listed if their difficulty significantly exceeds the rating of that portion of the river. For example, on Otter Creek (Champlain Watershed) the class III ledges at South Wallingford are listed as a portage because the North Dorset — Wallingford segment is billed in the chart as being only class I. Unlisted portages include lift-overs necessitated by fallen trees and low, temporary bridges. There may also be additional carries around rapids you do not wish to run.

4½ mi L **Gilsum Gorge** (cross river is 200 yds) — ¾ mi
7½ mi e **Maplewood Dam** — 100 yds

---

a) The first portage is on the left, 4½ miles from the beginning of the section. The second carry may be made on either side.
b) The location of a portage may be followed by a special notation (cross river in 200 yds).
c) The lengths of these portages are ¾ mile and 100 yards.

Campsites

There are few established campsites for water-borne campers in the area covered by this book. The notable exceptions are on the Pawcatuck River (Southeastern Watersheds) and on the Saco River (Saco Watershed). Available information is presented in this manner:

---

4 mi L **Carolina Management Area** — state
10 mi R **Swan's Falls** — AMC $ car

---

a) All campsites listed are open to the general public.
b) An "L" or "R" indicates which side of the river.
c) Administrating organizations are noted, in these cases the state of Rhode Island and the Appalachian Mountain Club (AMC).
d) Fees are charged where the symbol "$" appears, and when a campsite is also accessible by road, the word "car" is written.

In most states and towns you are obliged to have permission to camp on private property and to have a permit to build a fire when not camped in an established campground. However, ownership is difficult to determine from the water, and it is sometimes hard to track down a local fire warden to obtain a permit.

International Scale of River Difficulty

These ratings form Part V of the American Whitewater Safety Code. If the water temperature is below 10°C or the trip is an extended one in a wilderness area, this code specifies that the river should be considered one class more difficult than normal. These two considerations, however, are not used in rating the rivers in this book.

Parts I through IV are reproduced in the Appendix.

Class I. Very Easy. Moving water with a few riffles and small waves. Few or no obstructions.

Class II. Easy. Easy rapids with waves up to three feet, and wide, clear channels that are obvious without scouting. Some maneuvering is required.

Class III. Intermediate. Rapids with high, irregular waves often capable of swamping an open canoe. Narrow passages that often require complex maneuvering. May require scouting from shore.

Difficulty Rating Chart for River Sections or Individual Rapids

Prepared By Guidebook Committee, American Whitewater Affiliation — H. J. Wilhoyte   February 12, 1956

	Factors Related Primarily To Success in Negotiating				Factors Affecting Both Success and Safety				Factors Related To Safe Rescue			
	SECONDARY FACTORS				PRIMARY FACTORS				SECONDARY FACTORS			
POINTS	Bends	Length, Ft.	Gradient, Ft./Mi.	Obstacles Rocks, Trees	Waves	Turbulence	Resting or Rescue Spots	Water Vol. Mi./Hr.	Width/Depth	Water Temp. °F	Accessibility
NONE	Few Very Gradual	Less Than 100	Less Than 5 Regular	None	Few Inches High Avoidable	None	Almost Anywhere	Less Than 3	Under 75' Under 3'	Above 65°	Road Along River
1	Many Gradual	100 - 700	5 - 15 Regular	Few Passage Almost Straight Through	Low (Up to 1') Regular Avoidable	Minor Eddies		3 - 6	Over 75' Under 3'	55° - 65°	Less Than 1 Hour By Foot or Water
2	Few Sharp-Blind Scouting Req'd	700 - 5000	15 - 40 Ledges Steep Drops	Courses Easily Recognizable	Low to Medium (Up to 3') Regular Avoidable	Medium Eddies		6 - 10	Under 75' Over 3'	45° - 55°	1 Hour to 1 Day By Foot or Water
3		5000+	40+ Steep Drops Small Falls	Maneuvering Required Course Not Easily Recognizable	Med. to Lge. (Up to 5') Mostly Regular Avoidable	Strong Eddies Cross Currents	A Good One Below Every Danger Spot	10+ or Flood	Over 75' Over 3'	Less Than 45°	Greater Than 1 Day By Foot or Water
4				Intricate Maneuvering Course Hard to Recognize	Lge.-Irreg. Avoid. or Medium to Large Unavoidable	V. Strong Eddies Strong Cross C's.					
5				Course Torturous Frequent Scouting Required	Large Irregular Unavoidable	Large Scale Eddies & Cross C's. Some Up & Down Currents					
6				Very Torturous Always Scout from Shore	V. Lg. (5'+) Irregular Unavoidable Special Equip.	V. Lge. Scale Strong Up & Down Currents	Almost None				

Total Points (From Above Chart)	Rating	Approximate Difficulty	Approximate Skill Required
0 - 7	I	Easy	Practiced Beginner
8 - 14	II	Requires Care	Intermediate
15 - 21	III	Difficult	Experienced
22 - 28	IV	Very Difficult	Highly Skilled (Several Years with Organized Group)
29 - 35	V	Exceedingly Difficult	Team of Experts
36 - 42	VI	Utmost Difficulty — Near Limit of Navigability	Team of Experts Taking Every Precaution

Class IV. Difficult. Long, difficult rapids with constricted passages that often require precise maneuvering in very turbulent waters. Scouting from shore is often necessary, and conditions make rescue difficult. Generally not possible for open canoes. Boaters in covered canoes and kayaks should be able to Eskimo roll.

Class V. Very Difficult. Extremely difficult, long, and very violent rapids with highly congested routes which nearly always must be scouted from shore. Rescue conditions are difficult and there is significant hazard to life in event of a mishap. Ability to Eskimo roll is essential for kayaks and canoes.

Class VI. Extraordinarily Difficult. Difficulties of class V carried to the extreme of navigability. Nearly impossible and very dangerous. For teams of experts only, after close study and with all precautions taken.

River Levels in New England

The water level information given in the charts of individual rivers includes approximate dates which are subject to wide variations from year to year. Some of the factors which influence water levels are discussed here.

Snow depth, temperature, rainfall, and transpiration are four seasonal factors which affect river levels. The farther south you get in New England, the less important become the first two, since snow depths are usually less and occasionally non-existent. As the snow cover disappears, so does the importance of temperature, although run-off is greater and swifter when the ground is frozen. Once the leaves are out, surface run-off decreases substantially because plants of all sizes use up so much water. The fall foliage season invariably signals a rise in water levels for the same reason. Significant rainfall in autumn is also more likely than it is in the summertime.

Terrain features must also be considered. A river flowing from steep-sided hills and mountains will quickly collect the run-off from rainfall and melting snow. On the other hand, gently rolling hills, lakes and swamps buffer the spring run-off and allow for an extended season in spite of the weather. If you can draw upon a knowledge of New England's topography, it will be as helpful to you as familiarity with its weather.

In addition, you must also take into account the nature of the river itself. If a river is flat, it does not matter too much what the weather has been like so far as canoeability is concerned. If the river is steep and full of rapids, then lots of snow, warm temperatures, and moderate rainfall may all be necessary to keep it runnable. Also, you must consider the size of the river itself. A large river will generally peak and ebb more gradually, providing a much longer season than a small stream.

Many of New England's rivers have just enough quickwater and easy rapids to make high or medium water necessary for good passage. In early March, rivers all over central and southern New England become runnable. Farther north, access to the water in early spring is hindered first by snow and later by mud. Furthermore, ice shelves along the banks are hazardous in rapids and an inconvenience elsewhere.

If you wish to run rapids in early March, Connecticut is the place. By late March the season in that state for good class II and class III rapids is fading, and you will probably be limited to some of the larger rivers. By the time May arrives, the rivers of northern New England that are fed by melting snow deposits in the high mountains are usually at optimal levels. Sometimes they are passable through Memorial Day, but there have been years when the season is over by late April.

Many of New England's rivers have gauges which have been set up by the U. S. Geological Survey. Through a network known as the "Telemark System," USGS district offices collect daily gauge readings for some of these rivers. This book contains occasional references to these gauges and to other water level indicators, but comprehensive and detailed information about their use has not been included.

River levels can vary tremendously from season to season, and unusually heavy rainfall can make any river passable at any time. If you do enough canoeing and kayaking, you will probably meet someone who will defend winter and claim that the season includes any sunny day when the temperature is near freezing.

Over a period of several years, a person who runs

a lot of rivers develops a sense of river levels. Fishermen and lobstermen acquire an instinct for the tides; those who live off the land can almost smell the weather. And so it is with river people; after a while they get to know when a river runs and when it does not.

Water Releases

With many of New England's rivers passable for only a few weeks in the spring or after an unusually heavy rainfall, releases of water from dams can provide an extended season in some localities. There are many dams on large New England Rivers, but unless there are rapids below them, as is the case with the examples given, the effects of releases from them may not be too noticeable.

The first type of release includes dams used in connection with power generation. Two dams on the Farmington River (Lower Connecticut Watershed) provide a relatively constant flow to hydroelectric dams downstream. On the Pemigewasset River (Merrimack Watershed), a dam which supplies peaking power usually provides ample water for fine class II boating on weekdays throughout the season.

The second type of release is one scheduled solely for the benefit of canoeists and kayakers. These are arranged by whitewater clubs, among them the AMC. They take place on weekends during the spring, summer, and fall, and the dates can be obtained from the AMC. The West River (Upper Connecticut Watershed), and the Westfield Rivers (Lower Connecticut Watershed) are two rivers on which there are recreational releases.

The third type of release is the annual drawdown of lakes used primarily for summer recreation. These generally take place in the middle of the fall and greatly augment the natural flow for that time of the year. It often takes several weeks for a drawdown to be completed. Rivers on which these releases provide ample water include the Mascoma River (Upper Connecticut Watershed), the upper Farmington River (Lower Connecticut Watershed), the Mousam River (Central Coastal Watersheds), the Winnipesaukee River (Merrimack Watershed), and the Pine River and the West Branch (Saco Watershed). In New Hampshire, many drawdowns are controlled by the Water Resources Board (37 Pleasant Street, Concord, NH 03301), and late in the summer you can obtain a schedule from them.

Water releases can also provide an augmented flow on several other rivers in the area covered by this book, but unfortunately the information on them is not available for inclusion here.

Safety

Although this book was prepared with care, it should not be used on blind faith — indeed no guidebook should be. It is a very helpful companion to have while running a river, but it will not solve every problem.

It will not protect you from yourself. Managing a boat in current requires a degree of skill which depends upon the nature of the river. Maneuvering with style and finesse is a lot different than just paddling hard. Sometimes the latter works, but the faster the current the less effective it is. Be realistic about your abilities, and do not underestimate the power and difficulty of a river. The safety code of the American Whitewater Affiliation is included in the Appendix, and it contains many good suggestions for safe boating.

It will not protect you from unexpected rapids or obstacles. Many permanent changes in rivers have taken place within the last few decades, and they often occurred when dams were washed out. New England still has many old dams which could collapse and expose whatever the millponds covered. There is always the possibility of encountering temporary obstructions. Snowmobile bridges on some small quickwater streams have become a considerable hazard. They are low, often awash, and sometimes partially washed-out. They usually block a river even more effectively than a tree.

It will not protect you from sudden changes in water level. A moderate spring or autumn rainfall will significantly effect a river with a large, mountainous watershed. In a matter of hours the river can rise several feet and by so doing become more difficult and hazardous. Unanticipated releases from dams can cause the same condition.

Boating, as a sport, has certain risks that can be minimized with the proper training, forethought, caution, and equipment.

River Protection

Existing federal clean water legislation has had or will soon have a significant impact upon several New England rivers. Protection of water quality has become an accepted national goal, but widespread protection of scenic qualities has not. A few severely polluted rivers escaped pressure for riverside development because they stunk so, but now such olfactory deterrents are diminishing. However, some piecemeal protection of rivers does exist.

Some segments of riverbanks are owned by state and federal agencies. In Connecticut, for example, the Salmon River (Lower Connecticut Watershed) flows along and through Salmon River State Forest, and in Massachusetts the Sudbury and Concord rivers (Merrimack Watershed) flow through the Great Meadows National Wildlife Refuge. In Rhode Island the Pawcatuck River (Southeastern Watersheds) flows through the Great Swamp Management Area and along the edge of the Carolina and Burlingame management areas. The land behind all flood control dams is controlled by the Army Corps of Engineers, and there are many such dry dams which impound water only during floods. Such is the case in New Hampshire on the Blackwater and Pemigewasset rivers (Merrimack Watershed). In some cases, however, flood control dams have destroyed significant portions of several rivers.

Private organizations also own land along rivers. The Nature Conservancy owns many acres of land along the Connecticut coast, and the Massachusetts Audubon Society has sanctuaries along the Charles and Ipswich rivers (Central Coastal Watersheds).

Wetlands legislation and flood plain zoning can have a significant impact on low-lying rivers. The Massachusetts Wetlands Protection Act, which puts restrictions on construction in wetlands, is one of the most effective in the nation. Flood plain zoning at the local level can also be effective, particularly if there are state laws to support it.

The National Flood Insurance Program also helps save riverbanks from development. In order for such coverage to be available in a community, there must first be adequate land use regulations to restrict development in the flood plain. Since 1973 all federal agencies have been prohibited from making financial assistance available in the flood plains of non-participating communities.

The best protection a river can presently hope for

is designation as a wild or scenic river. The Housatonic and Shepaug rivers (Housatonic Watershed) are presently being considered for inclusion in the National Wild and Scenic River System. Weak legislation exists in Massachusetts to protect some scenic rivers, among them the North. In New Hampshire the AMC has become actively involved in an attempt to secure state legislation to set up a wild and scenic river system. Initial efforts are being made in behalf of the Baker, Blackwater, Contoocook, and Pemigewasset rivers (Merrimack Watershed) and the Saco River (Saco Watershed). Unfortunately, protected rivers have a tendency to grow fees and regulations.

For most rivers, however, there are no means of protection.

Rentals

There are many places to rent canoes in New England, and they are easy to find. Begin your search in the *Yellow Pages* under "Canoes." Grumman and Old Town dealers may be able to help you locate distant outfitters. If not, you can obtain a copy of the *Rent-a-Canoe Directory* by writing to Grumman Boats, Marathon, NY 13803. The Mad River Canoe Company (Box 363, Waitsfield, VT 05673) and the Old Town Canoe Company (Old Town, ME 04468) can also supply you with smaller lists of dealers who rent their canoes.

Around the Bend . . .

There are three ways that you — the reader and user of this book — can assist the AMC in the preparation of the next edition. Such assistance is earnestly solicited.

The first and most important way to help is to offer your comments about the manner in which the new descriptions are written. Does the new format present the material in a readable fashion? Can you easily obtain the information needed to select a river? Are the charts for each individual section helpful, and should they contain other types of information? Are the detailed descriptions useful to you on the river? Response of a general nature concerning the worth of this book would be most helpful.

The second way to help is to comment on the accuracy of the new descriptions. Hopefully there are no mistakes, but this book covers literally thousands of miles of rivers and streams, and perfection is not easily obtained. There may also be recent changes in the rivers themselves which should be noted. Just the knowledge that someone has run a river on a particular date and found the description to be accurate is helpful. Additional information about water levels, the length of the canoeing season, and other related data are as welcome as corrections.

The third way involves the old descriptions that appear in serif type. When the next edition is prepared, most rivers for which no new descriptions are available will be dropped. Since complete write-ups are needed for these rivers, individual corrections will not really be helpful; but a recommendation to keep or delete a river would be. If you want to write a new description, you are needed; but first contact the AMC to be sure that you are not duplicating someone else's effort.

Send your comments and suggestions to the AMC River Guide Committee, 5 Joy Street, Boston, MA 02108.

Steep Falls
Photo: Philip Preston

Tariffville Gorge, Farmington River
Photo: Pat Powning

Photo: Burt Porter
Can you identify this photograph. See page 66.

Suggested Rivers with Flatwater and Quickwater Canoeing

chapter	page	river	state(s)	miles	portage(s)	lake	flatwater	quickwater	class I rapids	short, easy class II rapids	tidal	passable at all water levels	scratchy sections in low water
2	45	**Lamoille River** (Morrisville — Fairfax Falls)	VT	34¼	4[1]	•		•	•				•
2	48	**Lemon Fair River and Otter Creek** (Route 74 — Lake Champlain)	VT	27¾	1		•	•					•
2	54	**Missisquoi River** (Sheldon Springs — Lake Champlain)	VT	21½	3		•	•		•			•
2	59	**Otter Creek** (Proctor — Threemile Bridge)	VT	32¼			•	•				•	
2	63	**Winooski River** (Montpelier — Essex Junction)	VT	38¼	2		•	•		•		•	
2	65	**Winooski River** (Winooski — Lake Champlain)	VT	9¼			•					•	
5	136	**Connecticut River** (Middletown — Old Saybrook)	CT	27½							•	•	
5	147	**Farmington River** (Farmington — Route 315)	CT	13½			•					•	
5	156	**Quaboag River** (Quaboag Pond — Warren)	MA	9		•	•		•				•
7	189	**East River** (North of and along Guilford/Madison Boundary)	CT	6							•		
8	203	**Shetucket River** (Willimantic — Baltic)	CT	10½	1		•	•					
9	214	**Chipuxet River** (West Kingston — Off Route 2)	RI	7¾		•	•						
9	219	**Nemasket and Taunton Rivers** (Assawompset Pond — Taunton)	MA	24¾			•		•			•	
9	223	**Pawcatuck River** (Richmond Dam — Westerly)	RI	18¾	2		•			•		•	
9	228	**Wood and Pawcatuck Rivers** (Route 165 — Westerly)	RI	29¼	7	•	•	•				•	
10	248	**Charles River** (Route 115 — Needham)	MA	21½	1		•					•	
10	237	**Crooked River** (Scribners Mill — Route 302)	ME	15	1		•	•		•			•
11	255	**Merrimack River** (Franklin — Manchester)	NH	42¼	3		•	•					•
11	263	**Baker and Pemigewasset Rivers** (West Rumney — Bristol)	NH	31		•	•	•		•			•
11	270	**Contoocook River** (Peterborough — Bennington)	NH	12	1		•		•				•
11	273	**Contoocook River** (Contoocook — Penacook)	NH	10¼			•	•				•	
11	301	**Sudbury and Concord Rivers** (Saxonville — North Billerica)	MA	27½			•					•	
13	336	**Saco River** (Center Conway — Cornish)	NH, ME	49½	1		•	•		•		•	
13	345	**Little Ossipee River** (Ledgemere Dam — East Limington)	ME	11¼	1		•	•		•			•

[1] includes one heavy rapid

Note: Only rivers with new descriptions have been included.

Suggested Rivers with Easy Rapids

chapter	page	river	state(s)	miles	portage(s)	short, intermittent rapids	several miles of continuous rapids	flatwater	quickwater	class I	class II	class III rapids
3	68	**Batten Kill** (Manchester — East Greenwich)	VT, NY	30½				•	•	•		
4	77	**Connecticut River** (Pittsburgh — North Stratford/Bloomfield)	NH, VT	33¾	1	•		•	•	•		
4	89	**Ashuelot River** (Gilsum Gorge — Shaw's Corner)	NH	4			•		•	•	1	
4	96	**Cold River** (South Acworth — Vilas Pool)	NH	5¼			•		•	•		
4	97	**Cold River** (Drewsville Gorge — Route 123)	NH	2¾			•		•	•	1	
4	116	**Sugar River** (North Newport — Claremont)	NH	9¾			•		•	•		
4	118	**Waits River** (Waits River Village — Bradford)	VT	10½			•		•	•		
4	122	**White River** (Granville — Bethel)	VT	25½			•		•	•	2	
5	141	**Eight Mile River** (Devils Hopyard — Hamburg)	CT	7¼	1	•			•	•	1	
5	144	**Farmington River** (Hogback Dam — Route 44)	CT	11	1	•	•		•	•		
5	159	**Blackledge and Salmon Rivers** (West Road — Route 16)	CT	11			•		•	•		
5	160	**Jeremy and Salmon Rivers** (Old Route 2 — Route 16)	CT	5¼	1		•	•	•	•		
6	183	**Shepaug River** (Bee Brook — Roxbury)	CT	9½			•	•	•	•		
8	197	**Mount Hope River** (Warrenville — Mansfield Hollow Reservoir)	CT	8	1	•		•	•	•		
8	198	**Natchaug River** (Phoenixville — North Windham)	CT	11	1	•		•	•	•		
10	246	**Crooked River** (Albany — Scribners Mill)	ME	38	4[1]			•	•	•	3	
11	261	**Assabet River** (Maynard — Route 27/62)	MA	1½	2			•	•	•		
11	269	**Contoocook River** (Jaffrey — Peterborough)	MA	6¾	2	•		•	•	•		
11	282	**Pemigewasset River** (North Woodstock — Blair Road)	NH	19				•	•	•		
12	319	**Isinglass River** (Route 126 — Country Farm Road)	NH	11¾	2[2]			•	•	•	1	
13	335	**Saco River** (Bartlett — Center Conway)	NH	22½				•	•	•	3	
13	343	**Little Ossipee River** (Davis Brook — Route 5)	ME	11¼		•		•	•	•		
13	347	**Ossipee and Saco Rivers** (Kezar Falls — East Limington)	ME	20¾	1			•	•	•	1	
13	348	**Pine River** (Pine River Pond — Elm Street)	NH	13				•	•	•		

[1] includes three class III rapids
[2] includes one class II rapid

Note: Only rivers with new descriptions have been included.

Suggested Whitewater Runs of Class III Difficulty

chapter	page	river	state	miles	portage(s)	difficult class IV rapids	water releases in summer or fall
4	85	**Ammonoosuc River** (River Bend — Pierce Bridge)	NH	2¾			
4	86	**Ammonoosuc River** (Pierce Bridge — above Littleton)	NH	8¼	1	2	
4	105	**Mascoma River** (Mascoma Lake — Lebanon)	NH	5½	1	1	•
4	112	**Otter Brook** (flood control dam — Keene)	NH	4¾			
4	127	**Winhall River** (off Route 30 — West River)	VT	7	1[1]	1[1]	
5	146	**Farmington River** (Punch Brook — Route 4)[3]	CT	2			
5	147	**Farmington River** (Tariffville — Route 187)	CT	1½			
5	150	**Millers River** (South Royalston — Athol)	MA	6¾			
5	156	**Quaboag River** (Mousehole/West Warren — Route 67 turn-off)	MA	2¾	1		
6	183	**Shepaug River** (Woodville — Bee Brook)	CT	6			
11	296	**Souhegan River** (Greenville — side road)	NH	3½	3[2]		
13	341	**Bearcamp River** (Bennett Corners — Whittier)	NH	3¾	2		

[1] Londonderry Rapids
[2] includes two class III-IV rapids
[3] class III at high water
Note: Only rivers with new descriptions have been included.

Suggested Whitewater Runs of Class IV Difficulty

chapter	page	river	state	miles	portage	covered boats only	water releases in summer or fall
4	88	**Ashuelot River** (Marlow — Gilsum Gorge)	NH	4½			
4	92	**Ashuelot River, South Branch** (Troy Gap — Webb)	NH	3		•	
4	98	**Gale River** (Jesseman Road — Ammonoosuc River)	NH	4		•	
4	111	**Otter Brook** (East Sullivan — Otter Brook State Park)	NH	3¾			
4	118	**Wardsboro Brook** (Wardsboro — Route 100)	VT	3½		•	
5	143	**Farmington River** (off Route 8 — New Boston)	CT	3			•
5	162	**Sandy Brook** (Campbell Road — Route 8)	CT	4		•[1]	
11	271	**Contoocook River** (off old Route 202 — West Henniker)	NH	3		•[2]	
11	275	**Mad River** (Waterville Valley — Campton)	NH	12			
11	281	**Pemigewasset River, East Branch** (Kan. Hwy. — N. Woodstock)	NH	6	1	•[3]	
11	293	**Smith River** (Route 104 — South Alexandria)	NH	3			
13	334	**Saco River** (Gorge — Sawyer's Rock)	NH	3¾			
13	351	**Swift River** (Rocky Gorge — Lower Falls)	NH	2½			
13	352	**Swift River** (Gorge — Darby Field)	NH	4		•	

[1] gauge reading of 3.0 or higher
[2] gauge reading of 8.0 or higher
[3] gauge reading over 1 foot at Kancamangus Highway
Note: Only rivers with new descriptions have been included.

West River
Photo: Pat Powning

Saco River
Photo: Philip Preston

CHAPTER 1

<u>MEMPHREMAGOG</u>
WATERSHED

Barton River   32
Black River   33
Clyde River   34

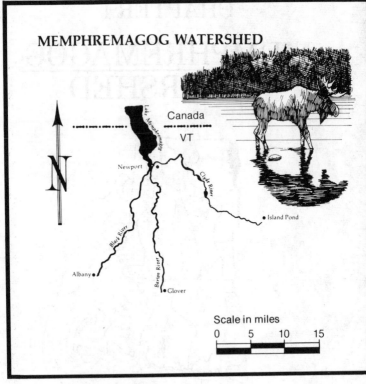

MEMPHREMAGOG WATERSHED

Scale in miles

0   5   10   15

BARTON RIVER

VT

The Barton River flows north into Lake Memphremagog.
The valley through which it flows is one of the main routes
to Canada, and it is followed all the way by a railroad and
part of the way by major highways, including I-91.

Glover — Orleans

9¼ miles

XXXX

Flatwater, **Class I–III**   15 km
High water: *spring*
Rural, Towns
    USGS: Lyndonville 15, Memphremagog 15
   Portages: 4 mi L **waterfall** — ¼–½ mi
          ca. 8¾ mi   **dam in Orleans**

      Begin on VT-16 at the first bridge N of Glover.
The river there is small but navigable. The first 2¼ miles to
the VT-16 bridge are class I.

Barton is located in a broad flood plain, and the river is flat as it passes the town, being degraded by raw sewage as it does. Two and a half miles N of Barton there is a section of class III–IV rapids which requires scouting. Stop just before the US-5 bridge (3¾ mi). **Caution!** Under no circumstances go under the second RR bridge (4 mi) at the end of the rapid because there is an 8-foot drop. Portage part or all of this rapid on the L along US-5, and put in at the next bridge.

One-half mile below the second US-5 bridge (4¼ mi) there is a low, private bridge which may block the stream in high water. In the next ½ mile to the third US-5 bridge, there are several class II–III drops for which scouting is recommended. The last 3¼ miles of winding river to the first bridge in Orleans are class I.

A take-out is recommended at the first bridge (8½ mi), but if you are continuing through town, there is a dam. Additional raw sewage also enters the river. There is a bridge across the river where the Willoughby River enters on the R (9¼ mi).

Orleans — Newport   12½ miles

XXXX

Lake, Flatwater, Class I   20¼ km
Passable at most water levels
Forested
    USGS: Memphremagog 15

From the bridge at the confluence of the Barton and Willoughby rivers just N of Orleans, there are no obstructions to Lake Memphremagog. The river meanders across a broad flood plain between low hills and in 10 miles reaches South Bay. From there it is 2½ miles to the US-5 bridge (12½ mi) in Newport.

BLACK RIVER   VT

    USGS: Hardwick 15, Irasburg 15, Memphremagog 15

This more northerly of the two Black Rivers in Vermont offers a large amount of easy canoeing and a short stretch of rapid running. The upper section is passable only at times of high water. The middle portion provides easy rapids but requires fairly high water conditions. The lowest part of the river may be passable later in the season but in dry seasons may be too low for summer running. The river has a number of lakes in its headwaters, so that

water levels should hold up late in the spring. It is possible to run from Eligo Pond, the most southerly part of the river at Craftsbury, to Albany, occasionally pushing one's way through reeds, but it is probably better to start a trip at Albany, where more water is available.

Albany — Irasburg   15 miles

Put in at a bridge on a side road 1 mile off Route 14. The river is a small meadow stream meandering down a pretty valley the 7½ miles to Irasburg, taking nearly twice as far as the direct distance. A little more than halfway down, the stream passes under the Route 14 bridge. At Irasburg take out either at the mill-dam or preferably above it at the Route 58 bridge, as below the dam there is an impassable gorge and it is best to carry around the town.

Irasburg — Coventry   6 miles

Put in just below Irasburg where the river swings north away from Route 58. Below the start 1 mile there is a covered bridge downstream from which there is often a barbed wire fence which must be carried. The next 3 miles are continuous easy rapids (class II) with attractive banks clothed with cedar and spruce. This portion is too low to run in the summer except after heavy rains, when the water is muddy. Those looking only for rapid running will probably wish to take out at the Route 14 bridge. Those desiring to continue down the river will, however, go on 2 miles to the third bridge beyond, below which there is an impassable fall. Take out here and carry around to the Route 5 bridge as there is another impassable fall in a gorge close to Coventry village.

Coventry — Newport   8 miles

Put in at the Route 5 bridge north of Coventry. From here there are 6 to 7 miles of deadwater to South Bay of Lake Memphremagog, and another 1 mile down the bay to Newport. The river banks are mostly wooded, and the stream provides a pleasant flatwater trip ofttimes possible in the summer.

CLYDE RIVER   VT

The Clyde River flows roughly northwest from Island Pond to Newport on Lake Memphremagog. At the beginning it is very obstructed, but it becomes more open below the VT-105/114 junction.

In the first section described here there are lovely marshes, cedar swamps, and farmlands. Trees droop their

branches, and occasionally their trunks as well, into the
river. Good boat control is required, and in low water it may
not be passable.

Island Pond — Pensioner Pond   13 miles

1976 Flatwater   21 km
High or medium water: *spring*
Forested, Rural, Town
    USGS: Island Pond 15, Memphremagog 15

The first 2½ miles beginning at Island Pond are
not recommended, for the "river" is very obstructed with
snowmobile bridges, fallen trees, rotten logs, and debris.
There is a short class II rapid.

The recommended put-in (0 mi) is near the
VT-105/114 junction. A hundred yards or so NE along
VT-105/114 there are places to pull off the road, and the
river is just beyond some bushes.

In ½ mile the river goes through a culvert on a
side road from which there is good access downstream on
the R. Soon you enter a marsh where there is little current
and many side channels. There are good views of the small
hills surrounding the river, but there is very little solid
shoreline in the first 5 miles to the VT-105 bridge.

Past the VT-105 bridge (5 mi) the river flows first
through a cedar swamp where there is likely to be a snowmobile bridge to lift over, and then it goes through
farmland to the next bridge on a side road in East
Charleston (6½ mi). There is more swamp and farmland,
and another bridge, in the remaining 6 miles to Pensioner
Pond (12½ mi).

It is ½ mile across Pensioner Pond to a fishing
access (13 mi) at the far end on the R. It cannot be seen
from a distance, but it is to the R of the obvious sandy
beach.

Pensioner Pond — Newport   10 miles

    USGS: Memphremagog 15

One-half mile below the pond there is a bridge on Route
105. Take out at that point and carry down a road on the
right ¼ mile to avoid a dam and a gorge. It is less than
a mile across another pond to a second dam. Below the
power station there are some easy rapids; then 2 miles of
flatwater to Salem Pond. It is 2¼ miles across Salem Pond
to the outlet at the northwest corner, and then 1 mile of

river to the Route 105 bridge at Derby Center. There are rapids with large boulders both above and below this bridge, but below these there are 2 miles of easy paddling with attractive cedar banks to Clyde Pond. It is about 1 mile down the pond to the outlet on the west shore. Many canoeists will probably elect to end the trip here in view of the carries and steep running involved in the last 2 miles to Newport. It is possible, however, to negotiate this section with some care and finesse. Take out at the red house near the end of the dam, carry past house on the right, cross the road, and continue down a dirt road ¾ mile. If there is sufficient water one may be able to put in at the bridge between the two powerhouses and shorten this carry. Otherwise put in again at the bridge below the lower powerhouse for the final 1 mile to Lake Memphremagog at Newport.

CHAPTER 2

CHAMPLAIN
WATERSHED

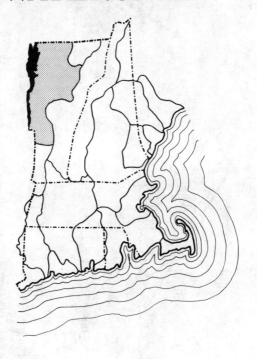

Dead Creek   40

Dog River   41

Huntington River   42

Lamoille River   43

Lemon Fair River   48

Lewis Creek   49

Mad River   50

Metawee River   51

Mill River   51

Missisquoi River   52

New Haven River   55

Otter Creek   57

Poultney River   60

Tinmouth Channel &
  Clarendon River   62

Winooski River   62

CHAMPLAIN WATERSHED

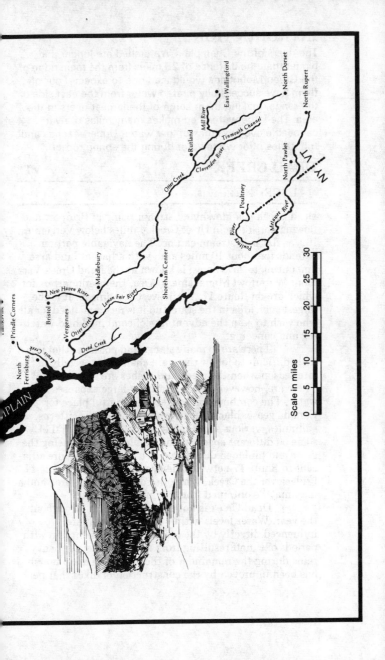

Scale in miles

0   5   10   15   20   25   30

North Ferrisburg

Prindle Corners

Bristol

New Haven River

Middlebury

Vergennes

Otter Creek

Lemon Fair River

Lewis Creek

Dead Creek

Shoreham Center

Otter Creek

Clarendon River

Rutland

Mill River

East Wallingford

Tinmouth Channel

Poultney

Poultney River

Mettawee River

North Pawlet

North Dorset

North Rupert

CHAMPLAIN

VT

N

INTRODUCTION

The rivers of the Champlain Watershed are longer and bigger than the distance of 25 miles from the main ridge of the Green Mountains would lead one to expect. Four of them have successfully pirated water from the east side of the range, making them some of the largest rivers in the area. The large watershed makes many miles of river canoeable even in times of low water. Upper reaches and tributaries offer whitewater during the spring run-off.

DEAD CREEK   VT

USGS: Port Henry 15

Dead Creek is a marshland stream rising in Bridport and flowing north to join Otter Creek 4 miles below Vergennes. It is as flat as a stream can be. The navigable portion extends for about 10 miles and, with adjacent land area amounting to 2578 acres, is known as the Dead Creek Vermont Waterfowl Management Area, the headquarters for which are on Route 17, 1 mile west of Addison. It is the largest such area in the state and it is recommended for all who wish to gain the advantages of combined bird watching and canoeing.

There are so many slangs and pot holes that it is a little difficult to follow the main channel, especially in the late season when the reeds and rushes are at full height. There are, however, many relatively large expanses of water. The combination makes a wonderful place for Canada geese, black ducks, wood ducks, teal, bitterns, gallinules, various shore birds, and others to a total of some 60 different species. One should not miss seeing the geese and pinioned ducks held in a 70-acre enclosure adjacent to Route 17 between the headquarters and Route 17 bridge over the Creek. A circular describing the area and a map may be obtained from the headquarters.

Dead Creek is not a flowing stream throughout the year. Water levels within the Creek itself are influenced directly by the levels of Lake Champlain with periods of runoff resulting from spring freshets or heavy rains during the remainder of the year. The main marsh has been improved by the construction of dikes that permit the flooding of 1000 acres of cattail marsh. These dikes divide the area into three major parts.

North Section   4 miles

This section may be visited as a side trip from Otter Creek or the trip may be begun at the mouth of Dead Creek from the bridge on the Vergennes—Basin Harbor road. Access may also be made from the bridge on the Vergennes—Panton road several miles farther upstream. Normally one can ascend the creek only 1 mile south of this road as the growth of reeds and rushes is very heavy in the ½ mile north of the dike which follows the line of the road running west from the East Panton School. A road has been opened to the dike from the road corner marked 125 on the USGS sheet. A better road for reaching this corner is the one from the Vergennes—Panton road directly south across the Holcombe Slang.

Middle Section   4 miles

This portion, running upstream from the dike above-mentioned to a dike about 1 mile south of Route 17, is perhaps the most interesting. The easiest approach is at the bridge on Route 17, but it may also be reached at the northern dike described above, or even more conveniently from the Farrell access road which leaves the country road at a point 2¾ miles south of Panton, a few feet south of the Panton—Addison line.

South Section   2 miles

Access to the south portion, as well as the middle, can be obtained at the Brilyea West and East dams, reachable by a road running south from Route 17 just west of the bridge. Access to the East Branch is easy from the road running west from Route 22A, ¾ mile south of Addison.

DOG RIVER   VT

This river is followed from its source in Roxbury to the Winooski River by a railroad and a main highway. Its most serious hazards are fallen trees and wire fences strung across it.

The best time to run this river is after a rainstorm in the spring before the middle of May.

xxxx   Flatwater, Class I–II   16½ km
High water: *April thru mid-May*
Rural, Towns
     USGS: Barre 15, Montpelier 15
    Portages: 1¼ mi   L   **pitch by 1st covered bridge** — 100 yds
              1¾ mi   **dam at Northfield Falls**
              3½ mi   L   **pitch past RR bridge**
              4¼ mi   **old wooden dam at Riverton**

Put in just below the dam at the Namtang Mill. There is about ½ mile of flatwater to a ledge obstruction just upstream of the concrete bridge on VT-12, from which it can be seen. At the correct water level this ledge can be run with scouting.

Flatwater continues past the first covered bridge to a 6-foot pitch (1¼ mi) which requires a short carry on the L. Take out again in ¼ mile at the next covered bridge and carry along the road past the dam in Northfield Falls at the Randall Wood Products Company.

Below Northfield Falls (1¾ mi), the river is flat for 1 mile to a high RR bridge, past which there is a minor obstruction which can be easily run on the far L. This is closely followed by two small ledge drops which can be run at the proper water level. Scouting is recommended.

Just past the next RR bridge (3½ mi) there is an 8-foot pitch which requires a short portage on the L. In ¼ mile there are two more ledge drops that can be run at the right water level. They, too, should be scouted. The remaining ¼ mile to Riverton is flat.

The old wooden dam in Riverton (4¼ mi) which can be seen from the VT-12 bridge in Riverton must be carried because of the obstructions provided by the timbers. The next 3½ miles are all flatwater to a short class II rapid which begins just past the Motorcycle and Gun Shop. The first section can be run on the L or R, but the second section is best run on the far R. The remaining 2½ miles to the Winooski River (10¼ mi) are flat with the exception of four minor ledge constrictions, each of which can be run straight through.

HUNTINGTON RIVER   **VT**

The Huntington River is a southern tributary of the Winooski River. It flows through woods and farmlands west of the Camel's Hump, and it consists mostly of class

I–II rapids. For the first 10 miles the gradient averages 20 feet per mile, but it is steeper after that.

The river can be run for most of its length at high water in April. At very high water it may be run from as far south as Hanksville.

Hanksville — Huntington Gorge   10½ miles

XXXX	Class I–II	17 km

High water: *April*
Forested, Rural, Towns
USGS: Huntington

Put in at the bridge which crosses the river E of the paved road in Hanksville. Just below there is a 4-foot drop which should be scouted and which can only be run at certain water levels. Watch for fallen trees and wire fences in the 4 miles to Huntington Center. A bridge (3 mi) on the paved road S of Huntington Center also makes a good put-in.

In medium water, begin at the bridge 3½ miles further N in Huntington (6½ mi), E from the center of town. Farther downstream the road to Richmond crosses twice (8¾ and 9¼ mi).

Caution! A rock wall on the R where the river bends L (10½ mi) marks the approach to Huntington Gorge, a treacherous cleft where swimmers regularly drown. There are many take-out spots on the L along the road, but be sure to obtain permission before carrying canoes or parking on the roadside strip. Parking at and carrying from the pool at the top of the gorge are permitted. Spectacular views of the falls in the gorge are seen from below.

Half a mile below this gorge is a lower gorge which is also impassable due to a series of waterfalls. Although the river is potentially canoeable for 1½ miles below the lower gorge, it is hard to reach and first-hand reports are not available.

LAMOILLE RIVER   VT

The Lamoille River rises in Horse Pond north of Greensboro Bend and flows for over 80 miles westward across northern Vermont to Lake Champlain, entering the latter north of Burlington. It was discovered by Samuel de Champlain in 1609 and put on his map as "La Mouette," the French word for gull. Either Champlain or a later engraver evidently forgot to cross his "t's," for it eventually became "Lamoille," a meaningless but melodious name.

The river used to originate a mile further north at Long Pond, which prior to June 6, 1810 was a mile and a half long and half a mile wide. On that day about sixty people went to the pond to open an outlet to the north so that the mills on the Barton River would receive an additional supply of water. A small channel was excavated and the water started running.

The northern barrier of the pond consisted entirely of quicksand except for an encrustment of clay next to the water. The quicksand was washed out and the unsupported clay broke away. The whole pond discharged to the north within fifteen minutes. The deluge advanced like a sixty-foot wall of water, sweeping along livestock, barns, houses, and mills for a distance of ten miles. A rock, estimated at a hundred tons, was moved half a mile. Nothing remains of the pond but its bottom, a meadow and swampy area off VT-16 called Runaway Pond, and it is now in the southern headwaters of the Barton River.

Greensboro Bend — Hardwick   8½ miles

XXXX   Flatwater, **Class I–III**   13¾ km
High water: *April thru May*
Forested, Rural, Towns
    USGS: Hardwick 15
    Portage: 4 mi   L   **ledges in East Hardwick**

Begin 7 miles below the outlet of Horse Pond in Greensboro Bend at the iron bridge (0 mi) just off VT-16. The river at that point is about 20 feet across and quiet but fast, and in the 4 miles to East Hardwick the difficulty reaches class III. This is a nice section that has a few sharp bends to make it interesting. Close to the road about halfway down there is a pitch that must be run on the L side because of a 4-foot drop. With caution it can be easily done.

Upon entering East Hardwick there is stillwater and the roar of some beautiful ledge falls which can be portaged on the L — a short carry between some houses, across the road, and down a large path to the river. There is a bridge (4 mi) going over the beginning of the falls.

From East Hardwick to Hardwick is a beautiful 4½-mile class I–III run with some stillwater for a breather. There are some ledges and rocks in this section which make the rapids exciting. When you get to Hardwick, open canoes have to run on the R side all the way to the second bridge (8½ mi) where there is a good parking area.

USGS: Hardwick 15, Hyde Park 15

One can start in Hardwick, off Route 12B on Alder Creek
at a convenient place above the head of beautiful
Hardwick Lake and enjoy a pleasant 2-mile paddle down
that sightly lake, or at Jackson Bridge at dam at foot of
lake. From here, there is an easy 5-mile run to the dam
above Pottersville where there is a 50-foot drop. When in
view of the bridge above Pottersville, land and look over
two ledges at a partly washed out dam below the bridge, in
order to decide whether to run or carry. At Pottersville
dam take out at the left end, carry ¼ mile down the trail
road and put in on the upper side of the powerhouse.
A short distance below, above the Route 15 bridge below
Pottersville, are the remains of an old dam with a 3-foot
drop. This may be run in high water, but land on left and
look over first, as a short carry may be desirable. From
Wolcott it is an easy 5 miles to the power dam above the
second bridge at Morrisville. **Caution!** Take out as near
the red building at the left end of the dam as safety permits. Carry down the road past the end of the bridge
250 yards to the transformer station, then make a sharp
reverse turn to the right 75 yards to the river and beautiful Lake Lamoille.

Morrisville — Johnson   9¾ miles

1975   Lake, **Quickwater**, Class I   15¾ km
         Passable at most water levels
         Forested, Rural
              USGS: Hyde Park 15
         Portages: 1¼ mi L **Cady's Falls Dam**
                      9¼ mi L **Dog's Head and Sloping Falls** — 350 yds

        Put in below the dam in Morrisville at the mouth
of Potash Brook. At first there is a pleasant paddle on Lake
Lamoille, the backwater from Cady's Falls Dam (1¼ mi).
Carry around the dam on the L for 100 yards to the main
road. Follow the road across the bridge, turn L, and follow
a road to an open field where a put-in is possible. This
makes an easy carry around the dam and the ledges.
        After Cady's Falls Dam (1¼ mi) there is a pleas-
ant, 8-mile run through meadowland to Dog's Head Falls, a
dangerous spot that can be most easily recognized by a
gravel pit on the R bank. Take out on the L and carry 350

yards around both Dog's Head Falls and Sloping Falls, two sharp drops that are separated by a pool.

One-quarter mile below the two falls you reach the Johnson bridge (9¾ mi).

Johnson — Fairfax Falls   24½ miles

This is a pleasant paddle through the delightful Vermont countryside. The Long Trail crosses on the VT-15 bridge, just beyond which the river cuts through the Green Mountains. Further on there are splendid views looking back to the east towards the highest of Vermont's mountains.

1975   Johnson — Fairfax Falls   24½ mi [39½ km]
          Quickwater, Class I
          Passable at all water levels
          Rural, Towns
              USGS: Hyde Park 15, Jeffersonville, Gilson Mountain
          Portages: 2¾ mi   **ledge below VT-15** (may be runnable)
                      3¼ mi   **Ithiel Falls** (may be runnable)
                      24¼ mi L **dam at Fairfax Falls** — ¼ mi

Put in ¼ mile above the Johnson bridge on the W side of the river. Immediately below it the Gihon River enters on the R. About ¼ mile below the VT-15 bridge (2½ mi) there is a ledge constriction with a 100-yard rapid through it. This pitch can cause trouble in low water, and it can be up to class IV in high water. About ½ mile further is Ithiel Falls which is also 100 yards long and up to class IV in high water. Both of these rapids should be scouted before running for the first time. Ithiel Falls was blasted out after the 1927 flood backed up water into Johnson village.

Immediately below Ithiel Falls there are huge and beautiful granite islands which make intricate channels that require alert paddlers. The best channel is to the L. A road follows this whole stretch along the N bank.

The river passes under the VT-108 (11½ mi) and VT-15 (12 mi) bridges in Jeffersonville. Then it meanders through farming country for 12¼ miles to the bridge at Fairfax Falls (24¼ mi). Take out on the L at the bridge, and portage around the dam to the river below (24½ mi).

Fairfax Falls — Milton   9¾ miles

The upper part of this section is an interesting series of rapids away from the road, and the remainder is flatwater through Arrowhead Mountain Lake.

Fairfax Falls — Milton   9¾ mi [15¾ km]
Lake, Quickwater, Class I–III
Passable at all water levels
Rural
    USGS: Gilson Mountain, Milton
    Portages: 9¼ mi R **1st dam in Milton**
                9½ mi L **2nd dam in Milton**

Quickwater extends past the VT-104 bridge at Fairfax (1½ mi) to a set of rapids which begin as the river bends to the L (3 mi). These rapids range from class I to class III, and they extend nearly continuously for 2½ miles.

At the beginning of these rapids, rocks appear in the streambed and increase in density over the next ¼ mile with a corresponding increase in the velocity of the flow. The main current — here class I — follows the R bank about 100 yards and leads into Two Island Rapids.

Two channels begin in another 100 yards. Very large rocks at the R bank signal a 2-foot and a 3-foot drop which are best run with care through the R channel. Two Island Rapids are class III at medium water, and at high water the whole set of rapids is more difficult because the rocks cause big eddies.

Class I rapids continue to another ¾-mile set of rapids which culminates at Five Chutes, a ledge that extends across the river. In another ½ mile you reach the East Georgia bridge (6 mi).

Arrowhead Mountain Lake is 3¼ miles long and shaped somewhat like a monkey-wrench. Paddle W and then S to Milton (9¼ mi).

Milton — Lake Champlain   8¼ miles

Flatwater, Quickwater, Class I   13¼ km
Passable at all water levels
Forested, Rural, Town
    USGS: *Milton*, Georgia Plains, Fort Ethan Allen
    Portage: 2¾ mi L **Peterson Dam**

Begin at the Milton hydroelectric station. Obtain access permission on location and notify the dam operator before running below the tailrace. It is 1 mile to the I-89 bridge where the backwater of Peterson Dam begins. The remaining 1¾ miles to the dam is very isolated and scenic. Be careful in approaching the dam, and take out on the L bank past the last large ledge outcrop. It is best to portage along the power station access road to the town road unless you wish to run the 100 yards of rapids immediately below the dam.

The remaining 5¼ miles lead past West Milton (3¼ mi) and the US-2 bridge (6¼ mi), and through a wildlife refuge to Lake Champlain (8¼ mi). There is a large island at the mouth of the river, and to take out you can paddle N for 1 mile to Sand Bar State Park (9¼ mi) on US-2.

LEMON FAIR RIVER   VT

The Lemon Fair River rises in the southeast corner of Orwell and flows north to join Otter Creek just a few miles below Weybridge. The canoeable part is composed of winding channels in a flat bottomland with splendid views of nearby hills and mountains.

According to a local story, the name of the river is derived from the remark of an early traveller who had lost his horse from miring in mud or quicksand as he crossed the stream. He referred to this episode as a "lamentable affair." Another legend is that the name is an anglicized version of "Les Monts Verts."

Shoreham Center — Route 74   7 miles

Scouted only. There is a canoeable reservoir above Shoreham Center (Rickville) which extends upstream beyond East Shoreham, but trips normally begin nearly ½ mile below the dam, or even farther if the water is too low.

Put in on the south side near the yellow house where the river comes close to the Shoreham road almost ½ mile below the dam. Except in the spring or after a good rainfall, this section may be too low to run. There are some light rapids and shallow places in the first 3½ miles to the bridge north of the Pinnacle. The last 3½ miles to the VT-74 bridge (7 mi) are flat. See the USGS Orwell and Bridport sheets.

Route 74 — Otter Creek   11½ miles

1976   Flatwater, Quickwater   18 km
High or medium water: *April and May*
Rural
       USGS: Bridport, Cornwall, Middletown, Port Henry 15

The river flows through farmland drained by ditches along both sides. Aquatic birds and animals live along it in abundance. It flows under VT-125 (5¼ mi) and two bridges on back roads before reaching VT-23 (11½ mi) at the confluence with Otter Creek.

LEWIS CREEK   VT

USGS: Hinesburg, Mt. Philo, Monkton, Port Henry 15

Lewis Creek offers interesting paddling in attractive, rough country during the spring runoff in the latter part of March and early April. The flow varies widely with temperature, recent rain and sunshine. If the water is right, a start can be made at the bridge on the Hinesburg–Monkton Ridge road or even higher up. The upper part is mostly flatwater with good current until just above a short fall above a covered bridge south of Prindle Corners, which should be portaged.

Prindle Corners — Lake Champlain   10 miles

The usual starting point is at the covered bridge south of Prindle Corners, about 2½ miles south of Hinesburg. A pitch just above the bridge should be looked over before running by those starting higher up. Easy rapids are encountered to the deadwater above the Scott Pond dam, where a short carry must be made. There is a good take-out place ½ mile below. This bit makes a lively class II, 3-mile run through rugged country.

In the 2 miles to North Ferrisburg there are two somewhat difficult ledges and as the village is approached the canoeist must take out on the left above the bend because of impassable ledges. The remaining 5 miles to Lake Champlain are far less interesting. There is no difficulty other than fallen trees, with the exception of a steep ledge below the railroad bridge just after passing under Route 7. This should be scouted but may be run in high water. Near this spot in the latter part of the 19th century Lewis Creek's last landlocked salmon was speared by a farm boy with a pitchfork. After reaching Lake Champlain the canoeist has several choices. He can return ½ mile to a state access, or go ½ north up the lake to take out on the narrow neck of Long Point, or go south a short distance on Little Otter Creek and the South Slang 2 miles to the state access at the bridge.

MAD RIVER VT

The Mad River flows northward on the east side of the Green Mountains from Granville Notch to the Winooski River below Middlesex. It offers a scenic, spring white-water run with crystal clear water over a rocky riverbed.

 Waitsfield — Moretown 8¼ miles

XXXX **Flatwater,** Class I–II 13¼ km
High or medium water: *April thru mid-May*
Forested, Rural, Towns
   USGS: Waitsfield, Waterbury
   Portage: 7½ mi L **Moretown Gorge** — ¾ mi

Begin at the Vermont highway garage 1.7 miles S of Waitsfield. There are 1½ miles of flatwater with a good current to the broken dam at Waitsfield which can be run straight through with no problems. The current is mild with no rapids to a class II drop in medium water where the river abuts VT-100, then bends 90° to the R, and makes an "S" shaped drop past a ledgy outcrop. It is best to scout this pitch the first time it is run.

The remaining distance to Moretown Gorge (7½ mi) is class I. The gorge is unrunnable, and to avoid it you should take out well above the VT-100B bridge.

If you are continuing downstream, portage along the highway past the dam in Moretown (8¼ mi).

Moretown — Winooski River 6¼ miles

XXXX **Flatwater,** Class II–III 10 km
High or medium water: *April thru mid-May*
Forested, Rural
   USGS: Waterbury, Montpelier 15
   Portages: 2¼ mi **gauging station**
                4¾ mi **dam**
                5¾ mi **dam**

Put in below the dam on the N side of Moretown. Flatwater extends for 2¼ miles to a gauging station which requires a short carry. Another ¾ mile of flatwater and a short section of class II rapids bring you to a 1½-mile section of backwater from a dam which affords a good trip-termination spot.

Below the second dam (4¾ mi) there is ¼ mile of class III–IV rapids which require scouting before running.

More flatwater follows to the third dam, ½ mile above the confluence with the Winooski River (6¼ mi).

METAWEE RIVER   VT

USGS: Pawlet 15

The river rises on the west slope of Dorset Mountain and passes under Route 30 in Dorset as a small brook. It is too small and brushy to run until 1 mile north of North Rupert. From here to North Pawlet is a good run in high spring water. Below there is a long stretch with easy paddling interspersed with impossible drops.

North Rupert — North Pawlet   8 miles

Put in at the Route 30 bridge 1 mile north of North Rupert. The stream is about 15 feet wide and runs through pasture land. Downed trees, old barbed wire fences, and low bridges are the worst problems; the current and rocks are easy. In Pawlet, Flower Brook joins the river and doubles its size. This section runs through attractive, high, wooded banks. After a mile the river returns to pasture land and after another 2 miles a large red bridge is reached. This is on a road which is the first left turn off Route 30 north of Pawlet. Another 1 mile may be run to the next bridge, but one should take out here or carefully scout the following pitch. **Caution!** Take out and check, as the river drops 25 feet through a narrow cleft just beyond. From here the river should be run only by those willing to check their course carefully.

MILL RIVER   VT

This is a small, rural class II–III stream southeast of Rutland. In the spring it provides 4–6 miles of intermittent whitewater paddling beginning at East Wallingford off VT-103. See USGS Wallingford 15 and Rutland sheets.

From East Wallingford, follow along the road and put in at any convenient point south of town. The best take-out is at a roadside picnic area on VT-103 north of Cuttingsville. You can paddle further, but the road pulls away from the stream, and there are no really good places to take out. If you do continue past the picnic area, take out as soon as you see the hanging bridge where the Long Trail crosses Clarendon Gorge. This gorge is impassable for open boats and perhaps for closed boats as well.

MISSISQUOI RIVER   VT, PQ

The Missisquoi River was an important Indian route. For
over 90 miles it flows westward across the top of Vermont
and through part of Quebec to Lake Champlain. It is in a
beautiful valley where there are views of hills and mountains all the time.

Most of the drops are impassable falls, and many
have been harnessed for power. Flatwater and quickwater
characterize most of the river, and only the section
upstream of North Troy requires high water. Roads are
convenient but not unduly noticeable from the river.

Lowell — North Troy   20 miles

USGS: Irasburg 15

Put in at stone bridge across Burgess Branch on Hazen
Notch Road, ¾ mile northwest of Lowell. A comfortably
fast meandering stream takes one 13 miles to the Route
100 bridge at Troy and then 1 mile more to Phelps Falls
(shown on old topographic sheet) beyond another bridge
1 mile northeast of Troy. Take out immediately beyond
bridge on right, cross bridge, and go straight ahead
through a gate. After 175 yards leave the road and follow
the powerline to the powerhouse or follow road 350 yards
around to the powerhouse, where one can put in at the tailrace. About 1 mile farther, the river narrows between steep
banks, demanding caution for the next 2 miles, especially
opposite the "E" in "RIVER" on the map, where there is a
very steep drop of 40 feet in ½ mile. One mile beyond the
next bridge the river comes close to the road 100 yards
below a red barn on the right at a bend. **Caution!** Do not
run below this spot because of Big Falls below. Take out
and carry along road ½ mile to the entrance to a picnic
area, where one should not fail to take the short walk to
look over Big Falls. After an additional 175 yards along the
road take an old road to left and follow it another 175 yards
to a gravel pit, where a sharp right turn for 10 yards brings
one to a good take-off place. A car would be useful at this
carry. Below here there are 2 miles of easy river to the dam
at North Troy, where one should land immediately above
a high bank on the right just above the bridge and carry
through a garden, across the road, and up a steep bank to
the northeast corner of a mill, next to the railroad track.
Then follow along track to left, through an underpass, over

a fence into a pasture, and then down the slope to the river. This route is obscure, so that it is better to scout it in advance.

North Troy — East Richford   16 miles

This loop of the Missisquoi circles through Quebec as it passes through the main ridge of the Green Mountains. It is a pleasant, enjoyable paddle which is quite popular.

1976	North Troy — East Richford	16 mi [25¾ km]

Flatwater, **Quickwater**
Passable at most water levels
Rural

USGS:	Irasbury 15, Jay Peak 15
CNTS:	Memphremagog 31 H/1, Sutton 31 H/2
Campsite:	6 mi R **campground**

Report to Canadian Customs at the border on VT-105A before launching your canoe below the dam at North Troy. The river meanders leisurely and extensively to Highwater, Quebec (5¾ mi) where there is a campground on the R shore. Below there the river is occasionally in sight of the road as it passes through farming country. Land on the L at the bridge in East Richford to report to US Customs.

East Richford — Enosburg Falls   19 miles

The river here consists mostly of pleasant riffles around islands, and much of it is close to the road. Two sections of class II and III rapids, one in Richford and the other 2¼ miles below East Berkshire, should be avoided by inexperienced canoeists.

1976	East Richford — Enosburg Falls	19 mi [30½ km]

Flatwater, Quickwater, Class I–II
High or medium water: *spring*
Low water: *some wading required above Richford*
Forested, Rural, Towns

USGS:	Jay Peak 15, Enosburg Falls 15
Portages:	5¼ mi L **class III rapids in Richford** (take out above factory)
	14 mi L **old dam in Samsonville**
	18½ mi L **dam at Enosburg Falls** — ½ mi

In the 5¼ miles to Richford there are riffles which may require some wading in low water. Below a RR bridge (4½ mi) the river approaches Richford. Rapids begin just below a factory (5¼ mi) on the L, and just above the bridge the river becomes confined within retaining walls where it drops over ledges near an old damsite. The most difficult ledge, a class III pitch, is below the bridge.

From Richford (6 mi) the river is mostly quickwater to the old dam at Samsonville (14 mi) which is in the process of washing out. It can be run in various places, or it can be portaged on the L. Then below it there is ¼ mile of class II ledges.

Between Samsonville and Enosburg Falls the river is mostly smoothwater. The best way around the dam at Enosburg Falls is to take out on the L under the first bridge (18½ mi). Walk up to the road along the river and follow it downstream past the second bridge about ¼ mile to a field with a gate. Go through the gate and down to the river (19 mi) to put in.

Enosburg Falls — Highgate Falls   18½ miles

Although largely quickwater, this section contains several sets of rapids. Below Sheldon Springs much of it is wild and away from the road.

1976   Enosburg Falls — Highgate Falls   18½ mi [30 km]
        Flatwater, **Quickwater, Class I–II**
        Passable at most water levels
        Forested, Rural
             USGS: Enosburg Falls 15, Highgate Center
          Portages: 10½ mi L **dam at Sheldon Springs** — ½ mi
                     17 mi R **ledge in Spring Rapid**
                     18¼ mi L **dam at Highgate Falls** — ¼ mi

---

From below the dam at Enosburg Falls there are 5½ miles of quickwater to the North Sheldon bridge. Then there are 3 miles of class II rapids, followed by 2 miles of quickwater and flatwater to the first dam.

At Sheldon Springs (10½ mi), take out on the L above the bridge and carry down the road past the mill on the R. Continue along the road to a crossroad and turn R. At a point 150 yards beyond a gully, leave the road, follow along the edge of the woods for 150 yards, and enter the woods at the birches below the transformer station, heading down to the river (11 mi) below the impassable cascade.

Below Sheldon Springs there is quickwater for 3¼ miles through woods to East Highgate (14¼ mi). Ledges start when the bridge is in sight. The abutments of an old dam are just below that bridge, and ledges of approximately class II in difficulty continue for ½ mile below it.

After East Highgate the river leaves the road again and flows through lovely woods. After a few miles there is a ledge which can be run, but just below it is another one 5 feet high (17 mi) which can be portaged on the R, but it is most easily lined on the L. This section is called Spring Rapid because of an old mineral spring on the hill above.

In another mile is the dam at Highgate Falls (18¼ mi) just above the old bridge. Carry on the L for ¼ mile to reach the river again (18½ mi).

Highgate Falls — Lake Champlain 14 miles

There are no difficulties in this section except a dam at Swanton, and the river is mostly away from the road. Naturalists will enjoy the last 5¼ miles through the Missisquoi National Wildlife Refuge.

1976	Highgate Falls — Lake Champlain	14 mi [22½ km]

Flatwater, Quickwater
Passable at all water levels
Forested, Rural, Town
USGS: Highgate Center, East Arlburg
Portage: 6½ mi R **dam at Swanton**

From Highgate Falls to Swanton there are 6½ miles of slow current, and in that distance you pass under I-89, US-7 (3½ mi) and an abandoned, covered RR bridge (4¼ mi).

Below Swanton (6½ mi) the river is flat. In 2¼ miles you enter Missisquoi National Wildlife Refuge at the entrance to Dead Creek (8¾ mi), which branches off to the R and leads in 2½ miles to Lake Champlain. The mouth of the Missisquoi has a number of islands in its delta. Once you reach Lake Champlain (14 mi), you can take out at a marina to the SW, or you can paddle to the SE and take out at Highgate Springs (16¼ mi).

NEW HAVEN RIVER VT

USGS: Bristol, South Mountain, Middlebury

The New Haven River, which flows from Lincoln Gap in the Green Mountains to Otter Creek is normally not run above Bristol. A small portion of the upper river can be run by experts at high water, and then preferably with covered boats. The middle and lower sections provide a pleasant paddle with a fall and a lively rapid down to its junction with Otter Creek.

Beaver Brook — Bristol   4 miles

This run is for experts only. In early spring or after a heavy rainfall one can put in from Route 116 at the junction of Beaver Brook and Baldwin Creek. For 2 miles Baldwin Creek offers swift current and pleasant paddling to its junction with the New Haven River, which rushes down from Lincoln Gap. As the New Haven is approached, the canoeist enters a continuous class III rapid and soon passes under the Route 116 bridge. There are steady class II and III rapids for the next 1½ miles to Bristol. Here above and under a cement bridge is a heavy, boulder-strewn, class IV or V rapid, which most paddlers will wish to portage although a passage on the left exists. Class III rapids continue through the village as the river makes a sweeping curve to the left and passes under an iron bridge.

Bristol — New Haven Mills   3 miles

From Bristol the river descends in a series of rapids of decreasing difficulty before taking a more moderate pace through the Bristol Flats, as the farming country is known. Less experienced paddlers may prefer to start near the iron bridge below the village or farther down along the road east of the river. In lower water, it is best to start about 2 miles below Bristol, where the river comes close to the road on the west. At New Haven Mills the former dam is now replaced by a steep pitch of several hundred feet, impassable except at medium to high water because of the boulders. This part can easily be seen from the bridge and should always be looked over in advance. If a carry is to be made, take out well above the bridge on the left.

New Haven Mills — Otter Creek   6 miles

Put in below the former dam at New Haven Mills. A short rapid is followed by easy paddling for 5½ miles to immediately below the third bridge, which is at Brookside on old Route 7 a short distance below the new Route 7 bridge. Nearby is the well known Dog Team Tavern. Take out here or carry around the falls just below the bridge and continue ½ mile to Otter Creek, where it may be possible to take out at a campsite on the right, otherwise the canoeist must go down Otter Creek 1½ miles to the next bridge at the power station on a side road to take out.

OTTER CREEK   VT

Otter Creek flows north from Dorset and drains a wide
valley between the Green Mountains and the Taconic
Range. North of Rutland it runs somewhat westward and
empties into Lake Champlain near Vergennes. At high
water it provides an easy trip of just over 100 miles, but
much of it can be run in medium or low water, making it
suitable for summer trips. It is highly recommended for its
pleasant paddling and its scenic views of the Green Mountains, the Taconics, and the Adirondacks in New York.

There are several dams on this river, and at many
of them the current is strong right up to the edge. Take out
well above all dams, especially in high water.

North Dorset — Wallingford   17¾ miles

High water is needed in the upper part where the river is
very narrow. Below South Wallingford at least medium
water is needed, and in that part the river may be
obstructed by an occasional, fallen tree. This whole section
is mostly quickwater, except for the rapids in South
Wallingford and Wallingford.

1973   North Dorset — Wallingford   17¾ mi [28½ km]
          Quickwater, Class I
          High water: *needed above South Wallingford, early spring*
          Medium water: *late spring*
          Forested, Rural, Towns
              USGS: Wallingford 15
          Portages: 11½ mi R **class III ledges** — ½ mi
                     17¼ mi   **class II rapids and rock dam**

Begin in North Dorset ¾ mile N of the Emerald
Lake dam by putting in from a farm road on the E side of
US-7. From there to Danby it is 5¾ miles with numerous
beaver dams and lodges. There are plenty of brushy
impediments, but there are no rapids to speak of.

Below the Mount Tabor road in Danby (5¾ mi),
there are riffles over a gravel bottom. The rapids at South
Wallingford (11½ mi) are class III for ½ mile, and they can
be most easily portaged on the R along the RR tracks.

Below South Wallingford quickwater continues to
Wallingford, where there are four bridges. The first one is
US-7 (16¼ mi). Class II rapids start below the second
bridge VT-140 (17¼ mi) and continue past a rock dam to
the fourth, where there is a ledge partially blocking the
L-hand span.

Wallingford — Rutland   13 miles

The winding river is still small here. There are roads on both sides of the valley, but they are hardly noticeable as the river is bordered by trees.

1976   Wallingford — Rutland   13 mi [18 km]
Quickwater
High or medium water: *spring*
Rural
    USGS: Wallingford 15, Rutland

       This pleasant quickwater run has an occasional fallen tree. Begin at the fourth (last) bridge in Wallingford. In 2¾ miles the Mill River enters on the R. This is the fourth and southernmost river which cuts through the Green Mountains, and it greatly augments the flow in Otter Creek.
       There is a bridge (5 mi) near Clarendon and another (9¾ mi) near North Clarendon. Take out at the River Street bridge (13 mi) in Rutland a short distance above the first dam in that city.

Rutland — Proctor   8¼ miles

The 6½ miles of flatwater in this section are set off from the rest of the river by high dams requiring long portages. Below Rutland the river is larger, and it can be run all summer.

1973   Rutland — Proctor   8¼ mi [13¼ km]
Flatwater, Quickwater, Class II
Passable at all water levels
Rural, Towns
    USGS: *Rutland*, West Rutland, Proctor
    Portages: ¼ mi e **dam in Rutland** — 100–400 yds
                1 mi e **dam in Center Rutland** (difficult) — ½ mi
                7¾ mi R **dam in Proctor** — ½ mi

       A quarter mile below the River Street bridge — the first one in Rutland — there is a low dam which is hard to see from the river. It can be portaged on either side, and it is followed by ½ mile of class II rapids. The current continues strong up to the dam in Center Rutland. Take out at the double bridge (1 mi). The carry up the steep bank and through the factory yards is difficult on either side.
       In Center Rutland, put in at the US-4 bridge (1¼ mi) below the dam, and pass the mouth of the Clarendon River (1½ mi) on the L. From there the river flows slowly

between wooded banks. Pass a RR bridge (6¼ mi) and take out at the next bridge (7¾ mi) to portage the dam in Proctor. Carry on the R down the hill on the highway, take the first L past the sewage treatment plant, and follow the dirt tracks down to the river (8¼ mi).

Proctor — Middlebury   35¾ miles

This is a beautiful paddle through farming country and under covered bridges. There are some mountain views. The river meanders through a broad valley with clear water and a sandy bottom.

1973   Proctor — Middlebury   35¾ mi [57¾ km]
Flatwater, **Quickwater**
Passable at all water levels
Rural
    USGS: Proctor, Brandon, Sudbury, Cornwall, Middlebury
    Portage: 35¾ mi L **dam in Middlebury** (take out well above)
                    — ¼ mi

In Proctor, put in on the E bank at the bottom of the hill by taking the first L past the sewage treatment plant. This trip is popular, and there are many bridges which offer access to the river. A few of them are listed here: the bridge in Florence (6¼ mi) ½ mile N of a RR bridge; two bridges SW of Brandon, Dean Bridge (13 mi) and Sanderson Bridge (14½ mi); the VT-73 bridge W of Brandon (18¼ mi); the bridge at Leicester Junction (21½ mi); and Threemile Bridge (32¼ mi). The latter, located next to the mouth of the Middlebury River, is the recommended take-out. It can be reached most easily from US-7 in East Middlebury by following Creek Road just to the N of the Middlebury River.

If you are continuing on to Middlebury, take out well above the VT-30/74 bridge (35¾ mi).

Middlebury — Weybridge   6 miles

xxxx   Flatwater, Quickwater, Class II–III   9¾ km
Passable at all water levels
Forested, Urban
    USGS: Middlebury
    Portages: 1 mi L **2nd dam in Middlebury** — 100 yds
                 3 mi R **Beldens Dam** — ¼ mi
           4¾ mi L **Huntington Falls Dam** — ¼ mi
              6 mi L **dam at Weybridge** — 100 yds

Three of these dams — all except Beldens Dam — are below bridges and should be portaged on the L. The banks consist of cliffs, ledges, and evergreen growth. There are rapids below the dams, and the most difficult ones are below Beldens, where there is a gorge. Three quarters of a mile below Beldens Dam the New Haven River (3¾ mi) enters on the R.

Weybridge — Lake Champlain   19¾ miles

This section is largely away from roads, but there are some buildings along the banks. The mouth of the river is very attractive, with views across the lake towards the Adirondacks.

The river below Vergennes is large enough for big boats, and there are many motorboats.

1976	Weybridge — Lake Champlain	19¾ mi [31¾ km]

Flatwater, Quickwater
Passable at all water levels
Forested, Rural
    USGS: Middlebury, Port Henry 15
    Portage: 12 mi R **dam in Vergennes** — ½+ mi

Put in from the end of the island below the dam at Weybridge or ½ mile downstream on the L if you wish to avoid the fastwater. The current is moderate past the mouth of the Lemon Fair River (3½ mi) to Vergennes (12 mi) where the take-out above the dam is difficult at high water. Carry on the R bank down a road.

Four miles below Vergennes, Dead Creek (16 mi) enters on the L. The best take-out is at the Fort Cassin Fishing Access ½ mile before the mouth of the river at Lake Champlain (19¾ mi).

POULTNEY RIVER   VT, NY

USGS: Poultney, Thorn Hill, Benson, Whitehall

The Poultney River rises in Tinmouth, Vermont and flows west to Poultney, where it turns north and becomes the boundary between Vermont and New York for the rest of its circuitous route to the East Bay of Lake Champlain. The upper reaches through the Taconic Range are too rough to canoe, but from Poultney down there is much easy paddling interspersed by difficult or impossible rapids. Much of it may be run in the summer, although the rapids may have to be carried.

Poultney — Hampton   2 miles

Put in at the Route 30 bridge south of town or at the
lower bridge southwest of town. It is an easy paddle down
to Hampton through pleasant meadow lands.
Caution! There is an unrunnable ledge under the bridge at
Hampton; pull out above and line down or carry.

Hampton — Route 4 Bridge   10 miles

This section provides easy quickwater paddling through
farmland and woods, but there are three ledges, with the
most difficult one being first. Many fallen trees block the
channel. **Caution!** There are some cascades just below the
Route 4 bridge. Take out at the bridge and look these over.

Route 4 Bridge — Carver Falls   3 miles

Put in below the cascades mentioned above. The river
from here to Carver Falls is a meandering stream largely
through meadowlands. One mile below the start there is a
rapid at the West Street Bridge. Just above this the
Castleton River enters, adding considerably to the flow in
the summer months if the Lake Bomoseen hydroelectric
plant is operating. In another 2 miles the pond of the
Carver Falls hydroelectric station of the Central Vermont
Public Service Company is reached, and canoes must be
taken out here for the carry around the dam and gorge on
the New York side, where the plant engineer's house
stands. Just above this point at the old bridge site there is
a rapid. Should this prove unrunnable canoes may be
taken out and carried down the old road 200 yards to the
engineer's house.

Carver Falls — Lake Champlain   10 miles

During the summer this section might be difficult if the
Carver Falls Station is not operating as no water is then
allowed to flow downstream. Check with the Central
Vermont Public Service Company in Rutland. Carver
Falls is reached by car from Fair Haven, Vermont. Take
West Street from the common 2 miles. After crossing the
Poultney River take first road right, ¼ mile, and follow
2 miles to dam. Put in below the power station in the
gorge. An old wood road goes down to the river at the lower
end of the gorge. It starts between the tool sheds back of
the engineer's house. It is not passable for cars, but canoes
may easily be carried down. The river runs west for
4 miles. In 2½ miles the Hubbardton River flows in on the
right, and in another 1½ miles the Coggman Creek is

reached. One may either pull out here on the road on the right bank or continue south another 6 miles down the East Bay of Lake Champlain. Except at high water this is now little more than a river rather than a wide bay and will provide a pleasant paddle between high hills. It is best to pull out at the bridge at the Elbow. This is only ½ mile above the confluence with Wood Creek, up which Whitehall, New York, may be reached in another mile.

TINMOUTH CHANNEL and CLARENDON RIVER VT

South of Rutland, Tinmouth Channel flows northward through the township of Tinmouth and into Clarendon, where it becomes the Clarendon River. It empties into Otter Creek just west of Rutland. There are two canoeable sections.

The first is a 5-mile section on Tinmouth Channel which is crossed by VT-140. It can be canoed in the spring, but it is overgrown with brush. Begin at a bridge on a road a short ways south of and parallel to VT-140 in Tinmouth, and paddle to another bridge at the north end of town. See the USGS Middletown Springs sheet.

The second section is separated from the first by a steep and unrunnable section. The last 3¼ miles of the Clarendon River can also be run in the spring. Begin from a bridge on a short side road less than 2 miles south of West Rutland on VT-133. The first half of the river is steep but then it becomes sluggish for the remaining distance past VT-4 (3 mi) to Otter Creek (3¼ mi). If you continue downstream on the latter, it is another 6¼ miles to Proctor. See the USGS West Rutland sheet.

WINOOSKI RIVER VT

The Winooski River rises in Cabot and flows westward through the Green Mountains to Lake Champlain near Burlington. Although its course circles some of the largest cities in Vermont, the banks are largely pastoral. Lovely mountain views are obtained in the middle portion. It offers 78¼ miles of canoeing.

Marshfield — Montpelier 24 miles

The river in this section is very small, and it can be run only in high water. The 8½ miles from Marshfield to Plainfield are a pleasant run ranging in difficulty from quickwater to class II. Most of the lower part consists of short sections between dams.

Marshfield — Montpelier   24 mi [38¾ km]
Flatwater, Quickwater, Class II–III
High water: *early spring*
Rural, Towns
    USGS: Plainfield 15, Barre 15, Montpelier 15
Portages: 1 mi   **dam in Marshfield**
               9½ mi   **dam in Plainfield**
               18 mi   **dam below East Montpelier**
                             three dams in Montpelier

      The rapids below the Green Mountain Power station above the town of Marshfield are class II–III, and they require very high water. The US-2 bridge (1 mi) is just above the dam in Marshfield.

      Access at the Twinfield Elementary School below the dam is followed by ½ mile of class II water. Then the river meanders for several miles of mixed flatwater and small rapids to Twinfield High School, where access is available at a bridge. From the high school through Onion River Campground, there is some class II water. Since access is difficult near the buildings at the dam in Plainfield (9½ mi), take out well above it.

      Below the Plainfield dam (9½ mi) is ½ mile of class III rapids. Then the river meanders with a good current and easy rapids past East Montpelier (16½ mi) to a dam (18 mi) which is a good place to end a trip on the upper river. Access is on the L bank off US-2.

      In the next 6 miles there are three dams. Above the first one there are class III rapids. Below it, class II rapids diminish to flatwater above a small dam which can be portaged on either side. You reach the third dam in the center of Montpelier after passing under four bridges.

Montpelier — Jonesville   22¾ miles

Below Montpelier the river can be run all year. The section described here has much quickwater with occasional rapids. The two dams are in scenic natural gorges, and the run is very attractive.

1977   Montpelier — Jonesville   22¾ mi [36½ km]
Flatwater, **Quickwater**, Class I–II
Passable at all water levels
Rural, Towns
    USGS: Montpelier 15, Waterbury, Richmond
Portages: 6 mi   L   **dam in Middlesex**
              16¼ mi   L   **Bolton Falls Dam** —½ mi

Access is at the Montpelier High School on the S bank just below the last bridge. About ¾ mile downstream from the high school, the Winooski goes under I-89 where the Dog River comes in from the L. There is another bridge 1¾ miles further downstream. The river continues with a slow current for another 3 miles to the bridge in Middlesex. Here the river divides. *Take the L channel* from which a portage can be made around the dam (6 mi).

Half a mile below the dam there is a chute followed by a large pool. With sufficient water this may cause open canoes some difficulty. There is quickwater for the next ½ mile to the mouth of the Mad River (7 mi) on the L just above the US-2 bridge. Below this is ½ mile of class II rapids, the first drop just around a corner being the most difficult. Then, 3½ miles of slow current bring you to the first bridge (11 mi) in Waterbury. Just after the third Waterbury bridge, the Little River (14 mi) enters on the R from Waterbury Reservoir.

Below the Little River 2¼ miles is Bolton Falls Dam (16¼ mi). **Caution!** This disused dam is in a natural gorge, and it is very dangerous to approach. Rapids start about ½ mile above the dam where the river swings to the R. Take out on the L at the southernmost part of the bend and carry across the field to the RR and the road. Take the first cart track to the R to reach the pool below the falls.

A little ways below the dam there is ¼ mile of class II rapids above the RR tressle (17 mi). The next 5¾ miles to Jonesville are quickwater. The Huntington River comes in on the L just below the bridge (22¾ mi).

Jonesville — Essex Junction   15½ miles

The river now leaves the mountains and follows a broad, smooth course through farmland. It is an easy, pleasant paddle.

1977   Jonesville — Essex Junction   15½ mi |25 km|
       Flatwater, **Quickwater**
       Passable at all water levels
       Rural
          USGS: Richmond, Essex Junction
          Portage: 15½ mi   e   **dam in Essex Junction** — 250 yds

---

There are 3½ miles of easy current to the bridge at Richmond and another 2½ miles past I-89 to the US-2 bridge (6 mi). Then you pass a RR bridge (8 mi), the bridge at North Williston (11 mi), another RR bridge (13¼ mi) before reaching the power dam (15½ mi) at Essex Junction. Portage on either side. The R side, although longer, is mostly on a road.

Essex Junction — Lake Champlain   16 miles

Most of the canoeable part of this run is smoothwater, but there are two difficult carries. Winooski Gorge is most easily enjoyed from the bank. In low water it is possible to visit the gorge by paddling down to it from a new access at the recreation area in Essex, returning back upstream to take out.

1977	Essex Junction — Lake Champlain	16 mi [25¾ km]

Flatwater, Quickwater
Passable at all water levels
Forested, Urban

USGS: Essex Junction, Burlington, Fort Ethan Allen, Colchester Point

Portages: 5¾ mi L **dam at Winooski Gorge** (see below)
6¾ mi   **dam in Winooski** (see below)

After ½ mile of class I rapids there are 4¾ miles of quickwater to Winooski Gorge which begins below Lime Kiln Bridge (5¼ mi). One-half mile further there is a RR bridge which precedes a dam. Take out on the L and carry up a steep bank and down the far side to the L beyond some cliffs. Below this first dam there is almost a mile of quickwater to the ledges above the next dam, but since there is no easy take-out above them, it is recommended that you portage both dams at one time by taking out at the launching ramp in Essex on the R bank and following the highway to Winooski. Such a portage by car is about 1½ miles long.

In Winooski there is access to the river on the R below the dam. The river meanders for 6½ miles to the VT-127 bridge (13¼ mi), and in another 2¾ miles it empties into Lake Champlain (16 mi). At the mouth of the river, there are cottages and a beautiful view across the lake towards the Adirondacks.

Bottom photo on page 25: The covered bridge crosses the West River near Jamaica, Vermont. The rapids are on the Pemigewasset River near Woodstock, New Hampshire. They are now spanned by a new bridge on NH-175.

CHAPTER 3
HUDSON
WATERSHED

Batten Kill   68
Hoosic River   70
Walloomsac River   71

HUDSON WATERSHED

Scale in miles
0   5   10   15   20   25   30

BATTEN KILL   VT, NY

The Batten Kill is a beautiful, clear stream which flows
west across southern Vermont from the Green Mountains
to the Hudson River. The water is clear and enjoyable for
swimming. It has a moderate current with riffles and only
two places — fairly close together and in the first section
— where a less skillful paddler might wish to line or carry.

	Manchester — Arlington	10½ miles
1976	**Flatwater, Quickwater**, Class I–II	17 km
	High or medium water: *spring and normal summers*	
	Rural	
	USGS: Equinox 15	

To put in, take the road E from the monument on US-7 in Manchester, and follow it for ¾ mile to a bridge. At the beginning the river is small and shallow. If there is enough water to run the rapid below the bridge, the river is runnable; but some fallen trees will have to be lined or lifted over.

It is 2¾ miles to the first bridge, below which the Batten Kill is generally slower and deeper. There is a mixture of flatwater and a few riffles. The river flows through farming country, much of which is posted. There is a good access to the river on the R bank just downstream of the US-7 bridge (8 mi).

After a mile of flatwater and just below the mouth of Roaring Branch (a large stream coming in on the L), there is a strong, fast current with class II rapids in high water where the river swings L and is divided into two channels by a big rock. If you wish to line or carry this spot, do so on the R.

Easy rapids continue past the VT-313 bridge (9¾ mi), which also provides good parking upstream on the L. One-half mile below, where the river takes a sharp turn to the R, there is a pool followed by a washed-out dam which can be scouted from the R bank if desired. Shortly beyond is Rochester Bridge (10½ mi) located off VT-313 just W of Arlington.

Arlington — East Greenwich   20 miles

The river here is a little wider, and it runs quickly and steadily, giving a fast ride through easy riffles. Except when it is very dry, it can be run all summer, and there are occasional, deep pools for swimming. This stretch is also very popular for float trips on rubber rafts, inner tubes, air mattresses, logs, and anything else which will float.

The river is crossed every couple of miles by a bridge, from any one of which there is access to the river.

1976   Arlington — East Greenwich   20 mi [32¼ km]
Quickwater, Class I
Passable at most water levels
Forested, Rural, Towns
     USGS: Equinox 15, Shushan, Salem, Cossayuna

In 3 miles you pass the mouth of the Green River near West Arlington, and 4½ miles farther is the NY-313 bridge (7½ mi). To improve the fishing on the Batten Kill, the state of New York has built several rock cribs and a low, sometimes-runnable weir. The latter extends across

the river above the County 61 bridge (8¾ mi) — the first
one below NY-313 and known as the "Tackle Box."

After several miles the river swings N, passes
Shushan (13¾ mi), goes under four RR bridges and NY-22
(17¾ mi), and then heads W again. Go under another RR
bridge near East Greenwich, and take out on the R above
the dam (20 mi).

HOOSIC RIVER   MA, VT, NY

USGS: Williamstown, Pownal, North Pownal, Hoosick Falls,
Eagle Bridge, Schaghticoke, Mechanicville

The Hoosic River rises in Lanesboro, Massachusetts, flows
north to North Adams, where it turns west to Williamstown, and then takes off northwesterly across a corner of
Vermont into New York, where it again turns north to
make a big loop to meet the Hudson River near Mechanicville. Its polluted water is most noticeable at low water.

North Adams — North Pownal   15 miles
Put in at the end of the dikes west of North Adams. This
section of the river flows through one of the most rural
areas of Massachusetts and provides a very pleasant
paddle. The valley is broad and open to Williamstown and
then turns north, narrowing as it passes into Vermont.
There are a number of easy riffles but no heavy rapids to
the dam at North Pownal, where there is a portage of less
than ½ mile.

North Pownal — Hoosick Falls   15 miles
This is a pleasant run through farming country with high
hills on either side of the valley. There are a few easy
riffles. On approaching Hoosick Falls take out on the left
just before the railroad bridge. **Caution!** Under no condition go below the railroad bridge as the steep rapid
beneath it is followed by rapids confined between concrete
retaining walls, which lead into impassable cataracts
below. As there is no convenient place to relaunch the
canoe below these falls and the power dam 1 mile below
involves another carry, it is better to portage by car
2 miles to Hoosick Junction.

Hoosick Junction — Valley Falls   17 miles

From Hoosick Junction the river provides a fast run for the
3½ miles to Eagle Bridge, where one should keep to the
right at the railroad bridge to avoid the heavy current
against the bridge pier. The current continues although
somewhat diminished another 3½ miles to Buskirk, but
below here the lake behind the high power dam at Johns-
ville is met. Carry this dam on the right ¼ mile. Below the
dam, the current picks up for 2 miles through pleasant
woodland until the slackwater from the dam at Valley
Falls is reached, and then another 2 miles down the lake
completes the trip to Valley Falls, where most canoeists
will elect to take out as there are numerous dams and
questionable gorges below.

WALLOOMSAC RIVER   VT, NY

The Walloomsac flows west from Bennington to the
Hoosic River. It provides a delightful paddle through beautiful and historic terrain. The river riffles over gravel beds
and around fallen trees, sometimes near the road or railroad, sometimes more remote. It is best to run it in the
spring, as stretches may be too shallow in the summer.

Bennington — Walloomsac Village   8¾ miles

XXXX   Flatwater, **Class I**   14 km
        High or medium water: *spring or after moderate rain*
        Rural, Towns
           USGS: Bennington, Hoosick Falls
        Portages: 1¼ mi   **dam at Paper Mill Village** (carry on island)
                 2¼ mi   L   **dam** — 30 yds

      Begin a couple of miles W of Bennington off
VT-67A by following Silk Road across the covered bridge.
Put in where the road comes close to the river opposite a
yellow house.
      Winding over riffles and passing under the
covered bridge, the stream becomes flat as it reaches the
first dam at Paper Mill Village in 1¼ miles. The dam is
under the second covered bridge. The stream divides here.
Both sides are dammed, and the carry is across an island.
      There is some class II water for a short distance
below the first dam (1¼ mi). The next dam, 1 mile farther,

is slightly above a bridge and it is not too conspicuous. A white colonial house on the L across an open field is a good landmark. Carry on the L. After about 2¼ miles more of pleasant riffles, the hamlet of Sodom is reached. Here there is a tiny dam or obstruction entirely across the river. This may be readily run at high water, but it might have to be carried at lower water levels.

About 4 miles below Sodom (4½ mi), the dam at the Columbia Products factory is reached. The riffles are almost continuous in the last ½ mile, and the dam (8¾ mi) appears suddenly around a bend to the R. The tall smoke-stack is very conspicuous, however; and as soon as it comes into view, caution should be observed. Canoes may be taken out on the L and carried uphill through a farm field to the road.

It is possible to relaunch well below the dam and the rapids, but there is only about a mile to the next dam (10 mi) at the Flomatic Valve Company where getting out is difficult. Carrying around it is even harder. There is no good take-out point below here, unless you continue down the Hoosic below the mouth of the Walloomsac (11¾ mi).

CHAPTER 4
UPPER CONNECTICUT
WATERSHED

Connecticut River   76
Ammonoosuc River   85
Ashuelot River   88
Ashuelot River,
   South Branch   92
Black River   94
Cold River   96
Gale River   97
Gale River, Ham Branch   99
Halls Stream   99
Indian Stream   101
Israel River   102
Little Sugar River   103
Mascoma River   103
Moose River   107
Nash Stream   108
Nulhegan River   108
Ompompanoosuc River   109

Ottauquechee River   109
Otter Brook   111
Passumpsic River   113
Phillips Brook   114
Saxtons River   114
Sugar River   115
Upper Ammonoosuc River   116
Waits River   117
Wardsboro Brook   118
Wells River   119
West River   120
White River   121
White River, First Branch   124
White River, Second Branch   124
White River, Third Branch   125
Williams River   125
Winhall River   127

UPPER CONNECTICUT WATERSHED

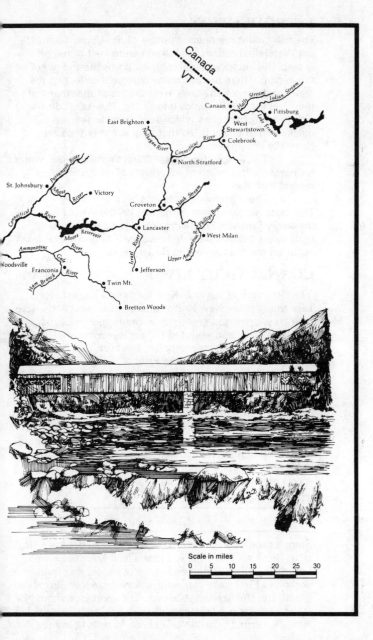

Canada
VT

Indian Stream
Hall Stream
Canaan
West Stewartstown
Pittsburg
Lake Francis
East Brighton
Mohegan River
Connecticut River
Colebrook
North Stratford
St. Johnsbury
Passumpsic River
Victory
Moose River
Groveton
Nash Stream
Connecticut River
Lancaster
Israel River
West Milan
Upper Ammonoosuc & Phillips Brook
Moore Reservoir
Ammonoosuc River
Woodsville
Franconia
Gale River
Ham Branch
Jefferson
Twin Mt.
Bretton Woods

Scale in miles
0   5   10   15   20   25   30

INTRODUCTION

The hilly and mountainous terrain of the Upper Connecticut Watershed causes rainfall and snowmelt to run off fairly fast. Thus quickwater and rapids dominate the rivers in this region. There are not many big rivers collecting the drainage from a large area, with the result that many of them get too low to run by late spring. There are some very nice flatwater sections which tend to be broken up by quickwater and rapids, so that long summer trips are generally not possible.

   The Connecticut River always has sufficient water for passage, but much of it consists of long, thin lakes behind high dams.

   There are water releases on a few of the rivers. The most widely known is the one on the West River that the Army Corps of Engineers schedules for a weekend early in the fall. Annual fall drawdowns of headwater lakes occur on the Mascoma and Sugar rivers.

CONNECTICUT RIVER   NH, VT

The Connecticut River is New England's longest river. Like many other New England rivers it is most attractive near its source, and gradually becomes more sluggish, industrialized, and polluted farther downstream. Canoeing on the lower river is popular, however, and it can be canoed in summer. From the head of navigation for the canoeist, the upper end of First Connecticut Lake, it offers about 400 miles of varied lake and river paddling with few unrunnable sections, but with fifteen dams requiring carries of varing lengths.

   The Connecticut River Watershed Council, 125 Combs Road, Easthampton, MA 01027, publishes a guidebook, *The Connecticut River Guide*, price $4.50, with maps showing the fishing sailing, boating, and water sports areas.

The Connecticut Lakes

USGS: Second Lake 15, Indian Stream 15

From its source at Fourth Lake, the Connecticut is a tiny trout brook to Third Lake. From Third Lake to Second Lake it is still too small and steep to canoe, and from Second to First Lake canoeing is not advised. Some canoeists do run this stretch, however, but great care should be taken as there is a tremendous drop halfway down, which must be carried. This drop is about ½ mile below the

Second Lake dam and about 50 yards below a left turn in the river. Although both Second and Third lakes offer pleasant canoeing, fishing, swimming, and other water sports, the canoeist wishing to run the river will probably start at the head of First Lake. A side road leading from Route 3 to Mettaluk Point offers easy access to that end of the lake. There is a launching area at the foot of the lake near the dam. Below First Lake the stream becomes canoeable for the first time, but as the level of First Lake is controlled by a dam there is apt to be insufficient water unless some is being let through for power. Water releases are, however, posted daily at the dam. Below the dam the river is very rough and steep for 1 mile, then easier rapids follow for ½ mile to the entrance of Perry Stream on the right. These easy rapids continue another 1 mile to Lake Francis, but under some water conditions this entire stretch can offer hard rapids, the last 150 yards of which will bear prior examination. Lake Francis is an artificial lake over what was formerly a less attractive stretch of river through farm lands. Below the Lake Francis dam there is rapid river to the bridge and dam at Pittsburg, where one must take out. **Caution!** Take out above the dam as there is an impassable gorge for 1½ miles below to a covered bridge. It is possible to line down this gorge in low water, but if a car is available it is much easier to carry and one must carry at medium to high water.

Pittsburg — North Stratford/Bloomfield 33¾ miles

The upper Connecticut River is apt to be a disappointment for would-be wilderness trippers. The solitude that can be found here is all too meager when you consider the long drive from the population centers of New England and the more isolated areas which are available not much more distant to the east. Nonetheless, an outing on this section can certainly be a pleasant one, although the river throughout even the uppermost parts is buccolic, not wild.

Opposite Colebrook, New Hampshire the river passes close to Monadnock Mountain. This 3,140-foot mountain offers fine views of the Connecticut River Valley to the north and south from the abandoned firetower at its summit. A climb of the mountain makes an excellent side trip. Plan on taking three to four hours. The trail is not well-maintained, and it is slippery and treacherous since the trail also doubles as a streambed in spots. Abandoned telephone wire is under foot at numerous places on the trail, and it is sometimes very difficult to see. A very pleasant

falls and a pool are located one-third of the way up the
2¼-mile trail, and they make a perfect lunch spot.

1976 Pittsburgh — North Stratford/Bloomfield   33¾ mi [54½ km]
Flatwater, **Quickwater**, Class I–II
Passable at most water levels
Forested, Rural, Towns
Monadnock Mountain Firetower: Stop at the bridge at Colebrook.
The 2¼-mile trail begins between the first two houses on
the W shore. It runs through an open field, and then heads
into the woods.

USGS: Indian Stream 15, Averill 15, *Dixville 15*
Portage: 9 mi R **Canaan Dam** — ½ mi
Campsites: 2 mi R **Indian Stream**
28½ mi L **Countryside Campgrounds**

Begin at the L of the covered bridge on Bacon
Road just off US-3 and 0.9 miles S of Pittsburgh. There is
also a small parking area here which is out-of-sight of the
main highway.

Starting immediately under the bridge, there are
150 yards of class II rapids in high water. Then for the next
2 miles the Connecticut has intermittent class I+ rapids.
The highway, US-3, follows almost constantly within sight
of the river on the R with an attractive, forested area rising
on the L. Two miles beyond Indian Stream (2½ mi), which
enters on the R, US-3 (4½ mi) passes over the river, and
below this point there are 350 yards of class I rips. The
boundary marker between New Hampshire and Vermont is
½ mile further, and S of this point the Connecticut River
forms the border between the two states.

In another 2¼ miles Halls Stream (7½ mi) enters
on the R, and shortly after passing under a bridge with
houses visible on each bank, you reach Beecher Falls
(8 mi). The falls are a short class II rapid that may be run at
any point, although passage on the extreme L or R is
probably drier and safer.

Canaan Dam lies 1 mile below Beecher Falls and
is most easily portaged on the Vermont side. In high water
more experienced boaters who are willing to do some
scrambling over the large wooden sluice pipe on the R
bank can put back in almost immediately below the dam.
The river should be taken to the R of the islands after the
dam, but the going is scratchy in high water and probably
impassable in low. A longer portage of ½ mile on the R is
the more conventional route around the dam.

After a level stretch there is a short, solid class III

drop before the NH/VT-114 bridge at West Stewarts-
town/Canaan (9½ mi).

From West Stewartstown/Canaan to Colebrook,
10 miles, the river is mostly flat and relatively shallow,
except for the Horserace, a 100-yard class I–II rapid
½ mile below the bridge. It meanders through level pasture
lands which border both sides of the river. Dairy cattle
graze along the banks for most of this section; reason
enough to bring along fresh-water if you plan to camp. At
Colebrook the river passes below Monadnock Mountain
which rises steeply on the Vermont side.

Below Colebrook (19½ mi) the river is flat for
3 miles; then it develops small rips for another 2 miles. It
continues mostly smooth for 4 miles below the Columbia
covered bridge to Countryside Campgrounds on the L
(28½ mi). About 1¾ miles below the campground, a stone
and earth works protrudes from the L shore. The river
should be taken on the R through small riffles.

Two and a half miles below Countryside Campgrounds are the remains of Lyman Falls Dam (31 mi). The
river has several islands on the L side, and canoeists can
put ashore here to scout the remains of the dam before
running. The river may be run to the L of these islands
through a passage which is narrow and scratchy in high
water and probably impassable in low. If run in this
manner, you are almost certainly committed to taking the
remains of the dam on the extreme L.

Caution! The remains of Lyman Dam should be
scouted, but to the moderately skilled whitewater canoeists it provides probably the most sport on the Connecticut
to this point. In high water the best run over the old dam is
directly below the log crib which lies 75 yards upstream.
The small curler below the dam can provide some very
interesting spots for canoeists to play and surf. In higher
water it should be approached cautiously, but the curler
should not present a problem to a strong class II boater.
Even so, it is probably best not to engage in too much play
at this point without being prepared for a swim.

There are riffles for the next 2¾ miles to North
Stratford/Bloomfield (33¾ mi).

North Stratford — Guildhall   25 miles

USGS: *Averill 15*, Guildhall 15

The river is placid with wide meanders from here to the
dam at Guildhall. It is 5 miles to Stratford Center opposite

which Paul Stream enters on the Vermont side, and
another 6 miles to the bridge at Stratford. It is then
11 miles with wide meanders on a flat river plain with fine
views of the mountains to the confluence with the Upper
Ammonoosuc River at Groveton. Only 3 miles farther on,
the bridge and dam at Guildhall is reached. As water is
spilled over the top at all times, this dam should not be
approached too closely without checking, especially at
high water when one might easily be inadvertently swept
over. The portage trail is on the Vermont side just to the
right of the power house, but less experienced canoeists
may prefer to take out farther upstream to avoid the risk of
being swept over.

Guildhall — Gilman   23 miles

USGS: Guildhall 15, Whitefield 15

The placid water continues for the next 23 miles to the
dam at Gilman. It is 10 miles to Lancaster, where the
Israel River enters ½ mile below the bridge, near which is
located on the left bank Treffrey's Campground with good
facilities. There follow 7 miles of winding river to the
bridge at South Lancaster and another 3 miles to the next
bridge at South Lunenburg. About ¼ mile below the railroad bridge one should watch carefully for large boulders
just beneath the surface, which could easily overturn a
laden canoe. From there it is only 3 miles more to the dam
and bridge at Gilman. One can easily take out on the New
Hampshire side at the end of the boom above the dam.
If prior arrangements are made with the Gilman Paper
Company, a vehicle can sometimes be made available for
the carry to the gravel pit on the Vermont side below the
bridge.

Gilman — East Ryegate   30 miles

USGS: Whitefield 15, Littleton 15, Saint Johnsbury 15,
Woodsville 15

The beautiful Fifteen-mile Falls section of the river
formerly began at Gilman, but these fine rapids, the best
on the river, are now completely inundated by the Moore
Reservoir and the Comerford Reservoir, although when the
former is low there are still a ¼ to ½ mile or more of fastwater with rocks and boulders. The New England Power
Company, which operates these two dams and the McIndoe Falls Dam below, has provided a number of boat

launching and picnic areas on the reservoirs, but no overnight camping is allowed at these points. One can put in at
Gilman on the Vermont side just below the bridge. From
here to the Moore Dam are 12 miles of paddling, mostly
lake travel on the reservoir, although when the water level
is low there may be as much as ½ mile or more of easy
rapids. Care should be observed, however, if the water
volume is large as the waves can be high. Once on the
reservoir the going is very pleasant but a head wind can
make progress a strenuous affair. It is, therefore, usually
best to start this section early in the morning before the
wind rises. There are three boat launching and picnic
areas on the south shore of the reservoir and one on the
north bank in Waterford near the dam. The carry at the
Moore Dam is on the Vermont side, about ½ mile long and
well marked by signs. The bank at the put-in place is
somewhat unstable so that care should be taken.

As the backwater from the Comerford Dam
comes practically to the Moore Dam, the 7 miles between
the dams are practically all lake paddling. There is a boat
launching and picnic area just below the Route 18 bridge
on the New Hampshire side and another one on the
Vermont side not far above the dam. The carry at the
Comerford Dam is on the New Hampshire side, about
½ mile long, and marked by signs.

The 7 miles from the Comerford Dam to the
McIndoe Falls Dam can be very interesting. If the Comerford Dam is discharging water the current will be swift and
the paddling easy although there are some large boulders
about 1 mile below the dam which present hazards to navigation. In another 1 mile the Passumpsic River enters on
the right and the river turns to a southerly course. The
next 5 miles are through a narrow wooded valley with high
hills on either side most of the way. The portage at the
McIndoe Falls Dam, on the New Hampshire side, is easy,
about 200 yards long, and well-marked.

The narrow wooded valley continues for the next
4 miles to the Ryegate Paper Company's dam at East Ryegate. This 15-foot high dam should be approached with
caution as water is often spilled over the top. It is just
below a left bend in the river and as the carry is on the
New Hampshire side it is best to approach it along this
bank. Several portage routes are available varying from a
few hundred feet if the current is slow to several hundred
yards if the current is fast and one cannot approach the
dam closely.

USGS: Woodsville 15, Mount Cube 15, *Mascoma 15*, Hanover

This is one of the more interesting and picturesque sections of the river and one on which one will find a certain amount of canoeing and boating, especially in the lower portion. Below the dam at East Ryegate there is some fast-water and the best channel is usually on the New Hampshire side. It is 4 miles to Wells River-Woodsville, where the Ammonoosuc River enters on the left and ¼ mile below the Wells River enters on the right just below the Route 302 and railroad bridges. There is a short but easy rip just below these bridges, then 10 miles of shallow winding river to the bridge at Newbury. This bridge is closed to traffic but the town of Newbury is only ¼ mile down the road on the Vermont side, where provisions may be obtained. It is another 2 miles to the covered bridge at South Newbury. The valley has now become wider with farmland in the level areas and views of the mountains appear in the background. The current now begins to slacken as the water backed up by the Wilder Dam 37 miles below is reached. This section is now known as Wilder Lake and provided with boat launching ramps and picnic areas. There is little perceptible widening of the river for many miles. It is 6 miles to Bradford and the entrance of the Waits River on the right bank. Bradford is most easily visited by paddling up the Waits River (There is a campground ¼ mile upstream.). In another 1 mile one passes under the Route 25 bridge and in 10 miles more the bridge from Fairlee to Orford. Here it was that Samuel Morey tested his steam propelled vessel in 1792–3. At Orford, New Hampshire, there is a municipal boat-launching area where one can camp with the permission of the selectmen. There is a campground on the New Hampshire side ¼ mile below the bridge. It is then 6 miles to the next bridge at North Thetford and 2 miles more to that at East Thetford. By now the river is obviously becoming wider. Here on the New Hampshire side, in Lyme, are the River Landing Campsites operated by Ralph Fisher of Lyme, New Hampshire, with all kinds of supplies including rental canoes. In 5 miles one passes the mouth of the Ompompanoosuc River on the right and in another 5 miles the bridge at Hanover, below which it is only 2 miles to the dam at Wilder.

USGS: Hanover, North Hartland, Claremont 15, Bellows Falls 15

It is 2 miles down Wilder Lake to the dam, which should be carried on the east side, where the ½ mile portage is well marked by signs. Below this dam the water levels can vary quite suddenly as the generators are started or stopped. The water is swift but shallow for 2 miles to White River Junction and the mouth of the White River on the right. The water becomes polluted by the sewage from the city but fortunately clears up after a few miles. Below the White River 1 mile the Mascoma River enters on the New Hampshire side, practically at the Route 89 bridge. Some 4 miles below here at North Hartland, the Ottauquechee River comes in on the Vermont side. It is then only 2 miles to the difficult and dangerous Hartland rapids, often called locally Sumner Falls, the scene of several drownings. A warning sign has been posted about 1½ miles upstream on the Vermont bank. If this sign is not noticed, the next warning is given by several huge boulders that emerge near the east bank of the river about ¾ mile above them. At the actual approach to the rapid, the river narrows and a wooded bank on the right juts out cutting off any view of the rapids below. Warning signs have been posted but are often removed by thoughtless vandals. **Caution!** These rapids should not be attempted in high water. They can be lined down or portaged on the right. The portage is marked and is about ½ mile long, ending at the picnic area at the foot of the rapid. At low water these rapids can be run by expert canoeists. At this time the entire river flows through two channels. That nearer the west bank, about 15 wide, has a drop too abrupt for loaded canoes. The other channel, near the center of river, is some 30 feet wide but narrows to only 7 feet at the bottom of the initial pitch where some large rocks must be avoided. Once through this pitch the haystacks can be ridden for 75 yards until an 180° turn right is made bringing the canoe into the western chute with only choppy water to the bottom of the rapid. Below the rapids it is 8 miles to the covered bridge at Windsor and then another 5 miles to the Route 103 bridge at Ascutney, just below which the Sugar River enters on the left, and Wilgus State Park offers camping areas on the Vermont shore. This whole stretch of river passes through fine hills with Mount Ascutney dominating the view. Below here there is a long stretch of river, 8 miles, around the Weathersfield

Bow to the entrance on the left of the Little Sugar River at North Charlestown. There follows 4 miles more of easy paddling down to the Cheshire Toll Bridge at Charlestown, just below which the Black River enters on the right. In 7 miles more one passes the mouth of the Williams River on the right, where there is a boat launching and picnic area, and then in 3 miles of deadwater the dam at Bellows Falls, where it is best to carry by car as it is a long portage, ½ to ¾ mile, right through the town. Either side of the river can be used but the easier route is probably on the east bank. Take out on the left above the arch bridge, and carry on New Hampshire side to below the falls.

Bellows Falls — Vernon Dam   31 miles

USGS: Bellows Falls 15, Keene 15, Brattleboro 15

Below the powerhouse at Bellows Falls one passes the mouth of the Saxtons River in ½ mile on the right bank and in another ¼ mile the Cold River on the left bank, and then in 2 miles more the bridge at Walpole. About 5 miles below this bridge there is a good campsite on the left just above Houghton's Brook in Walpole. There are then 14 miles of unobstructed river through open farming country to the Route 9A bridge above Brattleboro. In 1 mile more the West River enters on the Vermont side and then in another 1 mile the Route 119 bridge is reached. From the double bridges at Brattleboro there are 7 miles of deadwater to the dam at Vernon, which requires a ¼-mile carry on the west shore from the log boom above the dam. The portage is marked by signs.

Vernon Dam — Turners Falls   20 miles

USGS: *Brattleboro 15*, Keene 15, Northfield, Millers Falls, Greenfield

Below the dam the going is swift and may be rocky if the water is low. It is only 2 miles to the mouth of the Ashuelot River in Hinsdale and in another 3 miles the Massachusetts border is crossed. All through here and for the next 10 miles to the gorge at French King the river flows through open farmland, which offers good camping spots. In 1½ miles from the border the Route 142 bridge is reached. From there it is 8½ miles to the gorge, at the upper end of which there is a large rock which causes turbulence even when the rest of the river is calm. A route close to either shore is to be preferred at this point. Here the current quickens and the river turns right under the French King Bridge at the confluence of the Millers River and continues heavy to Turners Falls, 4 miles. At high water this section of river can become extremely rough and under these conditions some canoeists may prefer to take out at the bridge which crosses the Millers River at its mouth. At Turners Falls one should take out at the steel bridge ¼ mile above the dam, on the right side.

AMMONOOSUC RIVER   NH

The Ammonoosuc River, one of the largest rivers in New Hampshire north of the White Mountains, flows from the western slopes of Mount Washington to the Connecticut River at Woodsville. It offers some of the finest white-water canoeing in New England. This river is famous for a strong, upstream wind; and even in rapids it may be necessary to paddle hard to progress downstream.

Bretton Woods — Twin Mountain,   **7 miles**

Scouted only. See the USGS Mount Washington 15 and Littleton 15 sheets.

Begin at the junction with Clinton Brook near the Bretton Woods church. The water is smooth but fast for 3½ miles to Lower Ammonoosuc Falls, a 30-foot cascade.

The next 3 miles after the falls contain several rapids which are normally impassable. The last of them is ½ mile east of Twin Mountain. Then there are moderate class III rapids to Twin Mountain where there is an especially rocky drop above the US-3 bridge (7 mi).

Twin Mountain — Littleton   **16 miles**

1976

Quickwater, **Class II–III**   25¾ km
High water: *late April thru May*
Forested, Rural, Towns
   USGS: Whitefield 15
   Portages: 7½ mi e **Maplewood Dam** — 100 yds
               16 mi   **dam at Littleton**

Put in at the US-3 bridge (or ½ mile above town off US-302). Below the bridge there are class II rapids with small waves at high levels and lots of rocks to dodge at lower levels. It is 3 miles to the River Bend Motel, where the road leaves the river and the difficulty of the rapids increases to class III and IV. At high levels the boater should hug the shore to avoid the large waves in the center, and when the water is lower, fast maneuvering is required.

It is 2¾ miles from the motel to the steel truss bridge on US-302 — the Pierce Bridge (5¾ mi) — which is preceded by a rocky patch that gives trouble at lower levels. Most of this run is away from the road, but one of the more difficult rapids can be inspected by driving E along the road on the S bank and looking upstream from the gauging station.

The first 1½ miles from Pierce Bridge to Maplewood Dam contain easier class II rapids that lead to the backwater of Maplewood Dam. It is possible to take out on the R at this point to avoid the dam and the gorge. Otherwise, paddle ¼ mile of deadwater to the abandoned 15-foot dam and portage on either side for 100 yards. The gorge below contains class IV rapids, and they are the most difficult ones normally run on this river. The hardest rapid begins 100 yards below the dam, and there is another difficult one adjacent to the old powerhouse. It is ¾ mile from the dam to the NH-142 bridge in Maplewood.

Below Maplewood (8¼ mi) the rapids begin as class III and gradually get easier. It is 1¾ miles to the Wing Road bridge, followed by 2¼ miles of class II rapids to Hatch Brook (12¼ mi) where you can see a small, pink house on the R bank and hear some rapids ahead. **Caution!** A short distance below is the class IV Alderbrook Rapid. At high water those wishing to avoid large waves can run down among the rocks on the R, while at lower levels the best channel starts near the L bank and moves in an "S" shape to the center. Scouting of either route is advisable.

It is ½ mile from the end of Alderbrook Rapid to the next rapid of consequence: a series of rocky class III drops adjacent to the RR tracks which is best run near the R bank. Then there is 1 mile of easier rapids past a RR bridge to a convenient take-out on the old road on the R bank (14 mi). Then there are 2 miles of quickwater to the 40-foot Littleton dam (16 mi) which spills water over the top.

Littleton — Lisbon	13 miles

1977	Class I–II	21 km
	High water: *late April thru May*	
	Rural, Towns	
	USGS: Whitefield 15, Littleton, Sugar Hill, Lisbon	
	Portages: 1¾ mi L **unrunnable ledges**	
	13 mi R **dam in Lisbon** — ¼ mi	

Put in below the dam or at the Redington Road bridge ¼ mile beyond. There are 1½ miles of class II rapids to the center of town where there is a girder bridge on US-302. Below it there is a series of granite ledges which are normally unrunnable, and which can be most easily lined or carried on the L. Below them is a short class III rapid followed by ½ mile of class II rapids to Bridge Street (2½ mi), an alternate starting point for those wishing to avoid the ledges

The remainder of the run to Lisbon is unusual in that different routes in a rapid often vary in difficulty from class I to class III, so that skillful canoeists can choose between thrills and a dry boat. It is 4½ miles to a bridge on a side road and then another ¼ mile to the Gale River which enters on the L under a RR bridge.

The mouth of the Gale River (7¼ mi) marks the beginning of a particularly heavy rapid which is about ½ mile long. In another ½ mile a yellow house on the R bank marks a ledge which extends across the river at an island, but this ledge can be run in several places. In another 2 miles you reach a US-302 bridge (10¼ mi). The last major rapid is just below it; then there are 2¾ miles of class I rapids to Lisbon (13 mi). Take out well above the bridge on the R, because there is a dam just before it.

Lisbon — Woodsville   11½ miles

1977   Flatwater, **Quickwater**, Class I   18½ km
          High or medium water: *April and May*
          Rural, Towns
              USGS: Lisbon, Woodsville 15
          Portages: 6¾ mi R **dam at Bath** — 200 yds
                      11½ mi   **dam at Woodsville**

Put in on the R at a ball field ¼ mile below the bridge. There is a fast current with occasional standing-wave rapids for 6½ miles to Bath. Take out above the covered bridge on the R and carry 200 yards to a cove below the dam. There is a mile of fast current with one rapid to the mouth of the Wild Ammonoosuc River (7¾ mi), which is followed in ¼ mile by a RR bridge.

Below the RR bridge (8 mi), keep to the R bank to avoid a large wave adjacent to the gauging station. There are another 2½ miles of fastwater to where a road on the R bank offers a potential take-out. Then a mile of smooth-water leads to the covered bridge (11½ mi) in Woodsville. Just below it there is a dam, and at the foot of the dam is the Connecticut River.

ASHUELOT RIVER

The Ashuelot River is a beautiful tributary of the Connecticut, entering from the east only a short distance above the Massachusetts line. The type of canoeing varies so widely that it is doubtful if any one canoeist will like the whole river, but shorter trips can be arranged to suit almost any taste.

The upper stretches are all rapid and rough. The middle reaches are largely winding, placid river, while the last few miles provide some of the wildest running in New Hampshire. The upper part must be done in the spring; the lower section can sometimes be run in summer or fall. The middle section can be paddled most of the year.

Marlow — Gilsum Gorge   4½ miles

This section is known as the "Upper Ashuelot" and makes a good whitewater run for intermediate or expert paddlers. The scenery is somewhat marred by the fact that NH-10 is almost always present on the bank, but this makes put-in and take-out easier.

There is a gauge near the beginning of Gilsum Gorge. It is located on the right retaining wall just upstream of an old stone bridge just off NH-10. This section is scratchy but passable at a reading of 3.5; at 5.5 the river is class IV. The gorge has been run at levels around 3.5 and 4.1

1976 | Marlow — Gilsum Gorge   4½ mi |7¼ km|
Class III–IV
High to medium water: *April*
Forested, Town
    USGS: Lovewell Mountain 15, Bellows Falls 15
    Portage: 4½ mi L **Gilsum Gorge** (cross river in 200 yds) — ¾ mi

Though it is sometimes possible to paddle on the Ashuelot around Marlow, the normal put-in is a couple of miles S of the town along NH-10. Just below a pond-like section in the river, known as "Lower Stillwater," there is a small bridge over the river that makes a possible put-in (0 mi). This spot is only recommended for those who like to start with a bang, as there is a difficult class IV rapid — the hardest regularly-run pitch on the river — a couple of hundred yards below the put-in. This "Surprise Rapids" can be examined from NH-10, and it should definitely be scouted.

Surprise Rapids is followed by much easier class II–III rapids. The river bends to the R and is followed by an old elbow of NH-10 (½ mi), while the newer road continues straight ahead. This old loop is the usual put-in, since most groups do not want to start off with Surprise Rapids. Here the rapids are easy class II. Another small bridge is passed, and the easy rapids flatten out to smoothwater (1 mi).

Below a short pool the current speeds up considerably, marking the beginning of continuous rapids. The river is narrowed by the road embankment on the L. The next 2 miles contain many difficult class III and IV rapids. There is much maneuvering to be done, even at high water levels. Fortunately, NH-10 and its older loops are always nearby for an emergency take-out.

At the end of this 2-mile stretch, the river becomes relatively calm and splits around an island. The R side should be taken to get in position for a small broken dam below. The broken dam is about 1½ feet in height, and it is best run on the far R. One hundred yards below it is the NH-10 bridge in Gilsum (3½ mi), where the sawmill on the L provides a possible take-out.

Rapids continue through Gilsum, with the road or houses fairly close on the R. The rapids in this section are less difficult than those above, but they can have heavier waves, particularly near the end. Take out just below the next NH-10 bridge (4½ mi) at a picnic area on the L. Plan and execute this landing with caution, as the current is strong and the gorge begins a couple of hundred yards below.

An old stone bridge just off NH-10 marks the actual entrance to the gorge. From the bridge the gorge and its first drop are very impressive. The main current undercuts and deflects off an enormous rock in the center. Gilsum Gorge has been run in relatively low water, but this is a difficult stunt.

Gilsum Gorge — Shaw's Corner   4 miles

This run begins just below the Gilsum Gorge, where the river has pounded between spectacular 30-foot rock walls. This section is often called the "Lower Ashuelot," despite the existence of another whitewater run farther downstream. The Lower Ashuelot is very popular for novice-intermediate whitewater trips.

Water levels required for this section are about the same as the stretch above Gilsum Gorge. If the gauge above the stone bridge at the head of the gorge reads 3.5, the river is low but runnable; at 5.5 or higher you can expect a number of class III rapids.

Gilsum Gorge — Shaw's Corner   4 mi |6½ km|
Flatwater, **Class II–III**
High to medium water: *April*
Forested
     USGS: Bellows Falls 15

A put-in can be made where the river first
approaches the road below Gilsum Gorge. The small May
Brook (0 mi) enters the river at this point, and there is a
short island in the stream.

Class II rapids continue to a small bridge (¼ mi).
Just below this bridge there is a shallow rapid; if this spot
is passable, then so is the rest of the run. The Ashuelot
bends L away from the road. The next stretch contains
many class II rapids and some tight turns. The river then
returns to the road (1¾ mi). The rapids increase slightly in
difficulty, approaching class III at water levels of 5.0 and
higher.

About 2½ miles from May Brook there is one spot
where the river goes around a R bend with large boulders
blocking the L side. Then the channel empties back to the
L. This is the most difficult spot other than Shaw's Corner
Rapids farther downstream.

For a long distance above Shaw's Corner, the
road remains close beside the river. The river turns L (3½
mi) and passes a long, straight stretch with a field on the R.
Then the stone remains of a bridge abutment are spotted
ahead on the R bank — this is the start of Shaw's Corner
Rapids. The river turns sharply L with a ledge on the L.
A short, rocky section is followed by three ledges, with
waves or hydraulics depending on the water level. Novice
and intermediate paddlers should look this spot over.

A suspension bridge (4 mi) just below Shaw's
Corner Rapids is the usual take-out.

Shaw's Corner — West Swanzey   20 miles

    USGS: Bellows Falls 15, Keene 15

From Shaw's Corner the rapids soon diminish, and
smoothwater continues for the remaining 4½ miles to the
Surry Mountain Flood Control Dam. Below this dam the
valley becomes wider and the stream meanders with high
cutbanks and sand flats. Gradually the river becomes
deeper and quieter until the houses of Keene appear on the
left. Fortunately the river flows around rather than

through Keene, and there is an easy portage on the right
of the only dam. A mile below here on the outskirts of the
city the Branch enters on the left. The current is slow
and the river is winding. A new channel cutting off some
meanders has been cut here. The Keene sewage plant
discharges its effluent here so this section should be
avoided at low water. In another 2 miles the Ashuelot
River, South Branch, enters on the left. In another 3 miles
West Swanzey is reached. The dam here is best portaged
on the left.

West Swanzey — Ashuelot   15 miles

USGS: Keene 15

Below the dam at West Swanzey the river continues placid
for 3 miles to a point ½ mile below the Westport bridge,
where there is a broken dam. This is easily run at ordinary
water stages. The next 8 miles to Winchester are all flatwater. The dam here can be carried to the left. Stillwater
continues for another 3 miles to Ashuelot.

Ashuelot — Connecticut River   5 miles

This section of the Ashuelot River has distinct advantages
and disadvantages. On the positive side, the rapids are
heavy and challenging, and the water level is often high
enough for summertime running. As drawbacks, the
frequent dams necessitate short and difficult portages, the
water is polluted, and many factories back right on the
river.

There is a Telemark System gauge a short ways
up the left bank from the NH-63 bridge in Hinsdale. A level
around 4.5 corresponds to medium water and 5.0 to high
water. At any runnable level the lower Ashuelot is one of
the larger and more forceful whitewater runs in New
England. Often, the waves are too large and the dams too
close together for safe sport in open boats.

1977   Ashuelot — Connecticut River   5 mi [8 km]
Flatwater, **Class III–IV**
Medium water: *spring and after heavy rains*
Forested, Urban
   USGS: Keene 15
Portages: ¼ mi e **first dam** — 30 yds
            ¾ mi R **second dam** — 50 yds
            1½ mi R **third dam** (difficult) — 50 yds
            2¼ mi R **fourth dam** (approach cautiously) — 30 yds
            3 mi   **fifth dam** — 30 yds

Put in at the covered bridge in Ashuelot. Here the river is wide with just a good current but no real rapids. Portage the first dam (¼ mi) on either side. Mostly smooth river continues to the second dam (¾ mi). There are several long, wavy class III rapids to the next dam (1½ mi) which requires a short but tough portage on the R. The rapids here are typical of the lower Ashuelot — turbulent and powerful in high water.

Below the third dam (1½ mi) the Ashuelot passes under a bridge to the Ashuelot Paper Company. In the next R turn lies the heaviest rapid of the trip, class III–IV even at lower water levels. This rapid should be looked over from the side road on the R bank. More rapids continue to the fourth dam (2¼ mi). This one is on a diagonal with respect to the river, from upstream L to downriver R. For the portage, use the R side. Approach with caution because of the strong current above the dam and because of the diversion canal on the R.

Several more large rapids bring the paddler to the backwater from the fifth dam. This last dam (3 mi) is just below a steel bridge in Hinsdale. Below it there is a sharp drop and then some easier rapids to the NH-63 bridge (3½ mi) in the town. Rapids diminish to smoothwater, and the river flows through a gap into the broad Connecticut River (5 mi).

ASHUELOT RIVER, South Branch   NH

The South Branch of the Ashuelot River is a small stream that rises in Troy, rushes steeply northwestward to Webb, and then flows more smoothly westward to a junction with the Ashuelot River in Keene. The rapid, upper part is only runnable a few days of the year.

Troy Gap — Webb   3 miles

This portion of the stream is hemmed in by very steep banks and it contains many difficult rapids. The river drops 300 feet in these 3 miles. The railroad and NH-12 follow the river closely, although they are not always visible. When runnable, the South Branch is narrow enough that it is a challenge just to keep paddlers from running on top of one another. This problem is accentuated by the potential for fallen trees which create a real hazard.

> The South Branch is a difficult run and it should not be attempted by inexperienced paddlers or open boats.

1977   Troy Gap — Webb   3 mi [4¾ km]
Class IV
High water: *April*
Forested
       USGS: Monadnock 15

Put in from NH-12 about 1½ miles N of the center of Troy. Here there are two bridges close together where the South Branch loops under the road. The stream passes immediately under a RR bridge with flatwater for the first 100 yards.

The rapids begin, become continuous, and increase to class IV in the next ½ mile. The river then turns L under a RR bridge and crosses twice under NH-12 (¾ mi). At these bridges are the most difficult rapids on the river. Paddlers must first contend with a large cross-wave off the RR bridge abutment, then a very steep drop followed by extremely rocky going between the two road bridges. Because this stretch has steep, rocky walls, it should be scouted from the road bridges *before* putting in.

The next 1¼ miles to a small pool and dam (2 mi) hold many more class IV rapids. The dam, easily visible from NH-12, has a notch in the center that makes it runnable. Rapids moderate in the next mile to a culvert that is on a construction company road in Webb. This spot is reached by leaving NH-12 and following the road toward East Swanzey for a few hundred yards to a side road on the L which leads 100 yards to the river.

Webb — Ashuelot River   9 miles

       USGS: Monadnock 15, Keene 15

Put in where the stream turns south away from Route 12 and follows the road to East Swanzey. It is some 2 miles to the millpond above the dam just below East Swanzey, with rapids much of the way. Below here the South Branch has good current and few rapids, winding through pasture land until it joins the main Ashuelot near Swanzey some 7 miles down.

BLACK RIVER   VT

USGS: Ludlow 15, Claremont 15

Few canoeists may care to do the whole Black River
because of the variety of running and length of the portages, but one can obtain easy paddling on the lakes and
upper river, a fine whitewater run from Whitesville to
Downers, or a good run over easier riffles on the lower river.

Black River Lakes   6 miles

These lakes, situated near Tyson, begin about 6 miles
south of the source of the river near Plymouth Union.
Deeply set among the hills they provide attractive canoeing at all seasons. Route 100 passes along the west side of
all four lakes. One can put in at the northern end of Lake
Amherst directly from the main highway and 1 mile below
lift over a low dam into the short river leading to Echo
Lake, 1 mile long. At the southern end of the lake a 1-mile-
long river, rocky and presenting problems except at high
water, leads through Tyson to Rescue Lake, which
provides another 2-mile-trip to Reservoir Pond, itself
1 mile in length. A low, 2-foot dam at the southern end
is easily crossed into the river, or one can take out on
Route 100.

Reservoir Pond — Whitesville   10 miles

Put in at the low dam at the southern end of Reservoir
Pond close to Route 100. This part of the river, passing
through farm country, is pleasant if not exciting, but there
are several mill towns and carries around dams. Water
conditions should be checked before running. It is mostly
placid with good current and several riffles. It is 3 miles
from the start to Ludlow, where there is a carry around the
dam. Another 4 miles brings one to Proctorsville, where
there is another dam and carry. In another 3 miles the
hydroelectric station at the head of Cavendish gorge is
reached. Pull out on the left and portage along the top of
the penstock ¼ mile, putting in below the power station.
To the right of the penstock is a spectacular gorge, which
should be visited. To the left of the power station is a
desolate field of boulders, now growing up with small
scrub, resulting from the flood of 1927, when the water rose
so high as to flow around the north side of Cavendish Hill
causing great destruction. Below the gorge the river is
much steeper, and is augmented at Whitesville, 1 mile
below, where there is a low dam, by Twentymile Stream.

Whitesville — North Springfield   12 miles

This stretch contains the heaviest rapids on the river as well as much easy and pleasant running. In 2½ miles the river passes under an iron bridge and in another ½ mile a picnic ground is reached. Here the river makes a left turn and heavier rapids (class III) begin. Those wishing only the exciting part may begin here. The beginning of this section is marked by an old bridge abutment. The river is narrowed by steep banks and passes over ledges and huge boulders. At moderate water this can all be run but is dangerous at high water. The rapids continue heavy for 3 miles to the covered bridge at Downers, where the river again turns to the right, south. Those wishing only the maximum excitement will probably take out here, but easy rapids and riffles continue another 2 miles to the bridge at Perkinsville. One can easily take out here on the old road on the left bank, reached from Route 106 at the bridge. Just below the bridge is a dam, best portaged on the right. At ¼ mile below is a chute which can be run. At 1 mile below Perkinsville there is a high power dam with fine cliffs on the left. Here there is a portage of 100 yards. The river continues without rapids 3 miles to the North Springfield Flood Control Dam. Unless one is continuing down the river, however, most canoeists will prefer to take out at the recreation area and boat launching ramp on the right bank near the Springfield airport at the head of the 1-mile-long lake behind the dam.

North Springfield — Connecticut River   9 miles

Put in below the dam, reached by a stub road from North Springfield. There is good current but no rapids 1 mile to the low dam at North Springfield, easily lifted over on the right. From here to Springfield, 3 miles, the river follows the highway through settled farming country. There is a fair current and several riffles to aid the paddler. At Springfield there are six dams and a nasty carry through the town that few will want to attempt without a car. **Caution!** Take out on the left above the dam at the Fellows Gear Shaper plant. Although this dam might be run under exceptional conditions the short rapid below ends in a 150-foot cascade and a series of dams in a narrow gorge which could easily kill the hardiest canoeist. The river can be reached again by carrying down the main street ¾ mile to the lower bridge. From this bridge it is an easy 2 miles with a few riffles to the small dam at Goulds Mill. This is easily carried and in another 1 mile the

Route 5 bridge is reached on the flowage from the Connecticut River. One can take out here or continue another 1 mile to the Connecticut River and paddle upstream ¼ mile to the Cheshire Toll Bridge, where Route 5 comes close to the river.

COLD RIVER   NH

There are many Cold Rivers in New Hampshire. This one originates in Acworth and flows west into the Connecticut River below Bellows Falls. It offers a fine set of fairly continuous rapids which are unfortunately broken into short segments by impassable obstructions. The 4 miles above South Acworth are class III; the 12 miles below it are mostly class II.

At high water most of the rocks are buried and standing waves appear. At lower levels a considerable amount of rock-dodging is required. There are many blind corners and fallen trees.

 East Acworth — Connecticut River   16½ miles

1975   Class II–III   26½ km
High water: *early April*
Medium water: *late April*
Rural, Towns
    USGS: Lovewell Mountain 15, Bellows Falls 15
    Portages: 4 mi R **dam and gorge at South Acworth** — ½ mi
                9¾ mi L **dam at Alstead** (difficult) — 100 yds
         9¾–10½ mi R **frequent obstructions** — ¾ mi
           13 mi R **Drewsville Gorge** — ¼ mi

In the first mile below East Acworth, the river drops 100 feet; all of it visible from the road. Put in at the first bridge where the rapids become easier. The river is very small and the gradient even, making a pleasant run with no special difficulties, just lots of rock-dodging. This portion requires more water than does the rest of the river. A mile above South Acworth NH-123A crosses. Take out on the R above the dam in the town. Portage the dam and the gorge for ½ mile along NH-123A.

Begin again ½ mile W of South Acworth where the river comes close to the road below a spectacular gorge. The first 4 miles to a covered bridge and a new adjacent bridge consist of frequent rapids with blind corners and fallen trees. Frequently, NH-123A is visible from the river, and there are many sugar maples lining the banks.

One-half mile below this pair of bridges, there is a particularly difficult spot with several channels and frequent fallen trees. Where a small slide appears on the L bank and the river turns R, get out to scout. In another ¾ mile the small pond and dam at Vilas Pool (9¾ mi) are reached.

It is best to take out on the L, break the trip, and begin again at the NH-123 bridge in Alstead, as the next ¾ mile consists of class III rapids mixed with broken dams and fallen trees.

From the NH-123 bridge (10½ mi) it is 2½ miles of easy class II rapids to the next NH-123 bridge (13 mi). Take out on the R well above the bridge, as underneath there is a 30-foot falls known as Drewsville Gorge. Familiarize yourself with this take-out before beginning a trip. With permission of the landowner, portage ¼ mile to the foot of the falls. The rapids below are class II–III at the start, and the river here is in a steep, rocky gorge. The rapids soon diminish to class II, except for one class III pitch 1½ miles below.

The river passes a large gravel pit where the quarrying equipment is visible from the river. Three miles below the falls you reach the third NH-123 bridge (16 mi) at Cold River. This is a good take-out for those not desiring to canoe the remaining ½ mile of quickwater past the NH-12 and RR bridges to the Connecticut River (16½ mi).

It is often possible to run the portion of the river below the waterfall when the water above it is too low.

GALE RIVER   NH

The Gale River drains the northern side of Franconia Notch and the surrounding mountains. Because the stream is confined in a narrow valley and the drainage area includes the steep slopes of Mount Garfield and Mount Lafayette, a summer rain sometimes raises the river to a runnable level. The stream's flow generally peaks twelve to twenty-four hours after a rain.

Off Route 18 — Jesseman Road   4 miles

This run is similar to the nearby Ammonoosuc River below Littleton. Half of it is through the village of Franconia.

1976   Off Route 18 — Jesseman Road   4 mi [6½ km]
           Class II
           High to medium water: *late April thru May and after heavy rain*
           Forested, Town
              USGS: Franconia, Sugar Hill

Put in a mile above NH-18 from a side road reached by taking Coal Hill Road up the S side of the river and following the L-most road at a three-way fork. There appears to be good canoeing above this point, but there is no convenient access.

The first mile to the NH-18 bridge is rocky with occasional fallen trees, so much boat-handling is required. Just below the bridge the river doubles in size as Lafayette Brook enters from the L at a heavy rapid. For the next 2 miles the river flows through Franconia Village with NH-18 on the R bank. The rapids are easy class II.

The Ham Branch enters from the L just above the NH-117 bridge (2½ mi). A concrete watergate on the R bank marks the point at which NH-18/116 leaves the river, although a side road continues on the R bank. Another mile of similar going brings you to the truss bridge on Jesseman Road (4 mi), the last take-out before the difficult rapids below.

Jesseman Road — Ammonoosuc River   4 miles

Below Franconia Village the Gale River drops through a winding valley to its confluence with the Ammonoosuc. The banks are uninhabited woods; the whole run is one of the more scenic and unspoiled in the White Mountains.

This run is for closed boats only. There is a hand-painted gauge on the rocks underneath the NH-116 bridge in Franconia. A reading of 0.5 constitutes a low but runnable level.

1977   Jesseman Road — Ammonoosuc River   4 mi [6½ km]
Quickwater, **Class III–IV**
High to medium water: *late April thru May and after heavy rain*
Wild, Rural
    USGS: Sugar Hill, Littleton 15

The put-in is reached by travelling N on NH-18 through Franconia. One mile past the center, go L onto Streeter Pond Road to Jesseman Road. Streeter Pond Road continues downstream to the take-out, but it does not follow the river.

The first ½ mile is quickwater through open fields. The rapids begin at a powerline crossing. They are class III with many large boulders in the streambed.

The rapids get a little harder. After 2 miles a sharp L turn brings you to the entrance of a gorge (2½ mi). This spot can be recognized when, below a pool, there are rock walls on both sides. Take out on the R well above the beginning of the gorge and scout. The gorge contains four drops, each followed by a short pool.

Below the gorge there is a short drop run on the far R. Then the boater should look for rock dikes extending from the R bank. Take out on the L to scout the next steep drop. The chute is on the far L, with a total drop of about 6 feet. A final drop must then be negotiated to a RR bridge where the Gale River joins the Ammonoosuc (4 mi).

GALE RIVER, Ham Branch   NH

This scenic tributary of the Gale River drains the western slopes of Kinsman Ridge. The highway, NH-116, runs parallel to the river, but it is not close.

 Route 116 — Franconia   **7 miles**

976
Class I–II   7 mi [11¼ km]
High water: *May*
Forested, Rural
   USGS: Sugar Hill

Put in at the northernmost NH-116 bridge, as the stream above is reported to contain impassable drops. The trip is initially a twisting, rocky class II with some small, fallen trees, so that care should be taken on blind corners. After 2¼ miles the river splits around an island, at the end of which are two barbed wire fences. In another ½ mile you reach a truss bridge on a road to a farm.

Below the bridge (2¾ mi) the river has easier class I–II rapids. There are good views of the Kinsman Ridge across the fields. Just above the third side road bridge, Bickford Hill Road (5¾ mi), there is a washed-out dam that is easily runnable. A short distance below, where the river approaches NH-116 on the R, there is a ledge which is best run on the L. In another 1¼ miles the Ham Branch enters the Gale River (7 mi) just above the NH-117 bridge in Franconia.

HALLS STREAM   PQ, NH, VT

Halls Stream is one of the northernmost rivers in New Hampshire. The canoeable portion of it was once the boundary between Quebec and New Hampshire, but due to channel changes the river presently meanders back and forth across the border. Most of the river is a pleasant run of easy rapids and a gravel bottom, with occasional problems caused by fallen trees.

Access to the upper river is best from the Canadian side, where gravel roads lead close to it in two places. There is a public road on the New Hampshire side along the lower river, and with four-wheel-drive vehicles it may be possible to reach the upper river via logging roads along Halls Stream or from Indian Stream.

The CNTS Malvina 21 E/3 map is best for the upper river as it shows the Canadian access. The USGS Indian Stream sheet is adequate for the lower river, but it shows only the American side of the border. The CNTS Coaticook 21 E/4 and Averill maps show the last mile. including the take-out.

Malvina Stream — Tabor Notch   9 miles

1976   Class I–II   14½ km
          High water: *April and May*
          Forested, Rural
              USGS: Indian Stream 15 — *see above*

The key to Canadian access is the village of Paquette (Saint Venant-de-Hereford), located about 10 miles N of Beechers Falls on PQ-27. Take the gravel road N out of the village up a long hill. After 5½ miles, go down a steep hill and turn R. Proceed ¾ mile to a bridge over Malvina Stream. Put in here or 1 mile downstream at a farm. If the water is too low, Halls Stream is probably too low as well.

Malvina Stream is a gravelly class I stream about a boat length wide. About ½ mile from the farm (0 mi), it passes an old RR and enters Halls Stream. The latter is mostly class I, but occasionally there are harder spots. One rocky drop adjacent to the old RR embankment should be looked over. The banks are mostly wooded.

Five and a half miles from Malvina Stream a large farm on the Canadian shore provides access. It is reached by taking the road E from Paquette for 1 mile.

The remainder of this section has not been run. In another 3 miles there is a farm (9 mi) on the New Hampshire shore and a gravel road adjacent to the river. This is at the foot of Tabor Notch, a deep pass on the New Hampshire side which has no road through it.

Tabor Notch — Connecticut River   9½ miles

1976   Quickwater, Class I   15¼ km
          High water: *spring and after moderate rain*
          Rural, Town
              USGS: Indian Stream 15, *Averill 15*

To put in on the New Hampshire side, follow the road up the E bank for 7 miles to a location adjacent to the river, after which the road ascends for ½ mile and ends at a farm.

There are occasional riffles and fallen trees. From time to time there is access on the New Hampshire shore. In 9 miles the international boundary runs W from the stream, which from that point flows through Vermont. Another ½ mile brings you to the bridge at Beechers Falls and, just below, the Connecticut River (9½ mi).

INDIAN STREAM   NH

This is the northernmost canoeable stream in New Hampshire, for it rises even further north than the Connecticut River into which it flows below Pittsburg. The river is formed by several branches joining near the former Depot Camp, an early logging headquarters which was so remote that it was supplied from the railroad in Malvina, Quebec.

Nearly the entire watershed is timberland owned by the Saint Regis Paper Company. The only habitations are occasional hunting camps and some farms in the valley adjacent to the Connecticut River. A gravel logging road leads up the east bank from US-3 to beyond Depot Camp, and a branch road connects to Back Lake.

The entire watershed lies within the town of Pittsburg. The region was claimed by both the United States and Canada, but each exercised only sporadic jurisdiction. In 1836 the settlers formed the Indian Stream Republic. This led to an immediate settlement of the boundary and brought an end to the dispute and the republic.

Depot Camp — Connecticut River	17 miles

1976 | Flatwater, Quickwater, Class I | 27½ km
High water: *May*
Forested, Rural
      USGS: Indian Stream 15

Put in by carrying to the river near Depot Camp or by coming down one of the branches if the water is high enough. There are a few easy rapids, then a long stretch of weaker current with meanders. The road is frequently nearby. The last 2½ miles to Camp Brook contain more rapids.

Camp Brook is about 0.5 miles N of the Indian Stream and Back Lake roads. The river is close to the road, and there is an old, unuseable bridge. South of this point

the road does not follow the stream. It is 2½ miles to the
site of Kim Day Dam (10½ mi).

Below the old damsite (10½ mi) there is a ledge
at the head of an island, followed by 200 yards of
class II–III rapids which can be portaged on an old road on
the L. Then there are about 3 miles of class I rapids
through woods. The last 3½ miles to the Connecticut River
consist of broad meanders through fields, passable in the
summer. The US-3 bridge is ¼ mile above the Connecticut (17 mi).

ISRAEL RIVER   NH

The Israel River originates on the slopes of Mount Jefferson in the Presidential Range. It flows northwest to the
Connecticut River near Lancaster. Called Sinoogawnock by
the Indians, it was renamed for Israel Glines, a hunter who
frequented the area before its settlement.

The upper portion is a pleasant class I run, while
below Riverton there are class II–III rapids. There are
occasional views of the Presidential Range looking back
upstream.

Jefferson — Connecticut River	13 miles

1977	Quickwater, **Class I–III**	21 km

High and medium water: *May*
Forested, Rural
  USGS: Mount Washington 15, Whitefield 15
  Portages: 9½ mi **ice control dam**
       11 mi **dam below Lancaster**

Put in at the NH-115A bridge 2½ miles S of
Jefferson Village. The river is a small stream flowing
through cultivated land with large trees along the banks.
There are some class I rapids and a few fine swimming
holes. It is 2½ miles to a side road bridge and another
3½ miles to the US-2 bridge in Riverton.

Below Riverton (6 mi) the banks become more
wooded and there are frequent class II rapids. It is 3½
miles to the mouth of Otter Brook, just below which is a
dam (9½ mi) built in 1975 by the Corps of Engineers to
trap floating ice and prevent flooding in Lancaster. It will be
necessary to carry it if the ice net has not been removed.

Just ½ mile below the ice control dam, there is a
washed-out dam with a 3-foot drop which can be run. This
begins a series of class II–III rapids which continue for
¾ mile to the covered bridge in Lancaster (10¾ mi). It is

another ¼ mile to the US-2/3 bridge, just below which is a low dam which can sometimes be run.

The last 2 miles to the Connecticut River (13 mi) are mostly smoothwater.

LITTLE SUGAR RIVER   NH

USGS: Claremont 15

The Little Sugar River rises in Unity and flows northwest and then west to reach the Connecticut River in North Charlestown. It is steep but can provide a sporty run in the spring with the right stage of water from Quaker City to North Charlestown. It runs through a wild and secluded valley with few houses or signs of civilization although a country road does run up the valley and provides access. As this road may be muddy in early spring it may be best to reach Quaker City over the hard road from Claremont or Crescent Lake.

Quaker City — North Charlestown   5 miles

One can put in at Quaker City below the bridge and dam. The stream is small and rocky requiring constant attention for the first 3 miles. There is then a much faster section which contains a 30-foot fall. **Caution!** Shortly below the Whiskey Road bridge, the third bridge below Quaker City, there is a sharp right turn and then a sharp drop to a sharp left turn next to two houses on the right bank. The canoeist should take out as soon as he recognizes this spot as the current is swift. Below the fall the rapids continue but lessen in severity to the Route 12 bridge. The new Route 12 crosses the river on a high fill pierced by a large culvert, which one can canoe through, but the opening should be inspected first to make sure there are no obstructions. About ½ mile below this the bridge at North Charlestown is reached and it is best to take out here as the river descends in a series of cascades to the flood plain of the Connecticut River less than 1 mile below.

MASCOMA RIVER   NH

The Mascoma River drains a large area west of Mount Cardigan and flows into the Connecticut near Lebanon. It is more removed from highways than road maps indicate.

For those interested primarily in running demanding class II and III rapids in attractive settings, there is a ¾-mile section on the upper river between the first and second US-4 bridges in Canaan. The 5 miles between

Mascoma Lake and Lebanon are highly recommended. All these rapids are scratchy but passable in medium water and very challenging in high water.

Canaan Center — Mascoma Lake   14¼ miles

The upper Mascoma River is small until it is joined by the Indian River which flows along US-4 from Canaan. Its scenery is a mixture of alder swamps, meadows, fields, forests, and a small town.

     The annual fall drawdown of Goose Pond in Canaan provides medium water for over 4 miles above Mascoma Lake. Put in at the second US-4 bridge, since the river just above Goose Pond Brook is flat and passable at all water levels. Check with the Water Resource Board (603-271-1110) for dates.

1977   Canaan Center — Mascoma Lake   14¼ mi [23 km]
Flatwater, Quickwater, Class II–III
High water: *recommended for first 3½ miles, April*
Medium water: *some rapids scratchy, May and after moderate rain*
Dam-controlled: *annual fall drawdown of Goose Pond (lower section passable)*
Forested, Rural, Town
     USGS: Mascoma 15
     Portage: 11 mi   L   **dam at dilapidated mill** — 100 yds
                 14¼ mi   R   **Mascoma Dam** — 20 yds

     Begin at Canaan Center. The stream is narrow, a boat-length wide; and in the first ¼ mile there are some continuous class II rapids. Some lining may be advisable, since it is not easy to see or maneuver near the beginning. There are two old, washed-out dams here. In the next ¼ mile the rapids ease up, to be followed by 3 miles of flat-water to the US-4 bridge W of Switch Road, which parallels the river to the E. The winding river is free of overhanging bushes, but there is apt to be an occasional, blocking tree that can be easily removed with the aid of a small saw.

     Below the US-4 bridge (3½ mi) there are 1½ miles of flatwater past the Indian River (4 mi) and a RR bridge (4¾ mi) to the beginning of a ¾-mile set of nearly continuous rapids. The first 400 yards to the second RR bridge are class III and these rapids begin with a very difficult drop, but there is a RR embankment close by on the R if you wish to carry. Between the second and third RR bridges, ¼ mile, the rapids are class II, and past the third RR bridge (5½ mi) they are easy class II, tapering to flatwater in another ¼ mile. There are short, easy rapids under and past the fourth RR bridge (6 mi), then ¼ mile of flat-water to the second US-4 bridge W of Goose Pond Road.

After the second US-4 bridge (6¼ mi) the river is flat with a good current as it makes a broad swing to the N past several fields and the mouth of the outlet of Goose Pond (7¾ mi). Watch out for electric fences strung across the water. Below the third US-4 bridge (9 mi) the river opens into a broad meadow. There are some easy rips before a millpond spanned by a RR bridge beside an abandoned factory. Portage the dam on the L.

Below the dam (11 mi) class II rapids run for ¼ mile past the next bridge to flatwater above Enfield. In the town there is a washed-out dam. Scout it. If you choose not to run the old log crib, it can be lined on the R in medium water; in high water that may not be so easy. It might be runnable in high water. This dam is located at a R turn shortly after the start of some easy class II rapids that extend for ¼ mile through town between three road bridges. A final ¼ mile of flatwater brings you to Mascoma Lake (12 mi). There is a good take-out point just past a motel on the R (12¼ mi).

If you are continuing to Lebanon, the dam is located 2 miles away at the NE end of the lake (14¼ mi).

Mascoma Lake — Lebanon   5½ miles

Below the dam on Mascoma Lake, there are 5 miles of excellent class II–III rapids. The river here flows in a deep, wooded ravine. Except for a short section near exit 17 on I-89, and again in the middle of Lebanon, the river provides a very scenic run, in addition to being continuously challenging. It is still a small river, typically ten to twenty yards wide and two to four feet deep in medium water. There are many bends, and the rapids seem to go on endlessly.

At high water this section is a difficult class III. There are many large boulders to create turbulence, and visibility around some of the turns is restricted, making it necessary to approach them cautiously. Furthermore, two or three trees are apt to inconveniently block some channels. A railroad crosses the river nine times, but it does not appreciably detract from the scenic quality of the valley. Neither does Heater Road, a dirt road above the L bank of the upper section which is helpful if you wish to scout the river.

At medium water the river is still exciting, but it only rates as a difficult class II. It is scratchy in places, but there is plenty of time and room to maneuver your boat. The annual fall drawdown of Mascoma Lake provides medium water. Check with the Water Resources Board (603-271-1110) for dates.

The river is not recommended below the center of Lebanon. There are three dams in the city, and three more near the crossing of US-4/NH-10 west of it. There are few rapids until you pass five of these dams. The river becomes polluted, and its banks are unattractive for most of the remaining distance to the Connecticut River.

1977 Mascoma Lake — Lebanon   5½ mi [8¾ km]
Quickwater, **Class II–III**
High water: *difficult, April*
Medium water: *May and mid-fall*
Dam-controlled: *annual fall drawdown of Mascoma Lake*
Forested, Urban
   USGS: Mascoma 15, Hanover
   Portage: 4 mi L **dam below RR bridge** — 20 yds

Begin at the dam on Mascoma Lake. The rapids start almost immediately, but they do not become difficult until after you pass under the high US-4 bridge. They are continuous and of varying difficulty — class II and III — for 2¾ miles to the I-89 bridge. Then the river is easier, mostly quickwater, for ¾ mile.

At an old, closed bridge (3½ mi) just above a RR bridge, the next section of continuous, hard rapids begins. The most difficult section is in ¼ mile: a demanding class III pitch — possibly class IV — a short ways above the remains of an old factory high on the R bank. The factory serves only to tell you that you have passed these rapids, in whatever fashion; you must be alert to the character of the river itself. This 50-yard section is very bouldery in medium water, and lining on the L bank, the inside of the turn, is recommended.

Below the old mill, the dam of which must have been very high, there is a RR bridge and then a 6-foot dam (4 mi). Portage on the L bank in high water; at medium water it is easier to lift over the R side of it.

After the dam the river is no longer in a narrow valley. It is much easier, being a mixture of quickwater and easy class II for 1 mile, with some flatwater as you approach the center of Lebanon. Take out at a large parking area (5½ mi) on the L above the NH-120 bridge.

If you wish to continue downstream, you have three dams within the next mile. Portage each on the L. At the first one, just past the NH-120 bridge, carry across the RR tracks and the street, and continue straight down Water Street past the brick and wooden factory before turning R to the water. Below the third dam, a collapsing wood and cement structure, there is a difficult, 50-yard class III rapid. For 1 mile below I-89 (7¾ mi), the river is flat. Just above and under the US-4/NH-10 bridge, there are two dams. Portage each on the L. The lower one is just past a RR bridge, and it is a low weir with a strong current as you approach the lip.

Below the high US-4/NH-10 bridge (9 mi) W of Lebanon, the rapids are class II. Except for a millpond above the sixth dam (9½ mi) which you portage on the R, they are continuous all the way past the NH-12A bridge. Then there is ¼ mile of flatwater to the Connecticut River (10¾ mi) where there is a good take-out on the R bank.

MOOSE RIVER   VT

USGS: *Burke 15*, Littleton 15, *Saint Johnsbury 15*

The Moose River flows through sparsely settled rural countryside of northern Vermont to the Passumpsic at Saint Johnsbury. The water is warm and the river bed murky.

Victory — Saint Johnsbury   18 miles

There are moderate rapids below Victory, but they become strong at least 1 mile upstream from the bridge a mile above North Concord. Just above and below this bridge are several, sharp class III drops over ledges and rocks. Rapids cease ¼ mile below this bridge; and they are followed by 2½ miles of flatwater to the Route 2 bridge.

The river from the North Concord bridge on Route 2 to East Saint Johnsbury is mostly fast current and moderate rapids. In East Saint Johnsbury there is an impassable drop under the railroad bridge: lining is necessary. The lower section of the river is not as attractive because the valley is more settled and the railroad and highway follow the river. The river from the East Saint Johnsbury railroad bridge to ½ mile above the railroad bridge in Saint Johnsbury contains continuous class II rapids. This section is delightful because there are many locations for practicing eddy turns, ferrying, etc.

Above the mills in Saint Johnsbury, all paddlers should pull out except those with covered boats or those who are expert open boat canoeists. There are several class IV drops which require scouting and intricate maneuvering. Strong cross currents and fairly large haystacks are added obstacles. Beyond the two bridges (rail and highway) and after the mills, all boats must take out on the right, for beyond there is an impassable drop hidden around the next corner.

NASH STREAM NH

This small mountain stream, once noted for its log drives, flows south from Nash Bog Pond in Odell to the Upper Ammonoosuc River below Stark. It drains a large, forested area which is undeveloped except around what used to be the pond. The floods of May 1969 washed out the dam at Nash Bog Pond, leaving only a large marsh.

A private road of the Groveton Paper Company follows the river, but it is usually closed during the canoeing season. The river flows for 9 miles from the pond to the Upper Ammonoosuc with an average gradient of 75 feet per mile. It is recommended that the river be scouted carefully before running.

Nash Stream has been run for 3½ miles from BM 1368 to the gate near BM 1061 (USGS: Percy 15). There is a mile of quickwater to an old, runnable log dam, then class IV rapids with multiple channels. Choose the ones where the water drops first. Due to the tight, rocky drops, short, closed boats are recommended. Very high water is necessary, but the clear water makes it appear like the water level is lower than it actually is.

NULHEGAN RIVER VT

USGS: Island Pond 15, Averill 15

The Nulhegan River and its numerous tributaries drain an extensive area of swamps, wooded hills, and mountains east of Island Pond in the least inhabited part of Vermont. The main river rises in Brighton just east of Island Pond. Both it and the north branch flow through high but swampy country.

East Brighton — Stone Dam 9 miles

From the first Route 105 bridge in East Brighton the river is brushy as it flows through a swamp. Halfway between the second Route 105 bridge and Stone Dam (the third Route 105 bridge), there is a gorge which would be class IV if it is runnable at all. There is no reasonable access to the river above or below this gorge.

Stone Dam — Bloomfield 4 miles

This portion has more water and has been run after heavy autumn rains as well as in the spring. From the Route 105 bridge for 1 mile downstream the rapids are continuous and difficult (class III–IV) with one turn apparently unrunnable, usually carried on the right bank. The river is then joined by the East Branch and levels out with easy rapids and flat stretches to Bloomfield, where the former dam has disappeared, and to the Connecticut River.

OMPOMPANOOSUC RIVER — VT

The main branch of the Ompompanoosuc rises in Vershire and flows generally south to meet the West Branch in Union Village. Below the confluence there is a large flood control dam. The section of the main river above the dam contains many rapids; below there is flatwater to the Connecticut. The water in the river is dark, possibly because of the many, active farms.

West Fairlee — Thetford Center	8 miles

1974

Flatwater, Class II–III   12¾ km
High to medium water: *April*
Forested
    USGS: Strafford 15, *Mount Cube 15*
    Portages: 2 mi R **waterfall at Post Mills** — 50 yds

The first 2 miles to Post Mills are mostly smooth. Just above the bridge in Post Mills is a 12-foot waterfall which should be portaged on the R. From here there are 4 miles of easy class II rapids that lead to a high bridge on a side road near Thetford Center (6 mi). There are three or four more difficult class III drops in this section, with the hardest being ½ mile above this bridge. In high water the standing waves are likely to swamp an open boat.

The last 2 miles to the covered bridge in Thetford Center (8 mi) meander considerably among many fallen trees. **Caution!** The river goes over a 40-foot cascade just below this covered bridge.

The 3 miles from Thetford Center to the 170-foot Union Village Flood Control Dam are not recommended. Past that dam, flatwater with a good current extends for 4 miles to the Connecticut River.

OTTAUQUECHEE RIVER — VT

The Ottauquechee River makes a very fine canoe run at the right stage of water. It flows through settled country, largely farm land except for small towns, and is closely followed by the road. The rapids are mostly mild except for the spectacular Quechee Gulf, which is unrunnable in its entirety for an open canoe and dangerous for a covered boat.

West Bridgewater — Woodstock   15 miles

USGS: *Killington Peak,* Plymouth, Woodstock South

There is an unrunnable drop just above the Route 4 bridge
north of town, then ½ mile of class III–IV rapids to the
Route 4 bridge in the center of town. Below this point are
class I–II rapids all the way to Woodstock, best run in
April or early May. Route 4 is often alongside, and there
are many bridge crossings. The dam at Bridgewater,
8 miles below, is completely gone on the left side and can
be run. It is best to take out above Woodstock.

Woodstock — Connecticut River   15 miles

USGS: *Woodstock South,* Woodstock North, Quechee, Hartland,
North Hartland

Car scouted. There is a 2-foot weir under the Route 4
bridge in Woodstock, caused by a pipe crossing. There are
easy rapids through town, followed by a 4-foot weir under
the Route 12 bridge at another pipe crossing. This is a
difficult spot to line or carry, best avoided entirely. There
are 2½ miles of riffles and 1¼ miles of smoothwater to the
dam and covered bridge at Taftsville, then 4 miles of
mixed rapids and smoothwater to the dam and covered
bridge at Quechee. An interesting terrain model of the
lower river can be seen at the offices of the Quechee Lakes
Corporation on the left bank. It is 1 mile to the dam and
cascade at Deweys Mills. The next mile is the spectacular
Quechee Gulf, best viewed from the Route 4 bridge
midway down.

   A dirt road on the left bank leads to the foot of the
gorge. The former class II–III lower gorge has been flooded
out, and there are 3½ miles of riffles and sandbanks to the
North Hartland Flood Control Dam. At maximum pool
Quechee Gulf will be filled nearly to the brim, and the
dams at Deweys Mills and Quechee will be under water.
There is a boat ramp above, but access below is blocked by
a chain link fence. About ¼ mile below is an unrunnable
falls above the Route 5 bridge. It is 1 mile to a side road
crossing at a rock island with a dam on each side. One of
the bridges is a covered bridge. It is then ¼ mile to the
Connecticut River.

OTTER BROOK NH

Otter Brook is a small tributary of the Ashuelot and is sometimes called the East Branch or just The Branch. The water is often clear, particularly above Otter Brook Flood Control Dam, making the stream very appealing. The upper part of Otter Brook is an excellent, advanced whitewater run when it has water. The lower portion holds intermediate rapids before giving way to quickwater in Keene.

East Sullivan — Otter Brook State Park   3¼ miles

For one or two weeks in the year, this section of Otter Brook is runnable. It is definitely a small stream, averaging ten to fifteen yards wide. Expert boaters who catch it will find Otter Brook an enjoyable but not intimidating class IV run.

There is a hand-painted gauge on the upstream side of the NH-9 bridge abutment, but unfortunately the water piles up against it, so meaningful readings are hard to get.

From East Sullivan to Otter Brook State Park, NH-9 is next to the brook.

1976 | East Sullivan — Otter Brook State Park   3¼ mi [5¼]
Class III–IV
High water only: *early April*
Forested
      USGS: Monadnock 15

Put in just below the NH-9 bridge in East Sullivan. The rapids are class II for the first 100 yards, and then the difficulty increases to class III. The rapids are quite continuous. A long stretch of easy class IV rapids follows with no pools in which to rest.

The most difficult drop in the river comes when it bears slightly L away from the road and plunges 1 foot and then 3 feet over an angled ledge (1 mi). There is another class IV drop shortly below where the river turns R and returns to the road. Rapids continue past an old iron bridge (1¾ mi) to the bridge at Pinnacle Ski Area.

Below the ski area (2½ mi) the rapids diminish in intensity, but they remain continuous. Here, as above in Otter Brook, a capsized boat can be carried a long ways downstream.

The suggested take-out is at the next bridge (3¼ mi), which is the access road to Otter Brook State Park. There are picnic tables on the L here, providing a pleasant lunch spot. Because the gate at the NH-9 entrance to the park is usually locked when the river is runnable, boats must be carried a couple of hundred yards from the river to NH-9.

The rapids flatten out quickly below Otter Brook State Park, with mostly quickwater continuing to the pool behind the flood control dam. A ½-mile flatwater paddle brings you to the dam itself (5 mi). To continue would necessitate a long, steep carry. Therefore, this last portion is not recommended.

Flood Control Dam — Ashuelot River   5 miles

Below the dam Otter Brook contains continuous, inter-mediate rapids. The amount of water for the run is controlled completely by the dam which is managed by the Corps of Engineers.

1973	Flood Control Dam — Ashuelot River	5 mi [8 km]

Quickwater, **Class III**
High to medium water: *April*
Dam-controlled
Forested
         USGS: Monadnock 15, Keene 15

Put in right below the spillway from the dam. Rapids begin immediately with a wavy class III drop in a R turn. Otter Brook passes the remaining stone abutments of an old bridge and continues southward with class II–III rapids. After 2 miles NH-101 is visible ahead. The brook turns sharp R, is joined by Minnewawa Brook on the L, and follows along NH-101. The next ½ mile to the NH-101 bridge is class III — quite rocky in medium water and full of waves in high water.

After the NH-101 bridge (3 mi) the rapids diminish quickly to a high RR bridge followed by a dam (3½ mi). This dam has cement flanges extending upstream on either side, and the stream has cut a new channel above the R flange. Before entering, scout this new passage for overhanging brush or fallen trees.

After the dam the brook is mostly quickwater with a good current and a sandy bottom. Take out at the NH-12 bridge in Keene (4¾ mi) or join the Ashuelot River (5 mi).

USGS: Burke 15, Lyndonville 15, Saint Johnsbury

The two branches of this stream probably provide more enjoyable canoeing than the main river. They must be run, however, at high water. The main stream itself, being largely dammed, can be run at most seasons of the year but provides less attractive surroundings and is not highly recommended. The West Branch rises in Westmore below the height of land at the south end of Lake Willoughby. It is too small to run except in its last few miles from Folsom to the junction with the East Branch. The East Branch, which rises in Newark, is longer and for its last 4 miles below East Burke to the junction provides canoeable water. With high enough water it might even be run from Hartwellville. The two branches meet about 1 mile above Lyndonville, and the main stream offers easy paddling for the remaining 22 miles to the Connecticut River.

East Burke — Route 114   4 miles
WEST BRANCH

Put in below the dam at East Burke. In the next 4 miles the river drops 100 feet to the Route 114 bridge at the mouth of the stream just above the junction with the East Branch. One may take out here or go on ½ mile to the lower Route 114 bridge over the main river.

Folsom — Route 114   3 miles
EAST BRANCH

Put in near Folsom above the mouth of Calendar Brook. Some riffles near the start are soon succeeded by easy, meandering stretches of river to the junction with the West Branch, and ½ mile below, the Route 114 bridge over the main river is reached where one can take out.

Route 114 — Connecticut River   22 miles

One can put in at the Route 114 bridge 2 miles above Lyndon Center. This is just below the junction of the two branches. The river from here down is mostly placid, as it is dammed at a number of spots and the backwaters from the dams are almost continuous. It is, therefore, not a sporty run, but on the other hand may be used even in the summer. The carries around the dams are mostly short. There is a dam about ½ mile above St. Johnsbury Center, and the rocky stretch and rapids below may have to be carried if the water is low. In St. Johnsbury, the Moose River enters adding to the water volume. Most canoeists, unless continuing on down the Connecticut River, will take out at East Barnet hydroelectric dam about ½ mile above the mouth of the river.

PHILLIPS BROOK   NH

Phillips Brook flows into the Upper Ammonoosuc River from the north 3¾ miles downstream from West Milan. It is smaller than Nash Stream to the west.

Above Paris there are 2½ miles of winding brook followed by 3 miles of rapids, but the only access is by a private road of the International Paper Company that is usually closed during the canoeing season.

It is a 4-mile run from the nearly abandoned settlement of Paris to the Upper Ammonoosuc River. A 50-yard portage around a cascade in Paris is followed by about ¾ mile of shallow class II–III rapids. Then the brook meanders through swamps and fields with a good current for ¾ mile to the Bell Hill Road bridge, then another 1½ miles to Crystal where you must portage around the spectacular cascade which terminates in a 6-foot wide, undercut slit beneath the bridge. This is followed by ¾ mile of class II–III rapids to the Upper Ammonoosuc. See the USGS Percy 15 sheet.

SAXTONS RIVER   VT

USGS: Saxtons River 15, Bellows Falls 15

In March or April the Saxtons River offers one of the sportiest, one-day whitewater runs in Vermont. There is a continuous drop of 50 feet per mile between Grafton and Saxtons River Village, yet all can be run with sufficient water. Although the highway follows the bank, the valley is narrow and wooded, the water limpid, and the few farmhouses and pastures have the picturesque beauty characteristic of Vermont. There are no lakes or swamps to stay the flood, and this trip is not feasible except after heavy rain or while the snow is melting. A flood control dam projected for Cambridgeport may spoil the upper river for canoeing.

Grafton — Saxtons River Village   7 miles

Put in where the stream forks or any place below. All of the dams above Saxtons River Village are washed out, only traces of them are still visible. The channel is full of large rocks and only by constant maneuvering can a canoeist avoid mishap. The setting pole can be invaluable here.

Just beyond the bridge, 3 miles from the start, is a particularly bad stretch with even steeper water and larger boulders than usual. At Cambridgeport the gradient becomes slightly less and the valley broader, but the rapids continue sporty. A flood control dam is proposed here. A mile below Cambridgeport one passes under a covered bridge. One-half mile below this bridge is a ledge impassable in high water. The best take out spot is ½ mile above Saxtons River Village.

Saxtons River Village — Connecticut River   4 miles

The canoeing is less exciting. At Saxtons River Village are two dams with easy carries, the upper to the left and the lower to the right. At Barber Park the river further slackens its pace and the running becomes easy. There is a wooden dam at Gageville, just below a covered bridge. This can be easily passed on the right, but in a ½ mile there is a cascade, the site of a former hydroelectric plant for Bellows Falls, where the river drops some 60 feet and the portage is difficult. It is best, therefore, if a car is available, to pull out at the bridge and carry down the road to below the cascade, and put in here, from whence there is easy running down to the Route 5 bridge at Bellows Falls. There is a dam just below the bridge easily carried on the left with a short rapid 200 yards to the Connecticut River, or one may take out at the bridge.

SUGAR RIVER   NH

This river drains Lake Sunapee. It begins with several dams and an unrunnable section, so the best part of the river begins at North Newport.

The river can often be run late in the season because the drainage area is large and the flow is dam-controlled. A good indication of the water level can be obtained from the NH-11 bridge at Kellyville as these rapids are typical.

The Water Resources Board (603-271-1110) draws down the level of Lake Sunapee every fall. The exact dates are apt to vary from year to year.

1975   Quickwater, **Class II**   15¾ km
             High water: *April*
             Medium water: *scratchy, May thru June and rainy fall*
             Dam-controlled: *annual fall drawdown of Lake Sunapee*
             Rural, Towns
                   USGS: Sunapee 15, Claremont 15

        Put in at the bridge in North Newport. If the water
is high, there will be standing waves and turbulence, with
relatively few rocks visible. At lower levels you must dodge
numerous moderately sized rocks.

        About 1 mile below the start, around the second
R turn below the second RR bridge, there is a difficult class
III drop among boulders. It should be scouted from the
R bank. It is another 1½ miles to the bridge at Kellyville.

        Below Kellyville (2½ mi) the rocks are smaller, so
the river tends to wash out at high levels, although rock
dodging continues at lower levels. A unique feature of this
lower section is the presence of two covered RR bridges.
The rapids continue for about 5 miles, and then they
degenerate to quickwater. It is possible to take out on the L
bank near the fire department training tower (7½ mi) or to
continue another 2 miles to the center of Claremont.

        In Claremont (9¾ mi), take out well upstream of
the NH-11 bridge as there is a dam above it and the river is
confined between retaining walls.

UPPER AMMONOOSUC RIVER   NH

The Upper Ammonoosuc River drains the Kilkenny region
of the White Mountains, flowing north and then west to
the Connecticut River at Groveton. It has no connection
with the Ammonoosuc or Wild Ammonoosuc rivers
further south.

 York Pond Road — West Milan   **6 miles**

1976   Quickwater, **Class II**   9¾ km
             High water: *late April and May*
             Forested
                   USGS: Percy 15

        Take the road to the York Pond Fish Hatchery
from NH-110. In about 3½ miles, put in at the bridge
where this road crosses the river, or take the road along the
E bank upstream a mile or so to an alternate starting point.

The rapids at the bridge (0 mi) are a good indication of what the rest of the run is like. In high water the river is a wavy class II; it is rocky at lower levels.

It is 4 miles to Higgins Brook where there is a class III rapid which should be scouted. There is a rock ledge on the L and a short sandbank on the R. The first drop is a ledge around a sharp L turn, followed by a rocky rapid in a R turn.

There are more class II rapids for 1¼ miles to a side road bridge (5¼ mi). Below this bridge there is ¾ mile of quickwater and riffles to the mouth of Pond Brook, near the bridge at West Milan (6 mi).

West Milan — Groveton   17¼ miles

1977   Flatwater, Quickwater, Class I   27¾ km
        High or medium water: *late April and May*
        Rural, Towns
            USGS: Percy 15, *Guildhall 15*

This stretch of the river begins with over 9 miles of smoothwater. The NH-110 bridge is reached in 1¼ miles and Crystal Bridge in another 2¼ miles, with the mouth of Phillips Brook a short distance below. It is 1½ miles to the Bell Hill Road bridge (5 mi) and another 2¼ miles to the bridge at Percy (7¼ mi). Then there are almost 2 miles of smoothwater followed by a 1-mile class II boulder patch which is often too low to run. The latter ends at a covered bridge in Stark, one of the most photographed bridges in the state.

Below Stark (10 mi) there are 4½ miles of quickwater and riffles to the mouth of Nash Stream; then ¼ mile of class II to the bridge on Emerson Road (14¾ mi). Then it is 2½ miles to the first dam in Groveton (17¼ mi) which is the usual take-out.

Below this, current information is not available, but there were once four dams in the 1¼ miles through Groveton. For 2½ miles below the town, the river meanders to the Connecticut River (21 mi).

WAITS RIVER   VT

This is a sporty run in high water. The valley is narrow, and consequently the river rises quickly when there is a moderate run-off. Do not attempt it when it is in flood.

The scenery consists of fine, wooded hills and some pastureland. The water is clear and the banks clean. The stream is followed by VT-25.

1976   Quickwater, Class II–III   17 km
High water: *recommended above East Corinth, late April to early May*
Medium water: *passable below East Corinth, late May*
Forested, Rural, Towns
        USGS: East Barre 15, Woodsville 15, Mount Cube 15

Put in from a bridge on a side road at the Waits River Post Office. The river is narrow, steep, and rocky, dropping 50 feet per mile. Below VT-25 there are three ledges. The first one is around a sharp bend to the L, and it is usually runnable in the center. The other two are recognizable from above. Look them over first, as the best channel changes with the water level. They may have to be lined.

The rapids below a bridge on a side road are class II and can be run later in the season. Below the second VT-25 bridge (7 mi) there is a bend to the L and another ledge which should be checked because usually there is only a narrow gap near the R bank. Below this there is a rocky patch and an occasional, less difficult ledge. The final 2 miles are easier.

Take out at the picnic area below the bridge on VT-25B (10½ mi). Below this there is a high dam at Bradford, followed by a mile of flatwater to the Connecticut River.

WARDSBORO BROOK   VT

This small stream enters the West River below Ball Mountain Dam and it is parallelled by VT-100. It is a demanding class IV run that requires high water. Since run-off here occurs rapidly, Wardsboro Brook is recommended for only a few weeks of the year.

Wardsboro — West River   4½ miles

1976   Class III–IV   7½ km
High water only: *mid-April*
Forested
        USGS: Londonderry 15, *Saxtons River 15*

A put-in can be made below the bridge and the waterfall in the town of Wardsboro. Class II and III rapids make up the first mile of this run. Wardsboro Brook then passes under VT-100 and turns R with the first of many difficult class IV rapids. The next 2½ miles are steep and continuous, and they should only be attempted by a strong party.

Below the next VT-100 bridge (3½ mi) the rapids are even more difficult than the preceding ones and only questionably runnable at certain water levels. Therefore, most paddlers take out at this bridge or onto the adjacent dirt road just below. If you do paddle the last mile, take out at the bridge just above the confluence (4½ mi).

WELLS RIVER   VT

The Wells River flows into the Connecticut opposite Woodsville, New Hampshire. It is paralleled by US-302, which is occasionally visible from the river.

Above the section described here it is a small, steep brook; and at the end there are a series of falls and ledges that most people consider a scenic attraction rather than a canoeing possibility.

Groton — Wells River (town)   9½ miles

1977

Flatwater, Quickwater, Class II–III   15¼ km
High water: *April and May*
Forested, Rural, Towns
  USGS: Woodsville 15
  Portage: 7 mi L **dam in Boltonville**
             7¼ mi L **gorge below Boltonville**

Put in from a side road ⅓ mile E of the Groton bridge and just below an old dam. Following ½ mile of class II rapids, the river is mostly flat as it meanders through pastureland. There are old RR pilings in South Ryegate.

Below South Ryegate (4 mi) class II rapids extend for 1½ miles. After that there is a series of four ledges visible from a side road on the L bank. The last one is past an old abutment. Another drop obstructed with old granite blocks starts just below an old route 302 bridge. Then the current slows down, and the river meanders the remaining distance to Boltonville.

Just below the bridge in Boltonville (7 mi), there is a 50-foot dam and cascade which must be portaged on the L. Put in below the old power station, now a summer cottage. One-quarter mile of rapids leads to the head of a small gorge where there is a 4-foot waterfall, best carried on the L. The ledges continue through the gorge, and they should be scouted while portaging the falls.

Below the high I-91 bridge (7¾ mi) the river becomes slow and meandering for 1¾ miles with a sandy bottom. Take out where the river first approaches US-302 on the R (9½ mi), for the next mile contains major water-falls and ledges.

WEST RIVER   VT

USGS: Londonderry 15, Saxtons River 15, Brattleboro 15

The West River, known by the Indians and the early set-tlers as the Wantastigeset, rises in Weston and can be run by canoe at high water from Londonderry, although it is more usual to put in at South Londonderry or Winhall Station for the run to Jamaica or East Jamaica. Below East Jamaica the river is quieter with only occasional rapids and can be run at lower water stages. Although the country is not wild except in the narrow valley above Jamaica, there are plenty of campsites, and the many farms along the flood plains are invisible from the stream. One is hardly conscious that a road follows the valley. The clear, quickwater, rocky bottom, fine banks, and wooded hillsides are what one sees from a canoe.

Londonderry — South Londonderry   3 miles

Put in near the junction of Routes 11 and 100. There are a number of heavy pitches in the next 3 miles to South Londonderry, and high water is necessary. Care should be taken in approaching the dam at South Londonderry as the river is confined between retaining walls.

South Londonderry — East Jamaica   13 miles

This is the classic West River whitewater run, but it has been spoiled by the construction of the Ball Mountain Flood Control Dam. It is, however, still runnable and the dam does enable authorities to provide a regulated amount of water for the Eastern Slalom Championships held at Jamaica.

One can put in below the dam at South London-derry, below the rapids at South Londonderry, Winhall Station at the mouth of the Winhall River, or at Rawson-ville on the Winhall. For the first 3 miles the rapids are not difficult but are continuous. The river is then enlarged by the addition of the Winhall, which enters on the right. Below the Winhall the valley narrows and gets gradually steeper with larger boulders. A jeep road follows the old railroad grade. The 265-foot dam at Ball Mountain must be carried, but the portage is very long and steep. The dam can be reached by a side road off Route 30 or by going up the old railroad grade from the Salmon Hole at Jamaica, but this road is usually blocked by snow when the water is high enough for canoeing in early spring.

Just below the dam, Cobb Brook enters from the left and a side trip to the high falls with their fine pot holes is well justified. From the dam down, the most difficult section is 1 mile above Jamaica, where the river drops among huge boulders known as the Dumplings. It is dangerous or impassable at high water. The annual West River Slalom Races are held just below the Dumplings. Some 200 yards upstream from the bridge at Jamaica is the Salmon Hole. There is a campground here. The rapids continue on for another 3 miles to East Jamaica, where canoes can be easily taken out at the Route 100 bridge, or one can continue on for 4 miles to the West Townshend Food Control Dam, behind which there is a small lake.

West Townshend — Brattleboro   21 miles

Put in below the flood control dam. This section is largely flatwater interspersed with riffles and short rapids at Newfane and Black Mountain.

The 6 miles to Townshend are easy river with good current and few riffles. Those desiring a somewhat shorter trip may wish to put in at the Route 30 bridge 2 miles below Townshend. From here it is largely flat stream through pleasant meadows with good current, 3 miles, to the iron bridge on the road to Brookline. There is an excellent picnic spot on the rocks at the right of the bridge. In another 5 miles there is a broken, runnable dam. Some 2 miles below the broken dam, in West Dummerston and under the slope of Black Mountain, is another rapid. For the next 4 or 5 miles there are a number of ledges in the river which at low water force the canoeist to pick a careful route. At high water they present no difficulty. Most canoeists will take out 1 mile upstream from Brattleboro about where the Route 91 bridge crosses, although one can continue on to the Route 5 bridge near the mouth or into the Connecticut River itself. The bridge 1 mile below, at Brattleboro, provides an alternative take-out spot.

WHITE RIVER   VT

There are probably more than 100 miles of good canoeing on this river system, with nearly every kind of water, some of which can be run even in the summer. The valleys are highly cultivated and much of the river may not be attractive to those in search of wild surroundings. However, in the tributary valleys especially, one can see rural Vermont at its very best, the First Branch being perhaps the prettiest.

The main river rises north of Granville, then flows south, then east, then southeast, finally emptying into the Connecticut River at White River Junction. When in freshet some of the faster parts are class III, but with the gauge at West Hartford reading 4.2 to 5.8 it is class II.

Granville — Stockbridge   14½ miles

1978   **Quickwater,** Class II   23½ km
High water: *early April*
Medium water: *scratchy near beginning, late April to mid-May*
Rural, Towns
   USGS: Hancock, Rochester

Begin on VT-100 at a bridge 1.9 miles N of the VT-100/125 junction in Hancock. The river above this point is small, but in high water it can be run for an additional 2 miles by beginning at another VT-100 bridge about ¾ miles S of Granville.

From the bridge near the Granville-Hancock town line, this shallow stream winds past farms at the bottom of the narrow valley for almost the entire distance to Stockbridge. There are only a limited number of short class II rapids; the first is just below a bridge in Hancock (2½ mi). After the VT-73 bridge (7¼ mi) it is ½ mile to the second and most difficult rapid at a bridge beside VT-100. There is one more pitch in the remaining 6¾ miles to Stockbridge (14½ mi).

Stockbridge — Bethel   11 miles

1978   Quickwater, Class II   17¾ km
High water: *early April*
Medium water: *late April thru May*
Forested, Settled
   USGS: *Rochester*, Randolph 15

There are intermittent class II rapids which extend over much of the distance to Bethel. Some of them can be scouted from VT-107, which occasionally is close on the R bank. In medium water this is not a difficult run, but in high water the currents are strong.

The most difficult section is 4½ miles below

Stockbridge at an "S" turn just above Gaysville. The river swings to the L away from the highway and passes through a narrow cut. There are heavy waves, a submerged rock near the center which often cannot be detected as you approach, and a strong whirlpool at the bottom just before the river turns R. Under the high bridge at Gaysville (5 mi) there is another strong current where a rock ledge on the R deflects the river to the L.

There is a good take-out on the R at the VT-12/107 bridge in Bethel (11 mi).

Bethel — Connecticut River   28 miles

USGS: Randolph 15, Strafford 15, Quechee, Hanover

The river is increased at Bethel by the Third Branch and becomes a much larger stream suitable to summer running if the season is not too dry. Put in at the Route 107 bridge. The river is less rapid, wider, and the valley more open. However, for a long distance there are numerous transverse ledges producing sharp drops with fair current between. In 4 miles North Royalton, where the Second Branch enters from the left, is reached. It is 2 miles more to Royalton and another 2 miles to South Royalton where the First Branch enters. About halfway between these two towns there are ledges and a sharp drop. Just below the bridge at South Royalton there is a rapid followed by 5 miles of easy river to Sharon, where there is a broken dam which can be run on the right or portaged on the left. Below Sharon the 5½ miles to West Hartford are characterized by numerous ledges with rather sharp pitches but with smooth river between. These ledges begin at a gravel pit below Sharon, and there are usually only one or two passable notches at each drop. The most difficult place is 1½ miles below the gravel pit at a part known as Quarter-mile Rapids, which should be scouted. After approaching near the right bank, one crosses to left of a large rock in the middle and to the left of haystacks below it. About 4 miles below Sharon there are several ledges: the first open in the middle, the second on the far left. At the island below, the right channel is better, and the last rapid above West Hartford is best run near the right bank. The 6 miles to Hartford are largely flat, uninteresting river except for some rapids below the railroad bridge halfway down. Then it is 1½ miles to the bridges at White River Junction, which are just above the entrance into the Connecticut River. This portion of the river is quite flat, but just above the bridges at White River Junction is a sharp drop over a ledge followed by a rapid.

WHITE RIVER, First Branch   VT

USGS: Strafford 15, Randolph 15

The First Branch is the largest of the three branches coming in from the north. It rises north of the town of Chelsea and empties into the main river at South Royalton. It flows through a very lovely, although highly cultivated, part of rural Vermont. The proposed Tunbridge Flood Control Dam may well spoil this run, at least as far as scenic values are concerned.

Chelsea — Tunbridge   9 miles

The first 3 miles below Chelsea provide a fine run during the few days in early April when the water is high enough. A dairy plant just below the bridge is a convenient place to put in, but one should request permission to the use the premises. With less water the recommended spot to put in is at the mouth of Crams Brook about 3 miles south of Chelsea on Route 110. There are many sharp drops over ledges, lively, but most can be run with sufficient water. In about 2 miles there is a dam at a sawmill where there is a short carry on the left and a rapid river below. Another dam 2 miles below at North Tunbridge can be carried on the left also. In another 2 miles the upper of the two dams at Tunbridge is reached.

Tunbridge — White River   8 miles

This section has only about one half the drop of the upper river and is considerably less rapid. Put in below the lower dam at Tunbridge. The next dam is 4 miles below at South Tunbridge, and 3 miles lower, there are two more dams. It is only another 1 mile to the confluence with the White River.

WHITE RIVER, Second Branch   VT

USGS: Randolph 15

Although this branch rises in Williamstown and flows through the famous Williamstown Gulf, it does not become canoeable until East Randolph. It flows through a well cultivated valley and is crossed at numerous points by Route 14. It is mild and probably best suited to those seeking streams with few, if any, rapids.

East Randolph — North Royalton   **10 miles**

One can put in below the dam. The river is a meandering stream for the 6 miles from here to East Bethel, where there is a dam. There is a fall with a carry about 1½ miles lower down. The rest of the 2½ miles to the confluence with the main White River at North Royalton provides no obstruction.

WHITE RIVER, Third Branch   VT

For 16 miles from Braintree to Bethel the Third Branch provides an attractive run in high water. The upper part above Randolph is very pretty; the water is clear and swiftly flowing. The lower part is less attractive and the water is more turbid. See the USGS Randolph 15 sheet.

Above Randolph there is a wooden bridge and a large amount of rip-rap which must be portaged. One-half mile below the large concrete bridge there is a low dam. Take out on the R and carry past the rapids below. After Randolph the river meanders in a broad valley. The gradient is less than on the upper section. Just past the RR bridge in Bethel, take out at the lumber yard above the dam (16 mi).

WILLIAMS RIVER   VT

USGS: Ludlow 15, Saxtons River 15, Bellows Falls 15

Above Chester the Williams River has three branches, but the North Branch, which rises in Andover, is the only one which appears inviting to the canoeist. At its source it is just a small brook descending steeply until it reaches Route 103 in Chester just below the Proctorsville Gulf. Several miles below it becomes navigable at high water and provides a sporty run to Brockway Mills. Below there is another 1 mile of sporty running to the backwater from the Connecticut River. The proposed flood control dam at Brockway Mills may spoil part of the upper river but may also make the lower river more accessible.

Gassetts — Brockway Mills   12 miles

Put in at Gassetts, at the junction of Routes 10 and 103.
The stream is still only a small brook but descends
rapidly with a swift current. A low bridge 1 mile down may
require a portage at very high water. Four miles from the
start the river passes under Route 103 in North Chester.
Just below the bridge is a dam at an old grist mill which
can be portaged easily. One mile below, the Middle
Branch flows in from the right doubling the size of the
stream. One could put in for the remainder of the run at
the Route 11 bridge just above this junction. From here the
river descends with easy rapids, riffles, and pools for about
3 miles. It then passes under the railroad, narrows down
with the railroad close to the right bank, and gets steeper.
About ¾ miles below the bridge is a chute which cannot be
run safely. **Caution!** Check this spot carefully and either
line down or portage 50 yards over rough ledges. In 1 mile
more the covered bridge at Bartonsville is reached and
then the river slackens its pace for the 2½ miles to Brockway Mills. **Caution!** Pull out well above the concrete
bridge as just beyond it the river drops 100 feet in a series
of cascades into a deep and narrow gorge well worth a visit.
The *very last chance* to get off the river is just above the
bridge at the gauging station on the left bank, but this is
hard to reach at high water. This is a difficult portage for
¾ mile around the falls and gorge.

Brockway Mills — Connecticut River   5 miles

Put in below the gorge. If portaging, the best route is to
follow the road on the left bank ½ mile turning in on the
right, by a cart path, just beyond a brook. Cross the railroad tracks, keep right across the brook and through a pine
grove, and then down a steep bank to a superb swimming
hole. The same spot can be reached from Route 103 by
turning in at the Rockingham Highway Department tool
house and bearing left to the farther edge of the sand pit,
whence an old wood road, rutted and overgrown, goes
down to the swimming hole. Launch here but beware of
the rapid below. In 1 mile the backwater from the Connecticut River is reached, and in 3 miles more the Route 5
bridge is reached, where one can take out. It is 1 mile more
to the Connecticut River, but there is no good take out
spot at the mouth. It is, therefore, necessary to continue on
another 3 miles to Bellows Falls or 1 mile down on the New
Hampshire side, where Route 12 approaches the river.

WINHALL RIVER   VT

The Winhall River is a small stream that rises on the north slope of Stratton Mountain and flows east to join the West River. With sufficient water it provides one of the longest, advanced whitewater runs in Vermont. All the rapids, except Londonderry Rapids, can be run by skilled canoeists in open boats.

Off Route 30 — West River   **7 miles**

1975   Class III–IV   11¼ km
        High or medium water: *April*
        Forested
            USGS: Londonderry 15

A dirt road leads up the N bank from Grahamville School, which is a mile W of Bondville on VT-30. From one put-in at a large field on this road, there are continuous class II–III rapids for a mile to the bridge at Grahamville School. The next mile to the VT-30 bridge (2 mi) is about the same, with a more difficult section around a big rock in the middle just above this bridge.

From Bondville to the VT-100 bridge in Rawsonville, 2 miles of class III–IV rapids keep the canoeist very alert. Another mile of similar rapids brings you to a bridge on the unpaved Londonderry Road (5 mi). **Caution!** Pull out at this bridge and look over the difficult Londonderry Rapids in the next L turn. These rapids, at an old damsite, can be portaged on either side. For the brave and skillful paddler, routes do exist on both the extreme L and the extreme R sides.

Below Londonderry Rapids (5 mi) there are 2 miles of easier class II–III rapids to the confluence with the West River (7 mi), but the waves can be heavy. Take out either just above or just below the confluence on the R. Here there is a campground that is accessible from VT-100 a little ways N of Rawsonville.

CHAPTER 5

LOWER CONNECTICUT

WATERSHED

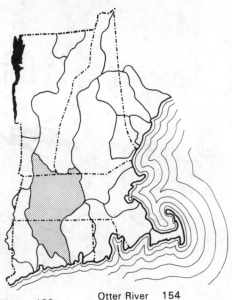

Connecticut River   132

Chicopee River   137

Coginchaug River   138

Deerfield River,
   North Branch   138

Deerfield River, Northwest
   Branch   139

Deerfield River   139

Eight Mile River   141

Falls River   142

Farmington River   142

Green River   149

Millers River   150

North River   153

Otter River   154

Quaboag River   154

Salmon River   158

Sandy Brook   162

Swift River   163

Tully River   164

Ware River   165

Westfield River,
   North Branch   168

Westfield River,
   Middle Branch   171

Westfield River,
   West Branch   171

Westfield River   172

LOWER CONNECTICUT WATERSHED

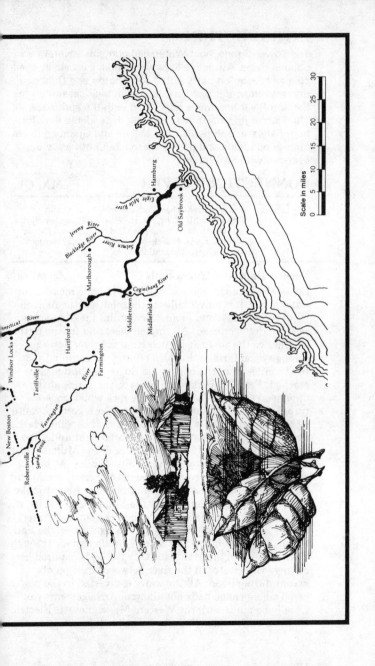

Scale in miles

0   5   10   15   20   25   30

New Boston
Windsor Locks
Robertsville
Tariffville
Sandy Brook
Farmington
Connecticut River
Farmington River
Hartford
Marlborough
Middletown
Middlefield
Coginchaug River
Jeremy River
Blackledge River
Salmon River
Eight Mile River
Hamburg
Old Saybrook

INTRODUCTION

The Lower Connecticut Watershed contains several very popular rivers. Attractive flatwater paddling is usually available all season on parts of the Farmington and Quaboag rivers. Whitewater paddlers can begin their season on the Salmon River and move northward with the spring thaw. The Farmington River has the most dependable flow for both flatwater and rapids. The Millers and Quaboag rivers offer good rapids and a long season, but both are more over-run with civilization.

CONNECTICUT RIVER   MA, CT

USGS: Keene 15, Brattleboro 15, Northfield, Millers Falls, Greenfield, Mt. Toby, Mt. Holyoke, *Easthampton*, Springfield North, Mt. Tom, Springfield South, Broad Brook, *Windsor Locks*, Manchester, Hartford North, Hartford South, Glastonbury, Middletown

Vernon Dam — Turners Falls   20 miles

Below the dam the going is swift and may be rocky if the water is low. It is only 2 miles to the mouth of the Ashuelot River in Hinsdale and in another 3 miles the Massachusetts border is crossed. All through here and for the next 10 miles to the gorge at French King the river flows through open farmland, which offers good camping spots. In 1½ miles from the border the Route 142 bridge is reached. From there it is 8½ miles to the gorge, at the upper end of which there is a large rock which causes turbulence even when the rest of the river is calm. A route close to either shore is to be preferred at this point. Here the current quickens and the river turns right under the French King Bridge at the confluence of the Millers River and continues heavy to Turners Falls, 4 miles. At high water this section of river can become extremely rough and under these conditions some canoeists may prefer to take out at the bridge which crosses the Millers River at its mouth. At Turners Falls one should take out at the steel bridge ¼ mile above the dam, on the right side. The Falls River enters just below the dam. A 3-mile portage through Turners Falls to the Montague City Bridge is required here as there is no water in the river between these points except during flood. All the water is diverted to the power canal where canoeing is not allowed. Arrangements can usually be made with the Western Massachusetts Electric Company in Turners Falls for a truck to take canoeing parties over this portage. Advance arrangements can be made through Supervisor of Hydraulic Maintenance, Western Massachusetts Electric Company, 45 Federal Street, Greenfield MA (413-774-2227).

Turners Falls — Holyoke   36 miles

At low water the 3½ miles from the dam to the Montague City bridge can be run by experienced canoeists, although short lifts or lining down will be required. It is an unpleasant bit, however, because of the paper mill effluent. Most canoeists will, therefore, make the long carry and put in at the Montague City bridge 3½ miles below the dam and just above the confluence with the Deerfield River. Camping is possible on the grounds of the Cabot Station of the Western Massachusetts Electric Company or on the island directly opposite. The next 32½ miles to the dam at Holyoke is easy paddling through farming country, but as the banks of the river are about 20 feet high little of the fields can be seen. As most of these fields are cultivated down to the river bank, the best camping spots on this stretch are on the islands in the river. In 1½ miles the B. & M. railroad bridge is passed. It is then 7½ miles to the Route 116 bridge in Sunderland, where there is a boat launching area at the east end of the bridge. An out-crop of conglomerate rock above the bridge offers a pleasant picnic spot and good views of the Sugar Loaves on the west and Mount Toby to the east. For the next 8 miles the river runs south through a wide valley. It then turns west for 1 mile and at this turn sandstone ledges on the left bank make a good picnic spot. A sandy beach in another ½ mile offers a good camping place if the owner's permission is obtained. The next 4 miles consist of a large oxbow around the village of Hadley. Canary Island near the west end of that bow makes a pleasant campsite. At Hadley there are a railroad and a Route 9 bridge. Just above these bridges Elwells Island offers a pleasant campsite. The Sportsman's Marina at the east end of the Route 9 bridge offers a launching area and permits camping.

The river now makes a large bend around Northampton. Below the bridge 2 miles Shepherd Island is suitable for camping. In 1 mile more there is a marina on the left bank with launching area and picnic tables. Below here 1 mile the Mill River, the scene of the great flood of May 16, 1874 in which 141 lives were lost, enters on the right, and just below is the entrance to the Ox Bow. One may paddle up this waterway 1½ miles to the Arcadia

Wildlife Sanctuary. At this point the river turns eastward for 1 mile and cuts through the Holyoke Range with Mounts Nonotuck and Tom on the southwest and Mount Holyoke to the northeast. Once through the range the river turns south and in 2 miles reaches Smith Ferry, where one may visit the famous Dinosaur Tracks just above some ledges where the highway is close to the river. Another 4 miles brings one to the Holyoke Dam. Here one should pull out on the left bank about 200 yards above the Route 202 bridge from Holyoke to South Hadley. The Holyoke Water Power Company will portage canoes for a reasonable charge if advance arrangements are made. Call the main office, 413-536-5520 during business hours a day ahead or on Fridays for a Saturday or Sunday portage.

Holyoke — Enfield Dam   18 miles

The usual launching place is on the South Hadley side ¼ mile below the Holyoke-South Hadley bridge and about ½ mile below the dam. Here a dirt road leads down to a riverbank terrace. The river here is shallow and quite swift. In 1 mile are the B & M railroad and Route 116 bridges. This is a heavily populated area with unattractive banks and at low water offensive pollution. As Holyoke is left behind the landscape becomes more attractive and 4½ miles below, just above the Massachusetts Turnpike bridge, a narrow wooded island offers a possible campsite. In 1 mile the Chicopee River enters on the left, and ¼ mile below is the Chicopee-West Springfield bridge. In another 3 miles the North End Bridge at Springfield is reached. Just below, Bassett's Marina on the left bank offers a good launching spot. In another 2 miles and only ¾ miles below the Memorial Bridge, the Westfield River enters on the right. In ½ mile more one reaches the South End Bridge to Agawam. Here the Agawam Yacht Club offers access on the right bank. From this point the river flows southward with low banks through a partly rural and partly suburban countryside passing under the Route 91 bridge in ½ mile and reaching the Massachusetts-Connecticut boundary in 3½ miles more. Below the border 2½ miles the old Route 190 bridge at Thompsonville is reached. From this point it is only 2¼ miles, mostly through tobacco farms, to the Enfield Dam. This is the last dam on the river and crosses diagonally, slanting downstream toward the right bank just above a steel bridge, and shortly below the new Route 190 bridge. This 9-foot high dam has been shot by canoes at low water. One

can lift over the dam and run the 4½ miles of easy rapids
through rough wooded country to the canal outlet opposite
Windsor Locks. Most canoeists, however, use the canal.

One should land on the west shore just above
the lock, lift the canoe over into the canal and paddle
down to the lower lock, which should not be approached
too closely because of the currents. The lift back into the
river is down over a steep bank on the left below the factory.

Enfield Dam — Wethersfield Cove   20 miles

From the dam one can canoe the river with its easy rapids
to Windsor Locks 4½ miles, with excellent campsites
along the way or use the canal as described above. The
remaining portion of this section of the river is in tobacco
farming country, but becomes more urban as Hartford is
approached. If one uses the canal the river is reentered
1 mile above the Route 91 bridge and in 3 miles the
Scantic River enters on the left. Below here 2 miles is
Windsor with its interesting old houses. Here the Farmington River enters on the right. In another 4 miles the
Podunk River enters on the left. For the next three miles to
the Charter Oak Bridge, under which the Hockanum River
enters on the left bringing in a certain amount of pollution, one has a fine view of the Hartford skyline on one's
right. In another 2½ miles the Wethersfield Cove opens up
on the right under the Route 91 bridge at its entrance.
There is a public landing on the south side of the Cove,
and some of the fine old houses of the town, which are open
to the public, are well worth a visit.

Wethersfield Cove — Middletown   15 miles

This lower part of the river is tidal, but no trouble will be
experienced with the tides until Middletown, and they are
not really important until one gets down as far as Had-
lyme. In the 7 miles to Rocky Hill Ferry, the river meanders across a broad flood plain. The banks are generally
low and sandy with fields and woods offering good picnic
or camping places. Just above Rocky Hill, below an abutment of large rocks, is a marina, Hall's Landing, on the
right. For the next 8 miles to Middletown the river's course
is straighter, through a somewhat more hilly country.
Gildersleeve Island, 5 miles below the Ferry offers suitable camping spots, while on the right bank Riverside
Marine Park, a launching area, has picnic tables. In

another 2½ miles, Wilcox Island, just above the mouth of the Mattabessett River at Middletown offers campsites. At the Route 6A bridge there is a landing place on the right.

Middletown — Old Saybrook   27½ miles

Below Middletown the river is very different. It is deeper and generally wider as it winds through the hilly country of southern Connecticut. The banks, high and ledgy, are more heavily forested. South of Middletown all property within the sight lines of the river is in the Connecticut River Gateway, an attempt by the state to maintain the scenic values of the river.

This lower part of the Connecticut River can be paddled anytime of the year whenever it is ice-free, but the best times are before Memorial Day and after Labor Day when powerboats with heavy wakes are less in evidence.

Rather than follow the main river all the way, a more interesting route is to paddle the "back alleys" that parallel the river. They lie along the east side of the river in East Haddam, Lyme, and Old Lyme. In addition there are several, attractive coves in the same area. The most helpful maps to have while paddling behind the islands and in the coves are the USGS Deep River and Old Lyme sheets.

1977	Middletown — Old Saybrook	27½ mi [44¼ km]

Tidal

Forested, Settled

USGS: Middletown, Middle Haddam, Haddam, Deep River, Essex, Old Lyme

Campsites:
4½ mi		**Dart Island State Park**
6¾ mi	L	**Hurd State Park**
17½+ mi	L	**Selden Neck State Park**

A few of the access points are listed here:

W bank —	0 mi	Middletown launching area off CT-9
W bank —	11 mi	Haddam Meadows State Park (S end) off CT-9A
E bank — ca.	11 mi	Haddam Neck nuclear plant
E bank —	13 mi	Salmon River launching area off CT-149
E bank —	13¾ mi	Goodspeed Opera parking lot off CT-149
W bank —	16½ mi	Chester ferry landing
W bank —	22¼ mi	Essex town dock
W bank —	27½ mi	mouth of South Cove in Old Saybrook from CT-154

The "back alleys" along the E shore begin below the CT-82 bridge (13¾ mi). Keep to the L of Rich Island (14½ mi) and enter Chapman Pond from the W and leave it at the S end. The next one is below the ferry crossing and goes to the E of Selden Neck (17¼ mi) via Selden Cove and Selden Creek. It is in Selden Cove that the citizens of Essex hid their ships from the British raiding parties during the War of 1812. There are more such passages above the Connecticut Turnpike (25 mi) and below the RR bridge.

CHICOPEE RIVER   MA

The Chicopee River springs full-grown at birth from the merger of the Quaboag and Ware rivers at Three Rivers in Palmer. It flows west to the Connecticut River at Chicopee. It drops 220 feet in 16¾ miles, but ten dams in that distance make nearly all of it smoothwater paddling. Because of all these dams, the appeal of this river is limited.

Three Rivers — Ludlow	8¼ miles

1973

Flatwater, Class I–III   13¼ km
Passable at most water levels
Forested, Urban
    USGS: *Palmer*, Ludlow, Springfield North
Portages: 2¾ mi L **Red Bridge Dam** — 100 yards
           5 mi R **dam at North Wilbraham** — 50 yards

Flood prevention work in Three Rivers has led to the removal of the old dams there. Considerable blasting has been done, so that the first ½ mile of the Chicopee consists of very sharp rocks and large haystacks. This section of class III rapids should be looked over before running. Below this drop is a 2-mile-long polluted impoundment which ends at Red Bridge Dam. In contrast to the water quality, beautiful hemlock, white pine, and mountain laurel line the shores.

At Red Bridge (2¾ mi), take out on the L bank just above the dam, portage along Red Bridge Road, and put in from the R bank just below the powerhouse. There is a short class II rapid and then more flatwater until you reach the dam at North Wilbraham (5 mi). Carry on the R bank. Below the dam is another brief class II rapid, followed by flatwater to the third dam (8¼ mi) in Ludlow. Take out on the L bank on River Road near the point where the boundaries of Ludlow, Springfield, and Wilbraham meet.

There are about a half-dozen dams in the remaining 8½ miles to the Connecticut River in Chicopee, so the last half of the river is not recommended.

COGINCHAUG RIVER   CT

This river flows northward towards Middletown where it joins the Mattabesset River. The recommended portion is a 2¾-mile section southwest of Middlefield that ends at Wadsworth Falls. It is a flatwater river in a forested and settled area, and high water is needed.

Begin at the CT-157 bridge in Middlefield close to the Durham town line. The river flows mostly through a swamp where the route is not always clearcut. Some logs must be lifted over, and there is one barbed wire fence. When houses start to appear, be alert for Wadsworth Falls, which is just below a bridge. Take out at that point as the stream below has a series of dams which must be carried, some with considerable difficulty. See the USGS Durham and Middletown sheets.

DEERFIELD RIVER, North Branch   VT

Known locally as the Dover Branch, this stream rises in Dover and flows southwesterly through Wilmington to the northeast corner of Harriman Reservoir. It flows through scenic farm country with fine views of Haystack Mountain, and the water itself is sparkling clear.

This branch provides a fine early spring run of moderate difficulty, being mainly fastwater with some class II rapids and two class III pitches of short duration. It is easier than the Northwest Branch.

Off Route 100 — Harriman Reservoir	6 miles

1976	Quickwater, Class I–III	9¾ km

High water: *late April thru mid-May*
Rural, Town
USGS: Wilmington 15

Put in 4.5 miles NE of the center of Wilmington Village off VT-100 where a farm road leads down to the river across the end of a meadow below a bridge. The stream is narrow but clear with a fast current. There are frequent riffles and mild class II rapids. After passing under the cement bridge on VT-100 (3 mi), the stream swings to the R around a large meadow and, after bearing L at the edge of a sugar orchard, descends over class II rapids of moderate difficulty. These are about ¼ mile long and are best run on the L.

The river then levels off until entering the narrow, steep class III chute that channels it through the center of the village. There is a sharp turn to the L at the head of this rapid; then a straight run down under the bridge in the center of town. This should be scouted before running.

Below the remains of an old milldam, the stream becomes wider and swifter as it parallels VT-9. There are some class II rapids which require caution in very high water. A short distance above Harriman Reservoir (the distance varies depending on the height of water impounded), there is another class III pitch that should be scouted carefully. Unless there is sufficient water to adequately cover the severe boulderly run-out below this rapid, take out opposite the electric power relay station on VT-9 (6 mi).

DEERFIELD RIVER, Northwest Branch
VT

This stream rises to the west of Somerset Reservoir and runs southerly to join the outlet of the reservoir a short distance above the lower dam where the penstock takes off to the Searsburg generating station. Take the road from VT-9 west of Wilmington toward Somerset Dam following the wooden penstock to the lower dam. Note carefully the conditions at the pond above this dam as canoes must be taken out well above the lip of the dam where the stream drops a sheer 120 feet. About 4 miles above, the road crosses the Northwest Branch, and this is a good launching spot.

The run from the put-in to the pond above the lower dam is about 5 miles of uninterrupted class II and class III rapids, making a fine whitewater run at the height of the spring run-off. The country here is wild and beautiful, the water clear over a rocky bottom, and herds of deer are often seen at this time of year. See the USGS Wilmington 15 sheet.

DEERFIELD RIVER
MA

USGS: Rowe, *Heath*, Ashfield, Shelburne Falls, Colrain, Greenfield

The Deerfield River rises east of the Green Mountains in southern Vermont, and flows south into Massachusetts, where it turns east to enter the Connecticut River at Greenfield. It is now largely developed for power. The upper waters have been impounded by two huge earthen dams: one at Somerset, Vermont, and another at Whitingham, Vermont, which form fine lakes for summer canoeing. There is another large dam a mile above Monroe Bridge, and a smaller one at Monroe Bridge. Below

Monroe Bridge there is the Bear Swamp pump-storage hydroelectric facility.

The water level in what remains of the river depends to a great extent upon electrical demand. Thus on Sundays and holidays, when power consumption is lowest, only a little water is released. Strangely enough, there is often more water in the river in dry weather than in wet, for in wet weather other hydroelectric stations of the New England Electric System can carry the whole load, whereas in dry weather these Deerfield stations can make use of the impounded waters.

The Deerfield was once a very beautiful valley, and was an important means of travel to the Indians. The white settlers occupied the fertile flood plains of the Deerfield and Connecticut rivers before 1700. The old Mohawk Trail followed the Deerfield to the mouth of the Cold River and then across Hoosac Mountain to the Hoosic River.

Loammi Baldwin, who built the Middlesex Canal, proposed to build a trans-Massachusetts canal in 1828, which was to have followed the Millers and Deerfield rivers and thence under Hoosac Mountain by a tunnel to the Hoosic River. The development of railroads frustrated the consummation of this plan, but the idea was carried over to the railroad era, and the Hoosac Tunnel was begun in 1856 and completed in 1873. Nearly five miles long, it was for many years the longest in the country. It is wide enough for two tracks, and is ventilated by a shaft running 1028 feet from the center of the tunnel to the surface above.

Hoosac Tunnel — Charlemont   8 miles

Put in near the Hoosac Tunnel entrance. From there the river provides an easy run with fine riffles except for one steep drop about 3 miles below Hoosac Tunnel. Zoar Gap, as it is called, should be looked over carefully before running and should not be attempted with a heavy canoe or an inexperienced party. The following 5 miles to Charlemont are good running with plenty of minor rapids and good current.

Charlemont — Connecticut River   26 miles

Below Charlemont, many of the rapids have been eliminated by dams. There are 7 miles of easy river to the first of four dams above and below Shelburne Falls. It is 6 miles to the last one, then 4 miles of river with a few rapids and riffles to the mouth of the South River on the right. The river continues unobstructed for another 3 miles in its narrow valley with the same average drop of 20 feet to the mile until near Wapping it suddenly breaks out into open farmland, and becomes mostly flat. The next 4 miles to the mouth of the Green River on the left near Greenfield and then another 2 miles to the Connecticut River make a good easy paddle.

EIGHT MILE RIVER   CT

This small, whitewater stream flows through Devils Hopyard State Park in East Haddam to Hamburg Cove on the Connecticut River in Lyme. North of CT-82 it flows through hemlocks and hardwoods in a narrow valley. The lower part is a mixture of fields, forests, and an occasional house.

Sawed blowdowns and rocks flecked with red, green, and aluminum attest to occasional usage.

	Devils Hopyard — Hamburg	7¼ miles

1977	Quickwater, Class I–II	11½ km
	High water: *recommended, early March*	
	Medium water: *scratchy, late March*	
	Forested, Rural	
	USGS: Hamburg	
	Portage: 6¼ mi L **dam at North Lyme** — 50 yds	

Put in beside the large picnic area just below the waterfall at the N end of Devils Hopyard State Park. Easy class II rapids begin immediately. After ½ mile there are a couple of ledges above another roadside picnic area that can be lined on the L if conditions are not such that they can be run. In another ¼ mile there is a small and runnable washed-out dam with the road close by on the R bank.

Within the next ½ mile the stream passes under a bridge and then for a short distance the road is again on the R. **Caution!** About 100 yards after it leaves the road, there is a cascade which should be lined on the L. Easy class I and II rapids continue for 1½ miles under several bridges to the CT-82 bridge.

Below the CT-82 bridge (3 mi) the river is mostly quickwater with some easy class II drops. Beside a cabin there is a small dam which can be lined on the R. The river flows under the CT-156 bridge (3¾ mi), and shortly the East Branch (also runnable from CT-82) enters on the L.

Past the CT-156 bridge (3¾ mi) there are three low, runnable roll dams before the deadwater above the dam (6¼ mi) near North Lyme. Portage the latter on the L.

There is quickwater for the remaining distance to Hamburg where there is a convenient take-out above the last bridge (7 ¼ mi).

FALLS RIVER   MA

USGS: Bernardston, Greenfield

The Falls River is a small stream which rises in Guilford, Vermont, and flows south through Bernardston to the Connecticut River, at Turners Falls. Above Bernardston village, it is too small for canoeing. There are long deadwaters caused by a dam in Bernardston, and a second dam 1 mile below at Hoe Shop Road. The best part of the river is below this second dam, but even here the trip is practicable only in high water. No roads follow the river and the banks are steep and wooded. Much of the land on both sides is posted against trespassing.

Bernardston — Factory Village   4 miles
From Route 10 bridge it is largely deadwater to the dam 1 mile below. The next mile to Bascom Road is mostly rapid, but not difficult. A quarter mile below the Bascom Road bridge, carry left around an impassable ledge. There are some good rapids a mile below here, near a Boy Scout camp on the right. Then the hills close in and form a small canyon. In less than a mile of easy paddling, one comes to a picnic ground and a dam, which is portaged on the right. Below the dam is ½ mile of fast current and easy rapids to the clearing above Gill Road. **Caution!** Proceed with care here, as the rapids increase to an impassable falls just above the bridge. Take out on the right. The last quarter mile to the Connecticut River is probably not canoeable.

FARMINGTON RIVER   MA, CT
The Farmington River for 65¼ miles — from near Otis, Massachusetts to Windsor, Connecticut — offers the recreational and racing canoeist a range of water conditions from peaceful flatwater to complex and challenging whitewater. The entire river valley suffered from abuse around the turn of the century, but today it provides pleasant scenery and interesting touring through a primarily rural, but civilized, countryside. Road accessability to most parts of the river is excellent with plenty of picnic and take-out spots. A most wonderful characteristic is its variety, making it possible to paddle a section of challenging whitewater in the morning and with little or no driving be able to

peacefully cruise on flatwater in the afternoon. The water quality is generally clear but not potable.

The water level above Colebrook Dam is dependent on natural flow and releases (generally in October) from Otis Reservoir. Below Hogback Dam the water level is dependent on releases from this dam and from natural runoff. Generally there is an adequate and constant release to power the generating station at Rainbow Dam. The river level rises quite rapidly after substantial rainstorms.

The Farmington River Watershed Association, 195 West Main Street, Avon, CT 06001 is an excellent source of river information. Their book *The Farmington River and Watershed Guide* ($2.75 postpaid) is an excellent reference for river descriptions, information on the wildlife and geology of the valley, and information on the trails, parks, and forests. The FRWA (203-678-1241) is a source for up-to-date reports on river levels, and it provides this information to the local media on Thursdays during the normal canoeing season.

Allen Road — Below New Boston   5 miles

The 3-mile section of the Farmington above New Boston is one of the nicest, expert whitewater runs in Massachusetts when it has water. The run can be made in early spring and also in the fall with the aid of water releases from Otis Reservoir. The rapids are quite continuous, with the difficulty usually class III–IV. The entire stretch is paralleled by MA-8, which facilitates scouting or impromptu take-outs.

In low to medium water, 250–350 cubic feet per second from the dam in Otis, this run is possible for open boats, paddled either solo or tandem. These flows correspond to approximately 3.6–4.0 on the gauge found on a side road off MA-8 a mile south of New Boston.

Otis Reservoir is controlled by the Massachusetts Department of Natural Resources. A few water releases for boaters are made in the fall. The dates can be obtained from the AMC.

1977 | Allen Road (Off Route 8) — Below New Boston   5 mi [8 km]
Class II–IV
High to medium water: *March thru April and selected fall weekends*
Dam-controlled: *scheduled releases on fall weekends*
Forested, Town
    USGS: *Otis*, Tolland Center

A put-in can be made from the green, iron Tolland State Forest bridge 3 miles N of New Boston on MA-8. The entire run consists of continuous turbulence and maneuvering, with the toughest rapids coming in the first ½ mile and in the two drops ½ mile above New Boston. The approach to these two last drops can be recognized when the remains of the arched, concrete bridge are spotted on the L bank. The second one is the harder, and its cross-currents have earned it the name of the "Corkscrew."

Below New Boston (3 mi) the Farmington is generally class II. From the CT-8 bridge there are 2 miles of rapids mixed with flat stretches that extend past the next CT-8 bridge (4¾ mi). One-quarter mile downstream of this bridge lies a rapid called the "Bear's Den." This class III drop should be scouted from the R bank before running. The best take-out is below this rapid (5 mi).

The river below the Bear's Dam is mildly riffled until it enters the backwater of Colebrook Dam (5¾ mi). The carries around Colebrook Dam and Hogback Dam (11 mi) are on the R and currently posted signs must be followed. See also the USGS Winsted sheet.

Hogback Dam — Farmington   25 miles

The upper part of this section from Hogback Dam to Satan's Kingdom is a beautiful run of mixed quickwater and class II rapids between hills and woods of People's State Forest on the left and American Legion State Forest on the right. There is a good road nearby on one side of the river or the other for much of the way to Farmington, making the river easily accessible from many locations.

The nature of this section is dependent upon rainfall and water releases from Hogback Dam. In summer and early fall the river provides many miles of easy class II rapids mixed with flatwater. In high water the river assumes a completely different character and can become very dangerous due to the water flowing around shoreside vegetation.

On the left abutment of the CT-4 bridge in Unionville, there is a gauge that gives readings which are applicable to that immediate area. At 2.0 the river is quite pleasant. When the gauge reads 3.0, it is quite swift with easy maneuvering eliminated because of powerful eddies and waves.

Hogback Dam — Farmington   25 mi [40¼ km]
Flatwater, **Quickwater**, Class II
High water: *spring*
Medium water: *summer*
Dam-controlled: *sufficient flow most of the year*
Forested, Rural, Settled

USGS: Winsted, New Hartford, Collinsville, Avon, New Britain

Portages: 15¼ mi R **1st dam in Collinsville**
16¼ mi R **2nd dam in Collinsville**
24½ mi L **dam in Farmington**

Campsites: 3–5 mi e **state forests** (contact resident forester)

Put in just below Hogback Dam at a little turnout on Hogback Road, which leaves CT-20 about 0.6 miles N of Riverton. The run to Riverton consists of 1¾ miles of class II rapids, and it can be easily scouted from the road. A state picnic area opposite the Hitchcock Chair Factory in Riverton provides another convenient access to the river.

The Still River enters on the R in ¼ mile. Class II rapids and flat stretches continue for about 4 miles until you reach a narrow stand of tall, straight pine trees on the L — on a high, wooded bank with a fence — and a L turn in the river. Beyond this is a class II–III rapid. This drop, the most difficult in this section, has big rocks in its midst, but there is a good pool just below. After the CT-181 bridge in Pleasant Valley (6 mi), the river broadens out but occasionally narrows down and produces riffles. The CT-219 bridge in New Hartford (8½ mi) is next. After going under a small bridge in New Hartford, be on the lookout for Riverrun Apartments on the R. In less than ½ mile a large rock to the R of middle and an outhouse on the R shore mark the entrance to Satan's Kingdom. There is a good take-out on the R bank 75 yards before the US-44 bridge and just downstream from the outhouse.

There is a small set of rapids under US-44 (11 mi) followed by 25 yards of flatwater before the big drop through the gorge of Satan's Kingdom. This drop is best run at medium levels, although it is runnable in the summer. In high water this becomes a severe class III drop and it must be run with extreme caution. It can be scouted and lined on the R bank. The drop is steep and the channel twists due to several large, partially submerged boulders critically positioned in mid-stream. The river forks in about a mile, and both forks are runnable.

Soon US-44 comes into view on the L bank, and the rest of the run to Collinsville Dam is intermittent, easy class II rapids until passing under a high silver bridge, where the river becomes flat for the remaining mile to the dam. This last mile is through a water skiing area, and canoes should keep to the R shore when skiers are present. Land on the L for take-out and on the R for portage.

There are two dams in Collinsville a mile apart, the upper one being at the CT-179 bridge (15¼ mi). Portage both along the road closest to the river on the R.

The river has some easy rapids until Punch Brook (17½ mi) enters on the R. From Punch Brook to the CT-4 bridge the river has a mixture of sometimes complex but moderate drops with good run-outs interspersed with stretches of flatwater. The initial rapid is quite soon after Punch Brook and should be run on the L side of the river, so an immediate crossing is recommended if the put-in is at the Punch Brook access. The remainder of the drops presents various river-reading problems which, if solved incorrectly, may easily lead to a broached boat. The last drop is the most complex, and it is above and just in sight of the CT-4 bridge (19½ mi). An exit from this drop on the R side of the river is best. There is a take-out on the R fork after the bridge at a sandy beach.

The first part of the lower section is not very pleasant, running as it does by the store and factory backs of Unionville. Opposite the restaurant "Auberge de Paris" the river becomes very ledgy and in ½ mile the oftentimes-called "Boateater Rapid," is encountered. At this point the river comes together and flows right against a high bank. The sluiceway has a large boulder hidden in a wave making the advisable route to the L of the main channel, very close to a gravel beach.

One-half mile of flat paddling after Boateater Rapid brings you to a RR bridge (22 mi) which is best run to the L of the L abutment. Then the river flattens out and flows through a large gravel pit. The Pequabuck River (24 mi) enters on the R where the river makes a 90° turn to the N at the foot of Talcott Mountain and close to Farmington with its white-steepled church. A dam at an old gristmill should be carried via a short trail on the L of the dam. There is a take-out on the L before the CT-4 bridge (25 mi).

Farmington — Connecticut River   29¼ miles

Flatwater characterizes this section. It is not a continuous flatwater trip, however, because it is broken very decisively halfway down by 1½ miles of class III rapids at Tariffville. Thus, flatwater trips usually begin or end near Tariffville.

From Farmington to Tariffville is a most pleasant flatwater paddle which can usually be made throughout the season. The river flows to the west of Talcott Mountain and gives fine views of these hills. The bank is sometimes high above the water level, but pleasant meadows near the water level can be found, particularly as you approach Tariffville.

Tariffville Gorge is 1½ miles of winding rapids which cut through a rock ridge. The rock cut is ledgy and contains sharp, angular rocks. The water level can be crucial and has the ability to make this gorge into an extremely turbulent area with huge souse holes and standing waves.

1977 Farmington — Connecticut River   29¼ mi [47¼ km]
Flatwater, Class III
High water: *spring*
Medium water: *summer*
Passable at all water levels
Rural, Towns
  USGS: New Britain, Avon, Tariffville, Windsor Locks, Hartford North
  Portage: 21¼ mi R **Rainbow Dam**

Access at Tariffville: Follow the main street to the end and turn R to a field by the sewage treatment plant.

It is 6 miles from the CT-4 bridge in Farmington to the US-44/CT-10 bridge and an additional 7½ miles to the silver iron bridge at CT-315 (13½ mi) N of Simsbury. The latter is the sixth bridge, counting the CT-4 bridge at the beginning, and it is the recommended take-out for flatwater paddlers. There is good access on the R, either by the CT-315 bridge or in ½ mile at the end of Curtiss Park.

One and a half miles from the CT-315 bridge (13½ mi), and after a bend in the river with a lawn on the L, high bridge abutments are seen. **Caution!** Unless the paddler is experienced and with a strong party, a take-out on the R should be made. This is the beginning of Tariffville Gorge, and difficult class III rapids are below.

After the CT-189 bridge (16½ mi) the gorge begins. The course is generally to the R until a set of low bridge abutments are passed. These abutments should be on your L, and once passed a very quick turn to the L must be made.

A stretch of flat but fast current leads to the largest drop. Scouting from the L shore is now advisable. The easiest route through this drop is on the extreme L into a large pool. After the pool, go to the L of the main current and over a small ledge; then proceed immediately to the L bank. This maneuver must be made very quickly in order to avoid a rocky hurdle. Setting or eddying maneuvers are indispensible. There is a small, vertical drop on the L bank that can be run; this current will turn R and then L, sweeping the boat through the rest of the gorge.

After a short flatwater stretch Spoonville Dam (17¼ mi) is reached. Land on the L to scout. This dam has been runnable, but the rocks in the sluice shift periodically so current inspection must be made. After the dam is run, the river turns L and flows hard against a rock wall creating extremely strong and tricky eddies and currents. The best route is on the L side of the island, to the R of the current, making a R turn after the island. In about 25 yards there is a low dam on the R bank which should be avoided due to its dangerous hydraulic actions. The rest of the run to the CT-187 bridge is through shallow water. Take out on the L before the bridge.

Below CT-187 (17¾ mi) the river continues shallow and broad until the backwater from Rainbow Dam (21¼ mi) is reached. The state-owned access is on the L bank about ½ mile before the dam, and the portage is on the R about 30 yards upstream of the dam. On the L side of the dam there is a fish ladder, opened in 1976, that is providing for re-entry of salmon into the river.

The water level for the remainder of the river is dependent on the water being released from Rainbow Dam. It is 1½ miles to the CT-75 bridge (23 mi) in Poquonock, below which there is ¼ mile of class II rapids. The river becomes flat and flows under I-91 (25½ mi) and the CT-159 bridge (28 mi) where there is a macadam ramp for take-out. There remain 1¼ miles to the Connecticut River (29¼ mi).

GREEN RIVER   VT, MA

USGS: Brattleboro, Colrain, Bernardston, Greenfield

The Green River is a crystal clear mountain stream
descending a narrow valley through the hills north of
Greenfield, Massachusetts, and emptying into the Deerfield River near that city. Rising to the west of Governors
Mountain in Guilford, Vermont, it is large enough to canoe
in freshet by the time it reaches Green River Post Office.
There are excellent swimming holes and plenty of opportunities for the trout fisherman. It is an unusually beautiful stream and a delight to the nature lover.

Green River — West Leyden   8 miles

A canoe can be launched a short distance below the mill-
dam at Green River. All the pitches in the first 4 miles
can be run at ordinary high water stages, but it is best to
proceed cautiously, inspecting each bad chute before
running it. A country road, which may be impassable
for cars in the springtime, follows down the valley close to
the right bank of the stream and affords an easy way
around any stretch which does not appeal to the canoeist.
Caution! This upper section should be attempted only
when the water is high and only then by those unafraid of
getting wet. The river is small, steep, and full of ledges,
particularly in the uppermost part where it rounds the east
slope of Pulpit Mountain. At Stewartville there is a dam at
a sawmill, where it is best to carry on the left.

West Leyden — Water Supply Dam   7 miles

From West Leyden to the next bridge is the best part of the
run. Here the rapids are almost continuous but never
severe. There are many clear, deep pools, beautiful banks,
and steep, wooded hillsides. Canoes may be launched from
the right bank just below the bridge at West Leyden. Pull
out 7 miles below on the left, just above the Greenfield
water supply dam. Here one can either end the run (the
road is nearby) or portage and put in again just above the
covered bridge in order to complete the more placid
reaches to Greenfield.

Covered Bridge — Greenfield   6 miles

The last 6 miles to Greenfield contain few rapids and the
banks are less interesting. Here the river has left its narrow
valley and passes through flat, farming country to its
junction with the Deerfield River.

MILLERS RIVER   MA

The Millers River flows west into the Connecticut River
near Greenfield. It has several sections which provide dis-
tinctly different types of canoeing. Above Royalston there
are many miles of smoothwater paddling; from South
Royalston to Athol there are continuous, intermediate
rapids; the stretch from Athol to Erving is mostly slackwater; and from Erving to Millers Falls the river has a
mixture of easy and heavy rapids.

     The water of the Millers is naturally dark, but it is
horribly polluted by the successive milltowns through
which it flows.

Winchendon — South Royalston   12 miles

USGS: Winchendon, *Royalston*

There are probably several miles of the river above Winchendon that are canoeable in high water, but they are
mostly through swamp. Through Winchendon, there is a
series of millponds, dams, and rapids. The last dam is at
Waterville on Route 202. One can put in just below this
dam on a side road, but the first mile is obstructed by
shallow rapids, a broken (but runnable) dam, and brush
jams. Below the rapids, a branch enters from the north.
It is small, but is canoeable in high water from the State
Line on Route 12, with some portages around dams and
obstructions. Below this junction, the Winchendon sewage
disposal plant is passed on the left, and there is a bridge at
Hydeville on a back road. This is the recommended starting point. The next bridge is on the New Boston Road,
5 miles along. The river winds through swamp and woodlands, with almost no current, but it is fairly pleasant if
the water is not too low. All of this section is in the reservoir of the Birch Hill flood control dam, in which the
Massachusetts Department of Conservation is pursuing an
extensive fish and wildlife management and improvement program. A mile below the New Boston Road, the
Otter River enters from the south. Then in 2 miles more
the Birch Hill Dam is reached and it is another 1½ miles
to the dam at South Royalston.

South Royalston — Athol   6¾ miles

This popular whitewater run, known as the "Upper
Millers," consists of a number of class III rapids. The
amount of water in this section is controlled by the Birch
Hill Flood Control Dam, and a check on the volume can be

made by calling the Army Corps of Engineers (617-249-4467) at the dam. A scratchy run can be made with as little as 500 cfs, but more water is really desirable. At 1200 cfs an open boat, singly paddled, is still a suitable boat; it is estimated that 1600 cfs would make it a closed-boat-only run.

1975	**South Royalston — Athol**	6¾ mi [11 km]
	Class III	
	High water: *late March or early April*	
	Medium water: *late April*	
	Forested	
	USGS: *Royalston,* Athol	

A put-in can be made at the green MA-68 bridge, but just above the next bridge in Royalston is a broken dam which can be rocky and dangerous at the wrong water level. Look it over carefully.

The better put-in is from a side road ½ mile below the MA-68 bridge on the R. Rapids begin immediately and pass around islands, then the pace slackens briefly before plunging into a wavy class III drop at the first RR bridge (1 mi). Another short flat stretch leads into a sharp L turn and a mile of continuous class III rapids.

Then there is a R turn and some smoothwater under the second RR bridge (3 mi). Just below is the site of the old Bear's Den Bridge. The easy rapids which follow include a little drop next to the RR. In the next mile the rapids increase through Hemlock Gorge, a class III section. The rapids then moderate, gradually flattening out in the pool above the dam in Athol (6¾ mi).

A rough take-out is necessary on the R bank — through the brush and along an old wood road to a side road. In Athol there are three dams to portage if you are continuing downstream.

Athol — Erving	**11 miles**
USGS: Athol, Orange, Millers Falls	

This part is not recommended. Below the dams in Athol, the river is flat and unattractive to the dam at Orange. Below Orange, the river leaves the flat valley and flows between steep hills again. The next dam is at Wendell Depot. There are only a few rapids in this section. The dam at Erving Paper Mills is broken, but it cannot be run. Then there is smoothwater to a low dam at Erving which can be run.

Erving — Millers Falls   6 miles

This section, consisting of the "Middle Millers" and the "Lower Millers," tends to hold water well. Most rapids are class II, with heavy waves in high water, but the rapid known as the "Funnel" is class IV at most levels.

Closely followed by a railroad and a highway, the Millers River descends between steep, wooded hills to the Connecticut River. Cars, a train, a few houses — even a dump — are continuing detractions from a river that offers nice, nearly continuous rapids. High water substantially dilutes the pollution that originates upstream.

1976   Erving — Millers Falls   6 mi [9¾ km]
        Quickwater, **Class II**
        High water: *March and April*
        Medium water: *May*
        Forested, Settled
            USGS: Millers Falls
            Portage: 3¼ mi e **Funnel** — 150 yds

From just below the dam at Erving behind the Erving Paper Company, there are rapids and then quickwater with the RR on the R bank. Below the RR bridge (¾ mi) MA-2 goes along the river as the rapids begin again with a class II chute that has large waves at high water. More easy rapids follow, and the river splits around an island with most of the water on the R. These rapids continue to the bridge at Farley (2¼ mi) which marks the end of the Middle Millers. A sandy beach on the L makes a good lunchsite. It is also a good place for less experienced paddlers to take out.

At Farley (2¼ mi) there is a class II rapid just below the bridge at an old damsite. It is most easily run on the far R. The next mile consists of calm sections and short class II rapids. A shallow, rocky class II rapid precedes the Funnel.

Caution! Be alert for the Funnel (3¼ mi), a class IV rapid which drops about 10 feet in 100 yards. It is located just upstream of the powerline crossing, but do not rely on spotting that landmark. The Funnel is a straight but heavy rapid which is sometimes too heavy for open canoes to run safely. A portage is possible on the R or along the high RR embankment on the L. At this point MA-2 is high up on the R bank, making scouting from the road impractical.

Below the Funnel a mile of fairly continuous class

II rapids leads to calmer water above the broken dam (5½ mi) in Millers Falls. This washed-out dam, with large timbers still underwater, is runnable anywhere, but the most abrupt drop is on the L and the center. Pass a small bridge and take out on the L just past a RR bridge (6 mi).

The rest of the description is not current. There are two dams in Millers Falls, followed by occasional rapids to the Connecticut River (7¾ mi). A bridge on a side road above the confluence provides a possible take-out.

NORTH RIVER   VT, MA

USGS: Colrain

The North River rises in southern Vermont and flows south to the Deerfield River. It is a small river in a not particularly attractive valley, but in the high water of early spring there are a few miles of whitewater canoeing. Above the Massachusetts—Vermont line, the river is too small and steep to canoe, but Halifax Gorge is worth a visit.

South Halifax — Colrain   3 miles

Experienced canoeists may elect to put in at South Halifax, Vermont, which is practically on the state line. The river is still very small but would offer a sporty run in high water to the bridge 1½ miles above Colrain.

Colrain — Deerfield River   7 miles

Most canoeists will start at a bridge 1½ miles above Colrain. The first 2 miles are all rapids, but not difficult. Just below Colrain is an unsightly dump, and a mile below Colrain is a broken dam which must be portaged or lined down on the right. There is an iron bridge just below the dam. For the next 1 mile the rapids diminish, the river goes under a covered bridge, and then soon one enters the slackwater of a large dam above Griswoldville. The West Branch enters on the right; it is small and steep, and is probably not canoeable. Portage left ¼ mile along Route 112 around the dam and mill. The river becomes polluted below here, and there are minor rapids 2 miles to Shattuckville. Here the river narrows and there is a small waterfall which must be portaged left. A short way below, just above the high bridge at Shattuckville, is a bad pitch which should be looked over or lined down on the right. Continuous rapids of intermediate difficulty continue 1 mile to the Deerfield River. One can take out at the bridge here, or continue down the Deerfield.

OTTER RIVER

The Otter River is a short stream rising in Templeton and flowing north into the Millers River above South Royalston. A water treatment plant under construction in Templeton is expected to improve the quality of the water in both rivers substantially.

From the MA-2A bridge it is 3¾ miles with moderate current past the MA-101 bridge and through mostly wooded countryside to the broken dam just above the River Street bridge in Otter River Village. Lift over the center of the 8-foot dam.

There is another dam above the Depot Street bridge (4¾ mi) in Otter River Village. Portage on the right or paddle along the canal on the left and carry out to the street.

There are a few rapids to the US-202 bridge in Baldwinsville (6½ mi). A couple of small class II–III drops are formed by the remains of an old dam just below this bridge.

In the last 3¼ miles to the Millers River (9¾ mi), there is a fair current with no hazards. The river is mostly in meadows and within the ponding area of the Birch Hill Flood Control Dam (11¼ mi) on the Millers River.

Scouted only. See the USGS Templeton and Winchendon sheets.

QUABOAG RIVER

The Quaboag River flows west from Quaboag Pond in Brookfield to Three Rivers, where it joins with the Ware River to form the Chicopee River. Its upper part provides a good flatwater trip, its middle section from Warren to Blanchardville is one of the best whitewater trips in central Massachusetts, and the lowest part is again smoothwater.

Due to the large lakes in its watershed, the Quaboag holds its water remarkably well, and it is little affected by a single rain or short dry spell. It can always be run up to the middle of June and frequently later.

The upper part of the Quaboag was used as a highway by the Indians. During King Philip's War, 1675–76, Brookfield was wiped out, and it was not re-established until 1686, when only one of the original settlers returned.

The Bay Path, which extended across the territory of the Massachusetts Bay Company from Boston to

Springfield, followed this valley and crossed the river by fords near West Brookfield and West Brimfield. Today, highways and a railroad follow the valley of the Quaboag.

Spencer — Quaboag Pond   6¼ miles
SEVEN MILE and BROOKFIELD RIVERS

In the early spring this trip in the headwaters of the Quaboag provides a nice, easy run for two to three hours. At the beginning there are many houses along or visible from the river, but the farther downstream you travel, the less you see of houses, buildings, and roads. Below East Brookfield the Seven Mile River enters a wide, isolated flood plain and empties into the Brookfield River, which in turn flows into Quaboag Pond.

1977 Spencer — Quaboag Pond   6¼ mi |10 km|
Flatwater, Quickwater, Class I
High water only: *March to early April*
Forested, Settled
    USGS: North Brookfield, East Brookfield

Put in next to the Pine Grove Cemetery where MA-31 crosses the river N of Spencer. The first 2 miles to the MA-9 bridge are flat. For most of this distance the river winds through a meadow. Portions of the stream are narrow, but encroaching alders are kept clipped back by canoeists who run it regularly. There are a few beaver dams which can be run at high water.

As the river passes a shopping center next to the MA-9 bridge (2 mi), the current picks up, and for the next 2 miles there is a mixture of quickwater and occasional class I rapids which end 100 yards below a high bridge over an old damsite in East Brookfield (4 mi). The river here is typically 10 yards wide, and it is shallow with a gravelly bottom.

The remainder of the trip is on flatwater. The Seven Mile River ends at the Brookfield River (4½ mi). The latter is almost all flatwater from the dam on Lake Lashaway (¾ mile upstream). To the L, it flows 1¾ miles to Quaboag Pond (6¼ mi).

Quaboag Pond — Warren   9 miles

This is an attractive flatwater trip that can be extended somewhat by beginning on the Brookfield River above Quaboag Pond. The Quaboag flows here in a broad valley in which towns and other built-up areas are for the most part hidden from the river. At the end of this section, the valley narrows, forcing roads, railroads, and towns closer to the river.

1971 Quaboag Pond — Warren   9 mi |14½ km|
Lake, **Flatwater**, Class I
Passable at most water levels
Forested, Rural
    USGS: East Brookfield, Warren

Begin from the road along the N shore of Quaboag Pond. The river begins after about a mile of paddling W along the N shore. The 5½-mile paddle from the pond's outlet to West Brookfield can be tedious in a head wind, as the river is fair-sized and leads through marshy meadows. Near West Brookfield the river passes under a RR bridge and the MA-67 bridge (6¾ mi), just below which the outlet from Wickaboag Pond enters from the R. For those who wish to avoid all rapids, this bridge makes a convenient take-out.

The last 2¼ miles to Warren have a stronger current and a few riffles. The first real rapid is just below the Old West Brookfield Road bridge (9 mi) at Lucy Stone Park, a good access point.

Warren — Blanchardville   10¼ miles

One attractive feature of this river is the fact that boating is not limited to the springtime — the water is often high enough to run in the fall. This applies especially to this section, where fine whitewater boating is available. The best part of this run is the whitewater, not the scenery.

There is a gauge located off MA-67 in West Brimfield 0.8 mile upstream from the Massachusetts Turnpike bridge. A reading of 3.9 represents low water, and anything over 5.0 represents high water.

Warren — Blanchardville   10¼ mi |16½ km|
Quickwater, **Class II–IV**
High or medium water: *March thru May and often in fall*
Forested, Settled, Town
    USGS: Warren, Palmer
  Portages: 1¾ mi R **broken dam and the Mousehole** — 30 yds
                2½ mi R **dam at West Warren** (difficult) — 50 yds

Just at Lucy Stone Park the river divides around an island in a little rapid with the L channel recommended. One and three-quarters miles of intermittent class II rapids follow to the broken dam above West Warren. **Caution!** Keep to the R. Do not even approach the canal on the other side, for it carries water into a pair of large tubes. On the far R of the collapsing dam is the Mousehole, a narrow channel which is sometimes runnable, but it should always be looked over for obstructions.

Below the Mousehole (1¾ mi) there is another short rapid leading to the first heavy rapid of the trip, a class III–IV pitch which is just below a RR bridge. This rapid should definitely be looked over. A broken dam, best run on the R, is next, followed by a rapid around an island. Then you reach the dam in West Warren where a tough carry on the R is necessary.

Below the West Warren dam (2½ mi) the rapids are class II. Another RR bridge and an island are passed. A broken dam is best run to the L of the two remaining stone columns. The river passes, in succession, a green bridge, a sewage plant, a RR bridge, a chute with heavy waves, a short pool, another RR bridge, and an island (3¾ mi).

The next mile is a challenging class III–IV run, with the first ½ mile comprising a long rapid leading uninterruptedly to a 3-foot drop which is difficult to see from above. At this point a large ledge blocks the middle, and both the far R and the far L are preferable. This drop can be looked over from MA-67 before putting in, but sometimes it is necessary to scout the entire ½-mile section that preceeds it. A short, smooth stretch leads into another ½ mile of similar difficulty. For those wishing only maximum excitement, one of the roadside turn-offs from adjacent MA-67 makes a possible take-out.

After the difficult rapids, 1¾ miles of riffles and easy class II rapids follow to the crossing (6½ mi) of the Massachusetts Turnpike, below which easy riffles and good current continue for the last 3¾ miles to Blanchardville (10¼ mi).

Blanchardville — Three Rivers   5¼ miles

The final segment of the Quaboag is almost entirely flat. This stretch, however, is not as attractive as the upper river because of the obstructions in the river and the towns along the banks.

| 1972 | Blanchardville — Three Rivers | 5¼ mi |8½ km| |

Flatwater, Class II
Passable whenever ice-free
Forested, Towns
    USGS: Palmer 15

The dam at Blanchardville was washed out by the 1955 flood, and only three stone bridge supports remain. A center route is recommended here. The cement blocks and protruding reinforcement rods just below can be avoided because the current is minimal. There are more obstacles at an island, with the R channel and its breached earthen dam more easily navigated than the jumble of steel and concrete at the end of the L channel. The earthen dam, constructed by the Palmer Paving Corporation, is usually washed out in the spring and rebuilt in the low water of summer.

After the problems in Blanchardville, 1½ miles of flatwater follow to Palmer (2 mi). The final 3¼ miles to Three Rivers are also smooth. Because of the rough water created by blasting and dredging below the confluence with the Ware River, a take-out is urged above the first bridge (5¼ mi) in Three Rivers.

SALMON RIVER   CT

For many people the season for whitewater begins on the Salmon River, which flows southward into the Connecticut between Middletown and Long Island Sound. Runs on the upper part of the river, where the rapids are, usually begin on the Blackledge and the Jeremy rivers, the two small streams which combine to form the Salmon. A large portion of the routes described here passes through or along the Salmon River State Forest, where the stream is flanked by stands of hemlock.

Just upstream from the CT-16 bridge over the Salmon River, there is a covered bridge, the old Comstock Bridge. On the downstream side of the right abutment there is a gauge. A reading of 1.4 corresponds to medium water.

West Road — Route 66   2¾ miles
BLACKLEDGE RIVER

1978   Quickwater, Class I–II   4½ km
High water: *early March*
Forested
     USGS: Marlborough
     Portages: ¼ mi   L   **culverts**   10 yds
                1½ mi   L   **dam**   20 yds

Begin N of the center of Marlborough at the bridge on West Road, just E of the intersection with Jones Hollow Road. The river here is small as it flows through a marsh. Soon it enters a thick alder swamp where there are two beaver dams. After scarcely more than 50 yards of thick bushes, you reach a set of culverts which must be carried. Beyond, the stream has been channelled through a gravel pit, and there are no obstructions for over ¼ mile.

Quickwater continues as the valley narrows beyond the gravel pit. The stream enters the woods where bushes occasionally crowd the channel. There are some class II rapids at an "S" turn above a small pond where a dam must be portaged.

Below the dam (1½ mi) the river flows through a very attractive, wooded valley with few obstructions. There are intermittent class I and II rapids for 1¼ miles to the CT-66 bridge (2¾ mi).

Route 66 — Route 16   8¼ miles
BLACKLEDGE and SALMON RIVERS

Of the two approaches to the Salmon River, this is the most frequently used. The rapids are also easier than those on the Jeremy. The most commonly used access to the river is at the old route 2 bridge southeast of Marlborough.

1978   Route 66 — Route 16   8¼ mi |13¼ km|
Quickwater, Class I–II
High water: *from CT-66, early March*
Medium water: *from old route 2, late March and after moderate rain*
Forested, Rural
     USGS: Marlborough, Moodus

In high water this stream can be run from the CT-66 bridge NE of Marlborough. A little diplomacy may be in order, because the stream is posted at this point. Connecticut law allows an owner of both banks to forbid passage on the stream. The first 3¼ miles are easy and can be run with little difficulty. The stream is narrow as it passes through a pretty area of woods and pastures. Be alert for fallen trees.

The put-in point is beside the old route 2 bridge for the run down the Blackledge and Salmon rivers. For 2½ miles past the River Road bridge (5¼ mi) to the confluence with the Jeremy River, the current is fast with occasional riffles and class I rapids.

Below the confluence (5¾ mi) there are continuous class II rapids which are easier in high water than in medium. A popular take-out is on River Road beside a brick fireplace (7½ mi) that is visible from the river. Below here a short distance there is a washed-out dam (7¾ mi) which should be scouted from the R bank. The clearest passage is on the R, but in medium water you are likely to run up on some rocks below. Class I rapids continue for ½ mile to the covered bridge just above CT-16 where there is a convenient take-out with parking on the R bank (8¼ mi).

Old Route 2 — Route 16   5¼ miles
JEREMY and SALMON RIVERS

The rapids in the approach to the Salmon via the Jeremy River are more difficult than those found on the Blackledge. They are also harder than those on the Salmon itself.

1977	Old Route 2 — Route 16	5¼ mi |8½ km|

Quickwater, **Class I–II**
High water: *early March*
Medium water: *late March*
Forested, Rural, Town
   USGS: Moodus
   Portage: 1½ mi L **dam at North Westchester** — 20 yds

The put-in point is beside the old route 2 bridge which is reached by turning R at the N end of CT-149 near Colchester. At first there is flatwater, but a short distance below the CT-2 bridge (¼ mi) the rapids begin. They are continuous class I and II for 1¼ miles to a bridge at North Westchester. There is a small millpond above a dam which must be portaged on the L.

Below the dam (1½ mi) class II rapids continue. There are a few short sections of quickwater as you approach the confluence with the Blackledge River, but for most of the 1¼ miles there are rapids. After a R turn there is a low ledge across the river which is runnable on the R.

Below the confluence (2¾ mi) there are continuous class II rapids which are easier in high water than in medium. A popular take-out is on River Road beside a brick fireplace (4½ mi) that is visible from the river. Below here a short distance there is a washed-out dam (4¾ mi) which should be scouted from the R bank. The clearest passage is on the R, but in medium water you are likely to run up on some rocks below. Class I rapids continue for ½ mile to the covered bridge just above CT-16 where there is a convenient take-out with parking on the R bank (5¼ mi).

Route 16 — Connecticut River   8¼ miles

Below the covered bridge next to CT-16, the Salmon River gradually flattens out. Above Leesville Dam there are no houses to be seen, and the river here makes a very attractive quickwater and flatwater run. Hemlocks line the steep banks and cover the hillsides. Below CT-151 the river is tidal, and there are some houses.

     A short distance below the CT-16 bridge, there is an imprinting pond where young salmon smolts are acclimated to the stream prior to being released into the river to swim to the sea and thereby restore the salmon fishery. Downstream, below Leesville Dam, the first salmon caught on rod and reel within Connecticut during this century was taken in 1977. The salmon released above the dam as young were unable to surmount it on their return from the sea, and they will be unable to do so until a fish ladder is built or until the shore owners downstream allow the dam to be breached.

Route 16 — Connecticut River   8¼ mi |13¼ km|
Flatwater, Quickwater; Tidal
High or medium water: *March and after moderate rain*
Forested, Town
    USGS: Moodus, Deep River
    Portage: 3½ mi L **Leesville Dam**

     Put in either below the covered bridge on the R, or below the new CT-16 bridge on the L at a picnic area. The current, which is strong here, gradually slows as you get nearer the dam at Leesville (3½ mi). Then, after a sharp L and R turn, you pass under the CT-151 bridge, the last place to take out above tidewater.

     One and three-quarters miles below CT-151 (3¾ mi), the river enters Salmon Cove (5½ mi), a tidal inlet on the Connecticut River. You can take out on the main river at the Salmon River boat launching area on the L

(7½ mi) or ¾ mile further at the parking area by the Good-speed Opera on the L just past the CT-82 bridge (8¼ mi) over the Connecticut.

SANDY BROOK   CT

Sandy Brook rises near South Sandisfield, Massachusetts and flows southeastward into Connecticut. It passes through Colebrook and reaches the Still River in the settlement of Robertsville, a mile up from the junction of that river with the Farmington at Riverton.

Above the CT-8 bridge Sandy Brook is very narrow, steep, and technical, providing one of the best whitewater runs in Connecticut. The rapids moderate from CT-8 down to the confluence with the Still River.

Sandy Brook has no major lakes or reservoirs in its headwaters, so that it rarely has enough water to be runnable.

Campbell Road Bridge — Route 8   4 miles

There is a gauge at the CT-8 bridge in Robertsville. This section of Sandy Brook is barely runnable at a reading of 2.3, while at 3.5 or higher it is a raging torrent. At water levels of approximately 2.3 to 3.0, it has been soloed in non-aluminum canoes (aluminum would stick too much), but it is normally a closed-boat run.

1977	Campbell Road Bridge — Route 8	4 mi [6½ km]

Class IV

High water: *March to early April*

Forested

USGS: Tolland Center, Winsted

To reach the put-in, turn W off of CT-8 onto Sandy Brook Road in Robertsville. The road follows the river closely and crosses it several times, facilitating scouting, putting in, and taking out. A start can be made wherever desired, with one possibility being the Campbell Road bridge 3.9 miles upstream from CT-8.

Rapids begin immediately, and a couple of small ledge drops are followed by a 4-foot ledge best run in the center. This drop can be viewed from Sandy Brook Road, and it should be looked over. Shortly below is another rapid, sometimes called the "Block," where a series of ledges and large holes finishes with an extremely tight drop around either side of a rock outcropping. The R side is about 6 feet wide with a rock narrowing the channel, while the L side is a canoe-width wide and only passable with the gauge at 2.8 or higher. Look over the Block also.

A bridge ¾ mile downstream of Campbell Road offers a put-in for those who do not want the difficulties above. However, below this is typical Sandy Brook — extremely steep and very narrow. Rocky class IV rapids follow upon each other's heels. The water is rarely heavy enough to be intimidating, but *fallen trees present a frequent and formidable hazard* to boaters throughout this run. Many rapids may require scouting, if only because the large rocks, tight turns, and steep gradient make it difficult to see ahead.

Route 8 — Riverton   2 miles

This section of Sandy Brook is still rapid but not nearly as difficult as the upper stretch. The river is considerably wider, with fallen trees presenting less of a hazard.

The water level for this lower part of the brook is less critical than for the upper section. A run can probably be made with less than the 2.3 reading (on the gauge at the CT-8 bridge) required for the upper section.

Route 8 — Riverton   2 mi [3¼ km]
Class II–III
High water: *March to early April*
Forested, Town
    USGS: Winsted

Put in from the CT-8 bridge in Robertsville. Rapids follow for a mile and are generally class II–III. Then it empties into the Still River, after which the rapids are even easier class II to the town of Riverton.

SWIFT RIVER   MA

The runnable upper stretches of the Swift River and its branches have all been inundated by the Quabbin Reservoir, which supplies Greater Boston with water. Regulations of the Metropolitan District Commission prohibit the use of canoes, sailboats, collapsible boats, and inboards on the Quabbin Reservoir. Therefore, boating is limited to the section of the Swift River below Winsor Dam.

The portion of the run immediately below the Quabbin Reservoir is the most attractive. The banks are heavily forested and the water is clear. Unfortunately, the river is quickly polluted and there are several dams in Bondsville.

xxxx   **Flatwater**, Class I   14 km
Passable anytime after ice-out
Dam-controlled
Forested, Towns
    USGS: Winsor Dam, Palmer
   Portages: 1± mi R **broken dam at West Ware**
               4½ mi L **1st dam in Bondsville** (take out well above)
                                   — ¼ mi
               4¾ mi   **2nd dam in Bondsville**
               5¼ mi R **dam below MA-181**
               6½± mi   **dam near Jabish Brook**

This description is the result of car scouting and second-hand reports. Although it is believed to be accurate, there may be errors or omissions.

At the MA-9 bridge the current is strong and the water clean. This type of running continues for a mile to the broken dam at West Ware, where a portage should be made on the R. Four miles of smoothwater follow to Bondsville, with some old bridge abutments about half-way down and a low steel road bridge with a big parking lot ½ mile further along on the R. Below West Ware the water quality deteriorates considerably.

Because canoeists are not allowed near the 12-foot dam in Bondsville (4½ mi), take out ¼ mile above it at a boat club on the L. This club is accessible from a road along the river. After putting in below the dam, a short paddle leads the canoeist under the Bay State Dyeing and Finishing Company's plant to a 3-foot dam just below.

The MA-181 bridge (5 mi) is passed, then another dam and a short, easy class II rapid. The Swift River then winds sluggishly to Jabish Brook (6½ mi), where a mill-dam necessitates another easy carry. The river continues for another 1½ miles through pretty country to its con-fluence with the Ware River. Take out either ½ mile up the Ware River at the MA-181 bridge or ¾ mile downstream in Three Rivers (8¾ mi).

TULLY RIVER   MA

The Tully River is a tributary of the Millers River just west of Athol. It is mostly smoothwater with some class I and II rapids. Start a trip by going about 2½ miles north of Athol on MA-32, and turning west onto Fryeville Road. Begin at the bridge over the East Branch.

The first ¼ mile below Fryeville Road is narrow,

shallow, and rapid, passable only at high water. The next mile to a broken dam is flat. The broken dam can be run single, or it can be portaged on the right. Then there is fast current for 200 yards to the Pinedale Avenue bridge (1¼ mi). The West Branch joins below, and there is mostly flatwater to the Millers River (3½ mi). There is a bridge less than ¼ mile downstream. *Scouted only.* See the USGS Royalston and Athol sheets.

WARE RIVER   MA

The Ware River rises near Hubbardston and flows in a southwesterly direction to Three Rivers, where within a mile it joins with the Quaboag and Swift rivers to form the Chicopee River. Much of it flows through a relatively unspoiled part of the state, but the upper section is very overgrown. Improvements have been made in the water quality, making summer canoeing, which is generally possible below MA-32 in Barre Plains, more pleasant than it once was.

North Rutland — Barre Falls   5½ miles

The stream above North Rutland is small and often badly obstructed. It has been run from MA-62, but brush and vines make passage down it difficult.

XXX   North Rutland — Barre Falls   5½ mi [8¾ km]
Flatwater, **Quickwater**, Class II
High water: *late March thru April*
Medium water: *May*
Forested, Town
    USGS: Wachusett Mountain, Barre
    Portage: 2½ mi L **dam at New Boston**

Information used to write the description of this 5½-mile section came from several sources. What follows is presumed to be accurate.

Put in below the last dam in North Rutland. The first 2½ miles to New Boston provide interesting and varied running, but some brush can be expected. At first there is a good class II rapid which is easier in higher water. The current continues strong with some easy, intermittent class II rapids that are followed by more strong current through swampy country. A 1-foot dam can be easily run, and then about a mile of smoothwater brings you to the millpond at New Boston. Portage on the L.

Below New Boston (2½ mi) there are 3 miles of smoothwater to the flood control dam at Barre Falls

(5½ mi). **Caution!** Do not cross the log boom or in any way enter the intake channel for the 885-foot long dam. There is no permanent lake behind this dam, and the stream is allowed to flow directly through a chute and tunnel in the dam. Five canoeists were injured here in 1975 when they were accidently washed through or became hung up upon the dam. Take-out on the L.

The section between the Barre Falls Flood Control Dam and South Barre is not recommended. There are tough portages at the flood control dam, around a short stretch above the Coldbrook Diversion Dam where boating is prohibited, and again in South Barre. Unless carrying a canoe is your sport, avoid the 6 miles below Barre Falls.

South Barre — Wheelwright	4¼ miles

XXXX | **Flatwater**, Class I–II | 6¾ km |

Passable at most water levels
Forested, Towns
    USGS: Barre, *North Brookfield*, Ware
    Portage: 4¼ mi L **dam at Wheelwright** — 20 yds

This description is believed to be accurate. There is a short rapid below the South Barre dam, and then the river divides, forcing the canoeists to choose the least obstructed channel. The last 3 miles from Barre Plains and the MA-32 bridge (1¼ mi) are pleasant flatwater behind the paper mill dam in Wheelwright (4¼ mi).

Wheelwright — Ware   10½ miles

This section of the Ware River is a pleasant flatwater trip broken in half by nearly 2 miles of rapids. It is possible for both flatwater and whitewater paddlers to arrange shorter trips to their liking.

    In Gilbertville there is a gauge on the downstream side of the right abutment of the Upper Church Street bridge. At a reading of 11.5 the rapids at Gilbertville are barely navigable. Note that on this particular gauge, higher numbers correspond to lower water levels.

1975 | Wheelwright — Ware | 10½ mi [17 km] |

Flatwater, Quickwater, Class II–III
High or medium water: *spring*
Low water: *passable for flatwater sections*
Forested
    USGS: Ware
    Portage: 10½ mi L **three dams in Ware** — ½ mi

From the Wheelwright dam 2 miles of flatwater and occasional riffles lead to the bridge on the Barre Airport road. After a little drop underneath this bridge, there is smoothwater for ½ mile to a RR bridge (2½ mi). Through wooded banks and mountain laurel, the river flows gently for 1¼ miles to a side road bridge (3¾ mi). Since there is no easy take-out right above the rapids, boaters desiring only flatwater should take out here.

In another 2 miles you reach the third RR bridge (5¾ mi), just below which class II–III rapids begin. These rapids can be impassable in low water. On the whole, the rapids above the MA-32 bridge (6½ mi) in Gilbertville are somewhat harder than the mile after this bridge, although the single most difficult drop comes right after the covered bridge (6¾ mi) in Gilbertville. This drop is best run on the far L, and it can be scouted, if desired, from that side. From this point the rapids diminish, giving way to quickwater for the remaining distance to the Upper Church Street bridge (8½ mi).

The last 2 miles to Ware are flat and somewhat wider. Grenville Park, ½ mile above the first dam (10½ mi) in Ware, provides a number of take-outs with easy automobile access.

If you are continuing downstream, the three dams in Ware should be portaged together. Under no conditions should you put in below the first dam, since heavy rapids and concrete retaining walls make the stretch hazardous. For a carry on foot, pull out on the L just above the first dam, cross the bridge below the dam, continue through the center of town, turn L on West Street, and take the first alley on the L leading to the river (11 mi).

Ware — Three Rivers   11¼ miles

xx | Flatwater, **Quickwater**, Class I–III   18 km
Passable whenever ice-free
Forested, Urban
    USGS: Ware, Palmer
    Portages: 8¼ mi L **1st dam at Thorndike** — 20 yds
                8¾ mi L **2nd dam at Thorndike**

This description is believed to be accurate. From Ware to Thorndike there are 8¼ miles of fine quickwater canoeing with a strong current and several good riffles. The MA-32 bridge is passed 3¼ miles below Ware. At Thorndike (8¼ mi) there are two dams, both of which should be portaged on the L. After the first dam and a road bridge, there is a short class III rapid which can be tricky in low water or heavy in high water.

The last 3 miles to Three Rivers contain a couple of class II–III rapids, particularly right after the second dam in Thorndike. Below MA-181 (10 mi) the Swift River enters on the R (10½ mi). Then it is ¾ mile to Three Rivers, where the Quaboag and Ware rivers meet to form the Chicopee River (11¼ mi).

WESTFIELD RIVER, North Branch   MA

USGS: Worthington, Goshen, Westhampton, Woronoco

The North Branch of the Westfield River rises in Windsor in the Hoosac Mountains, and flows southeast to Cummington, then south to meet the main Westfield River at Huntington. It provides one of the longest whitewater runs in Massachusetts. Above West Cummington it is too small for canoeing but from there it offers a fine run in the spring and later if the season is wet enough. Route 9 follows the valley from Swift River to West Cummington, so that one can judge the most suitable starting point for the existing water conditions. If the water is high enough it is best to start just below Berkshire Snow Basin Ski Area in West Cummington.

West Cummington — Swift River   9 miles
From West Cummington to Swift River, the stream is continuously rapid, but these rapids are not difficult (class II). This section is, therefore, a good place for the novice to try his hand and the expert to get his hand back as the road along the river provides an easy out in case of trouble.

Swift River — Knightsville Dam   18 miles
This stretch has more difficult rapids and, as it is entirely away from roads except for the crossing at West Chesterfield, it should be attempted only by thoroughly competent canoeists. The rapids are class III with easier going between. At Swift River village, also called Babylon, the river makes a sharp turn to the right, south, and after receiving the waters of the Swift River, which drops steeply down the hill from Goshen in a series of cascades, runs through a narrow twisting valley for 5 miles to West Chesterfield. This is a beautiful, wild valley hemmed in on both sides by high forested hills, and much of it has been protected by the Nature Conservancy. The straight

stretches are generally easy rapids, although shallow, but there are sharp drops at almost every turn. About ¼ mile above the West Chesterfield bridge there is a broken dam which is easily runnable on the right. This is the first point where a car can reach the river, and it is often used as a take-out. The bridge below here, Route 143, was originally the tollgate of the Third Massachusetts Turnpike. The water shoals near the bridge, and a passage is sometimes difficult to pick. If there is enough water at this point there is plenty for the rest of the river. The river flows through the town of West Chesterfield and 1 mile below the bridge makes a sharp right turn with a heavy rapid. The beach on the right offers a good lunch spot with a swimming hole below. The beach can also be used as a take-out, if the access road to it is not too muddy. About ¼ mile below this spot the river turns left with a sharp rapid and enters the West Chesterfield Gorge which is unrunnable except perhaps at certain water stages as a stunt. **Caution!** Take out on the right bank just above the curve. This may be a difficult maneuver, and it is easy to be swept into the gorge, so be sure to plan the landing carefully.

The West Chesterfield Gorge is a spectacular box canyon between sheer granite cliffs which are topped by tall hemlocks and spruce. At the upper end of the gorge are the remains of a high bridge, which carried the old stage road from 1769 until about 1875, when it was abandoned. Both banks are now owned by the Trustees of Reservations, who have torn down the old houses there and now have a fine park for the public to view the gorge. The carry is ¼ mile by the road which follows the right bank downstream. A car is handy for this chore. In low water, one can line down on the left, carry the bad drop, and run the rest of the gorge.

For the next 7 miles below the gorge the river continues in a steep narrow valley with heavy rapids for the first 4 miles. It then enters what were once lush farmlands for the last 4 miles to the Knightsville Dam. About 200 yards below the gorge there is a heavy rapid through some ledges which can be dangerous at high water. This can best be run by keeping well to the left and taking advantage of back eddies between the pitches. After about 1 mile of easier rapids the Boulder Patch is reached. **Caution!** Take out on right bank when large white boulders are noticed ahead as the route is intricate and ends in only one usable chute at the finish. Scouting is necessary here as the route may change with the stage of water. The steepest pitch can be lined down or portaged on the right if one prefers not to run it. Not far below here the river passes under a large telephone cable, beyond which there are several very good campsites on the left bank among open pine and hemlock groves. The rapids are easier here, and one is apt to be lulled into a false sense of security rudely shattered 1 mile below where there is another bad drop at a right turn. About 2 miles below this rapid the river enters a stillwater gorge, very spectacular and a fine swimming hole. This is the end of the heavy going, but there are still lively bits for the next 4 miles to the Knightsville Dam, but it is not as attractive as formerly, since the once pretty farmlands are apt to be covered with silt from the flooding caused by the dam. The old roads are still in use in the dam area and one from Route 112 just above the dam can be used to take out the canoes. If conditions are unattractive, the canoeist may prefer to take out about 2 miles below the stillwater gorge, where the old road borders the river on the right.

Knightsville Dam — Huntington   5 miles

There is still some fine running below the Knightsville Flood Control Dam. This section has class III rapids and is runnable throughout May, when the upper river and Middle Branch may be too low. Water releases from the dam for races and race practice often aid canoeing in the spring. Put in from a side road off Route 112 north of Route 66. The rapids continue with some severity for 1 mile, then the river turns left and passes through some vertical strata of rock where a minor gorge has been formed. This section starts with a 40-foot chute between angled ledges ending in a beautiful pool. The next pitch is below this pool, a direct drop of 2 to 3 feet with a back wave, best run on the far right. The next drop features a low island with a shallow, twisting passage on the left recommended. The right side has a large hydraulic and haystacks which will fill an open boat in high water. A short distance below this gorge the Middle Branch of the Westfield River enters on the right and the volume increases noticeably. In about 1 mile the Route 112 bridge is reached and many canoeists may wish to take out there. The rapids continue, however, for another 1 mile to the main Westfield River, which begins here at the junction with the West Branch of the Westfield River.

WESTFIELD RIVER, Middle Branch MA

USGS: Worthington, Chester, *Westhampton*

The Middle Branch of the Westfield River rises in Peru
and flows southeasterly to the North Branch of the Westfield River a few miles above the town of Huntington. It is
much smaller than the North Branch and is followed by a
road, so that it is less suited to camping. The stream is
continuously rapid, but the water is rarely heavy enough
to be dangerous. The valley is wooded, the stream crystal
clear, full of fish and fine for swimming. It is canoeable
from Smiths Hollow near the mouth of Tuttle Brook in
Middlefield to the North Branch, but high water is
necessary, so that early spring is preferable.

Smiths Hollow — North Branch   12 miles

To reach the Middle Branch, go north from Route 20 on
Route 112, cross the West Branch, and take a left onto
Basket Road. Follow the latter along the West Branch and
then take a road to the right that leads to the Dayville
Recreation Area.

    A put-in is possible anywhere along the road that
follows the Middle Branch. There is an average drop in
this section of about 30 feet per mile. The 6 miles to North
Chester are all rapid (class III), but just above the bridge
in North Chester there is a difficult gorge. The next 2 miles
to Dayville are also class III rapids, but the following
1 mile has heavier rapids. Most paddlers take out in Dayville because of the difficult access below. Below Dayville
there were 3 miles of rapids to the junction with the
Westfield River, North Branch, now eliminated by a flood
control dam. The dam is at Littleville, 1 mile above the
junction with the North Beach.

WESTFIELD RIVER, West Branch   MA

USGS: Becket, Chester, Blandford, *Woronoco*

The West Branch of the Westfield River rises in Washington and flows southeasterly to join the North Branch at
Huntington to form the main river there. It was once a
very wild and beautiful valley, but it is followed throughout its length by the main line of the Boston and Albany
Railroad and for a good deal of its length by a major highway, Route 20. Severe flood damage has also helped to mar

the natural beauty of the valley. Above Middlefield the West Branch is too steep to canoe. It is all rapid, but the upper part is quite steep and difficult. The run should be made in the early spring.

Middlefield — Chester   6 miles

The going is very rough (class IV) and inaccessible, so this stretch is suitable only for a strong party of expert canoeists. The start can be made about ½ mile below the Middlefield station, but about 1½ miles below the start there is a gorge with the railroad on the right bank high above the stream. In the gorge two ledges can be run in the center, but they are barely passable for an open boat because of high backwaves. Because of the difficult portage, some parties will elect to put in below it. The rapids are easier, class III, after the gorge. The railroad crosses and recrosses the stream repeatedly. A road runs by the river for the last mile to Chester — this is the first automobile access after Middlefield.

Chester — Huntington   6 miles

At Chester the river is joined by Walker Brook, which adds considerably to its volume. It becomes less rough (class II–III), but is continuously rapid to Huntington another 6 miles. About 3 miles below Chester after it passes under a railroad bridge there is a fine long rapid, steep but easily run at moderate water stages. Above Huntington there are two broken dams. The first one is easily run on the right: a sharp drop and backwave in the center and to the left should be avoided. The second one is best portaged on the left, although it is sometimes possible to run the class IV drop found on the right. At Huntington the West Branch joins the North Branch of the Westfield River to form the main Westfield River.

WESTFIELD RIVER   MA

USGS: Woronoco, *Mt. Tom*, West Springfield, Springfield South

The Westfield River is one of the principal tributaries of the Connecticut River from the west. It has four important branches: the North Branch, Middle Branch, and the West Branch, which meet at Huntington to form the main river, and the Westfield Little River, which enters at Westfield. The river flows southeasterly to meet the Connecticut River in West Springfield. Most of the valley is not very beautiful with many signs of human use and misuse. The water starts clear but gradually becomes more polluted, so that even in the lower section it is best to run early in the year.

Huntington — Connecticut River   21 miles

The first dam is 1 mile below Huntington, where the dam at the paper mill can be portaged by carrying on the left side down a steep bank. There are many rapids but none of them difficult (class I) in the next 2 miles to the dam at Russell, which should be carried on the right side. Below this the rapids are fewer and there are a number of stretches of flatwater in the 3 miles to the dam at Woronoco (Salmon Falls), which provides a difficult portage best made on the right bank around the mill. About 2 miles below here the river runs out of the mountains into a broad valley and meanders over shingle flats 4 miles to Westfield. Below Westfield the river is mainly slackwater. In 1 mile the Westfield Little River enters on the right, and in 2 miles more the river cuts through the low hills north of Proven Mountain into the Connecticut Valley, which it crosses for 6 miles to reach the Connecticut River just south of West Springfield.

CHAPTER 6

HOUSATONIC
WATERSHED

Housatonic River   177
Bantam River   179
Green River   180
Konkapot River   181
Naugatuck River   182
Shepaug River   182
Tenmile River   184

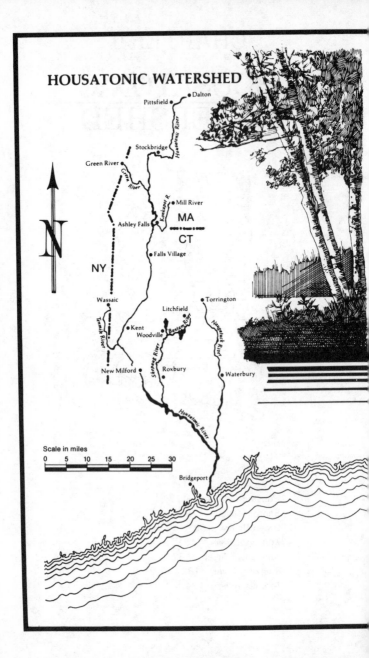

HOUSATONIC WATERSHED

Dalton

Pittsfield

Stockbridge

Green River

Ashley Falls

Mill River

MA

CT

Falls Village

NY

Wassaic

Torrington

Litchfield

Kent

Woodville

New Milford

Roxbury

Waterbury

Scale in miles

0 5 10 15 20 25 30

Bridgeport

HOUSATONIC RIVER   MA, CT

USGS: Pittsfield East, *Pittsfield West*, East Lee, Stockbridge,
Great Barrington, Ashley Falls, South Canaan, Cornwall,
Ellsworth, Kent, Dover Plains, New Milford, *Danbury*,
Newtown, Southbury, Long Hill, Ansonia, Milford

The Housatonic River rises near Pittsfield, Massachusetts, flows south through the wide valley between the
Berkshire Hills on the east and the Taconic Range on the
west, and continues through Connecticut to reach the sea
between Stratford and Milford. It is called by its Indian
name, which means "river beyond the mountains." Its
total length from Hinsdale, Massachusetts, to the sea
is 142 miles.

Dalton — Lenox   19 miles
There are several dams in Dalton, so that one should put
in below the last one. The river is somewhat polluted by
the paper mills there and again at Pittsfield by the Pittsfield sewage plant, so that this section is not particularly
recommended. Below Dalton and all the way down to
Lenox it is mostly a flat, winding river, but there are
stimulating views of Greylock from the meandering
stream. This section is best canoed in the spring when
the water is high, the current fast, and the pollution at a
minimum.

Lenox — Stockbridge   12 miles
Below Lenox ½ mile there is a dam and again in 1 mile at
Lee there are two more dams. This part is flat with some
rapids. Below here to Stockbridge the river is wilder and
more attractive, with the stream winding through a
swampy, overgrown section with some small rips.

Stockbridge — Great Barrington   13 miles
The first few miles through the Stockbridge meadows to
Glendale is very winding, but at high water there is a fast
current. There are two dams below Glendale with a bad
rapid below the second. The river then widens into a lake
for 1½ miles to another dam, and just above Housatonic,
there is another dam with a bad rapid below and 1 mile
of lake to the dam at Risingdale. The remaining 5 miles
to the dam in Great Barrington are flat water, with the
Williams River entering on the right 1 mile down.

Great Barrington — Falls Village 25 miles

This stretch is mostly flatwater with only two dams. Below the dam in Great Barrington it is 2 miles to the mouth of the Green River, which enters on the right. It is then some 15 miles to the mouth of the Konkapot River, which enters on the left at Ashley Falls just above the Connecticut line. Another 2 miles brings one to the old dam west of Canaan and another 5 miles to the dam only 1 mile above Falls Village. At this dam one can carry over into the intake canal, about ½ mile in length, which will save much carrying. There was a gristmill at Falls Village as early as 1740. Here in 1744 was built the first bridge in this section across the Housatonic, later known as Burral's Bridge.

Falls Village — Kent 19 miles

This is a favorite one-day trip with much smoothwater with fast current, some rips, and a rapid halfway down at Cornwall Bridge. It is a beautiful section of the river with high, steep, wooded hills most of the way. The river is broad and straight with plenty of room to maneuver. On Sundays during low water periods the powerhouse at Falls Village shuts down, and the river may then be too low for pleasant canoeing. Water is, however, sometimes released beginning at noon on Sundays. Put in below the power plant at Falls Village. There is a tricky corner just below this which should be checked before starting. There are no particular problems but many small rips which can be dangerous in high water until West Cornwall is reached 10 miles downstream. **Caution!** There is a long wooden bridge here and one should pull out well above it to look over the ¼ mile of rapid (class III) which starts just above the bridge and runs down to the corner below. This rapid can be dangerous (class IV) at high water. For some miles below this point the river runs through the Housatonic Meadows State Park. The next 9 miles to Kent are mostly flatwater with a good current except for a drop over a ledge about 1 mile below Cornwall Bridge.

Kent — New Milford 17 miles

The first 5 miles to the dam at Bulls Bridge are stillwater. The Kent School crews practice on this section. The lake at this dam leads into a 2-mile-long diversion canal, in which boats and canoes are not allowed. Below the dam, there is a ½-mile stretch of class IV rapids for which high water is needed. These rapids end near the mouth of the Tenmile River. About ¼ mile before reaching the power-house there is a particularly rough pitch, which had best be looked over first and may have to be lined down in high water. And ½ mile below the powerhouse there is another heavy pitch, which may require lining in high water. The rapids continue for some miles to Gaylordsville, with a particularly good one under the bridge there. The strong current continues the remaining 10 miles to the dam at New Milford. Just above that town the two Aspetuck rivers enter on the left.

New Milford — Long Island Sound   35 miles

This stretch has now all been dammed or is tidewater, so that it can be done at any season, being all lake or tide-water paddling.

The Shepaug Dam in Newtown, which forms Lake Lillinonah, is built about 2 miles below the mouth of the Shepaug River and floods back some 10 miles of the Housatonic nearly to New Milford, part way up the Still River, as well as several miles of the Shepaug, nearly to Roxbury Falls.

The Stevenson Dam in Monroe, which forms Lake Zoar, floods back up the river some 8 miles nearly to the Shepaug Dam. Not far below Sandy Hook at the head of the lake the Pomperaug River enters in the north side. For some miles on the south side of Lake Zoar is the Paugussett State Forest.

The Shelton Dam at Derby backs the water up some 5 miles nearly to the Stevenson Dam. The Indian Well State Park is located along the south shore of this lake, and it is at Derby that the Yale crews have their rowing practice, and the Derby Day races are held.

Below the Shelton Dam the river is tidal. In 1 mile the Naugatuck River enters from the north and the river becomes very large and deep.

BANTAM RIVER   CT

The Bantam River is a small stream that rises in Litchfield and joins the Shepaug in Washington. It is one of the early whitewater runs in New England — the first weekends of March bring many groups to the Bantam. Because of the river's small size, it is sometimes plagued by fallen trees and dangerous ice ledges.

1972   Lake, Flatwater, **Class I–III**   22½ km
             High water: *March*
             Forested
                 USGS: *West Torrington,* Litchfield, New Preston
             Portages: 8 mi   **dam in Bantam**
                          11½ mi   **broken dam at West Morris** — 30 yds

Put in at the CT-25 bridge NE of Litchfield. The pretty, narrow stream winds slowly through swampland to Bantam Lake (5¾ mi). It is about ¾ mile along the N shore around a promontory to the outlet (6½ mi). It is then a little over 1½ miles to the town of Bantam, where there is a dam. *This first paragraph is not current.*

Paddlers can put in where the river turns sharp L in Bantam (8½ mi), but novice groups desiring whitewater would be better off further down. The first ¾ mile from Bantam to a bridge on Stoddard Road is class III, with a high probability of tree obstructions.

The best start for an easy whitewater trip is at the Stoddard Road bridge (9¼ mi), reached by going S on West Morris Road from CT-25 in Bantam and following the former until Stoddard Road leaves on the L. There are easy class II rapids for ½ mile to the next bridge and another 1¾ miles of similar rapids to a broken dam and a bridge in West Morris. This dam is occasionally run, but it should be looked over. It is generally carried.

Below West Morris (11½ mi) there are 2 miles of more difficult class II rapids to the steel bridge at Rumsey Hall School (13½ mi). One-half mile of more rapids brings the boater to the confluence with the Shepaug River (14 mi). A take-out may be made either at Rumsey Hall School or at CT-47, which is 3 miles down the Shepaug.

GREEN RIVER   NY, MA

USGS: State Line, Egremont, Great Barrington

The Green River rises in Austerlitz, New York, and flows southeastward to enter the Housatonic just below Great Barrington. It is a beautiful, clear, limestone brook with Route 71 following it most of the way. It is small and must be canoed during freshet or after heavy rains.

Green River — Housatonic River　　　　　　12 miles

A start can be made at Green River village, but the first
1½ miles to a bridge on the side road off Route 71 are
extremely rough. The going then becomes easier, 2 miles,
to the Route 71 bridge, all quickwater with numerous short
rapids, very shallow in places. The valley is all open farmland along here, where the state line is crossed into Massachusetts. It is then only 2 miles to North Egremont, during
which two bridges are passed. **Caution!** All through the
lower part of this river watch for barbed wire. From North
Egremont to the Egremont Plains road bridge it is 2 miles
through broad meadows but with some logs to lift over.
The current continues strong for another 2 miles to the
Route 23 bridge. The remaining 2 miles to the Route 7
bridge, at the mouth where the river joins the Housatonic
River, are through broad meadows.

KONKAPOT RIVER　　　　　　　　　　MA, CT

USGS:　Great Barrington, Ashley Falls

The Konkapot River rises in Lake Buel in Monterey as a
rather famous trout stream and flows south across the
Connecticut line, where it turns west and north recrossing
into Massachusetts to flow into the Housatonic at Ashley
Falls. It is a small stream and should be run in the spring
or after heavy rains.

Mill River — Ashley Falls　　　　　　　　11 miles

The first 4 miles to Konkapot village are very rough and
not recommended. In the first 1 mile there are sharp rapids
which must be looked over, then a mill site with a carry on
the left, another sharp drop which can be run, a second
mill site with a carry on the left, another very sharp rapid
through a third mill site, and finally a short carry left
around a high dam. There is then a very sharp drop under
a bridge 2 miles below Mill River. In another ¼ mile there
are some splendid falls on the left and a pleasant picnic
spot, where the Umpachene River enters. The next 2 miles
to Konkapot village involve strong current and frequent
rapids, all runnable to the bridge at the town. It is then
1 mile to the Southfield Road bridge. The river is now a
broad, strong meadow brook, not exciting but fast paddling 2 miles to the two bridges at Clayton practically on
the Massachusetts—Connecticut line. In 1 mile the Sodom

bridge is reached, and the river turns north for 1 mile to the Route 124 bridge, which is almost on the state line. Below this bridge there are 2 miles of sluggish, winding stream to the dam at Ashley Falls, where one can take out or go 1 mile to the Housatonic River.

NAUGATUCK RIVER   CT

USGS: Torrington, Thomaston, Waterbury, Naugatuck, Ansonia

The Naugatuck River is formed in northern Torrington by the junction of a number of brooks. It is not navigable, however, until the town of Torrington, from whence it flows south to the Housatonic River at Derby. The Naugatuck Valley is densely populated with one of the major industrial concentrations of the nation. A number of short, steep tributaries flow into the deforested valley causing an extremely fast run-off with consequent severe flooding. The August, 1955, flood, which was four times more severe than any previous flood, took 42 lives and caused $220 million damage. As a result seven flood control dams and four local protection works have been built or authorized. These dams added to those already existing and the extreme pollution make the river unattractive, although it may be run with some enjoyment in the spring when pollution is at a minimum.

Torrington — Waterbury   **21 miles**

This section is not particularly interesting from a quick-water point of view, but there are a few short rapids and a very difficult one. There is a 142-foot high flood control dam just above Thomaston about halfway down. It is well to take out above the Waterbury dam as the section below is especially odoriferous.

Waterbury — Derby   **22 miles**

From Waterbury to Seymour there are seven dams and two more below that to the last dam at Ansonia, below which it is tidal for the remaining 2 miles to Derby, where it joins the Housatonic River.

SHEPAUG RIVER   CT

The Shepaug River rises in Cornwall and flows south to the Housatonic in Southbury at the former village of Shepaug, now drowned out by Lake Lillinonah behind the Shepaug Dam. The name "Shepaug" is from the Mohegan Indian word meaning "Rocky River."

This river provides two attractive, whitewater runs: one of intermediate difficulty and the other for novices. Since the river is small, these runs are only available in the early spring.

Woodville — Bee Brook (Route 47)   6 miles

1973   Class III   9¾ km
            High and medium water: *March*
            Forested
                USGS: New Preston 15

When the water is high enough, a put-in can be made below the Shepaug Reservoir in Woodville. To reach this spot, go N on CT-341 from its junction with CT-25. Take the first R turn off CT-341 onto Romford Road and follow this road to the river. There are two dams just above the put-in.

The first mile below the start is fast, twisty, and class III. Several islands complicate the choice of routes. The high CT-25 bridge (1 mi) is a possible put-in if there is insufficient water above. Two more miles with numerous class III rapids lead to the junction with the Bantam River. Romford Road follows the Shepaug closely for almost all of the distance.

After the confluence with the Bantam (3 mi), the Shepaug's volume is much greater. Rapids continue, sometimes reaching class III in difficulty, for 3 miles to the CT-47 bridge (6 mi) a mile above Washington Depot. This bridge is called "Bee Brook" for the small stream that enters on the R just upstream of the bridge.

Bee Brook (Route 47) — Roxbury   9½ miles

The 8-mile section from Washington Depot to Roxbury is one of the most attractive whitewater runs in Connecticut. Beautiful, steep, hemlock-covered banks rise three to five hundred feet above the river; in a few places there are scenic cliffs. Evidence of civilization is minimal. The rapids are continuous class II, permitting easy running without need for scouting.

Below Roxbury Station, the recommended take-out, is the scenic but unrunnable Roxbury Falls. Unfortunately, there is no easily accessible take-out above it because it is located in a narrow gorge. Many canoeists have found themselves unable to stop above the falls, and they have lost their canoes.

Roxbury was settled as the town of Pomeraug in 1713, and it was here that Ethan Allen was born in 1738.

1972	Bee Brook (Route 47) — Roxbury	9½ mi [15¼ km]

Class II
High and medium water: *March*
Forested
     USGS: New Preston, Roxbury

Below the first CT-47 bridge (Bee Brook), the Shepaug is gentler than above. One and a half miles of class II rapids lead past two more CT-47 bridges in Washington Depot. Then there are 8 miles of scenic class II rapids to Roxbury Station. Take out at Hodge Park (9½ mi) where the road on the E bank is close to the river, ¼ mile above the dam.

Caution! Four miles below the dam at Roxbury Station is Roxbury Falls. It is a trap. The approach is blind, and many canoeists, caught in the swift current as they approached it, have been swept over it. The steep walls and strong current at the top make a safe landing and exit both difficult and unlikely.

TENMILE RIVER   NY, CT

    USGS: Amenia, Dover Plains

The Tenmile River rises in Salisbury, Connecticut, where it is known as Webatuck Creek. It flows southwest into New York, where just below Wassaic, it is joined by Wassaic Creek and becomes known as the Tenmile River. It then flows south and finally turns east to meet the Housatonic just below Bulls Bridge in Connecticut. Although it starts and ends in Connecticut, most of the running on the river is in New York. This river has a number of difficult rapids and should not be attempted by novices, especially at the lower end. It is best run during medium water stages, as at high water some pitches can be difficult, and at low water impassable.

Wassaic — Housatonic River   **18 miles**

Put in about ½ mile below Wassaic, near the bridge at the Wassaic State School. At high water one can put in a mile farther upstream near South Amenia. There are two difficult pitches just below the start, then fast, smooth current around sharp turns in the meadows 5 miles to Dover Plains, where there is a dam which must be carried. Just below there is a broken dam which can usually be run, followed by 8 miles of easy, pleasant running to the dam at South Dover. The next 5 miles from here to the Housatonic, the stream is deeper and more sporting where it cuts through the hills. There are some rough turns 1 mile below the bridge at South Dover and again below at Webatuck. In 1½ miles more there is a steep chute with bad waves and a tricky outrun. **Caution!** The waves are high here and the pitch should be looked over carefully before running. Below here the rapids increase in severity and in the last 1 mile before the Housatonic River are quite severe. There is no pause on entering that river as the difficult rapids continue.

CHAPTER 7

SOUTH COASTAL
WATERSHEDS

Norwalk River   189
Saugatuck River   189
East River   189
Hammonasset River   190

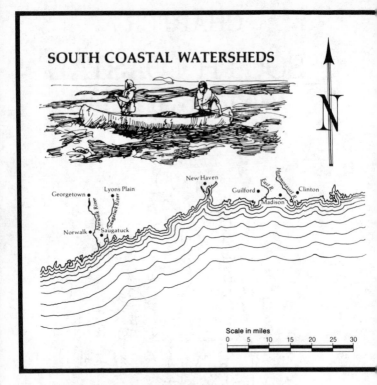

SOUTH COASTAL WATERSHEDS

Georgetown • Lyons Plain   New Haven   Guilford •   Hammonasset R. Clinton
Norwalk •   Saugatuck   Madison   East R.

Scale in miles
0   5   10   15   20   25   30

INTRODUCTION

Three major rivers reach the sea in Connecticut: the
Housatonic, the Connecticut, and the Thames. These and
their tributaries drain a major portion of the interior,
leaving little area to be drained by the coastal rivers. Thus
the latter tend to be short, but several of them have nice
tidal sections.

Tidal streams are of particular interest for the flora
and wildlife which are more visible there than in most
places, especially if you are alone and moving quietly. But
it is necessary to watch the tide so as not to be caught on
mudflats as the tide goes out. Many tidal streams are short
and, being of local interest only, they are not included here.

Two of the best rivers on the Connecticut coast
are the East and the Hammonasset.

NORWALK RIVER CT

The Norwalk River is paralleled by US-7 and flows into Long Island Sound at Norwalk. In spite of its length, it is small and shallow, and it can only be run when there is a heavy run-off. A fair amount of the upper river is enjoyable, but not necessarily scenic. Much of the lower section through Norwalk is unattractive. See the USGS Norwalk North sheet.

One suggested 7-mile run begins at Old Mill Road about a mile below Georgetown. From there to the bridge in Cannondale, it is class I and occasionally blocked by debris. From Cannondale to the take-out just a few yards south of the Norwalk-Wilton line, the difficulty reaches class II, and there are only a few carries.

Below the Norwalk-Wilton line the rapids are considerably more difficult.

SAUGATUCK RIVER CT

USGS: Westport, *Sherwood Point*

The Saugatuck River flows south into Long Island Sound at Saugatuck in Westport. It is best to canoe the river early in the year, March and early April.

Lyons Plain — Saugatuck 9 miles

Put in at Lyons Plain in Weston. It is a pleasant, 7-mile paddle with easy current through woodlands to tidewater, ½ mile above Westport. There are a few small dams with short carries. Take out at the bridge at tidewater, continue another ½ mile to Westport, or continue an additional 1½ miles to Saugatuck, where you can take out near Route 1. There are no good take-out spots near the mouth of the river.

EAST RIVER CT

This river, which forms a part of the boundary between Guilford and Madison, is one of the nicest tidal streams along the Connecticut coast. It provides a pleasant and easy 6-mile paddle.

It flows through the woods to farmland, past some houses, and then out into the salt marshes. The houses are attractive: some are very old; none are obtrusive. Most of the salt marsh is owned and preserved by the state or the Audubon Society.

Access upstream is from the upper end of Nut

Plains Road which is east of CT-77 and north of the Turnpike. Near the ocean there is access at the US-1 bridge,
the Guilford Town Dock, and the state launching ramp at
the end of Neck Road in Madison. See the USGS Guilford
sheet.

HAMMONASSET RIVER   CT

The Hammonasset River runs south into Long Island
Sound between Clinton and Madison. It is a pretty stream,
and the Madison Land Trust has been acquiring land along
the upper part in order to protect it. Unfortunately, filling
and dredging at US-1 have ruined many acres of salt
marsh, but there are still long stretches to the north and
south of the highway where none of this is visible.

If you plan to paddle in the tidal portion immediately below the old fish hatchery, plan your trip for mid-tide
or higher, or be ready to carry and drag over some rocks
where the stream is too shallow. Tides run about a half
hour earlier than Boston.

Off Route 79 — Route 1		**7¼ miles**

1973   Flatwater, Quickwater, Class I–II; Tidal   11¾ km
High water: *needed above Green Hill Road, early March*
Medium water: *passable below Green Hill Road, spring and fall*
Forested, Settled
    USGS: Clinton

Follow Chestnut Hill Road NE from CT-79 in
Madison. Just before the bridge, turn N up Summer Hill
Road and put in where it follows along the river.

At first the river drops gradually in easy class II
rapids. Just around the bend below Chestnut Hill Road,
there is a footbridge which can be passed on the R if the
water is too high for you to pass under it. After about
½ mile of rapids, the stream runs for a while through a
swamp and then into a pool above a broken, runnable dam.
Then, in about 100 yards you reach Green Hill Road.

Below Green Hill Road (1½ mi) there is a long
stretch which is flat, deep, and meandering. A broken,
washed-out dam by the Connecticut Turnpike — at the
site of an old fish hatchery — marks the beginning of tidewater.

There is a road on the L and a bridge just above
the Connecticut Turnpike (5½ mi) next to exit 62, with salt
marshes the rest of the way to US-1 (7¼ mi). In another
mile the river opens into Clinton Harbor (8¼ mi).

CHAPTER 8

THAMES
WATERSHED

Five Mile River   193
French River   194
Hop River   195
Moosup River   196
Mount Hope River   197
Natchaug River   198
Quinebaug River   199

Shetucket River   203
Susquetonscut Brook   204
Willimantic River   204
Yantic River   205

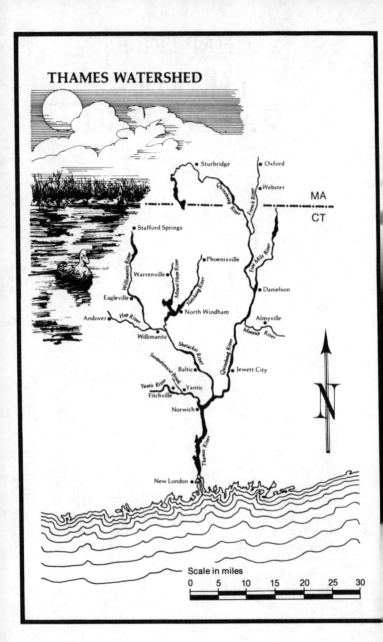

THAMES WATERSHED

Sturbridge • Oxford
• Webster

Quinebaug River
French River

MA
CT

• Stafford Springs

Willimantic River
Mount Hope River
Natchaug River
Five Mile River

• Phoenixville

Warrenville •
• Danielson

Eagleville •
Hop River
• North Windham
Almyville •
Moosup River
Andover •

Willimantic •
Shetucket River
Quinebaug River

Susquetonscut Brook
Baltic •
• Jewett City

Yantic River
• Yantic
Fitchville •

Norwich •

Thames River

New London •

N

Scale in miles

0   5   10   15   20   25   30

192

INTRODUCTION

The rivers of the Thames Watershed are relatively unknown by comparison with others close at hand. But for spring and fall canoeing, there are several good alternatives from which to choose. If you want a gentle stream with a good current, try the Willimantic. The Hop River is more difficult — narrower and faster with sharper turns. The Natchaug River has many scenic miles of intermittent quickwater and class I–II rapids.

Apparently this area is overlooked because better alternatives lie nearby or equally suitable rivers are closer to population centers. Whitewater in the Thames Watershed does not equal that found on the Quaboag and Salmon rivers to the north and west, and to the east there are many fine flatwater rivers. Perhaps this explains why this area attracts less attention.

The Thames River is a wide, tidal river which flows south from Norwich to Long Island Sound at New London. It is not described in this book.

FIVE MILE RIVER   CT

USGS: Thompson, *East Killingly, Danielson*

The Five Mile River rises in Thompson near the south end of Webster Lake. It flows south into Quaddick Reservoir, continues south through Putnam into Killingly, where it swings southwest and then south again to meet the Quinebaug River at Danielson. Much of it flows through wild, unspoiled country, mostly woods, but some of it through open farmland. It appears to hold its water well, and parts of it can probably be run even in summer.

Quaddick Reservoir — Ballouville   8 miles

At the outlet of Quaddick Reservoir, one has a choice. One can carry over the dam into the small pond below, and carry over the next dam and through the brush into the stream below. Or one can bypass the small pond and second dam by carrying 400 yards along the road on the right. From the road bridge just below the second dam, there are 200 yards of brook to the next pond, and this may be a scratchy stretch if the water is low. One can continue the portage through open field to the pond if necessary. The next 5 miles of stream will have some shallow scratchy spots if the water is not well up, until one reaches the slackwater at the bridge 1 mile above Pineville dam. The run is narrow and winding, through farmland and well-wooded areas. At Pineville there is a fine swimming hole above the stone dam, and an easy portage, left. If the water is too low to navigate the riffles below the dam, one can carry 700 yards along the paved road to the next bridge, where the slackwater above Ballouville dam begins.

Ballouville — Danielson   7 miles

At Ballouville, one should land between the dam spillway and the gatehouse on the left. If the water is too low to run the riffles below the dam, one portages 600 yards left around the mill via streets and puts in at the canal below the mill. About 1 mile beyond Ballouville there is a drop which should be looked at before running. There are a number of little drops over ledges throughout this 1½ mile to Attawaugan, which can be exasperating or impassable during low water. There is a low dam to be portaged just above Route 12, and a good flow of water is needed to navigate the next mile to the slackwater above Killingly. There are probably two short portages around obstructions in this stretch. At Killingly, one can portage 600 yards via streets starting from the first spillway and sluice gates and going around the right side of the factory. Or one can portage 300 yards along the embankment left of the mill pool to the second spillway, scrambling down through the poison ivy to enter the river at the foot of the spillway. The river below is shallow and scratchy during low water until slackwater is reached again above the Rock Avenue bridge 1½ miles below Killingly. Another 2½ miles through slackwater brings one into the center of Danielson, where there is a dam.

FRENCH RIVER   MA

USGS: Leicester, Webster, *Oxford*

The French River rises in a cluster of ponds on the border between Leicester and Spencer, where the canoeist can find some pleasant lake-paddling. From there it flows south through a rapid succession of shallow brooks, mill ponds and dams to Hodges Village Flood Control Dam in Oxford. The run from there to Webster is quite pretty and without dams. Below Webster the dams are frequent and the water vile until the river joins the Quinebaug just below West Thompson dam.

Oxford — Webster   8 miles

When there is a good flow of water, a start can be made from the area in North Oxford west of Route 12 opposite Old Worcester Road, about 2¾ miles above Hodges Village Flood Control Dam. Another good starting point is in the pond just below the dam. The river is placid and pretty for the next 5½ miles to the dam at North Village in Webster. Mill Brook, the outlet of Webster Lake, enters from the left 200 yards upstream from the high abandoned railroad bridge at North Village. At this point, the water becomes opaque, odorous and disgusting. A take out at this point is recommended.

HOP RIVER   CT

This is a clear, medium-sized stream which flows east into the lower end of the Willimantic River. It runs through hardwood forests for most of its length; occasionally there are fields on one side or the other. The first 9 miles are the most isolated. Few houses or buildings are visible from the river in that section, even though a major highway follows the valley.

This is a good river for the beginning canoeist. There are few obstacles, but there are many turns and a few very easy rapids in which to practice. The only class II rapids are short and can be easily avoided.

Andover — Willimantic   12 miles

977   **Flatwater, Quickwater**, Class I   19¼ km
High or medium water: *early spring and late fall*
Forested, Rural
   USGS: *Rockville, Marlborough*, Columbia, *Willimantic*
   Portage: 7 mi L **dam at Hop River Road** — 10 yds

Near the NW corner of Andover, leave US-6 on Hendee Road and put in at the bridge. The current is fast; the stream about ten yards wide. After 1½ miles the river comes near the road just above a washed-out dam where there are some easy class II rapids with small rocks. There are two class I rapids and two bridges before a tricky class II drop at a set of cement culverts that are still in the river, although the road has been completely washed away.

There is a rock dam just past Parker Bridge (5½ mi), and just after a RR bridge there are some class I rapids as the river drops into the millpond above a dam at Hop River Road. Portage on the L.

After Hop River Road (7 mi) there are 100 yards of very easy class II rapids followed by more class I drops. There is another bridge (8¼ mi), the access ramps to I-84, a powerline (10 mi), and then the second RR bridge (10½ mi), underneath which there are some short class II rapids (the hardest on the river) as you approach the embankment of I-84. There are class I rips under the bridge on Flanders River Road (11 mi), a half mile above the confluence with the Willimantic River.

From the end of the Hop River, there is ¼ mile of flatwater and quickwater to a convenient take-out on the R just past a RR bridge at a roadside picnic area off US-6 (12 mi).

MOOSUP RIVER RI, CT

USGS: Oneco, Plainfield

The Moosup River rises in Rhode Island, flowing south at first, then swinging westward through the towns of Moosup and Central Village to join the Quinebaug below Wauregan. Its upper portion offers remote, wilderness canoeing. However, above Almyville there are many fallen trees, and it should only be run in the spring. Its central part has frequent dams, and its final stretch is wooded and remote.

Moosup Valley — Quinebaug River   23 miles

Start at Route 14 bridge near Fairbanks Corner. From there the river runs a good 6 miles to Oneco, meandering through isolated, wild, wooded country most of the way. The dam at Oneco is portaged starting at the landing on the left side above the highway bridge, crossing the bridge, and putting in behind the mill on the right. It is then 2 miles with riffles to the dam at Sterling, where the portage is on the far right near the mill, and runs 100 yards along Route 14 to the Main St. bridge. In another 3 miles the high upper dam at Almyville is reached. Here the portage can be made on either side, carrying around the mill buildings. The topographic map (1953) shows 5 dams in the next 3½ miles, but 2 of these have since broken, making a reasonably fast river with some boulder-dodging. The dam below Almyville is easily portaged on the right, if one is not concerned about poison ivy. The river runs fast for the next 1 mile to the broken upper dam at Moosup, which experienced whitewater canoeists will likely find runnable, and others can easily lift over on the left. The lower dam at Moosup is broken, and has been replaced by a low dam, easily portaged, located at the head of the old pond. The river continues through the dry bed of the old pond to a 1-foot drop located at the site of the old dam. This and the short rubble pile below are easily portaged. Just beyond the Connecticut Turnpike there is a brief portage over the left end of a low dam. The map does not show the next low dam just ahead, located 150 yards above the Route 12 bridge. At Central Village there is a 1-foot drop at the railroad bridge to run or lift over. Fifty yards ahead are the remains of the old dam shown on the map, which can be run. One-half mile farther are two road bridges, which are the last take-out points on the Moosup River. If one passes these bridges, he must run 6 miles more. There are 2 miles of the Moosup River to its junction with the Quinebaug, plus 4 miles on the Quinebaug to reach the next take-out at Route 14.

MOUNT HOPE RIVER   CT

This river is a tributary of the Natchaug River a short distance north of Willimantic. It is a small, clear stream in a predominately rural setting. In difficulty it resembles the Natchaug, but relatively higher water is needed for good passage.

There are some nice class II rapids in the last 1¾ miles of the river, but the only convenient take-out at the end is from the Mansfield Hollow Reservoir, and the latter may still be frozen early in the season.

Warrenville — Mansfield Hollow Reservoir   8 miles

Lake, **Flatwater, Quickwater**, Class I–II	12¾ km
High water: *March*	
Forested, Rural, Settled	
USGS: Spring Hill	

Begin from the CT-89 bridge N of US-44 at Warrenville. Above that point access to the river is restricted, and passage down it is obstructed by fences.

A mixture of flatwater and quickwater extends for 3¼ miles past the US-44 bridge (½ mi) and the next CT-89 bridge (2¼ mi). Then there is a narrow, 100-yard class II rapid that extends around a L turn. Easier, intermittent rapids are to be found in the next ¼ mile to Mount Hope Bridge (3½ mi), which is next to a traffic light.

For 2¼ miles flatwater and quickwater continue almost all the way to the second small bridge below

Mount Hope Bridge. Then there are nearly continuous class I and II rapids for 1 mile to Atwoodville, where there is a sharp R turn from which a high bridge is visible. Below this turn, but above the bridge, there is a sharp drop over a ledge which can be lined or portaged on the L. Access to the river near this bridge is poor.

There are more class II rapids after the ledge in Atwoodville (6¾ mi), and they culminate in a short, steep class II–III pitch just before you reach the normal pool (7½ mi) behind the Mansfield Hollow Flood Control Dam. The most convenient take-out is at the bridge (8 mi) on Bassett Bridge Road off CT-195 in Mansfield Center.

NATCHAUG RIVER CT

This is a very scenic river that flows south through a lightly settled valley to Willimantic. The lower section has been ponded by a flood control dam and a reservoir. What remains above provides an excellent, one-day canoe trip for novice whitewater canoeists.

A moderate run-off is needed for this river. The rapids are generally short, and they occur intermittently all the way down it. Along the upper portion Natchaug State Forest borders one or both of the banks. The west bank has several campgrounds (public and private) where many small and runnable rock dams have been built to form swimming holes and wading pools.

The 2¾-mile section from the CT-198 bridge in South Chaplin to North Windham is the best part of the river. The rapids are the longest, and the countryside the wildest. For most of this distance the river valley is within the area of potential inundation from the flood control dam during times of severe and dangerous run-off.

 Phoenixville — North Windham **11 miles**

1977	Flatwater, **Quickwater**, Class I–II	17¾ km
	High and medium water: *early spring and late fall*	
	Forested, Rural	
	USGS: Hampton, Spring Hill	
	Portage: 8 mi L **Diana's Pool** — ¼ mi	

Put in below the junction of CT-198 and US-44 at the bridge just off General Lyons Road to avoid a dam. At the start there are 200 yards of class II rapids which ease up to a 2-mile mix of quickwater and flatwater that is broken occasionally by class I drops over rock dams. As the river passes a state campground on the R, there are intermittent class I and II rapids that last for ¾ mile. Then, as you pass a private campground, there are two large rock dams, one of which must be lined in medium water.

The second bridge is Morey Road (4 mi), and ½ mile below it there is a high rock dam which should be lined in medium water. Just past the dam there are intermittent class II rapids that continue past the third bridge (4¾ mi) and ease up as you approach the crossing of Bear Hill Road (6¼ mi). The next mile to the bridge on England Road is flat.

Just at the England Road bridge (7¼ mi) there is a short drop, and soon thereafter there are some easy, intermittent class II rapids that lead into a large pool. **Caution!** After the short rapids leading out of the pool, stop on the L bank and portage ¼ mile along paths beside a very beautiful area of large boulders and ledges above Diana's Pool. At certain water levels this part would probably be a class IV run.

Put in again just above the CT-198 bridge (8¼ mi) and run a nice ¾-mile section of class II rapids that are followed by 2 miles of mostly quickwater to North Windham. The last convenient take-out is at the bridge in North Windham (11 mi), upstream and on the L.

After another ½ mile of mixed quickwater and class I rapids, the Natchaug flows into the backwater behind the Mansfield Hollow Flood Control Dam. You can take out at Mansfield Hollow State Park (11¼ mi), but you should spot the take-out in advance so that you will recognize it from the river. The only good take-out from the lake is at the landing on Bassett Bridge Road (12¾ mi) which can be reached by continuing straight along the road which crosses the river at North Windham.

QUINEBAUG RIVER   MA, CT

USGS: Wales, Southbridge, Webster, Putnam, Danielson, Plainfield, Jewett City, Norwich

The Quinebaug River rises in Holland on the Massachusetts-Connecticut line and flows in a big loop to the north and east through Brimfield, Sturbridge and Southbridge to cross the state line flowing southeast at Dudley. It then flows south through Putnam, Danielson and Jewett City until it turns west to join the Shetucket River near Taftville and the Thames River at Norwich. There are a number of dams, some of which are no problem and others, particularly in urban areas, that must be approached with considerable caution. The water is dark and in places somewhat polluted, but there is much pleasant canoeing available on this stream.

Hamilton Reservoir — East Brimfield   5 miles

If water is high enough, the 1½ mile stream below Hamilton Reservoir is a pretty run, but one must be prepared to lift across a few shallow, rocky places and ledges. If water is low (one judges by the flow over the dam) a portage can be made by foot or by auto 1.1 miles via Dug Hill Road to Holland Pond Recreation Area (USCE), which is a good put-in place at any water stage. From the outlet of Holland Pond the river flows as a broad, placid stream. In ½ mile there is a road bridge and a camping spot on the left. Mill Brook enters from the left here, and can be used as an alternate starting point from Brimfield. The Quinebaug continues as a broad stream through open marshes bordered by pretty hills, and soon widens into the permanent pool behind East Brimfield flood control dam, the distance to the dam being three miles from the junction of Mill Brook. A bay of the lake extends north of Route 20 1¾ miles into what was formerly Long Pond, and there is a good take-out place at its north tip.

East Brimfield Dam — Sturbridge   2¾ miles

Below the East Brimfield flood control dam there is ¾ mile of riffles, easily run if release from the dam is around 120 CFS (2.7 feet on tailrace marker). A broken dam just around the bend below Holland Road bridge should be looked over before running. The dams in Fiskdale can be portaged via the island between them, into the right branch. The river is then fast-flowing for 1 mile to Leadmine Road bridge and the pond at Old Sturbridge Village.

Sturbridge — Westville Dam   5¾ miles

At Old Sturbridge Village, there is a dam that is portaged easily on the left. For the next 4 miles the Quinebaug is a pretty stream with few rapids and mostly placid running through woods and marshy meadows. There is then a low dam to portage, left, or take out onto autos, right. The river descends 20 feet in the next ¾ mile to the head of the permanent lake, 1 mile long, at Westville Flood Control Dam. This 20-foot descent has heavy spots and thin spots, with much depending on the amount of water being released from East Brimfield dam. It is well to scout ahead before running this section.

Westville Dam — West Dudley 5½ miles

This section is not pleasant. It is best to take out at the head of the lake at Westville dam, where there is a boat ramp and parking area on the left, or at the low dam ¾ mile upriver, and portage by auto around the entire city of Southbridge. For those who are willing to labor up and over Westville dam, there is ½ mile of rapids, easy if water release is adequate, to a small mill pond below Mill Street bridge in Southbridge, where there is another dam to portage, then another ½ mile of easy rapids to the mill pond at American Optical Co. Canoes must be taken out at the Mechanic Street Bridge at the head of this pond and portaged 1 mile via Mechanic Street and Route 131. This bypasses one dam on the A/O grounds and another 0.4 - mile below, canoes returning to the river below the second dam. It is then 2½ miles, mostly slack water and foul, to the dam at West Dudley.

West Dudley — West Thompson 10 miles

Below Southbridge the river runs through a broad valley with bushes on the banks and cultivated fields or meadows on the flood plain. The bridge at Dudley Hill Road is a possible place to put in if one has portaged around Southbridge by auto, or one can drive on 2 miles and put in below the dam at West Dudley, avoiding some of the foul water below Southbridge. From West Dudley the river runs with fair current to the broken dam at Fabyan, which can be run through the open sluice. It is then 6 miles to the flood control dam at West Thompson. The French River enters just below this dam.

West Thompson — Jewett City 33 miles

One can put in below the dam at West Thompson and run down 2 miles to Putnam, but as there are three dams in quick succession there, many will prefer to put in below Putnam. One must be cautious approaching the upper dam at Putnam, and make a landing on the left, well upstream from the dam. A single carry of ¾ mile via city streets puts one back into the river below the third dam. The river meanders somewhat for the next 12 miles to Danielson, flowing through broad flood plains for much of the distance. The only interruptions come about midway where there are two road bridges ½ mile apart, the second being Route 101, and ½ mile farther there is a dam which can be portaged easily on either side. Care must be taken at Danielson. The first dam can be portaged on the left, starting on the downriver side of the new Route 6 bridge, but be cautious about currents. The Fivemile River enters here from the left through culverts under the new rotary. The next ¼ mile involves broken dams and heavy rapids that should not be attempted without first walking ahead their entire length to look them over carefully. One can portage around them on the left, and should do so if he is not thoroughly expert in such water. One and a half miles below Danielson are the broken remains of Dyer dam, which should be scouted from the right bank. Another 2½ miles brings one to Wauregan, where the jagged remains of a broken dam must be avoided. It is best portaged left, near the sluice gates, where one is safe from the fast current sweeping into the jaws of the break. The section from Wauregan to Jewett City offers pleasant canoeing. It is 6 miles without interruption through well-wooded country to the Route 14 bridge near Canterbury, with the Moosup River entering from the left early in this stretch, and it is 5 miles through broad flood plain with some meanders from Route 14 to the next road bridge and railroad crossing near the head of Aspinook Pond. Another three miles of lake paddling brings one to the dam at Jewett City, where the drop is vertical for 20 feet. Portage here is on the right, starting well upstream from the strong current at the masonry wing wall at the approach to the crest of the dam.

Jewett City — Norwich   11 miles

The river now flows through a narrow valley between steep, wooded hills. It is a picturesque stretch but not an area for novices, as there are problems with rocks and currents, and considerable difficulty in taking out along the way. About 3 miles below Jewett City the river makes a sharp right bend to flow west for 1 mile, then south 1 mile, and then west again for 1 mile entering a narrow gorge at the far end of which is the tall and dangerous power dam at Connecticut Light and Power Company's Tunnel Plant. This gorge and dam can be a trap if the water is high enough to flow over the crest of the dam, this being dependent partly on general water levels and partly on operations at the power plant, and subject to unexpected change. There are no stillwaters in which to take refuge. The current will sweep full force through the gorge and over the dam. One should not venture into this gorge

without having first walked in to the dam, accessible by a
dirt road and footbridge from Route 12, to see for himself
what the situation is on the day of his trip, and having
inquired about what will be the case at the hour of his
expected arrival. If water is being taken through the plant
to the extent that there is little or no flow over the crest of
the dam at arrival time, a landing can be made against the
rock cliff at the right end of the crest, followed by a difficult and very hazardous portage 200 yards along the
middle of the railroad track to the far end of its masonry
retaining wall, which drops off vertically 20 feet into the
river bed, then scrambling down the steep rock fill to
water's edge, and loading and launching from the rocks in
deep water. The railroad track is in active use, and has
blind curves at both approaches to the portage area. The
best advice is to stay away from this area entirely. One-
quarter mile below the power dam the Shetucket River
enters from the right. One mile farther is the dam at
Norwich, which is best portaged on the left. Another
1½ miles through Norwich brings one to the junction of
the Yantic River on the right, which junction forms the
start of the Thames River.

SHETUCKET RIVER   CT

This river begins at the confluence of the Natchaug and
Willimantic rivers and flows into the Quinebaug near
Norwich. It makes a pleasant, easy run with no rapids. The
wooded banks over much of the way make this an attractive trip, although there is no outstanding scenery.

Willimantic — Baltic   **10½ miles**

976

Flatwater, Quickwater   17 km
Passable at most water levels
Forested, Settled
   USGS: Willimantic, Scotland, Baltic
   Portage: 6½ mi R **dam**

Begin at the CT-14 bridge over the Natchaug
River. The CT-203 bridge (3¼ mi) in South Windham is
halfway to the first dam (6½ mi), and it is the last one
before the dam in Baltic (10½ mi).
   The following information is not current. In addition to the dam at
Baltic, which should be portaged on the R, there are two more dams: one at Occum
(12¾ mi) and the other at Taftville (14½ mi). Five and a quarter miles below Baltic,
the Shetucket meets the Quinebaug River (15¾ mi).

SUSQUETONSCUT BROOK CT

This small stream flows through Franklin and into the Yantic River near Norwich. Less than 2 miles from CT-32, Champion Road leads off CT-87 and soon crosses the brook and a RR. Access to the stream below a series of low waterfalls is down a steep bank. For much of the next 1½ miles the river flows through a very secluded valley. There are a few trees down (1977). Do not continue past the bridge on Murphy Road located just before you reach a large mill. Below this point the brook is frequently blocked by debris and trash. Furthermore, it stinks.

This run is almost all quickwater and class I, for which high water is required. Barring an usually large run-off, it is not recommended after mid-March. USGS: Fitchville.

WILLIMANTIC RIVER CT

The Willimantic River begins at Stafford Springs and flows south to the Natchaug River which it joins in the city of Willimantic to form the Shetucket River.

This stream has a good current with alternate riffles and quickwater. It provides a good introduction for canoeists, such as family groups, wishing to try river paddling for the first time. There are no tricky drops, and a road is always nearby.

The scenery is attractive for most of the way, but there are occasional sand and gravel operations and at least one modern sewage treatment plant which is not obtrusive. The stream is stocked with trout by the state, so the water is relatively clean.

 Stafford Springs — Eagleville 14¾ miles

1977   Lake, **Flatwater, Quickwater**   23¾ km
High or medium water: *spring and fall*
Forested, Towns, Settled
     USGS: Stafford Springs, South Coventry

Put in just below the center of Stafford Springs where CT-32 comes close to the river. After a short distance there is a broken dam with large, concrete abutments on each side. It can be run on the L. The current remains steady until the backwater of the Eagleville dam.

At the beginning the river runs for several miles in a narrow valley that widens somewhat as you approach

the I-86/CT-15 bridge (4¾ mi). In West Willington
US-44 (6 mi) crosses the river, as do several
other roads before Mansfield Depot (12½ mi) where
US-44A crosses. After another 1½ miles you reach
Eagleville Lake. Take out next to the dam (14¾ mi) where
there is a large parking area.

The following description is not current. Below the Eagleville dam the
river winds with less of a current for 6 miles past the mouth of the Hop River
(20½ mi), which enters on the R just below I-84, to a good take-out on the R at a
roadside picnic area off US-6 (20¾ mi). Farther downstream in Willimantic there are
dams and difficult rapids. See also the USGS Columbia and Willimantic sheets.

YANTIC RIVER   CT

The Yantic flows eastward and joins the Thames River in
Norwich. In the early spring it has some excellent whitewater, but to run all of it you must portage around two
dams. The portages are not difficult. It takes two to three
hours to run the section described here.

The Yantic River is smaller than the Salmon River
(nearby in the Lower Connecticut Watershed), although the
rapids are somewhat harder. The scenery is not as nice, but
some sections are attractive.

Camp Moween Road — Fitchville   **5¼ miles**

1977   Lake, Flatwater, Quickwater, **Class I–II**   8½ km
       High water: *early March*
       Medium water: *sufficient for most rapids, late March*
       Forested, Rural, Town
          USGS: Fitchville
       Portages: 2 mi   L   dam — 150 yds
                    2½ mi e   **dam at Gilman** — 70–300 yds

From exit 22 off CT-2, follow the road upstream
along the N side of the Yantic River for 1.3 miles to Camp
Moween Road on the L.

At the beginning the current is fast, and there are
a few trees down over the river. After a mile, however,
rapids begin, and there is a sharp class II drop as the river
passes alongside CT-2. Soon you reach the short deadwater behind the first dam (2 mi). Take out on the L bank
just before a large boulder and carry across the road and
put in below the second bridge. Class II rapids continue for
¼ mile to the next bridge where the deadwater behind the
dam at Gilman begins. Portage the latter on the L.

Just below this second dam (2½ mi) it will probably be necessary to line down a ledge beside a factory. If the river is too high, there may be no place to stand beside the river, making it necessary to portage on the R from the dam to the bridge below it, about 300 yards.

Below Gilman (2¾ mi) there are easier class II rapids that continue for ½ mile to a powerline crossing. The remaining 1¾ miles to Fitchville Pond are mostly quickwater with a few class I rapids which begin beside a cemetery and continue a short way past a road bridge below. Take out at the road leading to exit 23 off CT-2 (5¼ mi).

The river below here is not as attractive. You must portage the dam on Fitchville Pond by going through a backyard on the L, and once back on the river there are several old dumps and many wrecked cars lining fields farther on. There are no rapids to speak of, but there is quickwater for 2 miles to the abandoned highway bridge just below the CT-32 bridge in Yantic. Beyond, the river soon flows into Norwich, where there is even less to recommend it.

CHAPTER 9

SOUTHEASTERN
WATERSHEDS

Agawam River   211

Blackstone River   212

Chipuxet River   214

Cohasset Tidal Rips   214

Copicut and Shingle Island
    Rivers   215

Hockomock and
    Town Rivers   215

Mattapoisett River   217

Nemasket River   219

North River   220

Pawcatuck River   222

Satucket and
    Matfield Rivers   225

Taunton River   226

Wading and Three
    Mile Rivers   22-7

Weweantic River   228

Wood River   228

SOUTHEASTERN WATERSHED

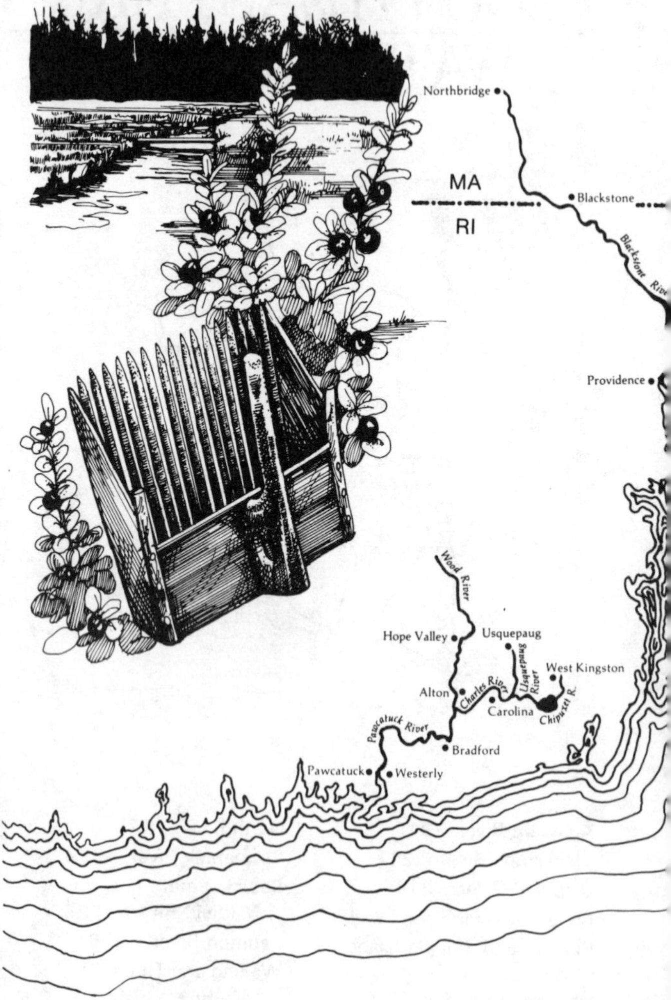

Northbridge •

MA

RI

• Blackstone

Blackstone River

Providence •

Wood River

Hope Valley •   Usquepaug

West Kingston

Alton   *Charles River*   *Usquepaug River*   Carolina   *Chipuxet R.*

Pawcatuck River

• Bradford

Pawcatuck •   • Westerly

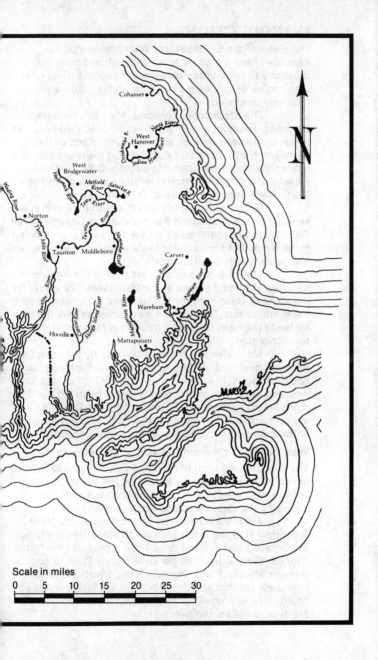

Cohasset

West Hanover

Drinkwater R.
North River
Indian Head River

West Bridgewater

Hockomock River
Matfield River
Saluckel R.
Town River
Taunton River

Norton

Three Mile River

Wading River

Taunton

Middleboro

Nemasket River

Carver

Weweantic River

Agawam River

Taunton River

Wareham

Copicut River
Shingle Island River

Mattapoisett River

Hixville

Mattapoisett

Marsh

holost

Scale in miles

0   5   10   15   20   25   30

INTRODUCTION

The rivers of the Southeastern Watersheds that are described here are all far more undeveloped than their proximity to large urban areas might suggest. They offer many miles of canoeing amid surroundings that are relatively unspoiled.

The Blackstone, Chipuxet, Matfield, Nemasket, Satucket, Taunton, and Town rivers as described here can be canoed whenever they are not frozen. Parts of the Agawam, North, Pawcatuck, and Wood rivers are also runnable throughout the canoeing season. Only the Drinkwater and Indian Head rivers, written-up as part of the North River, require high water for easy passage.

Good rapids, though short, are to be found at all seasons on the Blackstone River and at the Cohasset Tidal Rips. There are some rapids on the Drinkwater and Indian Head rivers, but they are not likely to satisfy a whitewater enthusiast's desire to run rapids.

The cleanest and clearest river is the Agawam, followed at some distance by the Nemasket. The award for the darkest, clean river (or the cleanest, dark river) goes to the Mattapoisett. The Taunton wins, uncontested, the prize for being the most polluted, although at high water it is not too noticeable.

Many rivers in the area covered by this chapter have not been included because no current information could be found. In addition, tidal rivers which do not have runnable, fresh-water sections have also been left out. Thus there are no descriptions for rivers on Cape Cod. Gathering up-to-date information for this book was not easy, and unfortunately the line had to be drawn somewhere.

Wampanoag Commemorative Canoe Passage

The Wampanoag Commemorative Canoe Passage follows inland waterways that were used by the Wampanoag Indians who lived in southeastern Massachusetts. It connects Massachusetts and Narragansett bays.

From Massachusetts Bay, it follows the North River past Hanover and heads south along Herring Brook to Furnace Pond in Pembroke. Then it crosses over to the Taunton River watershed via Little Sandy Pond. It goes through Stetson Pond, the twin Monponsett Ponds, and ultimately reaches Robbins Pond in East Bridgewater via Stump Brook. From Robbins Pond it follows the Satucket, Matfield, and Taunton rivers.

In this chapter there are descriptions of those portions of the Canoe Passage that follow the North River at the Massachusetts Bay end and the Satucket, Matfield, and Taunton rivers from Robbins Pond to the city of Taunton: a total of almost 41 miles. The connecting link of about 12 miles is described in *Wampanoag Commemorative Canoe Passage,* a booklet available free from the Plymouth County Development Council, Box 1620, Pembroke, MA 02359.

AGAWAM RIVER   MA

This river flows south through cranberry country to Buzzards Bay. It is a small stream with unusually clear water and a fairly dependable flow as it leaves Halfway Pond in Plymouth. However, this flow is subject to interruption in the fall because the river is dammed in several places to provide water for flooding the cranberry bogs when there is a danger of frost.

The first 3½ miles down to Glen Charlie Pond are the most attractive. The scenery is varied: cranberry bogs, ponds, pitch pine forests, and a winding stream. Large sections of the two lakes at the end are developed, especially on the east shores.

The river is a delight in November after the cranberry-picking season, when the bogs are a dark maroon color. There are a few places where bogs are right next to the river, and overlooked cranberries can be gathered from the canoe.

Halfway Pond — Wareham   8 miles

1977   Lakes, Flatwater, Quickwater; Tidal   13 km
        High or medium water: *spring and fall*
        Forested, Rural, Settled
          USGS: *Sagamore,* Wareham
        Portages: ¼ mi R **low bridge** — 10 yds
                     ½ mi L **diversion dam** — 20 yds
                    1¼ mi L **reservoir dam** — 20 yds
                    3¼ mi L **dam on Stump Lake** — 10 yds
                     5 mi L **dam on Glen Charlie Pond** — 10 yds
                    5¼ mi R **dam** — 10 yds
                     7 mi R **dam on Mill Pond** — 20 yds

Begin at Halfway Pond which is E of Miles Standish State Forest in Plymouth. The river leaves the S end of the pond and in 200 yards a dirt road along the shore is passed. Soon there is a small cranberry bog on the R, and then the first carry. In a short distance the stream passes through a cranberry bog for ½ mile. Part way along there is a carry around a diversion dam. At the end of the bog (¾ mi), the canoe must be dragged over boards in a large culvert. Soon the stream opens into a reservoir.

Below the reservoir dam (1¼ mi) there is another large cranberry bog which extends along the river for ¾ mile. Then there is a very nice ½-mile quickwater run through an open pitch pine forest. Just before you enter Stump Lake (2½ mi) there is an old bridge which canoes can be dragged over.

Stump Lake has many surprises just below the surface for those who paddle too fast across it. In spite of the crystal clear water, the submerged stumps are not easy to spot. Below the dam (3¼ mi) a short stretch of quickwater leads to Glen Charlie Pond. After you pass a number of houses on the L, leave a wide bay on the L, continuing more or less straight to the dam (5 mi).

Shortly after Glen Charlie Pond there is another dam (5¼ mi), some quickwater; then you are in Mill Pond. Follow the L shore as the lake winds for over 1½ miles to the dam.

At the end of Mill Pond (7 mi), carry across the westbound lane of US-6/MA-28 and run quickwater past the bridge carrying the eastbound lane, below which you reach tidewater. The river swings to the R through salt marshes and passes under US-6 (8 mi), just past which there is good access on the R.

BLACKSTONE RIVER MA

This river connects the second and third most populous cities in New England, Worcester and Providence. The Blackstone River Basin, with many small milltowns on the main river and its tributaries, is one of the most heavily industrialized in New England. Thus a certain amount of pollution is to be expected, but this is an era of river clean-up, and the Blackstone is not being left out.

Nonetheless, the Blackstone does have many scenic stretches that are away from roads and mills. A large area around Rice City Pond has been set aside as a state recreation area. There are also some challenging rapids. Parts of the canal that was built to handle commerce between Worcester and Providence are still intact.

1977   Lake, **Flatwater**, Quickwater, Class II–III   20½ km
        Dam-controlled: *good flow all year*
        Forested, Towns
             USGS: *Grafton, Uxbridge,* Blackstone
        Portages: 3 mi   **dam on Rice City Pond** — 200 yds
                     12 mi L **dam above Blackstone Gorge** — 100 yds

Access at Church Street: Between Northbridge
and North Uxbridge, Church Street crosses MA-122 and
goes E to and over the river in 0.6 miles.
Access at Blackstone Gorge: The gorge can be
reached from Stables Street off MA-122 between Blackstone and Millville. Below the gorge the take-out is at the
baseball field behind the Tupperware mill. It can be
reached off Stables Street.

Put in at the bridge on Church Street. The dump
for the town of Northbridge is on the L, but it is generally
unseen from the river. There are 2¼ miles of flatwater with
a good current and many turns to Rice City Pond. At the
S end (3 mi) the river divides and both parts spill over
dams. The R channel, a section of the old Blackstone
Canal, takes you close to the MA-16 bridge, with one carry
of 100 yards to get back onto the river. The river below the
R-hand dam winds for 1¾ miles with a fast current around
sharp corners and past log jams to MA-16, just above
which there is a mill on the R.

One-quarter mile below MA-16 (4¾ mi) the
Mumford River enters on the R. The Blackstone meanders
for most of the next 2¼ miles past the mouth of the West
River (6¼ mi) to the MA-122 bridge (7¼ mi). The river
straightens out somewhat for the next 3¼ miles to the
bridge at Millville. Here the river divides. There are rapids
on each side, with the L side being the sportiest (class II).

A little over 1½ miles below the Millville bridge
(10½ mi), there is a large dam that is most easily portaged
on the L. Below the dam the river runs through Blackstone
Gorge. This is an isolated, granite gorge with 600 yards of
class III rapids that are difficult and dangerous in high
water. They begin just below the dam and run through an
"S" turn that begins to the L. They end with a turbulent
chute that is best run in the middle. Scout these rapids
from the L bank.

At the end of the Blackstone Gorge, the Branch
River (12½ mi) enters on the R. Then, ¼ mile further on
there is a 5-foot dam under a bridge (12¾ mi).

CHIPUXET RIVER

The Chipuxet River flows south through the Great Swamp to Worden Pond. From there it flows west a short distance through the swamp to join the Usquepaug River to form the Charles River. Though the river is passable, the banks are overgrown with bushes.

Worden Pond is a large body of water which must be crossed heading towards the west. A strong, afternoon southwest wind, common in this area, can make the paddle a strenuous one.

West Kingston — Off Route 2   **7¾ miles**

1977   Lake, **Flatwater**   12½ km
          Passable at all water levels
          Forested
              USGS: Kingston

Put in at the RI-138 bridge just W of the junction with RI-110 in West Kingston. The current is slow as the river winds through bushes for 3 miles to Worden Pond. As you head W along the N shore, the first prominent point is Stony Point (4 mi). Past the next point the river leaves the pond (4¾ mi).

From the outlet the Chipuxet River winds for 2¼ miles to the confluence with the Usquepaug River where the Charles River begins (7 mi), ¾ mile above the Biscuit City Road Fishermen's Access.

There is a Fishermen's Access on the S shore of Worden Pond. From there it is 1½ miles to the outlet.

COHASSET TIDAL RIPS   MA

Situated between Cohasset Harbor and The Gulf, this is a place frequently used for whitewater instruction and practice by canoeists and kayakers. It is located on the south side of Cohasset Harbor just below the Border Street bridge and near Hugo's Lighthouse (restaurant).

Beginning at high tide, the water flows out for nine hours. As the level of Cohasset Harbor drops, a short, narrow, and turbulent rapid is exposed. At its most difficult stage, near low tide, it is class VI and too rough for open canoes. Kayakers attempting it have got to know what they are doing, for there is a danger of both boat and body getting banged up on the ledges.

The best conditions for practice in canoes begin when the rapids reverse midway on the incoming tide.

Within the three hours preceding high tide, the rapids build up to a wide class II pitch with heavy waves and strong eddies. The current begins to lessen about one hour before high tide, when the flow reverses again. Tide times are about the same as at Boston.

COPICUT and SHINGLE ISLAND RIVERS   MA

These two rivers in Dartmouth are part of the drainage of the East Branch of the Westport River. The mile on the Copicut River from Cornell Pond on Hixville Road to the confluence with the Shingle Island River is reported to have been cleared in recent years. The mile on the Shingle Island River below the confluence to Lake Noquochoke is also reported to be open. High water is recommended. See the USGS Fall River East sheet.

HOCKOMOCK and TOWN RIVERS   MA

The Hockomock River flows south from Brockton to the Town River. The latter flows generally eastward to Bridgewater where it joins the Matfield River to form the Taunton River.

The Hockomock is a small, meandering stream that flows for much of its length through meadows and along the edges of fields. It winds so much in the open that a strong wind from almost any direction can make paddling difficult. Bushes that grow along the banks are regularly clipped.

The Town River flows out of Nippenicket Pond in Bridgewater and within a mile it is joined by the Hockomock River. However, this upper section is very overgrown, and passage down it is difficult. The rest of the river is noticeably wider than the Hockomock.

When the water is high enough, a good 9½-mile trip on these rivers begins at Walnut Street in West Bridgewater and ends at the first dam in the same town. When the water is low, begin at the Scotland Street bridge (West Bridgewater) and continue for 5 miles to the High Street bridge in Bridgewater.

The last 4 miles from the High Street dam to MA-104 are not so nice. The river is polluted and occasionally clogged with debris.

1977   **Flatwater**, Quickwater   25¾ km
         High and medium water: *recommended, March thru May*
         Low water: *E of MA-24 only*
         Rural, Settled
            USGS: Brockton, Taunton, Whitman, Bridgewater
            Portages: 5½ mi e **culvert at Maple Street** — 10 yds
                        9½ mi L **dam at War Memorial Park** — 10–100 yds
                        12 mi R **dam at High Street** — 100 yds

---

Access at Walnut Street: Head W from the
MA-106 exit off MA-24. Take the first R (N) and turn L at
the second intersection, from which the river and bridge
are visible.

Access at Scotland Street: Go E on MA-106 from
MA-24. Take the first R (Lincoln Street), bear R onto Elm
Street, and then bear L onto Scotland Street.

Access at War Memorial Park: Follow River
Street SW from the junction of MA-18 and 106.

Access at High Street: From the N end of Central
Square in Bridgewater, where MA-18/28 and 106 cross,
follow Main Street to the NW for about a mile and turn R
onto High Street.

Below the Walnut Street bridge the river has a
strong current. In 1 mile it is necessary to drag your canoe
over the grass to the L of a low bridge. After 2¼ miles
there is some very fast current as you approach and pass
under the third highway crossing, MA-106.

One-half mile below the MA-106 bridge (3½ mi),
there is another grassy drag on the R at a culvert located
just downstream from a low mound of earth from which
you can look out over the extensive meadows. After
1½ miles of more meadows, you reach Maple Street where
the culverts must be portaged.

Below Maple Street (5½ mi) the river flows for a
while through a maple swamp, followed by more
meadows. Soon the Hockomock empties into the Town
River (6¼ mi), but you will not notice the location if the
area is flooded. Pass under the MA-24 bridge (no access)
to the Scotland Street bridge.

After the Scotland Street bridge (7 mi) the river is
somewhat wider, deeper, and more sluggish. There is an
old stone bridge and three road bridges before you reach
the first dam.

Take out on either side of the dam at War Memorial Park (9½ mi) and carry to the main river below the spillway. If the water is too shallow, put in past the bridge; do not run the canals. There is a rock dam after the bridge; then more flatwater.

The following description is believed to be accurate. There is flatwater for 2½ miles through marshes to the dam at High Street. Portage 100 yards from the R-hand channel across the island and put in below the L-hand dam. Low water may require a longer carry. After 200 yards of quickwater the two channels rejoin. The river is flat as it passes N of Bridgewater in a little valley. Debris in the river becomes more noticeable, especially near a shopping center adjacent to the MA-18 bridge. The river passes under Hayward Street (15 mi) before entering the deadwater at the confluence of the Matfield and Town rivers. Follow the R shore and continue S down the Taunton River for ½ mile to the bridge on MA-104 (16 mi).

MATTAPOISETT RIVER   MA

The Mattapoisett River is a small stream that flows from Snipatuit Pond in Rochester to Buzzards Bay. The water is very dark, and for most of the distance the river flows through impenetrable swamps of catbriar, rosebushes, and other shrubs. There are occasional houses, farms, and cranberry bogs only when it flows near roads.

The best part of the river is the 4¼ miles from Snipatuit Pond to MA-105. High water is recommended because in the first mile the river winds through a meadow with turns so sharp that a long canoe is in trouble if it is confined within the grassy banks. Fortunately, a dam used to divert water into some cranberry bogs helps to keep the water level up.

The section below MA-105 is a class V bushwack. For much of that distance, the river is overgrown with bushes that require determination to get through. If you should decide to canoe this part, either your character will be strengthened, or your will to persist broken.

Every year on Memorial Day, a locally sponsored race is held between Snipatuit Pond and Mattapoisett. Contestants, who enter in pairs, must travel down the river in a boat of their own making.

1977   Lake, **Flatwater**, Quickwater   19¾ km
              High water: *above MA-105, early spring*
              Passable at most water levels: *below MA-105*
              Forested, Rural
                 USGS: Snipatuit Pond, Marion
              Portages: 2¾ mi e **road culvert** — 10 yds
                          5¾ or 7¾ mi e **road culvert** — 10 yds

Neck Road in Rochester crosses the N end of Snipatuit Pond. From the bridge it is 1¾ miles to the SE corner of the pond (to the L of a farm) where the Mattapoisett River begins. When the water is high, you can run the small dam at the outlet. After about ¼ mile in woods the stream enters a meadow. The streambed is so narrow, and the turns so sharp, that it is difficult to maneuver a large canoe unless the area is flooded. The channel is occasionally marked by rags tied to branches. One mile from Snipatuit Pond the river flows under Snipatuit Road in a culvert. A short portage is necessary.

South of Snipatuit Road (2¾ mi) there is a small reservoir to supply water to the adjacent cranberry bogs. The outlet is on the L alongside the road, and the low dam is runnable in high water. In the next ½ mile there is a good current and a short class I rapid as the river flows past the cranberry bogs, but there are three or four obstructions to lift around. There is another class I rapid at the bridge on Hartley Road (3¼ mi). The stream is unobstructed as it flows across the bottom of an empty millpond to the remains of Rounseville Dam (4¼ mi) which must be lined because of debris in the river.

At MA-105 the Mattapoisett River looks open enough for easy passage, but it does not stay that way for long. The next 7 miles will probably take 4 hours or more. Most large obstructions, such as fallen trees, have been cleared away, but there is a lot of dense growth through which it is necessary to force your canoe. There are several short sections where the passage is clear, but most of your time will be spent battling the bushes.

One and a half miles below MA-105 (4¼ mi) you reach Perry Hill Road (5¾ mi), and 1½ miles after that you enter an old millpond. The broken dam is runnable in high water — a short class I drop. On the other side of Wolf Island Road (7¾ mi), there is a cranberry bog on the R, and you will have to drag your canoe around small diversion dams and low bridges. Then you head back into the

bushes, passing between two old bridge abutments
(9¾ mi), and finally breaking out into the clear at the
Acushnet Road bridge (11¼ mi).

The rest is easy. The river passes under I-195, and
there are some class I rapids before you reach a stone
bridge (12 mi). The fish weir just above the MA-6 bridge
(12¼ mi) can be run, and at low tide there is some quickwater on the other side.

NEMASKET RIVER   MA

The Nemasket flows north from a series of ponds in Lake-
ville through Middleboro to the Taunton River. It is one of
the prettiest rivers in eastern Massachusetts. The water as
it leaves Assawompset Pond is quite clear. It becomes
darker as it flows downstream, but it is noticeably lighter
than the water of the Taunton River at the point where
they meet. A sewage treatment plant in Middleboro does
not noticeably affect the quality of the water.

Assawompset Pond — Taunton River	11¼ miles

1977

Flatwater, Quickwater   18¼ km
Passable at all water levels
Forested, Rural, Town
    USGS: Assawompset Pond, Bridgewater
    Portages: 3½ mi R **dams at Municipal Light Plant** — 50 yds
                     5½ mi e **dam at Oliver Mill Park** (low water) — 30 yds

If you are coming across Assawompset Pond
from MA-18/105, the old dam can be run or lined, depending upon the water level. The river winds through marshes
and under Vaughan Street (½ mi) and Bridge Street
(1¾ mi). Both are popular points of access to the river.

At the Municipal Light Plant in Middleboro
(3½ mi), do not go under the bridge, but take out by the
fish ladder on the R, carry across the road, and put in below
the second dam.

There is ¾ mile of quickwater as the river passes
E of Middleboro. Portions of this may require lining in low
water. There is a rocky class I drop as the river passes
through a breech in an old canal wall. Then, with occasional steep banks bordering the river, the Nemasket flows
for 1¼ miles around the N side of Middleboro, reaching
Oliver Mill Park just before the US-44 bridge. Line or portage the dam and shallows depending upon the water
level.

Below US-44 (5¾ mi) the river winds past a sewage treatment plant and through forests and marshes for 4½ miles to the Taunton River. The two bridges, Plymouth Street (7¼ mi) and Murdock Street (8 mi), can be reached by following roads on either side of the river N from US-44. There are large meanders under a powerline as you approach a RR bridge (10 mi) and the confluence with the Taunton River (10¼ mi).

The first take-out from the Taunton River is 1 mile downstream at Titicut Street (11¼ mi), S of the Bridgewater State Prison and reachable from MA-18/28 via Plymouth Street.

NORTH RIVER   MA

This river has a fresh-water and a tidal section. Under the name of the Drinkwater River, it flows south in the western part of Hanover, and as the Indian Head River it runs eastward forming the boundary between Hanover and Hanson. The tidewater portion is called the North River.

Easy passage on the Drinkwater and Indian Head rivers requires high water, because there are several sections of class II rapids for which lower levels are insufficient. It is scratchy in medium water and not recommended in low water. The North River is passable at high or low tide, but the former is the preferred level.

The fresh-water rivers are contrasts of unspoiled woods and growing suburbs, of quiet millponds and commercial districts, of clean, dark water and carelessly discarded junk.

The North River, all of it tidal, is the most attractive part of this river system. It is being considered for protection under the state's Scenic Rivers Act, and it is rich in the history of early American shipping. The Wampanoag Commemorative Canoe Passage follows the North River and one of its tributaries from the south, Herring Brook.

West Hanover — Route 3A   **15¾ miles**

1977   Lakes, Flatwater, Class I–II; **Tidal**   25½ km
            High water: *recommended for fresh-water sections, early spring*
            Medium water: *scratchy in fresh-water sections, spring and late fall*
            Forested, Settled
               USGS: Whitman, Hanover, Cohasset, Scituate
               Portages: 1¼ mi L **2nd King Street bridge** — 30 yds
                          2¾ mi R **dam on Factory Pond** — 10 yds
                            4 mi L **dam in South Hanover** — 100 yds
                          5½ mi e **dam at Elm Street** — 30 yds

Put in on the Drinkwater River from MA-139 in West Hanover. At the start the river is smooth. After King Street (½ mi) there is ¼ mile of easy class II rapids that are scratchy in medium water. Then the stream turns sharp L and soon enters Forge Pond. At the second King Street crossing (1¼ mi) there is a bridge which may have to be portaged because of low clearance in high water. Carry as needed on the L.

The dam at the outlet of Forge Pond can be run, and it leads to a narrow, shallow class II rapid that would be nice were it not for large pieces of jetsam in the river. Halfway down at an old bridge there is a dam with a 1-foot drop that can be lined. A canal rejoins the river at the foot of the rapids, ¼ mile below the dam. Flatwater continues for ¼ mile to Factory Pond.

There is a bridge across Factory Pond just before the latter hooks around to the L. Portage the dam (2¾ mi) on the R beside the factory. Now as the Indian Head River, flatwater continues as the stream passes under a bridge and through a swampy area with some small, passable debris dams and many houses on the R bank. At the South Hanover dam, take out at the culvert on the L if the water is high.

Below the dam in South Hanover (4 mi), there are 100 yards of class II rapids, with flatwater for ¼ mile to a shorter class II drop that is runnable if not blocked. After another ½ mile of mostly flatwater, there is a class II drop at an old damsite beside a factory up on the L bank. The river soon enters the deadwater behind the dam at Elm Street, where there is good access.

Below Elm Street (5½ mi) the river soon enters the tidal marshes. The river generally winds towards a wooded hill, then turns L where Herring Brook enters on the R (6¼ mi). Pass under MA-53/139. An easier take-out is a few hundred yards further at the next bridge (7 mi).

For 10½ miles below Hanover the North River flows through nearly continuous tidal marshes to Massachusetts Bay. The first highway crossing is MA-3 (no access). The best access is next at Bridge Street, Norwell (13½ mi); then comes MA-3A (15¾ mi). The open ocean is 1¾ miles further at New Inlet where the North and South rivers meet. **Caution!** There are strong tidal currents in New Inlet, and they present a hazard to inexperienced canoeists.

PAWCATUCK RIVER

RI, CT

The Pawcatuck River drains much of southern Rhode Island. It rises under the name of the Queens River in West Greenwich and flows south to Usquepaug Village in South Kingstown. It is known as the Usquepaug River from here through the Great Swamp to the outlet from Worden Pond; then it is called the Charles River until it meets the Wood River south of Alton. From there it is the Pawcatuck as it flows south to the sea at Watch Hill, Rhode Island.

This is a very pleasant and interesting trip through three Rhode Island management areas, where there is good warm water fishing. There are campsites along the river in the Carolina and Burlingame management areas. It is 29½ miles from Usquepaug to Westerly.

Exeter — Usquepaug
QUEENS RIVER

The Queens River is not recommended because of legal problems that could land a trespasser in court. The passage is overgrown in many areas and barricaded in others with barbed wire, metal fences, and steel beams.

Usquepaug — Off Route 2   5½ miles
USQUEPAUG RIVER

This part is canoed less frequently than the sections farther downstream. It is heavily overgrown with bushes, and passage through it is difficult.

1976   Usquepaug — Off Route 2   5½ mi [9 km]
Flatwater, Quickwater
High or medium water: *March thru June*
Forested
     USGS: *Slocum*, Kingston

Park off the highway at the SW side of the RI-138 bridge. The first 2½ miles to the RI-2 bridge are mostly flatwater as the river flows through a big maple swamp. The Great Swamp begins below RI-2, and it is also flatwater. In about 1¼ miles you reach a RR bridge, and here the stream breaks up into numerous channels, making it difficult to pick the best one. In another mile the Chipuxet River (4¾ mi) from Worden Pond enters on the L.

At this confluence the name changes to the Charles River. After ¾ mile — about thirteen turns — take a R off the main river and pass under a low, steel RR bridge to reach the Fishermen's Access on Biscuit City Road in Richmond (5½ mi).

Off Route 2 — Wood River   8¾ miles
CHARLES RIVER

The old mill towns along the way are much the same as
they were in the 1700's. From the parking lot at the
Kenyon Mill, walk up the hill and visit the mill store. In
Shannock the house on the high dam was built in 1709.

A suggested two- or three-day trip of about
18 miles starts at the Worden Pond Fishermen's Access on
the southern shore and ends at the Bradford Fishermen's
Access of RI-91/216.

1976

Off Route 2 — Wood River	8¾ mi [14 km]

Flatwater, Class II

High water: *January thru early April*
Medium water: *late April thru mid-June and after heavy rains*

Forested, Towns

USGS:	Kingston, Carolina		
Portages:	¾ mi		**dam in Kenyon** — 100 yds
	1½ mi	L	**high dam in Shannock** — 100 yds
	1¾ mi	e	**low dam in Shannock** — 200 yds
	3½ mi	L	**dam in Carolina** — 70 yds
Campsite:	4 mi	L	**Carolina Management Area** — state

To reach the Fishermen's Access off RI-2, take
Biscuit City Road 0.4 miles N of the RR crossing in
Kenyon.

There is flatwater past the high, arched, concrete
RI-2 bridge (½ mi) to the dam at Kenyon (¾ mi). Portage
under the bridge through the mill. There is under a mile of
flatwater to the high dam at Shannock. Portage on the L
across the road 100 yards. A short distance beyond is the
low dam. Portage on the R or L. The former is easier but
longer — about 200 yards. Then there is flatwater to
Carolina (3½ mi), where there is a dam at RI-112 which
crosses the river on three bridges.

Below the L-hand bridge at Carolina, there is a
class II chute in high water that should be scouted. It is
followed by ¼ mile of easy class II rapids that are very
scratchy in low water. At Richmond (5¼ mi) there is a
Fishermen's Access off RI-91 next to a dam that is runnable in the center.

Below the Richmond dam (5¼ mi) there is a
good current for 1¼ miles to a wooden bridge (6½ mi). In
the last 2¼ miles to the confluence with the Wood River
(8¾ mi), there are about half-a-dozen large trees across
the river.

Wood River — Westerly   15¼ miles

With occasional, broad meanders the Pawcatuck River winds past open fields and swamps from the confluence of the Charles and Wood rivers to Westerly. There is an abandoned milltown at Burdickville near the beginning, but most of the river is remote with relatively few houses.

The section through Westerly is not recommended. Near the Stillman Avenue bridge the river is confined within walls at a broken dam that cannot be avoided. In high water it is dangerous.

1976	Wood River — Westerly	15¼ mi [24½ km]
	Flatwater, Class I–II	
	Passable at all water levels	
	Forested, Rural, Town	
	USGS: Carolina, Ashaway	
	Portages: 4¾ mi R **Bradford Dam** — 20 yds	
	11¼ mi R **Potter Hill Dam** — 100 yds	
	Campsites: 2¼ mi L **Burlingame Management Area** — state	
	2¾ mi L **Indian Acres Canoe Camp**	

Below the confluence where the Charles and Wood rivers join to form the Pawcatuck, it is a mile to the broken dam at Burdickville. Run it on the R or carry 30 yards on the L. Then the river is wide and flat. At the Burlingame Management Area, where the river runs due S, there is a campsite on the L bank. Then in about ½ mile, where the river runs due N, you reach Indian Acres Canoe Campsite. The river meanders for 2 miles to Bradford where there is a Fisherman's Access at the RI-91/216 bridge (4¾ mi). About 50 yards past the bridge, portage 20 yards on the R around a broken 4-foot milldam. Then there are 6½ miles of flatwater past the RI-3 bridge (10 - mi) to the dam at Potter Hill (11¼ mi). Take out on the R just before the bridge. Carry 100 yards down Laurel Street, past the fish ladder at the 8-foot dam.

Below the Potter Hill bridge (11¼ mi) there is a short stretch of rapids, then flatwater to Boom Bridge (13¼ mi). From there it is 1¼ miles to White Rock.

Caution! At White Rock there is an old debris-covered dam which shunts most of the river into a canal on the L. The current then becomes strong with some occasional rocks. The rapids are an easy class II, but there are few places to land once you are in the canal. Keep to the R. After 500 yards the river flows through a breach in the canal wall and returns to the old streambed. At the quick "S" turn there are some class II rapids which present no problem to capable canoeists as long as the channel is not blocked by debris. If you wish to scout this area, stop on the L above the old dam.

The best take-out is just before the new RI-78 bridge (15¼ mi). It can be reached from White Rock Road on the E bank.

The remainder of the river flows between Pawcatuck and Westerly. **Caution!** Just below the Stillman Avenue bridge, there is an old, breached dam that can be run on the L at certain water levels, when it is class II with large waves. Scout this in advance. Presumably there are no more dams between the Stillman Avenue dam and tidewater. *This last section was not run for this write-up,* and the river is not easily checked from the shore.

SATUCKET and MATFIELD RIVERS   MA

The Satucket River flows into the Matfield in East Bridge-water. Both rivers form a part of the Wampanoag Commemorative Canoe Passage from the coast near Scituate to Narragansett Bay. In Bridgewater the Matfield and Town rivers join to form the Taunton River.

The Satucket is a small river that winds past active farms and through woods. The water is fairly clean, but it is very dark. The Matfield is a dirty river, and its water has the smell of pollution even at high water levels.

The roads in this area are lined with houses. The route described here is through the backlands quite removed from them, and only a few of them are visible from the water. The woods and meadows along the rivers are very attractive and seemingly isolated. The only place where you can see many houses and buildings is near the portage at MA-106. Below that point there is some debris in the river and along its banks. It becomes more noticeable below the confluence of the two rivers.

Robbins Pond — Route 104   **8¼ miles**

977   Flatwater   13¼ km
Passable at most water levels
Forested, Rural, Town
USGS: Whitman, *Bridgewater*
Portage: 4½ mi e **dam at Plymouth Street** — 100 yds

Follow Pond Street NE from MA-106 to the outlet of Robbins Pond. The Satucket River winds around pastures on the L. Almost immediately, there is a barbed wire fence to slide under, and soon thereafter a low bridge which cannot be cleared in high water.

Poor Meadow Brook, which enters ½ mile from Robbins Pond, is reported passable from MA-27 in Hanson.

After the Washington Street bridge (1¾ mi) the river is noticeably wider. Past Bridge Street (3¼ mi) the river widens out even more as it reaches the backwater behind the dam at Plymouth Street, MA-106. If you can pass under the MA-106 bridge, then take out on the L just above the dam and portage past all the buildings. If the water is too high, take out on the R, cross over or around the fence, and portage along MA-106 to the R of the factory and put in from the parking lot.

Below the dam (4½ mi) the river winds in a small wooded valley. After 1¼ miles the Satucket River flows into the Matfield in a wide marsh. The Matfield, which enters on the R, is noticeably cloudier and odorous. After passing under Pond Street (6¾ mi) and High Street (7½ mi), the Matfield River goes under some powerlines and joins the Town River in a wide deadwater. Past a small, visible dump and a peninsula on the L, the Taunton River flows for ½ mile S to the MA-104 bridge (8¼ mi). It is easy to miss this turn.

TAUNTON RIVER   MA

The Taunton River flows to the sea at Fall River. It is the lower segment of the largest drainage system in southeastern Massachusetts, and it forms a part of the Wampanoag Commemorative Canoe Passage.

Southwest of Brockton the Hockomock flows into the Town River, and southeast of Brockton the Satucket flows into the Matfield. In Bridgewater the Matfield and the Town rivers join to form the Taunton River. Below the city of Taunton the river is tidal, and many large cabin cruisers are berthed in Taunton.

There are many towns in the region through which the Taunton flows, but it manages to avoid almost all of them. It flows along the edge of some fields, but most of the way the river is lined with thick woods and tangled underbrush. It makes a nice trip if you want flatwater and are willing to overlook the fact that the water is severely polluted. At low water the smell is especially noticeable.

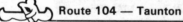

Route 104 — Taunton	21¼ miles

1977 | **Flatwater**, Class I | 34¼ km |

Passable at all water levels
Forested, Rural, Towns
USGS: Bridgewater, Taunton
Portage: 0 mi R **dam below MA-104** — 20 yds

East of Bridgewater MA-104 crosses the Taunton River near some old factories. Just below the bridge there is a dam which backs up water on both the Matfield and Town rivers. Portage 20 yards on the R. The Winnetuxet River enters on the L after 3¼ miles.

There are many bridges across the river. The second one is partially collapsed (3¾ mi). The fourth is a RR bridge beside a brick factory, and then on the L, just below a powerline, is the mouth of the Nemasket River (6¾ mi).

Under the fifth bridge, Titicut Road (7¾ mi), there are some class I riffles. Then comes MA 18/28 (8¼ mi). Above the next two bridges are riffles that are flooded out in high water. Then you pass under MA-25 (no access) and US-44 (12¾ mi).

The biggest rapids, but still only class I, are under the Church Street bridge, an old stone structure which constricts the flow of the river into several narrow passages. Many canoeists on the Taunton River lack whitewater skills, and this is where they run into trouble. The waves are biggest, and the current trickiest, in high water.

There is a bridge in East Taunton beside a factory (15¼ mi). You will probably notice many long, overgrown stonewall embankments lining the riverbank as you continue downstream. After considerable winding the river flows under MA-24 (no access). In the city of Taunton there are several more bridges beyond a closed girder bridge (19¾ mi) next to US-44. The first bridge below the two RR bridges is MA-140 (21¼ mi), and the Mill River enters on the R just beyond.

At high tide there are no rapids as you pass through Taunton. High tide occurs about 2½ hours earlier than Boston; low tide about 1 hour earlier. The tide varies between 2½ and 3½ feet.

WADING and THREE MILE RIVERS   MA

The Wading River flows from Lake Mirimichi off MA-106 in Foxboro southeast through Mansfield and into Norton where it meets the Rumford River. At that point it becomes the Three Mile River which flows through Taunton. These two small, isolated streams wind through woodlands, swamps, and small millponds. There are few houses or buildings near them.

These rivers are passable for 18 miles from Lake Mirimichi to MA-140 just outside Taunton. The first 4 miles to Otis Street in Mansfield are passable at most water levels. The mile between Otis Street and Elm Street/Richardson Avenue is difficult because it is overgrown, but the next 13 miles to MA-140 are clear and recommended in early spring and late fall. See the USGS Wrentham, Attleboro, and Norton sheets.

WEWEANTIC RIVER   MA

It is about 16 miles from Carver to US-6 at Wareham. This river has been recently run, but it is not an easy trip. Begin on South Meadow Brook where it is crossed by MA-58 in Carver. Many sections of South Meadow Brook and the Weweantic River are overgrown, and some others are blocked by trees. Occasionally the channel is not easy to find, so the current must be carefully followed. See the USGS Plympton, Snipatuit Pond, and Onset sheets.

WOOD RIVER   RI

The Wood River rises in western Rhode Island and flows south to Alton, where it joins the Pawcatuck. It is one of the most attractive streams in this area. This clean river flows alternately through thick brush and open valleys, and its banks are lined with blueberry bushes, laurel, oaks, and pines. It flows through the Arcadia Management Area, and it is a truly delightful run in summer or winter.

The portion of the river north of RI-165 is called the Fall River on the Rhode Island State Map. It is narrow, with low, hanging branches and sharp turns.

The most popular section begins at the RI-165 bridge and runs for 13¼ miles to Alton. The water is clean and clear, and there is always plenty of it. There are fields mixed with deep woods, with some cottages in the lower section.

 West Greenwich — Pawcatuck River   **16½ miles**

1976   Lakes, **Flatwater**, Quickwater, Class I   26½ km
        High water or medium water: *January thru May*
        Passable at all water levels: *below RI-165*
        Forested, Rural, Towns
            USGS: Hope Valley, Carolina
            Portages: 6 mi L **Barberville Dam** — 70 yds
                       8½ mi L **Wyoming Dam** — 200 yds
                       9½ mi R **Hope Valley Dam** — 100 yds
                       13¼ mi e **Woodville Dam** — 70 yds
                       15¾ mi R **Alton Dam** — 100 yds

From US-3, head W on RI-165 for 5.3 miles to Escoheag Hill Road. Go N for 0.9 mile to the first R; the entrance to the Arcadia Management Area at a log rail fence. Take the dirt road down a steep hill to the river.

In the first 2½ miles to RI-165, the river is narrow and shallow. Most of the way there is quickwater with sharp turns.

There is a good access at the RI-165 bridge (2½ mi). Below it there are 2 miles of fast current, followed by 1½ miles of deadwater to Barberville Dam. **Caution!** Do not run under the bridge. Take out on the L and portage 70 yards across the road and launch on the R below the bend in the river.

Below Barberville Dam (6 mi) there is ½ mile of class I rapids. Then there is about a mile of flatwater to Wyoming Pond at Skunk Hill Road (7¾ mi). It is ¾ mile across the millpond to the dam in Wyoming at the junction of RI-3 and 138. On the L, take out and portage 70 yards down RI-3 to the concrete bridge. Launch on the L.

Below the dam at Wyoming (8½ mi) there is quickwater, followed by flatwater. After a mile, take out on the R and portage 160 yards around an old mill and dam. Cross the bridge and put in on the L down a steep bank in the millyard. Then in about ½ mile the river passes under I-95. On the R there is a state launching ramp. The river then flows through woods and a swamp before reaching the deadwater above the dam at Woodville. Portage on either side. The L side is shorter but more difficult.

After Woodville Dam (13¼ mi) there is a good current for ½ mile. At a fork in the river (13½ mi), bear L. To the R, 100 yards, there is an old mill. The river is deep here, soon becoming shallow as it winds through a marsh above Alton Pond. The latter is ¾ mile long. Close to the edge of the dam on the R, there is a launching ramp and a parking area at the junction of RI-91 and the road from Alton to Woodville.

At Alton (15¾ mi) a portage of 100 yards on the R is followed by ¾ mile of flatwater to the confluence with the Pawcatuck River (16½ mi).

CHAPTER 10
CENTRAL
COASTAL
WATERSHEDS

Neponset River   234
Charles River   235
Mystic River   241
Ipswich River   242
Parker River   243
Mousam River   244
Crooked River   245

CENTRAL COASTAL WATERSHEDS

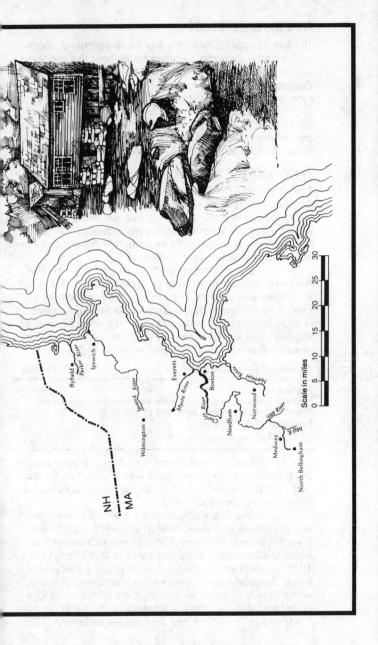

Scale in miles
0   5   10   15   20   25   30

INTRODUCTION

The five coastal rivers in the Bay State described in this chapter offer flatwater paddling throughout the canoeing season. The most scenic miles are to be found on the upper Charles and the lower Ipswich rivers. The Parker River is nice too, but it is very short.

The Crooked River in Maine offers a mixture of challenging rapids and pleasant flatwater in settings that are not unlike northern Maine; but to be enjoyable throughout its length, high or medium water is needed.

NEPONSET RIVER   MA

This river flows from the Neponset Reservoir in Foxboro to Dorchester Bay in Boston Harbor. Years ago it powered many mills as it descended to the ocean. Most of them were in Walpole where ten sites were developed. Its summer flow is minimal, so its primary industrial use now is for process water. Enter pollution.

The water is dark and polluted by the time the Neponset has left East Walpole. Below Norwood it is flat and canoeable all year. The scenery is a combination of mostly marsh and sloppy suburban. Generally, however, it is more attractive than its proximity to a large city would suggest. You will find litter (floating and sinking varieties), noise, and some smell; but then what do you expect?

Norwood — Hyde Park   **9½ miles**

1973   **Flatwater**, Class I   13½ km
High and medium water: *January thru May and after moderate rain*
Passable at all water levels: *below exit 11 off I-95*
Forested, Settled, Urban
    USGS: Norwood, *Blue Hills*

Put in at Morse Street, which leaves US-1 next to Boch Motors in Norwood. If the water is too low for the first part, put in at Pleasant Street, which crosses Morse Street before you reach the river.

Below Morse Street there are some easy class I rapids that are thin in low water. In ½ mile, pass under Pleasant Street. The current diminishes as the river passes under US-1 near the shopping areas at Dean Street (1 mi). Then the river enters the marshland where I-95 crosses it twice. Between the crossings Neponset Street (3½ mi), which is exit 11, provides access if the water is too low upstream. After passing the Norwood Airport and the main RR tracks to New York, the river passes under MA-128 (no access) and enters the Neponset River Reservation (7¼ mi) where Fowl Meadow is located.

The attractive section of the river ends at the Neponset Valley Parkway (9½ mi). There is a good take-out here at an MDC picnic area. A small parking area is located near the R bank S of the bridge.

The rest of the river is not recommended. Once you leave the Neponset River Reservation it is ugly. Most of it is fenced-in, so access is difficult.
Caution! There is no good landing spot as you approach the dam at Milton Lower Falls, and in high water, especially, it is difficult to get off the river.

CHARLES RIVER   MA

The Charles River is the major recreational waterway in Metropolitan Boston. The winding, 64-mile river passes many towns, offering some good canoeing, sailing, fishing, and picnic areas for a large population. The Indian name for the river was Quinobequin, meaning meandering river — an appropriate name.

Clean-up campaigns, storm drain diversion projects, and tighter pollution laws have all helped to make the Charles a cleaner river. However, because of its slow and meandering nature, the water will always be dark and oftentimes plain muddy — especially in low water. The nearly twenty dams and ninety-odd bridges have slowed up the flow of the river so that it cannot flush itself. In the summer the water tends to stagnate behind the dams; but they do help maintain the water level, so that canoeing is possible throughout the season.

In 1967 the Army Corps of Engineers began to study flood control in the Charles River Basin. Past favorites, such as reservoirs, dikes, and channels were dismissed in favor of a new program of land acquisition to prevent development. The watershed contains about 20,000 acres of flood plain, of which the Corps plans to acquire control of 8,500 acres.

Congress authorized the Natural Valley Storage Project in 1974. Land acquisitions are expected to be completed in 1979. This soft approach to preventing or limiting flood damage depends upon state and local cooperation to restrict development of the remaining 11,500 acres through implementation and enforcement of flood plain zoning.

The Metropolitan District Commission has a large interest in the recreational development of the river. They publish a folder showing their many recreational facilities on the Charles and other local waterways. This is free for the asking from the MDC Headquarters (20 Somerset Street, Boston, MA 02108).

The Charles River Watershed Association (2391) Commonwealth Avenue, Auburndale, MA 02166) is a non-profit organization dedicated to the welfare of the river. They publish the *Charles River Canoe Guide* ($1.50) and can furnish more information about the Charles River Natural Valley Storage Project.

North Bellingham — Route 109   14½ miles

The portion of the Charles starting at Medway is especially recommended. The put-in is a bit rough, but once accomplished you will find it worth the effort. You will be treated to occasional rapids in a setting that is very attractive, being mostly woods and meadows with only occasional patches of housing. There are no portages, and the only wide meadow is near the end, an important consideration if the wind is strong.

The source of the Charles is north of Echo Lake in Hopkinton. Above North Bellingham there are some sections that are too narrow and steep to canoe and others that are fenced-in and unattractive. At one of the crossings of I-495, passage is not possible in high water.

1976   North Bellingham — Route 109   14½ mi [23½ km]
Flatwater, Class I–II
High water: *recommended above MA-115, March thru mid-April*
Medium water: *rapids above MA-115 bony, late April to June and fall*
Low water: *some spots thin below MA-115*
Forested, Rural, Settled
    USGS: Franklin, Holliston, Medfield
Portages: 1¼ mi R **Caryville Dam**
           3¼ mi R **dam**
           5¼ mi R **Medway Dam** (difficult) — 30 yds

Access at Medway: Put in from the bridge on Franklin Street (Lincoln Street in Franklin) which crosses Village Street next to the Cumberland Farms store in Medway.

In North Bellingham, begin on the L bank from a parking lot behind a mill on Maple Street. There are some class I rapids at the start. In 1¼ miles you reach a small pond behind a dam. Carry on the R. In 2 miles there is another pond and dam, with the third dam 2 miles beyond that. Carry the last dam on the R, using one of two poor choices. You must either lower your boats down a steep ledge, or carry them up to Franklin Street and put in down on the other side of the bridge.

Immediately below the Franklin Street bridge (5¼ mi), the river enters a steep valley where there are some easy class II rapids. Part way down there is an old, washed-out, wooden dam which is runnable. The current slackens to flatwater by the time you reach the next bridge at Populatic Street (5½ mi) where there is easy access. After 1½ miles the river enters Populatic Lake (7 mi). Follow the L shore for 200 yards to the outlet.

Below Populatic Lake the river is noticeably wider and deeper. After 1¼ miles **Mill River** (8¼ mi) enters on the R through a culvert. This small tributary can be canoed in high water for 2 miles from just below City Mills Pond off Main Street in Norfolk.

Just beyond the Mill River there are class I rapids at a bridge. Rockville Rips (8¾ mi) at the Pleasant Street bridge in Millis begin at a broken dam with narrow channels that require quick maneuvering. The L is recommended for high water; the R for medium water. The quickwater below the bridge is followed by ¾ mile of flatwater to the MA-115 bridge.

Below the MA-115 bridge (9½ mi) there is a short section of quickwater. The remaining 5 miles to MA-109 are flat, except when broken in low water by an occasional ford, boulder, or block from an old abutment. For much of the distance, meadows line one or more of the banks. There is one bridge (11 mi) — Forest Street, Millis/Orchard Street, Medfield — and it provides good access with parking.

Stop River is a tributary of the Charles in Medfield. It enters ¾ mile above MA-109 on the R. In high or medium water it is canoeable for 2½ miles from South Street in Medfield.

Route 109 — Needham   16½ miles

Above South Natick Dam is one of the best parts of the river. Large meadows in Medfield and Mills give way to wooded banks and smaller meadows in Dover and Sherborn. Land on the north side at Rocky Narrows is owned by the Trustees of Reservations. Farther downstream in Natick, the river borders the Massachusetts Audubon Society's Broadmoor Sanctuary.

Since the river meanders every-which-way in the large meadow between MA-109 and MA-27, headwinds and crosswinds are inevitable in a strong blow. At low water, unseen rocks are a problem between Broadmoor Sanctuary and South Natick Dam.

1976

Route 109 — Needham   16½ mi [26½ km]
Flatwater
Passable at all water levels
Forested, Settled, Urban
  USGS: Medfield, Natick
 Portages: 10½ mi R **South Natick Dam**
     16½ mi **Cochrane Dam**

   There are many sharp meanders in the first
3½ miles past the mouth of Bogastow Brook (2½ mi) on
the L to MA-27 (3½ mi). In 2 miles you pass through
Rocky Narrows, then it is 1½ miles to the Bridge Street,
Dover/Farm Road, Sherborn bridge (7 mi) where there is
good access. Three and a half more miles bring you to
South Natick where you take out on the R.
   Put in on the R from the Coatings Engineering
parking lot (10½ mi). In the next few miles the river
wanders erratically, so a map is handy. After 5½ miles
there is a road bridge followed closely by a RR bridge. Take
out on the L at an MDC parking area just above the dam
(16½ mi) at South Street in Charles River Village,
Needham.

Needham — Norumbega Park   **18¼ miles**

XXXX **Flatwater,** Class II   29½ km
Passable at all water levels: *except at the beginning*
Forested, Urban
  USGS: Natick, Newton
 Portages: 13½ mi L **Silk Mill Dam**
     13¾ mi R **Metropolitan Circular Dam**
     15½ mi L **Cordingly Dam**
     15¾ mi L **dam at Newton Lower Falls**

   Put in below Cochrane Dam, which is at the W
end of South Street in Needham. In high water there are
400 yards of class II rapids below the dam, and they are
often used for practicing whitewater maneuvers. If the
water is too low, or these rapids are not to your liking,
put in where it is suitable. At the Chestnut Street bridge
(1½ mi) there are more, short rapids that are shallow in
low water.
   Below Chestnut Street in Needham, the Charles
River flows generally eastward and passes under MA-135
(3 mi) and MA-128. Soon it swings in a big loop to the S
through Dedham, passing several bridges including two on
MA-109 (7 and 8¾ mi).
   The Dedham Loop can be by-passed by following

Long Ditch, which leaves on the L below MA-128 and rejoins the Charles at the RR bridge below Dedham. It is ¾ mile long and it cuts off 5¼ miles of the river.

Below the lower end of Long Ditch (9¾ mi) the river flows through an attractive marsh area known as Cutler Park before it reaches the industrial area above the two dams in Newton Upper Falls. Portage the first one (13½ mi) across the grassy area on the L and put in before Echo Bridge. Portage the second (13¾ mi) on the R and carry down Quinobequin Road under MA-9.

The 1½ miles from Newton Upper Falls to Newton Lower Falls are close to MA-128. Cordingly Dam (15½ mi) is portaged on the L through the parking lot of the Walnut Street industrial area. At the put-in there are a few whitewater rips, and they are followed in a few hundred yards by the Washington Street dam which must be carried on the L over the street.

From Newton Lower Falls it is 2½ miles past MA-128 to the MA-30 bridge (18¼ mi) at Norumbega.

Norumbega Park — Charles River Dam   14¾ miles

Just below the intersection of MA-128 and the Massachusetts Turnpike the Charles River widens into an impoundment formed by Moody Street Dam. The deep inlets and bays formed by the dam are bordered by park and reservation land, and the scenery here is as beautiful as any to be found on the river. Unfortunately, traffic noise from the nearby expressways intrudes into these otherwise pleasant surroundings. Motorboats are also more common at this point on the river, and the speed limit of 10 mph seems to be honored more in the breach than in the observance.

The Metropolitan District Commission is well along in a multi-million dollar project mandated by recent federal legislation to clean up the basin. Several projects have already been completed which will reduce substantially the flow of polluted water into the basin by decreasing the frequency at which combined storm and sanitary sewers overflow into the river. Present water-quality projections for the basin provide that, at least through the late 1980's, the water quality will be suitable for boating but still not for swimming.

An historic point of interest in this section is the stone tower on a hill in the Charles River Reservation on the left bank about ½ mile below the put-in. The tower marks the spot where Norsemen supposedly settled in 1543.

Norumbega Park — Charles River Dam   14¾ mi [21 km]
Lakes, **Flatwater**
Passable at all water levels
Settled, Urban

USGS: Natick, Newton, Boston South

Portages: 2¾ mi   R   **Moody Street Dam** — 300 yds
             3¾ mi   R   **Bleachery Dam** — 100 yds
             5¾ mi   R   **Watertown Dam** — 50 yds

The put-in point may be reached by following the signs to MA-30 from MA-128 or the Mass Pike and then by following the signs to the duck feeding station across from the Marriott Hotel. The put-in is at the extreme L. An alternate put-in is available at Recreation Road off MA-128.

The river narrows dramatically after 2 miles at the Prospect Street bridge in Watertown. There is a cluster of cement piles just up-river of the bridge that mark the site of a turn-of-the-century ballroom which attracted a large water-borne clientele. Below the Prospect Street bridge the river assumes a more urban character with a number of commercial and residential buildings crowded along both banks. Moody Street Dam lies ¾ mile below the Prospect Street bridge. It can be portaged by taking out at the wooden dock just above the Moody Street bridge. Cross the street and then go through a small plaza halfway down the block on the L. The put-in is below the parking lot.

The river flows smoothly for 1 mile to Bleachery Dam (3¾ mi), which lies 100 yards below a wooden RR bridge. The dam is little more than a spillway with a drop of only about 2 feet. Depending on the experience of the canoeist and the debris below the dam it may be possible to avoid a portage by lining the dam from the bank on the R. If a portage is necessary, it involves a carry of about 100 yards along the R bank.

After another mile Rolling Stone Dam (4¾ mi) just above Bridge Street is reached. The dam has been breached and it should be run on the L. There is quick-water for about 10 yards below the dam. In another mile Watertown Dam (5¾ mi) is reached. The approach to the dam is indicated by a modern, steel-beam foot bridge which lies about 40 yards up-stream. The dam can be easily portaged through the park on the R.

Below the Galen Street bridge in Watertown (6 mi) the Charles begins to widen. As one paddles farther into the river basin there is increasing traffic from power-boats, scullers, crews, and below Boston University Bridge, sailboats. The Metropolitan District Commission does not prohibit canoes below Larz Anderson Bridge so canoeists can paddle the entire basin, through the locks (14¾ mi) and out into Boston Harbor.

MYSTIC RIVER   MA

The Mystic River flows from Wedge Pond in Winchester roughly southeast to tidewater at Amelia Earhart Dam in Everett. It is short, easily canoeable, and flat. Above Everett the river is urban, but generally pleasant. The tidal portion is heavily industrial, polluted, and filled with heavy shipping.

Mystic Lakes — Everett   6½ miles

1976   Flatwater   10½ km
        Passable at all water levels
        Settled, Urban
           USGS: Lexington, Boston North
           Portage: 4 mi R Cradock Dam

While the ½ mile from Wedge Pond to Upper Mystic Lake can be canoed in high water, most usually the Mystic Lakes will provide the better start.

From the entrance of the river into Upper Mystic Lake at its NE corner, it is 1¼ miles S to Lower Lake and then ½ mile to the river's exit at the SE corner of Lower Lake. In ¼ mile the stream passes under the MA-60 bridge (2 mi). In another ½ mile the Harvard Avenue bridge is passed. Alewife Brook enters on the R in another 500 yards. This stream is passable for some distance upstream, but it is little more than a refuse-laden, fenced-in ditch for much of its length. In the next mile the Mystic River is largely contained by parkways. It passes beneath seven bridges before it reaches Cradock Dam in Medford. Portage on the R.

Below Cradock Dam (4 mi) is the basin formed by the dam in Everett. Formerly tidal, this stretch is now largely in the process of development. At present much of it is surrounded by grasslands and highways. The 2½ miles from Cradock Dam to Amelia Earhart Dam is broader than the upper river. The Malden River enters on the L just above the dam (6½ mi).

IPSWICH RIVER
MA

The Ipswich River winds from Burlington to the ocean near the south end of Plum Island. It runs through many miles of wetlands in an area dotted with drumlins and other glacial formations.

Housing developments and urban areas are scattered all along the river, but they are separated by long sections of woods, swamps, and meadows. In particular, the 8¾-mile section from I-95 eastward through Bradley Palmer State Park is especially attractive because large segments of the river corridor are protected due to ownership by the Audubon Society and local, county, and state agencies, as well as through easements obtained by the Essex County Greenbelt Association.

From source to mouth there is a varying amount of debris and junk in and along the river. The section along MA-62 in North Reading is the most cluttered.

The material for this write-up was obtained from several sources, including topographic maps and letters that commented on the description in the old guidebook. Most of the information, however, came from the "River Systems Study — Ipswich River" which was prepared by the Metropolitan Area Planning Council. An expected description of this river was not received, and what follows represents the best information available in January, 1978.

 Wilmington — Ipswich **30¼ miles**

XXXX Flatwater 48¾ km
Passable at most water levels
Forested, Settled
   USGS: Wilmington, Reading, Salem, Georgetown, Ipswich
   Portages: 7½ mi L **dam in Peabody** — 20 yds
        24¼ mi   **Willowdale Dam**
        30¼ mi   **1st dam in Ipswich**

This information is believed to be accurate.
Put in from the bridge on Woburn Street, which parallels I-93 W of exit 27 (Concord Street). The river is very small as it passes through Hundred Acre Swamp before I-93 (½ mi). Then it winds for 7 miles, passing under Haverhill Street in North Reading (4½ mi) about halfway to the dam in Peabody. Then the river becomes more isolated as it flows in wide wetlands past the MA-114 bridge (10¼ mi).

There is good access at the MA-62 bridge
(12½ mi). The river flows under several bridges, among
them I-95 (15½ mi), US-1 (17¾ mi), and MA-97 (18¾ mi)
— before it reaches Wenham Swamp. As it does (just after
a RR bridge), the Salem-Beverly Waterway Canal leaves on
the R. In very high water the river may be difficult to follow
through Wenham Swamp.

The river valley narrows as the river flows N of
Bradley Palmer State Park to Willowdale Dam (24¼ mi).
Below there, one or two short drops and shallow sections
may require lining or portaging. There is access to the river
on the L above the first of two dams in Ipswich (30¼ mi).

The rest of the river is tidal.

PARKER RIVER   MA

The Parker River is a small, pleasant river beginning at
Pentucket Pond in Groveland and flowing to Plum Island
Sound at Newbury. The upper river above Thurlow Street,
Georgetown is too overgrown to canoe at any time, but
below it there is a 2½-mile section that is passable at most
water levels. The section through Byfield is not recommended because there are many dams separated by
shallow stretches that are only canoeable in high water.
Shortly below the town the river becomes tidal.

Georgetown — Byfield   2½ miles

◀1974   Lake, Flatwater   4 km
          Passable at most water levels
          Forested, Town
              USGS: Georgetown, Newburyport West

From Thurlow Street to Crane Pond, the small
stream meanders through pleasant meadows. In early
spring the pond will be frozen long after the river is open,
thus requiring a retreat or an over-ice portage. Crane Pond
is roughly circular and less than ¼ mile in diameter. The
river enters the pond in the SW corner and exits (¾ mi) on
the N side where the marsh grasses begin to be super-
ceded by alders.

The river continues to meander past the pond for
1¾ miles to the upper dam of the Byfield Snuff Company.
Half of this portion is meadow, but shortly after the
entrance of Beaver Brook (1½ mi) on the L, the river
passes between wooded knolls, and the land becomes
more elevated on the L. As Byfield is approached, the
powerline running along the old RR grade will become evi-

dent on the R. At the small, upper dam (2½ mi), exit can be made on the L to Forrest Street, Byfield along a short side road. Since this portion has very little current, it can be paddled in either direction with little difficulty.

MOUSAM RIVER ME

The Mousam River flows into the sea at Kennebuck. There is usually not enough water in the upper section for good canoeing except in the spring and just after Labor Day when Mousam Lake is drawn down to permit lakeshore work to be done.

 Mousam Lake — Estes Lake   **14 miles**

1975

Lakes, Quickwater, Class I–II   22½ km
High water: *early spring and early September*
Dam-controlled: *annual drawdown of Mousam Lake*
Forested, Rural, Settled
    USGS: Berwick 15, Kennebunk 15
    Portages: 3½ mi   L   **1st and 2nd dams in Springvale**
                     4 mi   R   **small dam in Springvale**
                    4½ mi   e   **1st dam in Sanford**
                     6 mi   L   **2nd dam in Sanford** (cross over 1st bridge)
                 14 mi   R   **Estes Lake Dam**

The river below the dam on Mousam Lake can be reached by turning off ME-11/109 at the Emery Mills Post Office. If there is a boiling flow at the base of the dam, there is sufficient water for this trip.

In the 3 miles to the first millpond in Springvale, there are three sharp drops to watch out for. The first is under a powerline, the second is a short distance below the ME-11/109 bridge (1¼ mi), and the third one is about a mile farther on.

At Holdsworth Park in Springvale, there is good access to the pond above the first dam. If continuing downstream, take out L of the dam (3½ mi), portage along Water Street, and put in below the second dam. There is a third dam (4 mi) just upstream of an abandoned, stone RR bridge.

The first dam in Sanford (4½ mi) is followed by quickwater to the millpond above the second dam (6 mi). Take out on the L, cross the river via Washington Street, follow Pioneer Avenue downstream, and put in by the Emery Street bridge. Then there is quickwater with some debris for 3 miles to the ME-4 bridge.

Below ME-4 (9 mi) it is ½ mile to the ruins of Jagger Mill Dam which can be run. Quickwater continues for most of the way to Mousam Lane (13 mi) which is near the head of Estes Lake. When the lake opens up, turn R to reach the dam (14 mi).

Estes Lake — Kennebunk   12 miles

USGS: Kennebunk 15

Below the powerhouse there is a short rapid, followed in ½ mile by a gauging station on the right, the Whichers Mills Road bridge, and a dam. This dam should be carried on the right and the put-in made below a sharp fall and rapid, at the head of Old Falls Pond. There are then 1½ miles of paddling down the pond to the high power dam at the end. This should be portaged on the left, down a steep hill 150 yards. Below the start, 200 yards, just around the bend, is a sharp rapid which should be scouted before running, if the river is in flood. Once through the rapid, the river becomes quiet with a fair current and good hemlock woods on the right bank. The valley soon widens out, and in 4½ miles the bridge at West Kennebunk is reached. The old dam just below the bridge has a short rapid just below it. In ½ mile more the railroad culvert is reached, and then in another 200 yards a dam at a mill, where there is a short, steep carry on the right bank to the rapids. These ¼-mile-long rapids are easily run to the slack-water, which continues for 1 mile to the Maine Turnpike bridge. The next 2 miles of meandering river to the Route 1 bridge in Kennebunk pass through farmlands on both sides. In Kennebunk, it is best to take out above the bridge and the rapids below which drop to tidewater.

CROOKED RIVER   ME

The Crooked River flows from Songo Pond near Bethel south to the Songo River and Sebago Lake. For the most part it is clean and attractive, and for 53 miles it has scenery that includes forests typical of northern Maine, alder swamps, and stands of red maples. There are many sections which have a remoteness which road and topographic maps do not suggest. From the river, North Waterford is not very pretty, but the settlements of Bolsters Mills and Scribners Mill farther downstream are slices from New England's past.

In the spring the river offers a pleasant combination of rapids and smoothwater. Below the ME-118 bridge in East Waterford, there are ten sets of rapids which are mostly class II with a few class III drops. In high water there are several sections with heavy waves. Because of the river's relatively small drainage area, the water level changes from hazardously high to undesirably low in a matter of weeks.

Albany — North Waterford   9 miles

The Crooked River here is small. In a few places fallen trees block the stream, and in the middle section alders crowd the channel. The current is fastest at the beginning where it flows through forests, portions of which have been selectively cut. Where the gradient lessens, the river meanders through alder thickets.

1975   Albany — North Waterford   9 mi [14½ km]
Flatwater, Class I–II
High water: *April*
Forested
    USGS: East Stoneham, North Waterford

A convenient starting point within sight of the highway is from a bridge on a logging road that leaves ME-5/35 just over 5 miles N of Lynchville. For ¾ mile there is a mixture of rapids and flatwater. Stop above an old bridge by an abandoned farm (1½ mi) to scout the rapids below. One-half mile below the second highway bridge, the stream enters an alder swamp through which it meanders for 2½ miles to the ME-5 bridge in Lynchville (7½ mi). For the next 1½ miles to the ME-35 bridge in North Waterford (9 mi), the river is flat and wider.

North Waterford — East Waterford   12 miles

The banks of the river in North Waterford are not very attractive, but beginning at the broken dam below town, there are a couple of miles of good rapids mixed with quickwater. The last 6 miles are very crooked, with leaning swamp maples crowding the stream.

1975   North Waterford — East Waterford   12 mi [19½ km]
Flatwater, Quickwater, Class II–III
High water: *April*
Medium water: *shallow rapids, May*
Forested, Towns
    USGS: North Waterford, Norway 15

Below the ME-35 bridge less than ½ mile, there is a broken dam which should be scouted. Then there are easy rapids as the river flows past a lumber yard. About 100 yards beyond the point where the stream approaches

the highway again, stop just above a cabin on the R (1 mi)
to scout the steep class III rapids beside the roadside rest
area. Near the top, large boulders produce heavy waves in
high water with no obvious channel. The lower section is
¾ mile long, and it contains two easier class II drops which
can be scouted from ME-118.

Below the last drop (2 mi) the river leaves the
highway and runs deep and slow. A jam of fallen trees by a
gravel pit on the L must be lifted over on the L. Two and a
half miles below the rapids, the outlet from Papoose Pond
enters on the R, and in another ¼ mile there is a bridge
(4¾ mi). After 1 mile the river passes below the cliffs of
Pulpit Rock (5¾ mi). The second bridge below the rock is
ME-118 in East Waterford (12 mi), and it is reached after
6¼ very crooked miles.

East Waterford — Scribners Mill   17 miles

This stretch makes a pleasant one-day trip with a mixture
of rapids and smoothwater. There are some cabins along
the river below East Waterford and Twin Bridges, and also
beside McDaniel's Rips near Sodom; but other than that
the river is secluded all the way to Bolsters Mills. The
section between Sodom (a name which originated in the
enmities aroused by a 19th century land feud) and Twin
Bridges is especially scenic.

The rapids between East Waterford and Sodom
provide nice whitewater runs for people with skill and
good judgment. Not all who try to run them possess these
qualities, and many canoes have been wracked up in
McDaniel's Rips.

1975 East Waterford — Scribners Mill   17 mi [27½ km]
Flatwater, Class II–III
High water: *April*
Medium water: *scratchy rapids, May*
Forested, Towns
    USGS: Norway
   Portages: 14 mi L **dam at Bolsters Mills — 30 yds**
               17 mi L **dam at Scribners Mill — 20 yds**
   Campsite: 4¾ mi L **bottom of 1st rapids**

Below the ME-118 bridge there are 4½ miles of
winding river that lead to a ¼-mile-long set of rapids that
begin innocently enough, but which soon lead to a very
sharp class III drop followed by easier rapids that have
heavy waves in high water. It should be scouted from the
L bank. Below it there are two pools separated by some

riffles, and then you reach McDaniel's Rips (5 mi). Stop on the R bank and scout them, because they begin with a drop over a ledge at the site of an early paper mill. Beyond, about 100 yards, they continue as class II or III rapids (depending on the water level) which are ½ mile long, and which taper to smoothwater at the Sodom bridge.

Below Sodom (5½ mi) there is slackwater for 3 miles to a powerline (8½ mi). Shortly after that there is a nice, 100-yard class II rapid with clear channels and large waves in high water, followed almost immediately by another, shorter pitch; also with heavy waves in high water. In about ½ mile there are more class II rapids at Twin Bridges.

For ¼ mile below ME-117 at Twin Bridges (9½ mi), the rapids continue; then there is smoothwater for 4¼ miles to the dam at Bolsters Mills (14 mi). Portage on the L. Past the dam there is ½ mile of class II rapids. The latter are followed by 2½ miles of slackwater that is broken by one short, easy pitch about halfway to Scribners Mill (17 mi). If you are continuing downstream, portage on the L.

Scribners Mill — Route 302   15 miles

This section is passable all summer, although there are a few short rapids that may have to be walked down. Between Scribners Mill and Edes Falls, the river meanders for many miles through a high banked flood plain where some sandy beaches are exposed in low water.

The portion of the river from US-302 to the Songo River is not recommended. The banks are lined with a veritable Hooverville of small cabins, and there are other encroachments of civilization, such as powerboats, that the sections upstream generally lack.

1976   Scribners Mill — Route 302   15 mi [24¼ km]
Flatwater, Class I–II
Passable at all water levels
Forested, Rural
    USGS: Norway 15, Sebago Lake 15
    Portage: 10 mi L **Edes Falls** — 10 yds

To reach Scribners Mill, head S from ME-35 from the junction with ME-117 in Harrison. In 2.7 miles, continue straight onto a side road when ME-35 bears R. Go straight past a crossroads in 1 mile, and turn R when the road ends in another mile. Take the first L and follow that road for 1.2 miles to the Crooked River.

Put in below the dam on the L. After ½ mile of rapids, the river is flat and winding for 9¼ miles. Near the end of the flatwater, there are a few camps on the L, then some class I rapids, and finally a portage on the L around the old dam at Edes Falls.

Below Edes Falls (10 mi) there is ¼ mile of class II rapids which end just below the bridge. The last 5 miles are mostly flatwater. There is good access on the L bank at the ME-11 bridge (12¾ mi), and fair access at the US-302 bridge (15 mi).

The last 4¼ miles to the Songo River (19¼ mi) are flat, crooked, and unattractive. From the mouth of the river, continue straight ahead through the locks to the Bay of Naples (20 mi), or turn L to Sebago Lake (21¾ mi).

CHAPTER 11

MERRIMACK
WATERSHED

Merrimack River   254
Assabet River   258
Baker River   262
Beaver Brook   263
Blackwater River   265
Cockermouth River   268
Cohas Brook   268
Contoocook River   269
Little River   274
Little Suncook River   275
Mad River   275
Nashua River   277
Newfound River   279
Nissitissit River   280
Pemigewasset River   280

Piscataquog River, North
  Branch   287
Piscataquog River, South
Branch   288
Powwow River   290
Salmon Brook   290
Shawsheen River   291
Smith River   292
Soucook River   295
Souhegan River   296
Stony Brook   298
Sudbury and Concord Rivers   299
Suncook River   304
Warner River   306
Winnipesaukee River   307

MERRIMACK WATERSHED

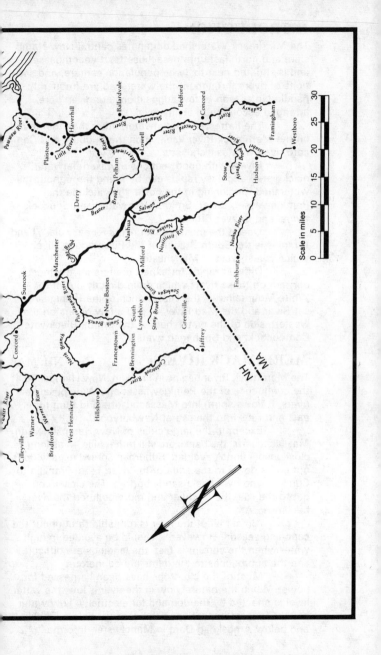

Scale in miles

0 5 10 15 20 25 30

NH
MA

INTRODUCTION

The Merrimack Watershed dominates central New Hampshire and northeastern Massachusetts. It encompasses, and is situated next to, large population centers; and sections of rivers throughout the watershed are frequently paddled in season. A few suggestions are given here, arranged according to ability level.

The flattest of the flatwater, other than that found on the Merrimack River itself, is on the Sudbury and Concord rivers in Massachusetts.

Rivers with good sections of mixed flatwater, quickwater, and easy rapids can be found throughout the watershed. Beginning in the north, they include the Pemigewasset, Baker, Smith, Blackwater, and Soucook rivers, and Beaver Brook.

One of the most popular rivers for easy class I and II rapids is the South Branch of the Piscataquog River, which is just west of Manchester.

Difficult rapids for expert boaters for the most part are on those rivers which drain directly out of the White Mountains — the East Branch of the Pemigewasset River and the Mad River — and a few others on the western side of the watershed — the Smith, Blackwater, Contoocook, and Souhegan rivers.

MERRIMACK RIVER   NH, MA

The Merrimack River begins in Franklin, New Hampshire at the confluence of the Pemigewasset and Winnipesaukee rivers. It flows south into Massachusetts and then turns east and runs into the sea at Newburyport.

Except in the large cities of New Hampshire and Massachusetts, the banks are still rather nice — as long as close inspection is avoided. Suburban sprawl usually does not come down to the edge of the river. From Franklin to Concord, the river has a sandy bottom. The closer you get to the sea, the muddier and more polluted the river becomes.

Almost all of the river is runnable throughout the canoeing season. However, it should be avoided in high water when the current is fast, the landings are difficult, and the approaches to the dams are dangerous.

Most of the big drops have been harnessed for power. When the natural flow in the river is low, the water level is affected by the demand for electricity. Low water has the biggest impact upon the canoeist below Franklin and below Amoskeag Dam in Manchester. Information on daily flows can be obtained by calling the dispatcher at the Public Service Company of New Hampshire (603-225-6182).

The Merrimack is close to many large centers of population, and launching ramps provide access to all sections of the river. Nonetheless, it gets limited use by canoes and motorboats.

In Penacook, at the mouth of the Contoocook River, sits Hannah Duston Island. There it was that Hannah Duston, who had been captured by the Indians in a raid on Haverhill, Massachusetts on March 15, 1697, a week after the delivery of her eighth child, escaped from her captors. On the morning of March 31, she, with the help of Mary Neff, who had been taken prisoner at the same time, and a youth who had been captured on a raid on Worcester, Massachusetts, killed and scalped ten of the twelve Indians guarding her. The other two Indians fled, and the three prisoners went downriver by canoe to reach Nashua that night. Hannah later received a bounty of twenty-five pounds per scalp from the Massachusetts General Court.

Franklin — Concord	24 miles

1976	Flatwater, Quickwater	38¾ km

Passable at most water levels
Dam-controlled: *peak power generation on Pemigewasset River*
Forested, Settled
    USGS: Penacook 15, Concord
    Portage: 18 mi L **Sewall Falls Dam**

Put in on the Pemigewasset River below Eastman Falls Dam if you want to begin with 1 mile of class II rapids, or on the Winnipesaukee River behind the high school in Franklin if you prefer ½ mile of flatwater.

From the confluence of the Pemigewasset and Winnipesaukee rivers (0 mi), there are class I rapids for the first ½ mile. Then there is a moderate current to Boscawen (10½ mi) where the first bridge (closed) is located. Another 4½ miles of meandering river bring you to Penacook, a bridge off exit 17 of I-93 (poor access), and the mouth of the Contoocook River on the R.

In the mouth of the Contoocook River (15 mi) there is an island — joined to the mainland by two RR bridges — on which is a monument to Hannah Duston. In 2 miles there is another bridge with a launching ramp downstream on the R. From that point it is 1 mile to Sewall Falls Dam which must be portaged on the L.

Below Sewall Falls Dam (18 mi) there is a class II rapid which is ¼ mile long and rocky in low water. In another 3½ miles there is a RR bridge and an I-93 bridge, just upstream from which there is a launching ramp that can be reached from exit 16. The remaining distance to the US-4/202/NH-9 bridge (24 mi) was shortened in 1976 when a new channel was cut across a meander.

Concord — Manchester 18¼ miles

1976	Flatwater, Quickwater	29½ km

Passable at all water levels
Dam-controlled: *good flow all year*
Forested, Settled

USGS: Concord 15, Suncook, Manchester North

Portages: 5 mi L **Garvin's Falls Dam** — 100 yds
10½ mi L **dam at Hooksett** — ¼ mi
18¼ mi R **Amoskeag Dam** —200 yds

There are boat launching ramps just below the US-4/202/NH-9 bridge (0 mi) and just above the US-3 bridge (1½ mi) on the L. After 2¼ miles of meanders, you pass under a RR bridge, below which there is some turbulence. Then Garvin's Falls Dam (5 mi) comes in sight. Portage on the L. There is a short class II rapid below it.

In the next 5½ miles to the dam at Hooksett, you pass the mouth of the Soucook River (5¾ mi) and the Suncook River (8¾ mi). One-fourth mile above the dam (10½ mi) there is a nice boat launching ramp on the L, but experienced canoeists who are carrying by hand can continue in low water as far as the abutment on the L. Carry past the parking area to another launching ramp below the dam.

There is some turbulence around the bridge abutments below the Hooksett dam, then 7¼ miles of smoothwater to Manchester. Amoskeag Bridge and the Manchester skyline can be seen from a long distance upstream. Take out above the bridge on the R to portage Amoskeag Dam.

Manchester — Nashua 17¾ miles

1976	**Flatwater**, Quickwater, Class II	28½ km

Passable at most water levels
Dam-controlled: *peak power generation*
Forested, Settled, Urban

USGS: *Manchester North*, Manchester South, Nashua North

There is a mile of class II rapids through Manchester. On the L bank the walls of old factories rise straight up from the river, and on the R there is a limited-access highway. In high water, keep to the R.

Past two highway bridges and shortly below the rapids, the Piscataquog River (2 mi) enters on the R in South Manchester. A cascade of sewage, attested to by a crowd of seagulls, comes in on the L just above the Queen City Bridge — the third highway bridge below Amoskeag Dam. In 1½ miles there is a riffle, and soon the I-193 bridge comes in sight.

Land under the I-193 bridge (4¼ mi) to scout the class III ledge which can be run on either side but not in the middle. This spot can be reached on the R via a dirt road. In another ¾ mile there is a RR bridge with a ledge starting just above it. It, too, can be run on either side but not in the middle where there is an island. This ledge can be inspected in advance from dirt roads on either side.

Below the RR bridge (5 mi) there is smoothwater for 1¼ miles to a short class II drop and then for another 2 miles to a longer class II rapid just below a big power line. After 2¼ miles of smoothwater the Souhegan River (10½ mi) enters on the R. There is another class II rapid in 4 miles, followed by 3¼ miles of easy paddling to the NH-111 bridge (17¾ mi) in Nashua just below the mouth of the Nashua River on the R.

Nashua — Lowell   14 miles

USGS: Nashua South, Lowell

From the Route 111 bridge in Nashua, it is only 1 mile to the south end of town, where Salmon Brook enters on the right. The river now is all flatwater. It passes between tilled fields and meadow land for some distance, finally entering a section with wooded banks before reaching the next bridge, Route 113, at Tyngsboro, 5 miles below. There are more signs of human habitation in the next 4 miles to North Chelmsford, where Stony Brook enters on the right. In another 3 miles one arrives at Lowell. At Lowell portage into the canal at the right and paddle down the canal beyond the cement bridge. Haul out at the floodgate and carry up the path to the road, turning left down the road to a dump. Put in and paddle down the pond. Then carry again over green slimy rocks, a nasty carry, to the clear current, which is below the entrance of Beaver Brook, and close to the mouth of the Concord River.

USGS: Lowell, Lawrence, South Groveland, Ayres Village,
       Haverhill

From below the dam in Lowell it is 10 miles by river with
no bridges (except the Route 93 bridge) to Lawrence. At
the dam at Lawrence portage on the right bank down the
fish run. There is shoalwater for the next 3 miles. In the
first 1 mile the Shawsheen River enters on the right, and
the Spicket River on the left. Below the shoalwater it is
another 7 miles to the bridge, Route 125, at Haverhill.
Just above this the Little River enters on the left.

Haverhill — Newburyport   20 miles

USGS: Haverhill, Newburyport West, Newburyport East

This stretch is tidal, and one should try to have the ebb
tide with one on a paddle downstream. It is 3 miles to the
Route 97 bridge in Groveland and 4 miles more to the
bridge at Rock Village. Another 5 miles of easy paddling
brings one to Amesbury and the mouth of the Powwow
River on the left. In another 1 mile one passes under the
Route 95 bridge and the Deer Island bridge, a most picturesque spot. It is then only 3 miles to Newburyport and
another 3 miles to the mouth of the river, where on the
right just before Plum Island is reached, the Plum Island
River, a tidal estuary, opens up behind several islands.

   The tidal rise and fall at the Merrimack River
entrance varies between 8½ and 9½ feet. High tide is
about 5 minutes later than Boston and low tide 10 minutes
later. At Newburyport, the respective differences increase
to 15 minutes and 55 minutes, with corresponding
increases farther up the river.

ASSABET RIVER   MA

The Assabet River rises in Westboro and flows northeastward to Concord, where its confluence with the Sudbury
creates the Concord River. Although many dams have
eliminated most of the rapids, there are still a number of
short, fairly attractive trips which can be made.

Westboro — Hudson   11¼ miles

In its upper stretches the Assabet is still a small stream.
Most of this portion is runnable all year, but shallow places
below the dam in Northboro and through Chapinville make

the spring preferable for a run. The scenery includes frequent views of marshes and farms, with only a few interruptions from road crossings and dams.

| 1976 | Westboro — Hudson | 11¼ mi [18 km] |

Flatwater, Quickwater, Class I
High water: *late March thru April*
Medium water: *May*
Forested, Rural, Towns
USGS: Shrewsbury, Marlboro, Hudson

Portages:	3¾ mi	R	**dam at Northboro** — 10 yds
	4¾ mi	R	**dam at Woodside** — 15 yds
	11¼ mi	L	**dam at Hudson** (difficult) — 200 yds

From the put-in at the MA-9 bridge, there are 3¾ miles of winding, marshy river to the dam in Northboro. This dam, the site of a gristmill around 1700, should be portaged on the R. If the water is high enough, the riffles under the US-20 bridge just below can be run; otherwise carry around the bridge also. Riffles continue below this bridge under an old mill. This mill actually draws its power from a dam on Cold Harbor Brook, which enters from the L, so that the main river is clear of obstructions. Just below, the river widens into a pond above the dam at Woodside. Just above this dam are a high stone aqueduct bridge and a low bridge on a side road. Portage the dam itself (4¾ mi), and the low bridge if necessary, on the R. Riffles continue below, and the river runs navigably under another mill and between stone walls.

For the next 6½ miles the banks alternate between marsh and farmland. The river is occasionally overhung and obstructed. A number of small bridges are passed, including those of I-495. The portage around the dam in Hudson (11¼ mi) is complicated by fences and concrete retaining walls. Carry on the L side through gas stations to a put-in just below the MA-85 bridge.

Hudson — Maynard   **8½ miles**
This section is probably the most attractive on the river for flatwater paddlers, with the only detrimental factors being the buildings and declining water quality in Hudson. This run is available all year, although the portage at Gleasondale may be a little longer in low water.

1976 Hudson — Maynard 8½ mi [13¾ km]
Flatwater, Class I
Passable at all water levels
Forested, Towns
  USGS: Hudson, Maynard
  Portages: 3¾ mi L **dam at Gleasondale** — 50 yds
  8½ mi L **first dam at Maynard** — 15 yds

One-half mile below the MA-85 bridge there is a dam which is low and easily run. Several marshy miles follow to a dam in Gleasondale (3¾ mi) which should be portaged on the L. The short shallow rapids below may have to be walked or carried in very low water. The MA-62 bridge is quickly passed, and then there are 4½ pleasant but sluggish miles past Assabet Brook (8 mi), which enters on the L, to the dam above Maynard (8½ mi). Portage on the L.

Stow — Maynard 4½ miles
ASSABET BROOK

This tributary of the Assabet River provides a short, pleasant run on a narrow stream. The water is moderately clean, in contrast to the main river which is darker and dirtier. There are a number of obstructions necessitating short portages.

1976 Stow — Maynard 4½ mi [7¼ km]
Lakes, Quickwater, Class I
High or medium water: *April thru July*
Forested
  USGS: Hudson, Maynard
  Portages: 1¼ mi R **dam on Wheeler Pond** — 20 yds
  2 mi R **dam on Fletcher Pond** — 20 yds

Put in at the MA-117 bridge about a mile W of Stow. The stream, with a good current at this point, splits immediately around an island. The woods give way to marshier banks, and the Stow Country Club is passed on the R. The brook leads into ½-mile-long Wheeler Pond. Portage the outlet dam (1¼ mi) on the R, and if necessary, because of low clearance, the stone bridge on Wheeler Road just below. Another marshy ½ mile brings the paddler to the MA-62 bridge, shortly below which Fletcher Pond is entered. After the portage at this outlet dam (2 mi), there are 1¾ miles of river with good current and occasional riffles. One low culvert usually must be por-

taged. The brook passes the Assabet Country Club —
where another low bridge will probably require lifting
around — just before joining the Assabet River (3¾ mi).
A take-out is possible at the bridge ¼ mile down the
Assabet or at the dam (4½ mi) just above the MA-117
bridge in Maynard.

Maynard — Concord   **8½ miles**

The rapids in Maynard provide good training for novice
whitewater boaters. The remainder of the run is smooth
and runnable all year. The pollution of the water, however,
is less offensive when the water level is up.

1977   Maynard — Concord   8½ mi [13¾ km]
Flatwater, Quickwater, Class I–II
High or medium water: *March thru May*
Low water: *rapids in Maynard impassable*
Forested, Settled
     USGS: Maynard, Concord
     Portage: 2¼ mi   L   **second dam in Maynard** — 50 yds

         Put in on the R bank from a dirt road next to the
Pace Company. There are 1½ miles of easy class II rapids
through Maynard. These can be odorous and impassable in
low water. Below the MA-27/62 bridge in Maynard
Center, the rapids end, followed by ¾ mile of flatwater to
the second Maynard dam (2¼ mi). Portage on the L.

         Below Maynard, swift current and two quick
crossings of MA-62 give way to another flatwater section
above the broken dam in West Concord (4 mi). The gatehouse has been washed out, so that the dam is runnable on
the far R. Before going down it, look this slot over for
obstructions. The next 2 miles contain a mixture of slow
and moderate current, of highway and RR bridges. After
the Concord Reformatory and the MA-2 bridge (6 mi), the
river has high banks on the L and meadows on the R.

         Spencer Brook, which enters on the L 1¼ miles
below MA-2, was often spoken of by Thoreau. This brook
can be ascended a short distance, but tall marsh grasses
overhang the canoe, and the abrupt turns make passage
difficult. Just past Spencer Brook there is a large rock in
mid-river called "Gibraltar," and there are several other
rocks which must be avoided. The river makes two grace-
ful curves with wooded banks. A short distance above the
junction with the Sudbury River is the site of the hemlocks
made famous by Hawthorne in *Mosses from an Old
Manse*. These were on the R bank at the foot of Nashaw-

tuc Hill, but they are now largely replaced by willows. The next take-out is 200 yards down the Concord River at the Lowell Street bridge (8½ mi).

BAKER RIVER   NH

This river was named for Thomas Baker, a lieutenant from Northampton, Massachusetts who travelled along it in 1712 on a raid against the Indians. It rises on the south slopes of Mount Moosilauke in Benton and runs south and then east to the Pemigewasset in Plymouth.

The scenery is rural and very attractive. A main highway follows up the valley, but it usually cannot be seen from the river. An abandoned railroad grade is scarcely noticeable.

Route 118 — Wentworth   6 miles

The river has been channelled from NH-118 through the town of Warren, an indication that run-offs frequently are fast and furious. The watershed is mountainous and at first the gradient is steep, making boating in the first 2 miles very dependent upon the weather. If the spring is early or dry, the water needed for the good class III rapids above Warren will already be in the Merrimack by mid-April.

1977 | Route 118 — Wentworth   6 mi [9¾ km]
Quickwater, Class II–III
High water: *April*
Medium water: *bony above Warren, early May*
Forested, Rural, Towns
   USGS: Rumney 15
   Portage: 6 mi L **ledge at Wentworth** — 100–200 yds

Put in at the NH-118 bridge N of Warren. The gradient is steepest in the first ¾ mile where there are class III rapids as the river drops steadily over small boulders. The river widens and the rapids become easier as the town of Warren comes into view.

The first bridge in Warren, Studio Road (1¼ mi), can be used as a starting point if the rapids above are too shallow. The current through Warren to the NH-25 bridge is swift. Much of the remaining distance is quickwater, with wide turns where overhanging trees are an occasional hazard. Below the second NH-25 bridge (3½ mi) there is a short class II rapid. In Wentworth (6 mi), take out above the old truss bridge, as underneath there is a very turbulent class IV drop. It can be carried on the L under the bridge unless the water is very high.

Wentworth — Plymouth   21 miles

The farther you start downstream on the Baker River, the more it becomes a leisurely float trip, with less and less water being needed to keep you off the bottom. The river is clean, and the riverbed is sandy in many locations. With a little helpful rain, the part below West Rumney makes a nice summer trip.

The river winds through a rural valley hemmed in by wooded hillsides. It frequently undercuts banks, dumping trees into the current. These are hazardous, but they can almost always be paddled around. Noise from the highway is most noticeable as you near the end. You do not miss much by taking out at the Smith Road covered bridge 4¼ miles above Plymouth.

1977 | Wentworth — Plymouth   21 mi [34 km]
Flatwater, Quickwater, Class I–II
High or medium water: *April thru May and after moderate rains*
Low water: *passable below West Rumney*
Forested, Rural Town
USGS: Rumney 15, Plymouth 15

Put in at the ballfield below the NH-25 bridge on the N bank. There are short class I–II rapids and quickwater for 6 miles past two bridges to the girder bridge on a side road in West Rumney. Below here the river is generally wider with less current. In 1¼ miles there is a highway rest area on the R, followed in ½ mile by an overhead cable at a gauging station which precedes a short class II rapid at the site of an old dam. More flatwater, but with good current, continues for 6¾ miles past the rusty Stinson Lake Road bridge (10 mi) to an old bridge site in an "S" turn by Polar Caves (14½ mi). Stinson Mountain with a firetower (now closed) on the top is occasionally visible. The river is more sluggish for the next 2¼ miles to the Smith Road covered bridge (16¾ mi).

There are 4 more miles of flatwater to the truss bridge on US-3 (20¾ mi) in Plymouth where there is a good take-out on the R bank. This point is also used as a starting point for trips on the Pemigewasset River, since the confluence is just ¼ mile below (21 mi).

BEAVER BROOK   NH, MA

Beaver Brook is a pleasant, winding stream which flows from Beaver Lake in Derry to the Merrimack River at Lowell. There is a good current for most of that distance with lots of small beaver dams, some minor rapids, and occasional carries. It flows through several suburban communities, but few of the settled areas are visible from the water.

 Derry — West Windham   **7 miles**

1977   Flatwater, Quickwater   11¼ km
       High water: *April*
       Forested, Towns
           USGS: *Derry,* Windham
           Portages: 4 mi R **dam at Kendall Pond** — 100 yds
                       7 mi R **dam at West Windham** — 40 yds

---

Put in at the high bridge on NH-28, as just above it is a large marsh where the water is diffused. Within the first ¾ mile there is a stone RR culvert, a highway bridge, and a pipe culvert on a side road above a sewage treatment plant. The sewage outfall is perhaps ¾ mile beyond, but the effluent is quickly diluted at high water levels. It is then ½ mile to the I-93 bridge and another ½ mile to the next side road bridge (2½ mi). One mile further Beaver Brook enters Kendall Pond (3½ mi).

One-half mile across the pond is the outlet (4 mi), where there are a dam and a bridge. Take out on the R and carry across the road. Beware of snowmobile bridges just past the dam. For the next 3 miles the stream winds through meadows where there are log jams and beaver dams. Portage the dam at West Windham (7 mi) on the R. The NH-128 bridge is just below it.

 West Windham — Dracut   **13½ miles**

1977   Flatwater, **Quickwater**, Class I–II   21¾ km
       High water: *April*
       Forested, Towns
           USGS: Windham, Lowell
           Portages: 3¾ mi L **broken dam**
                       6¾ mi e **dam**

Below the NH-128 bridge (0 mi) the river bottom is gravelly, and considerable rock picking is required in low water. It is 1¾ miles to the NH-111 bridge, ¼ mile more to the next bridge, and then 1 mile to the second NH-128 bridge.

Three-quarters of a mile below the second NH-128 bridge (3 mi), land on L above a rock ledge where the river makes a blind L turn. Line or carry past a broken dam with jagged masonry. Soon there are two closely spaced bridges, and then 1½ miles of river to another bridge, now closed. In another 1½ miles there is a small concrete dam (6¾ mi) which can be lifted over on either side or run in the middle.

One-half mile past the second dam a steel beam bridge (7¼ mi) on NH-111A may have to be carried at high water due to low clearance. It is ¾ mile to a stone arch bridge and another ½ mile to the bridge on Bridge Street (8½ mi) opposite the shopping center in Pelham.

From the shopping center it is ¾ mile to the Willow Street bridge, and from there the river winds for 4¼ miles mostly through meadowlands. There are some class II rapids above the dam and bridge at Collinsville (13½ mi) in Dracut. Take out 200 yards above the dam.

BLACKWATER RIVER   NH

The sandy soil of the Blackwater Valley is not as rich for farming as other parts of New Hampshire, a factor which perhaps explains why it is so sparsely settled. The river rises in Wilmot north of Mount Kearsarge (Merrimack County) and flows southeast to meet the Contoocook River not far from Concord. Most of the river is a delightful, easy paddle in a scenic area. The quality of its water is high, since the Blackwater is one of the few large rivers which the New Hampshire legislature has designated as class A.

Medium water of the spring or fall is needed. The river should be avoided in high water, as the many fallen trees are a definite hazard. Inexperienced canoeists often have to be rescued from them.

Cilleyville — West Salisbury   **9 miles**

977   Flatwater, Quickwater, Class I–II   14½ km
High water: *needed above Andover, early spring*
Medium water: *late spring and wet fall*
Forested, Town
USGS: Mount Kearsarge 15
Portage: 9½ mi   **broken dam at West Salisbury**

Put in from the old route 11 bridge, since there is a dam just below the new one. The river begins with small, easy class II rapids, rock dams, and fallen trees. At Andover (3 mi), where there is a covered bridge on a side road, the rapids are over. Many people, choosing to avoid white-water, put in here.

The current becomes slower with occasional riffles as the river wends its way, passing twice beneath US-4. After 4½ miles it enters the slackwater of The Bay,

where the river broadens into a series of marshy ponds for
1½ miles. You can take out at the end of The Bay on a dirt
road to the L.

| **West Salisbury — Flood Control Dam** | **12 miles** |

xxxx   Flatwater, Quickwater   19¼ km
        Medium water: *late spring and wet fall*
        Wild
            USGS: Mount Kearsarge 15, Penacook 15
            Portage: 12 mi   **Flood Control Dam**

        There is a steep, rocky drop at the end of The Bay.
Then it is less than ½ mile to the next bridge where there is
a broken dam with jagged masonry in the river. The class II
rapids below the dam diminish to quickwater within the
next mile to Peters Bridge, the best place to put in for
this section.
        From Peters Bridge (1½ mi) there are 4 miles of
quickwater to Sawyers Bridge (5½ mi). It is a beautiful
stream which meanders through a swamp above and
below Sawyers Bridge, but there are many fallen trees.
Some of them are dangerous in high water because you
may get swept under them; others are a nuisance at low
water because they must be lifted over.
        The best take-out above the dam is on a dirt road
on the R just E of Littles Hill (11 mi). Below here there are
some class II rapids, followed by the backwater from the
flood control dam (12 mi).

Flood Control Dam — Contoocook River   10 miles

The middle part of this section is recommended for covered
boats only. Open boats are sometimes used in the first
2½ miles through a set of rapids near Dingit Corner, but
below that closed boats are needed. People who never tip
over on the Contoocook above Henniker often swim in one
of the two class IV rapids above Snyder's Mill.

1975   Flood Control Dam — Contoocook River   10 mi [16 km]
        Flatwater, **Quickwater, Class III–IV**
        High water: *April*
        Forested
            USGS: Penacook 15, Hopkinton

        Put in on the R at the foot of the cascade under
Swett's Mills Bridge on NH-127. Below the cascade the
river splits around an island where there is a shallow, rocky
rapid. There is more water on the R. If you do not hit any

rocks here, the rapids farther down the river past Dingit Corner will be extremely exciting. Below the island there is an easier put-in behind the Webster Elementary School (¼ mi).

Then the river riffles through an attractive, forested area. One and a half miles below the school the river turns L and tumbles through a class III rapid with a couple of large rocks and a nice set of 3-foot standing waves. There is a pool at the bottom, at the outlet of which there is a 30-yard chute which terminates with a 6-foot drop which can be seen upstream of Clothespin Bridge (2 mi).

At that point the river squeezes through a 15-foot-wide notch in a ledge and drops into a messy hole. Runnable by covered boats and kayaks, it is quite exciting, often resulting in nosestands and Eskimo rolls. The water below it is fast and deep.

Below Clothespin Bridge (2 mi) there is a class III ledge. The river rounds a sharp L corner, passes the USGS gauge (2½ mi), and drops over a rocky class III rapid best run near the L bank.

Open canoes should take out on the L past the USGS gauging station. Below that point the road is away from the river, and the next two rapids are dandies: each about ½ mile long and separated by ¼ mile of flatwater.

The first set of class IV rapids (2¾ mi) is rocky and continuous, with only small eddies big enough for one boat. The river swishes from side to side around the rocks, reminding one of a downhill ski run. After rounding a sharp R-hand turn, the river drops into the ¼ mile of flatwater which is the lull between the storms. If the first rapids are not to your liking, do not run the next set.

The second set of class IV rapids is very turbulent, tricky to run upright, and bad news indeed to swim. It could be described as a hard class IV washing machine followed by a 4-foot ledge onto a ¼-mile washboard. The latter consists of shallow, bony rapids that run down under Snyder's Mill Bridge (4 mi). There is a dirt access road at the end of the rapids on the R.

Below Snyder's Mill there are 6 miles of quick-water to the mouth of the river. There are two bridges (8½, 9½ mi) before the Contoocook River (10 mi).

COCKERMOUTH RIVER   NH

This small river empties into the northwest end of Newfound Lake. Its water is clear, and the valley through which
it flows typifies rural New England at its best. It takes
about two hours to run.

| Groton — Newfound Lake | 3½ miles |

| 1977 | Flatwater, **Quickwater** | 5¾ km |

High and medium water: *early spring, after heavy rain*
Rural
    USGS: Cardigan 15

Start in Groton where the road to North Groton
crosses the river, which here is about a canoe-length wide.
The current is fast as the stream winds along the edges of
fields. Just above the second bridge (2 mi) there is a short
and easy class II rapid. In the last ¾ mile the river is flat
and wide. It flows under a road along the N end of Newfound Lake ½ mile before it empties into Hebron Bay
(3½ mi).

COHAS BROOK   NH

Cohas Brook flows along the south end of Manchester and
enters the Merrimack at Goffs Falls. The banks are so
thickly wooded that nearby urban areas are usually out of
both sight and sound. See the USGS Manchester North
sheet.

The upper portion is a nightmare of dense
thickets, fallen trees, garbage, raw sewage, wire mesh, and
an electric fence. Also in store for you is a mile of the
median strip of I-93.

There is an acceptable, 4-mile portion that begins
at the second Bodwell Road bridge, just after the river
leaves the median. The stream, soon enlarged by the outlet
of Massabesic Lake, passes the NH-28A bridge in
1¼ miles and meanders through a large marsh west of
NH-28A. Approach the NH-28 bridge (4 mi) cautiously
and take out on a high steep bank. Around the corner
below is a difficult rapid.

The lower portion is also not recommended. It
contains smoothwater and rapids, but there is no
convenient take-out before ¼ mile of cascades to the
Merrimack that are unrunnable.

CONTOOCOOK RIVER   NH

The Contoocook is one of the principal tributaries of the
Merrimack River. It rises in Rindge east of Mount Monadnock and flows generally northeast to join the Merrimack
at Penacook.

　　　The greatly differing sections of the Contoocook
hold appeal for both flatwater and whitewater paddlers. In
the upper section there are easy rapids which are only
available in the early spring. Much flatwater follows as the
river's volume increases. Heavy rapids above Henniker give
way to pleasant flatwater, with a few rapids near the confluence. The calm stretches and even some of the rapids
provide opportunities for summer boating.

Jaffrey — Peterborough   6¾ miles

From Jaffrey the Contoocook flows through easy rapids
interrupted only by a small gorge. The rapids make a good
training ground for beginning whitewater paddlers. This
section, very small and winding, contrasts noticeably with
the breadth and volume of the lower river.

　　　It is possible to get through the swamps of
Rindge and Jaffrey from Contoocook Pond or Pool Pond,
but few will want to canoe above Cheshire Pond in Jaffrey.

77　Jaffrey — Peterborough   6¾ mi [11 km]
Class II
High water: *late March thru early April*
Forested
　　USGS:　*Monadnock 15,* Peterborough 15
　Portages:　2 mi　L　**class IV gorge** — 400 yds
　　　　　　5 mi　R　**Noone Dam** — 10 yds
　　　　　　6¾ mi　L　**Peterborough Dam** — 30 yds

　　　There is a dam at the outlet of Cheshire Pond, and
a put-in can be made from the US-202 bridge just below.
Easy class II rapids start immediately. The river crosses
several times beneath the RR and old route 202 bridges.
The old road can be followed beside the river. After 2 miles
the river makes a sharp R turn into a hemlock grove and
there is a wooden bridge 30 yards beyond.

　　　Caution! Make a steep, short take-out on the L
above the bridge (2 mi), as a gorge starts below it. The
gorge contains difficult rapids that can be run at certain
water stages. At higher water levels the rapids are class IV
and can be navigated by closed boats. At somewhat lower

levels open boats can proceed from drop to drop in the gorge, lining or lifting around any drops deemed impassable. The gorge should be scouted, particularly since a fallen tree or jammed log would create a bad situation. To portage, carry down the road on the L for ¼ mile and, upon passing the first house on the R, return to the river. A car certainly eases this portage.

Below the gorge there is another 1½ miles of class II rapids. In the succeeding mile the rapids alternate with smooth stretches to a side road bridge (4½ mi) above the millpond in Noone. The dam at Noone (5 mi) requires a short portage on the R. Another mile of mixed rapids and flatwater continues to Peterborough, where there is a little drop next to the Peterborough Plaza. A take-out can be made at the new NH-101 bridge (6¼ mi), or, for those desiring a little more smooth paddling, at the dam above a stone bridge in Peterborough (6¾ mi).

Peterborough — Bennington   12 miles

The flatwater paddle from Peterborough to Bennington is one of the prettiest on the river. Most of this stretch, particularly the second half, is navigable whenever the river is ice-free.

1977	Peterborough — Bennington	12 mi [19½ km]

Flatwater, Class I
Passable at most water levels: *especially towards Bennington*
Forested

USGS: Peterborough 15

Portages: 2 mi R **North Village Dam** — 10 yds
             12 mi R **1st of several dams in Bennington**

From the stone bridge and dam, it is a 2-mile paddle to the dam in North Village. Portage on the R. The Contoocook then flows under US-202 and snakes swiftly around some low islands. This portion might be impassable in low water. Five and a half miles of smooth paddling by woods and meadows lead to a small side road bridge (7½ mi). In another mile the Contoocook empties into Powder Mill Pond, the back-up from a dam in Bennington. A half mile down the pond there is a covered bridge at a narrowing of the river (9 mi). Continuing down the pond, a RR bridge crosses at another narrows (10¾ mi), and the first dam in Bennington is reached (12 mi). Take out on the R bank.

In the next 1½ miles through Bennington there are at least four dams and impassable rapids; in addition, the Monadnock Paper Mill sometimes diverts the water and leaves the riverbed almost dry.

Bennington — Hillsboro   12 miles

This stretch is also flatwater, but not quite as appealing as that above Bennington. The current is sluggish, the river winds considerably, and the paper mill in Bennington contributes to the decline in water quality.

---

977 Bennington — Hillsboro   12 mi [19½ km]
Flatwater, Class I
Passable at all water levels
Forested
    USGS: Hillsboro 15
    Portage: 12 mi   **two dams in Hillsboro** — ½ mi

Put in below the last dam in Bennington at the bridge near the Monadnock Paper Company, visible from US-202. It is 2½ miles to Antrim, and another 8¼ miles to the entrance of the North Branch of the Contoocook (10¾ mi). About ½ miles past the North Branch, class II rapids begin and continue right up to the dam (12 mi) in Hillsboro, making approach to it difficult and dangerous.

Take out on the R where the river comes close to the road ½ mile above the dam and just before the mill buildings. It is also possible — with permission — to take out upstream before the rapids at private docks.

Hillsboro — West Henniker   6½ miles

The heaviest rapids on the Contoocook are found in this section — the river is at this point one of the largest whitewater rivers in New England. The water level here is more reliable than on other rivers, making the rapids runnable all spring and after heavy rains.

There is a USGS gauge on the right bank a mile above the dam in West Henniker. When it reads up to 8.0, all rapids except Freight Train Rapids near the end are difficult class III and can be run in open boats. Freight Train Rapids are always class IV. Although they have been run open at this level, that is not recommended. At water levels above 8.0, all the rapids become more turbulent and should be left to closed boats. At virtually any level a tipover in the Contoocook can lead to a long swim and a difficult rescue.

xxxx   Hillsboro — West Henniker   6½ mi [10½ km]
Flatwater, Quickwater, **Class III–IV**
High and medium water: *spring and after heavy rains*
Forested, Settled
  USGS: Hillsboro 15
  Portage: 6½ mi R **West Henniker Dam** — 10 yds

A milldam directly under the NH-149 bridge in
Hillsboro makes it advisable to put in just below the village.
Reach the river from the L bank near the RR trestle. The
first ½ mile consists of class III rapids, and then the river
becomes smooth, with one rapid shortly above the old
route 202 bridge. From there quickwater continues to the
bridge (3 mi). The older road is still kept up, and it provides
the best access to most of the rapid sections below.
Another smooth ½ mile leads to the start of the rapids. For
those just starting a trip, the beginning of the rapids can be
reached from old route 202 by going through the woods. A
dirt road follows the L bank from the old route 202 bridge
to Freight Train Rapids, but it may be impassable in the
spring.

The first rapid of the lower section (3½ mi) begins
in a slight L turn where the current goes from impercep-
tible to irresistible. There are no rocks here, but the waves
can be very turbulent at high water. The river bends R with
rapids and returns to the road (4 mi). The next L turn holds
another difficult rapid, the shallowest in this portion: if this
rapid is passable, then the whole stretch can be run.

When the river leaves the road, a very challenging rapid is ahead. The R turn is the beginning of a heavy
and continuous ½-mile rapid known as the "S-turn." In this
rapid, swimming and rescue are extremely difficult. There
are then easier rapids with a USGS gauge on the R bank
(5 mi). Any paddlers wishing to avoid the last and
toughest of the Contoocook rapids should take out here
where the road is near.

From this calm spot (5 mi) the river turns L with
easy class II rapids. Where it turns R, the Contoocook
begins the ferocious Freight Train Rapids, a class IV pitch
in medium water. Take out on the L bank on the dirt road at
the turn to scout. The route is basically through the biggest waves and holes in the center. The last ½ mile is flatwater with current to the dam in West Henniker (6½ mi).
A take-out can be made on the R bank on old route 202.

West Henniker — Penacook   **26½ miles**

The placid lower Contoocook is interrupted only by rapids
at the beginning and the end, with a flood control dam in
the middle. There are long stretches for a pleasant flatwater outing in the spring, summer, or fall.

1977   West Henniker — Penacook   26½ mi [42¾ km]
        Flatwater, Quickwater, Class II–III
        Pasable at all water levels
        Forested, Settled
            USGS: Hillsboro 15, Hopkinton, Penacook 15, *Concord*
            Portages: 2 mi   R   **broken dam** — 20 yds
                        8½ mi   L   **flood control dam; older dam below** — ¼ mi
                        13¾ mi R   **dam at Contoocook Village** — 10 yds
                        24 mi   **dam at the Island** (land at tip)
                        25¾ mi R   **difficult rapids** — 400 yds

---

From the old route 202 crossing in West Henniker
(just below the dam), there are 1½ mostly smooth miles to
Henniker. At Henniker the river passes under the stone
NH-114 bridge and through a few class II–III rapids to a
broken dam ¼ mile below Henniker. This dam may
possibly be runnable under the right conditions, but most
paddlers will opt for the short portage on the R. In
100 yards a steel truss bridge is passed. This bridge (2 mi)
makes a better start for a flatwater trip.

The next 6½ miles past the US-202/NH-9 bridge
to the West Hopkinton flood control dam (8½ mi) are flat,
but the scenic attractiveness depends on recent fluctuations in the water level at the dam. This is one of the larger
flood control projects in New England, potentially backing
water all the way up to Henniker. The portage on the L is
arduous. There is an older dam that also must be portaged
100 yards below the flood control dam.

After a few easy rapids and a covered bridge in
the small town of West Hopkinton (8¾ mi), 5 miles of
smoothwater follow to Contoocook Village (13¾ mi).
Portage a small dam on the R and paddle through class I
rapids under a stone and a covered bridge where canoe
rentals are available. Flatwater continues as the Warner
River joins (14¾ mi) and the bridge at Tyler is passed
(16¼ mi). On the S bank near the bridge are Gould and
Rattlesnake hills, where timber for the Civil War warship
USS Kearsarge was cut.

Whereas the river banks had been uninhabited
above the Blackwater River (17¾ mi), a few cabins are
now seen on the way to a side road bridge in the locality

known as Riverhill (22½ mi). The river is lined with houses in the next 1½ miles to a park in Penacook known appropriately as the "Island" (24 mi). The Island is reached by taking Washington Street out of Penacook and following a marked turn-off. There is a public boat landing on the upstream tip of the Island for easy take-out. Though it is possible to continue to the Merrimack, the dams and the rapids will make most paddlers want to terminate their trip here.

There are dams on both sides of the Island, requiring a short portage. The next mile to the US-3/4 bridge in Penacook (25¼ mi) has some class II–III rapids. Just below this bridge is a broken dam that can sometimes be run as a stunt, but it should generally be portaged. In low water one can land on the R just above the dam to portage, but this should be avoided in high water when the current is stronger.

One-half mile of easy rapids follows to another bridge (25¾ mi), where a take-out should be made above the bridge on either side. Directly below this bridge is an island with an old bridge abutment. To the L side of the island, there is a very sharp drop followed by an unrunnable dam. On the R of the island, the descent is more gradual — a possibly runnable but difficult class IV. Look this over carefully. The R bank offers a long but gradual portage of 400 yards, enabling the paddler to avoid all the difficult rapids. When the two channels rejoin, there are more class IV rapids with a line of old mill buildings on the L bank. Rapids diminish quickly to the confluence with the Merrimack River (26½ mi).

LITTLE RIVER   NH, MA

This stream is runnable from Plaistow, New Hampshire to within a mile of the Merrimack River in Haverhill, Massachusetts, at which point it runs into a culvert. It is a small quickwater stream that is canoeable only at high water.

Begin the run from Main Street in Plaistow (NH-121A) just E of NH-125. In ½ mile the stream passes beneath Westville Road, and within another ½ mile beneath two bridges, the second of which is NH-125. It passes under NH-121 (1½ mi) just above the state line. The stream remains small until it passes underneath I-495 (3 mi) and enters the backwater of a dam in Haverhill. Much of this flowage is paralleled by railroad tracks. The best take out points in Haverhill are at a playground (5 mi) on the right 150 yards past a railroad bridge and ½ mile above the dam, or at Benjamin and Apple streets just above the dam. See the USGS Haverhill sheet.

LITTLE SUNCOOK RIVER   NH

This small, exciting stream is the outlet of Northwood Lake in Northwood. It flows almost due west to the Suncook River just below the Epsom traffic circle. It is followed nearby on the right bank by US-4, but the highway is usually out-of-sight. See USGS Gossville sheet.

The first 1½ miles from the dam on Northwood Lake to a small concrete dam visible from US-4 may be runnable by experts, but no information is available. Below, there are rocky class III–IV rapids which require just the right water stage, often found in early April. There are many sharp corners which sometimes hide a snowmobile bridge or fallen tree. It is ½ mile to the first road bridge, then another ¾ mile to the bridge at Gossville. Below Gossville the rapids taper off quickly. Another ½ mile brings you to the Suncook River, ¼ mile below the US-4 bridge.

There is an annual fall drawdown of Northwood Lake by the Water Resources Board (603-271-1110).

MAD RIVER   NH

The Mad River, a tributary of the Pemigewasset River north of Plymouth, provides expert paddlers with many miles of continuous rapids. The steepness of the terrain around it means that run-off takes place quickly.

Waterville Valley — Campton   12 miles

This portion of the river flows through Waterville Valley, one of the most beautiful in the White Mountains. It does not often have enough water in it for boating, but on a few days of the year it provides a long and continuously interesting whitewater run. Flexible boats have a somewhat extended season. In general, it contains a multitude of small and medium-sized rocks that force paddlers to constantly move their boats.

At Six-Mile Bridge there is a hand-painted gauge on a rock that is just upstream of the left abutment. It is estimated that a reading of 1.5 on this gauge would be medium water, while a reading of 2.5 would represent high water.

1977   Waterville Valley — Campton   12 mi [19½ km]
             Lake, **Class III–IV**
             High or medium water: *mid-April to early May*
             Forested
                 USGS: Plymouth 15
                 Portage: 12 mi L **dam at Campton** — 30 yds

---

Begin near the town of Waterville Valley. Follow NH-49 through the town and, shortly after passing the tennis courts, make a sharp L turn by the library. This road soon crosses the river and continues to join the Tripoli Road to North Woodstock. The Tripoli Road is not plowed in the winter, so that NH-49 from the S is usually the only route into the Mad River basin in the spring.

From the put-in the West Branch of the Mad River is also visible, and it adds its waters shortly below. Rapids begin almost immediately, with the difficulty reaching class III. A mile and a half of rapids brings you to the Mount Tecumseh Ski Area bridge. The latter can also be used as a put-in, but the access is more difficult.

Below the ski area bridge (1½ mi) there are 3 miles of continuous class III–IV rapids with a couple of drops slightly harder than the rest. The hardest rapid is in a R-hand turn about 1½ miles below the bridge. It is actually a little easier than it looks, a fairly straight course in the center being the best route in medium to high water. A roadside turn-off facilitates scouting this drop from the road.

There is a nice view of Welch Mountain on the R bank (4½ mi), after which the rapids become tougher — class IV. The river becomes narrow, and resting or rescue places are even harder to find. The rapids are continuous for 2 miles to Six-Mile Bridge.

From Six-Mile bridge (6½ mi) there are 2 miles of class III–IV rapids with larger waves but with fewer rocks. At Goose Hollow (8½ mi) there is a double bridge — one for trucks which not too long ago had to ford the river. In the next 3 miles to Campton Pond, the rapids steadily ease up from class III to class I. Take out at NH-49 which follows along the western shoreline.

If you are continuing downstream, portage the dam (12 mi) on the L.

Campton — Pemigewasset River 2½ miles

In Campton there is a steep gorge that is sometimes the site of whitewater slalom races. The rapids there are caused by steep drops over and around ledges as well as boulders. Campton Pond tends to make the flow in this section steadier and more dependable.

---

977   Campton — Pemigewasset River   2½ mi [4 km]
Quickwater, Class III–IV
High or medium water: *mid-April to mid-May*
Forested, Town
      USGS: Plymouth 15

Just below the bridge there is a partially washed-out dam which should be scouted and probably lifted over. Past an old factory on the L, the river swings to the R and enters Campton Gorge where there is ½ mile of class III–IV rapids. They can be run by skilled boaters, but they should be looked over.

Below Campton Gorge there are 2 miles of quickwater to the Pemigewasset River (2½ mi). The first take-out is 1½ mile downstream on US-3 (4 mi) a short distance above the I-93 bridges.

NASHUA RIVER   MA, NH

USGS: Fitchburg, Shirley, Clinton, Ayer, Pepperell, *Milford 15*, Manchester 15

The Nashua River has two principal branches, the south, or main river, rising near Worcester, and the North Branch formed by the junction of the Whitman and Nookagee rivers in West Fitchburg. The two branches meet at Lancaster Common and flow north to the Merrimack River at Nashua, New Hampshire. The main river is dammed at Clinton to form the Wachusett Reservoir, which supplies water to Boston. There is, therefore, usually little or no flow through the old river bed between Clinton and the junction with the North Branch at Lancaster Common, so this branch has now become the principal headwater of the river.

Fitchburg — Lancaster   15 miles
NORTH BRANCH

The North Branch flows over many dams through Fitchburg, and the entire river is ruined by the extreme pollution from the many paper mills there, although the pollution is less noticeable in spring high water. Because of the
dams in Fitchburg it is better to put in below, at South
Fitchburg, if this portion is to be run. From there it is 2½
miles of easy paddling in an open valley to North
Leominster. Below North Leominster the valley becomes
more attractive and the river has good current and several
riffles, passing between wooded banks. Despite the filthy
water, this portion, from South Fitchburg or North
Leominster, can make a very pleasant canoe trip in the
spring when the water is high.

Lancaster — Nashua   32 miles

There are no rapids, the dams are rather far apart, and but
for the dirty water this would be a fine smoothwater trip.
From Lancaster through Groton the country is at first
pastoral, then wooded. About 9 miles below Lancaster
Common the river passes under a railroad bridge, and just
below Nonacoicus Brook enters on the right. In another
1½ miles Mulpus Brook enters on the left and shortly
below it the river passes under the Route 2A bridge at
Woodsville. Only ¼ mile below this bridge the Squanna-
cook River enters on the left. At the Route 119 bridge there
was a broken dam, but the water backed up from East
Pepperell has now covered it. From here to East Pepperell, the river is not attractive, as the increase in water
level has flooded swampland and killed the trees. At East
Pepperell there is a long carry around the Nashua River
Paper Company dam. Pull out on the left and carry
½ mile via Mill Street to the bridge below.

At this bridge, on April 19, 1775, when the men of
Pepperell had gone to Concord to answer the alarm, the
women dressed themselves in their husbands' clothing and
armed themselves with whatever they could find. They
patrolled the bridge and arrested a Tory, Captain Leonard
Whiting of Hollis, who was bearing dispatches to the
British in Boston.

From the Mill Street bridge in East Pepperell,
where one puts in below the dam, it is only ¾ mile to the
junction with the Nissitissit. There is moderate current as

far as the broken dam of Ronnell's Mills just below the next bridge, northwest of Hollis Depot. There is an easy portage on the right. Do not run this drop without careful scouting. From here to the upper Nashua dam, there is little current and the banks are mostly wooded, with some pasture land here and there. The upper dam at Nashua is a mile west of town; it is a difficult portage to the right, around the powerhouse. There is a footpath along the river.

There are rapids below the upper dam, then the river goes through housing developments, under the Everett Turnpike, and into the center of Nashua. At the dam, take out above it on the right to run the rapids below or on the left if you intend to portage them. The Nashua shortly empties into the Merrimack River.

NEWFOUND RIVER   NH

This river drains Newfound Lake and flows into the Pemigewasset River at Bristol. It is a short, narrow river of continuous and difficult rapids. In one section the drop is 50 feet in half a mile, and it provides a challenging run in high water for covered boats. In medium water, it is an ideal section for a small inflatable canoe which, being flexible, can easily slither past the rounded boulders.

The annual fall drawdown of Newfound Lake does not provide sufficient water for this run.

Newfound Lake — Bristol   1¾ miles

977 Class II–IV   2¾ km
     High water: *early April*
     Medium water: *late April*
     Forested, Settled
         USGS: Cardigan 15
         Portage: 1¼ mi L **hydroelectric dam — 20 yds**

Begin on the L bank below the dam at the S end of Newfound Lake. The rapids that follow are class II–III for 1 mile to the first millpond. The most difficult drop in this section is just above the first bridge. Portage the dam on the L.

Below the first, small hydroelectric dam (1¼ mi), the rapids soon become class IV. **Caution!** Just 50 yards below the first US-3A bridge, there are two large, nasty spikes sticking straight up from a shoal in the middle of the river waiting patiently for the unsuspecting. Fortunately for the inflatables, they are exposed at medium water. The class IV rapids extend for ½ mile on the E side of the highway, from which the whole section can be scouted. The most difficult pitch is behind a restaurant near the end. Take out at the second millpond beside the lower bridge (1¾ mi).

The remainder of the river is tame by comparison. If curiosity impells you to run it, carry the second hydroelectric dam on the L and begin again in the millrace, which is deeper and more accessible than the main channel. The class I rapids soon end, and they are followed by quickwater. Take out at the NH-104 bridge (2¾ mi), the second in this section. Do not continue, because the river is not easily accessible from the Main Street bridge, and below the latter there is a steep, unrunnable cascade that continues the rest of the way to the Pemigewasset River.

NISSITISSIT RIVER   NH, MA

USGS: Townsend, Pepperell

The Nissitissit River rises in Potanopa Pond, Brookline, New Hampshire, and flows southeast to the Nashua River at Pepperell, Massachusetts. This river is a pleasant quickwater run in high water, except for a few dams and other obstructions. The best time to run is in the spring, or after heavy rains in the summer or fall.

Bohannon Bridge — Pepperell   7 miles

The 2½ mile run from Bohannon Bridge through Campbell's Meadows to West Hollis may have some beaver dams. Some of these can be run, others may require a lift-over. A small fieldstone dam can usually be run. The river has clear water with mostly muddy bottom, and flows through woods and swamps. From West Hollis the 2½ miles to the Prescott Street bridge in North Pepperell is the best part of the river, with good current and wooded banks. It is another 1½ miles to the dam in Pepperell, with some shallow rapids and a long deadwater above the dam. Take out on the left and carry canoes out to the road which crosses just below. There are rapids below the dam. If one continues to the confluence with the Nashua the next point to take out would be the bridge northwest of Hollis Depot, New Hampshire, 3½ miles down the Nashua River.

PEMIGEWASSET RIVER   NH

The Pemi is a born-again river. In the mid-twentieth century, much of it was fetid and frowzy. Today it is clean and clear.

Analysis of the river water in the mid-sixties yielded results typical of severe pollution. Some tests in 1966–67 showed less than a 10% saturation of oxygen. Completion of several waste water treatment facilities has resulted in a significant improvement in water quality during this decade. The Pemigewasset is now a class B river, and it is suitable for swimming and fishing.

The Weeks Act of 1911 authorized the federal government to purchase land in the White Mountains in order to protect watersheds. By that time, many of the steep slopes in the Pemigewasset Watershed had been denuded by logging which in some cases was followed by forest fires. Thus there existed the possibility of serious flooding caused by rapid run-off into the Pemigewasset River. This potential threat to the many communities downstream along the Pemigewasset and Merrimack rivers helped lead to the establishment of the White Mountain National Forest.

Kancamagus Highway — North Woodstock   6 miles
EAST BRANCH

This large, clear river drains the Pemigewasset Wilderness. There are several miles of difficult whitewater above the Kancamagus Highway bridge, but the only way to reach them is to carry up the west bank on the Wilderness Trail or along the east bank following an old road. Below this bridge the rapids are continuous.

There is a fairly even gradient of over 70 feet per mile in this section, but the large drainage basin gives the East Branch a comparatively long season. There is a painted gauge on the center bridge abutment; if it reads a foot or more, the waves and holes will probably be too much for an open boat.

1977   Kancamagus Highway — North Woodstock   6 mi [9¾ km]
Class IV
High water: *difficult, April*
Medium water: *May and after heavy rains*
Forested, Town
   USGS: Mount Osceola, Lincoln
   Portage: 4½ mi L dam at Lincoln

From the bridge on the Kancamagus Highway, the first 2 miles contain broad class III–IV rapids. In the next mile there are more difficult rapids around islands followed by a very rocky and congested section just above the bridge to Loon Mountain.

The 1½ miles from Loon Mountain (3 mi) to the dam in Lincoln contain the most difficult rapids on the river — class IV. Just below the bridge, the rapid created when the dam washed out in 1973 should be looked over carefully, because the waves and holes can be very large. About ½ mile below the bridge there is a steep rapid around islands with a choice of channels. This section should be looked over, as the best route changes from year to year and depends on the water level. Two more heavy rapids lead to a broken dam in Lincoln. **Caution!** The current continues all the way to this dam. Be careful to spot it and pull out on the L to portage. It is sometimes possible to make a scratchy run on the L.

Below the dam (4½ mi) the rapids are easier — class III. There is an "S" turn with very large waves just before the I-93 bridge, followed by easy class II rapids to the confluence with the main river (6 mi).

North Woodstock — Plymouth   23 miles

This section of the Pemigewasset is the most responsive to rainfall and melting snow. The gradient is not so steep that it requires a heavy run-off, as is the case with the East Branch, yet it is just enough to require a good flow for easy passage. A good soaking summer rain can be counted upon to raise the river to medium levels and provide a few days of pleasant boating. Most of the river below Woodstock remains passable at moderately low water, although travel may be slow because some walking down will be necessary. Between Plymouth and Woodstock, I-93 crosses the river four times, so you have a good opportunity to check the water level as you drive along it.

During and after a heavy rain the level of the river can change very quickly. Sometimes in a couple of hours it can amount to several feet. Be conscious of this if you are camping along the river, for there is plenty of evidence that the islands are flooded each year.

Most of this section consists of swift current over a gravel bottom, but there are two stretches with challenging rapids. The most popular one begins at North Woodstock. It is usually a good class II run, but in very high water there are large waves and usually a few fallen trees sticking hazardously out into the main current. Above Livermore Falls in Campton, there are more fine rapids, but high water produces large waves which must be handled carefully in open boats. The danger is that the pools of calm water which are present at medium water cease to exist when the water is high, so that heavy rapids and fast-moving water continue right up to the lip of the falls.

The river is attractive and seemingly remote; that is surprising considering that there are three highways, a railroad, and transmission lines following the narrow valley. All of these are occasionally obvious, but as a whole the trip is a scenic one. In many respects this section is similar to the Saco River from Bartlett to North Conway.

1976   North Woodstock — Plymouth   23 mi |37 km|
Quickwater, Class II–III
High water: *April and after heavy rains*
Medium water: *May and after moderate rains*
Forested, Rural
    USGS: Lincoln, Plymouth 15
Portage: 21 mi R Livermore Falls (difficult) — 300 yds
Campsites: **several islands above West Campton**
       21¼ mi L **beach below Livermore Falls**

Put in at the end of a dirt road that goes to the L of a supermarket near the W end of the Kancamagus Highway. Almost immediately there is a class II rapid with big waves as the East Branch joins the main river coming in on the R. There is a bridge at the end of these rapids (½ mi). For the next 4 miles the river flows through intermittent class II rapids and around islands where the channel is frequently changing. After a RR bridge and a new NH-175 bridge in Woodstock, there is a ledge which should be scouted and possibly carried. The easiest passage is an obscure channel on the L. A second, new NH-175 bridge has been built at these rapids.

Below the ledge in Woodstock (4½ mi) there are quickwater and class I rapids for 5 miles to a bridge in West Thornton past I-93 where there is a put-in on the R reached by a side road to the Robbins Nest Motel. There is more of the same past the second RR bridge (13½ mi), the second crossing of I-93, a bridge in West Campton near a gravel mill (15¾ mi), the mouth of the Mad River (16¾ mi), the third crossing of I-93, and finally the Blair Road covered bridge — exit 27 off I-93.

The Blair Road covered bridge (19 mi) is the first sign of the rapids that precede Livermore Falls. **Caution!** In high water, continue beyond here with care, because a boat that becomes swamped or capsized in these rapids might be swept over Livermore Falls. There is much less danger of this in medium water. The rapids begin 1 mile below the covered bridge, and they are class II in medium water. When the water is high, they are class III

with heavy waves under the third RR bridge (20¼ mi), followed by a straight stretch of fast-moving water for ½ mile
before the R turn that precedes Livermore Falls (21 mi). In
high water it is advisable to hug the R bank before the turn
and to avoid some class II rapids by lining around the corner to the sandy beach to the R of the falls. The trail up
from the river is a difficult one, for it follows a route across
a ledge beside the beach and up to the infrequently used
RR tracks. Livermore Falls can be reached via a short tar
road that leads down off US-3 about 1 mile N of the I-93
overpass in Plymouth.

If you are continuing downstream, follow the RR
tracks past the cut. Take either the steep trail that leads
down to the pool below the falls, or continue on to a woods
road that descends at an easier grade to the river at the
bottom of the next set of rapids. You can also portage
along the ledges beside the river.

Below the pool at the base of Livermore Falls,
there is an island. The class II rapids around to the L are
easier than those on the R. There is quickwater in the last
1¾ miles to Plymouth. A little past the fourth crossing of
I-93 is the mouth of the Baker River (22¾ mi). Access to
the river at the bridge in Plymouth (23 mi) is poor.

Plymouth — Bristol   15¾ miles

This is an attractive and easy section. There are only a few
houses along the banks, and roads are only occasionally
visible. For much of the distance, however, I-93 lies close
enough to the L bank so the traffic is frequently heard even
though it is seldom seen.

For two-thirds of the distance there is a good
current, but after that you are in the deadwater behind
Ayres Island Dam above Bristol. On very rare occasions in
the fall the water level behind the dam is drawn down,
exposing wide mud and sand banks that are visible from
the interstate highway. The effect is noticeable as far back
as the Squam River where a ledge becomes exposed and is
difficult to pass.

1976   Plymouth — Bristol   15¾ mi [25½ km]
        Lake, Flatwater, Quickwater
        Passable at most water levels
        Forested. Rural
            USGS: Plymouth 15, Holderness 15
            Portage: 15¾ mi R **Ayres Island Dam** — ½ mi

There is an easy put-in on the S bank of the Baker River at the US-3 bridge. It is about ½ mile to the bridge in Plymouth (0 mi).

From the bridge in Plymouth the river has fast current for many miles. Good current continues past the US-3 bridge in Ashland (4¼ mi) to the mouth of the Squam River (6¼ mi) where there is a small ledgy island. Low water at this point exposes some more ledges which are not normally noticeable. The current weakens in the next 3 miles as you approach the deadwater behind Ayres Island Dam.

There is a public access to the river on the W bank beside the NH-104 bridge in New Hampton (12¼ mi). Portage the dam (15¾ mi) on the R.

Bristol — Franklin   15 miles

Below Ayres Island Dam in Bristol, there are 1½ miles of heavy rapids which vary in difficulty with the water level. Usually they are class II, but during periods of heavy runoff the current is powerful and the waves are large.

This dam supplies peaking power, so when the flow in the river is low you must time your trip with the demand for electricity. During the week there is usually a medium water flow of 1500 cubic feet per second from 9–12 AM and from 1–3 PM. On Sundays there is often a low water flow of 500 cfs from 9 AM to 3 PM. A call to the dispatcher at the Public Service Company of New Hampshire (603-225-6182) can give you current information.

Eastman Falls Dam at Franklin is also operated by the Public Service Company. The generation schedule is about the same as at Ayres Island Dam in Bristol.

The best run on this portion of the river is the 7½-mile section from the Bristol dam to Hill. There are rapids and quickwater most of the way. It is a scenic trip with secluded shorelines altered somewhat by the effects of periodic flooding.

Hill has a ghost-like atmosphere. Back from the river a short distance, the main street, somewhat dilapidated but complete with a sidewalk, is lined with maples and elms that are aged and in poor health. The driveways are also lined with old trees, and lone apple trees dot the farmyards. But there are no houses, no telephone poles, and no people; only cows and corn. The town is gone; moved when the Franklin Falls Flood Control Dam was built downstream. Today, standing in the still fertile fields, you can almost feel the past.

The trip below Hill is not as attractive. The effects of flooding are more noticeable, and the flood control dam necessitates an uninteresting and somewhat difficult portage. Shortly beyond there is another portage around Eastman Falls Dam. The rapids at Franklin, easier than those in Bristol, would be a more logical part of a trip down the Merrimack River.

It is interesting to note that normal spring run-off causes the pool behind the flood control dam to rise only 7 or 8 feet from late March through April. In this decade the high levels have been recorded at other times of the year. In early July 1973 the pool was 70 feet deep, or 66% of capacity. The next highest was in December of that year: 48 feet or 33% of capacity. For two days in August 1976, the aftermath of Hurricane Belle resulted in a pool 24 feet deep that took two days to drain off.

1976	Bristol — Franklin	15 mi [24¼ km]

Lake, Flatwater, Quickwater, Class II
High water: *heavy waves, spring run-off*
Medium water: *1500 cfs*
Low water: *scratchy, 500 cfs*
Dam-controlled: *peak load hydroelectric stations*
Forested, Rural
USGS: Holderness 15, Penacook 15
Portages: 12½ mi L **Franklin Falls Flood Control Dam** — ½ mi
14 mi R **Eastman Falls Dam** — 200 yds
No camping

One mile E of the center of Bristol on NH-104 a road R leads past some highway department buildings and down the hill. Take a L turn near a water treatment facility and follow the dirt road to the river just below the dam.

In the first 1½ miles there are several nice class II rapids which have heavy class III waves at high water levels. The last important drop is ½ mile below the Bristol bridge at a R turn. This rapid should be run on the inside of the bend. If you wish to run only the rapids, there is a road along the L bank.

Quickwater continues for the next 3½ miles past the mouth of the Smith River (3½ mi) and around a large island. One mile after the flatwater begins, the valley widens; and there are fields on the R. This is Hill, at the other end of which there are some old bridge abutments (7½ mi). The river at this point can be reached from US-3A.

Flatwater continues to the Franklin Falls Flood Control Dam (12¼ mi). Road access to this dam is off NH-127 at a sign N of Franklin. If you are continuing down the river, portage on the L from the log boom up over the dam and down to either of the two bays of the deadwater below. After this dam there is a deadwater above the power dam at Franklin (14 mi). Portage on the R. There is a 1-mile class II rapid in the remaining distance to the confluence with the Winnipesaukee River (15 mi).

PISCATAQUOG RIVER, North Branch NH

The North Branch rises to the southwest of Concord in Deering and flows east and south to join with the South Branch just above Goffstown. The upper part is steep and rocky with several obstacles, while the lower portion is a pleasant quickwater run. They are separated by a large flood control dam at Everett.

Lake Horace — Everett   9 miles

Scouted only. The upper river appears to be about class III, with several potentially rough spots. Fortunately there is nearly always a road nearby, although it is often out-of-sight because the banks are thickly wooded. High water is necessary, and early April is probably the best time to run it. See the USGS Hillsboro 15 and Weare sheets.

Put in below the dam on Lake Horace. The first mile is especially rough due to several old damsites. There is a 20-foot dam in North Weare. The rapids ease up until a mile below North Weare, where it may be necessary to line around three difficult chutes. The river below here is within the maximum pool of the flood control dam, but the permanent pool does not begin for another 3 miles.

Take out on the left near the junction of Choate Brook (8 mi). This point can be reached by proceeding westward for 3 miles on NH-77 from Pages Corner (the NH 13/77 junction), turning south on Sugar Hill Road, and continuing past the "Road Closed" sign. It is also possible to paddle a mile down the permanent lake to the dam.

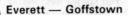

Everett — Goffstown   8½ miles

976 Quickwater   13¾ km
High or medium water: *spring and after moderate rain*
Rural
    USGS: Weare, *Goffstown*
    Portage: 5¼ mi R **dam in Riverdale**

Put in just below the flood control dam by carrying past the "Road Closed" sign. The bridge ½ mile below offers an alternate put-in. The river winds with a gentle current through meadowlands to Riverdale, where the dam above the bridge should be carried on the R. Be considerate of the landowner.

Below the dam (5¼ mi) there are 1¼ miles of easy river to the NH-114 bridge (6½ mi), where there is a boat ramp, and another ½ mile to the junction with the South Branch (7 mi). The bridge at Goffstown (8½ mi) is 1½ miles below.

PISCATAQUOG RIVER, South Branch NH

The South Branch rises southwest of Concord in Francestown and flows east and northeast to join the North Branch just above Goffstown. The upper river has too many obstructions to be popular, but the lower river is frequently used as a whitewater practice run. Someone who is going to run the "Piscataquog" is usually refering to the section below New Boston.

Francestown — Old Bridge   7½ miles

Scouted only. This portion contains mixed rapids and smoothwater. There are several sharp drops, some of which must be carried. See the Peterborough 15 and New Boston sheets.

Put in at the NH-136 bridge east of Francestown. There are 1½ miles of beaver swamp to the first bridge on the Francestown-to-Mount Vernon road — the Second New Hampshire Turnpike — below which there is a steep rapid that is runnable only in high water. There is a sharp drop under a side road bridge ¼ mile further, then 1¾ miles of mixed smoothwater and rapids to the next turnpike bridge (3½ mi). In ½ mile there is another side road bridge followed by a partially broken dam and a difficult rapid emptying into a marshy pond.

Below the pond there is a bridge in the middle of an impassable gorge which must be portaged for ¼ mile. Then there are 1½ miles of mixed smoothwater and rapids to a high brick chimney which marks an old paper mill site where there is a chute full of old iron machinery. From that point it is a mile to an abandoned bridge where a side road parallels the river (7½ mi).

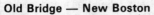
976   Class I–II   5¾ km
                High water: *March thru early April*
                Rural, Towns
                    USGS: New Boston
                Portages: ¾ mi R **small dam** (lift over)
                             2½ mi R **1st dam in New Boston** — 50 yds
                             3¼ mi R **2nd dam in New Boston** — 300 yds

     This bridge can be reached by taking a side road
to the W off NH-13 a mile S of New Boston and proceeding for approximately 2 miles, crossing the river midway.
Put in wherever it is convenient.

     From the abandoned bridge (0 mi) there is ¾ mile
of class I rapids to a small dam which can sometimes be
run, followed by another ½ mile to a side road bridge.
Below this bridge class II rapids lead in 1¼ miles to a dam
which should be portaged on the R. Rapids continue for
¼ mile to the NH-13 bridge, just below which there is a
millpond. Carry the dam in the center of New Boston
(3¼ mi) on the R down the street for 300 yards, and put in
near the next NH-13 bridge. In ¼ mile, pass a bridge by the
old RR station (3½ mi).

976   Quickwater, **Class I–II**   12 km
                High water: *March thru early April*
                Rural, Towns
                    USGS: New Boston, Weare, *Goffstown*

     The most convenient starting point in New
Boston is the old RR station across the second bridge
below the dam. In about ¼ mile there is a class II rapid at
an old damsite, and after another ¼ mile there is a side
road bridge.

     For the next 5 miles NH-13 is often in sight on
the R bank. Many of the rapids in this section are artificial
because rocks have been placed in the river to improve the
fish habitat. These present no problems at high water, but
they require careful route selection at lower levels. It is
2½ miles to the next bridge, below which the Middle
Branch (3 mi) enters on the L. The next 1½ miles to a
bridge (4½ mi) and a gauging station are somewhat easier.

     One mile below the gauging station the road
leaves the river, and the rapids end. There are numerous

meanders with a fast current, fallen trees, and many channels. The North Branch (6 mi), indistinguishable from other channels, enters on the L. From there it is 1½ miles to the bridge at Goffstown (7½ mi).

POWWOW RIVER   NH, MA

This small stream in southeastern New Hampshire has two sections which offer pleasant canoeing in areas that are largely isolated. See the USGS Haverhill 15, Exeter, and Newburyport West sheets.

The first section begins in Kingston. Put in just below the outlet of Great Pond where NH-111/125 crosses the river. One and a half miles of narrow stream in a picturesque marsh give way to 1¼ miles of more open water above Powwow Pond, where there are many cottages. Take out at the east end of the pond to the left of a railroad bridge (4 mi). A short dirt road leads out to NH-107A.

The second section begins off NH-107A on Chase Road. There are about 2 miles of stream — narrow at first — before the river reaches Tuxbury Pond. The dam at the outlet (3½ mi) is just over the state line in Amesbury, Massachusetts.

SALMON BROOK   MA, NH

Salmon Brook is a very small stream which rises in Groton, Massachusetts, and flows northward to enter the Merrimack River in Nashua, New Hampshire. There are no long rapids or difficult portages, but there are some short carries around jams, dams, and culverts. The section above Massapoag Pond is very difficult because of obstructions, but the rest of the river is relatively easy.

 Route 40 — Nashua   **10½ miles**

xxxx	Lakes, **Flatwater**, Quickwater, Class I 15 km

High to medium water: *March and April*

Forested, Rural, Settled

USGS: Ayer, Pepperell, Nashua South

Portages: 2½ mi R **dam above Massapoag Pond** — 20 yds
                4 mi   **dam on Massapoag Pond**
                5 mi   **culvert at MA-113** — 20 yds

Scouted only. Begin in Groton on MA-40 near the N end of Cow Pond — Whitney Pond on the Ayer Quadrangle. Put in at the marshy outlet of a tiny private pond just N of the highway.

Cow Pond Brook, as Salmon Brook is called at the beginning, provides a bushy ride for several miles to a pond. There is a dam at the outlet (2½ mi) which requires a short portage on the R. After another 100 yards the brook empties into Massapoag Pond, a narrow lake 1¼ miles long. The next body of water, following shortly, is Lower Massapoag Pond.

Below Lower Massapoag Road a culvert at MA-113 (5 mi) in Dunstable usually requires a short portage. For most of the remaining 5½ miles the course of the brook is through woods, swamps, and farmlands. There are many possible take-outs as Nashua is approached. One is on Harris Road (10½ mi), which is the last bridge before the Everett Turnpike. It is located just S of exit 4.

The remainder of the stream through Nashua is unattractive.

SHAWSHEEN RIVER   MA

This quiet little meadow stream rises in Bedford and flows roughly northeast into the Merrimack at Lawrence. The section above the mill at Ballardvale in Andover makes one of the better one-day paddles close to Boston. All but the uppermost part of the river (MA-4 to US-3) can be run through the spring in most years. Dams, factories, and pollution below Ballardvale become increasingly offensive, making the lower part of the river less pleasant.

Bedford — Ballardvale   **15¼ miles**

1975   **Flatwater**, Class I   24½ km
       High water: *April*
       Medium water: *May and June*
       Forested, Settled
          USGS: Concord, *Billerica*, Wilmington, *Lawrence*
          Portage: 1+ mi R **rapids below MA-62** (rough) — 250 yds

With high enough water a put-in can be made at the concrete MA-4 bridge in Bedford. The Bedford sewage pumping and water pollution control station on the L provides a convenient if unaesthetic start. The river is shallow and rocky as it heads through woods and marshes. This type of running continues past the Page Road bridge to the green-railed MA-62 bridge.

While the riffles beneath the MA-62 bridge (1 mi) require less water than those above, the rapids just out-of-sight below this bridge are usually unrunnable. It is possible to carry your canoe on the R bank — a tough,

250-yard portage amidst boulders and trees. Sometimes a canoe can be lined or walked through in medium water. After these rapids ¾ mile of smoothwater through marshes follows to the US-3 bridge (2 mi), and then there is another similar meandering mile to the double-barreled culvert at the Middlesex Turnpike (3 mi). More smoothwater with current brings the paddler to MA-3A (4½ mi), where the low bridge may necessitate a portage on the R. Three and a quarter miles with wooded or marshy banks lead to the MA-129 bridge (7¾ mi), just below which there is a rapid formed by the collapsed ruins of the Middlesex Canal. Fallen trees in this section may require short lift-overs.

Enter the rapid by the old Middlesex Canal on the R side of the abutment, and turn sharply L at the end of the channel to avoid sharp-cornered stone blocks. Since this passage may be obstructed, it should be looked over first. In the next mile a RR bridge, the low Whipple Road bridge, and the mouth of Content Brook (8¾ mi) on the L are passed. The MA-38 bridge (10 mi) is next, followed in about a mile by a short class II rapid just after a minor road bridge. Follow a smaller R channel which is both deep and steep. There is an occasional riffle and the I-93 bridge in the remaining 4 miles to the dam in Andover at Ballardvale (15¼ mi). After a low bridge just above the dam, a take-out can be made on either side.

If continuing downstream, take out on the L above the low bridge and carry through the Spectrametrics Company parking lot to the stream.

The remainder of this description is not current. The 2½ miles to the center of Andover consist of smoothwater with current. The banks are steeper and more heavily wooded in this stretch than elsewhere on the river. The first of the two dams in Andover is complicated by wire fencing which limits access, the L side is probably better. Another ½ mile brings you to the next dam. After about a mile there are two 2-foot drops.

After leaving Andover the river passes under the MA-114 bridge (20¼ mi) and continues on through South Lawrence to the Merrimack River (22¾ mi).

SMITH RIVER   NH

The Smith River rises near Grafton as a small stream and flows east to the Pemigewasset River near Bristol. The upper part is a pleasant quickwater trip, while the lower part contains difficult rapids. There is a scenic waterfall below the part normally run. The banks are wooded, and there are frequent road and railroad crossings, so trips of varying length can be planned.

976   Flatwater, **Quickwater** Class I   21 km
        High water: *April*
        Forested, Rural
            USGS: Cardigan 15

        Put in from the road to the Ruggles Mine just W
of Grafton Center. In the first 6½ miles to Fords Crossing,
where there are adjacent RR and road bridges (the first of
two such pairs), the river is a winding meadow brook with
overhanging bushes and occasional, fallen trees. There is
often quickwater under bridges. The next 6½ miles are
more open and less obstructed, and they lead you past the
US-4 bridge (9¼ mi) to the girder bridge on NH-104.
        Just above the NH-104 bridge (13 mi) there is a
short class II rapid which can be avoided by taking out just
above it at the Eastern District Road bridge.

NH-104 — Profile Gorge   8 miles

The river in this section offers some very fine whitewater
boating. The rapids above South Alexandria are the most
challenging, but the nearby Smith River Road provides an
easy retreat. Below South Alexandria the pitch is more
moderate, and civilization is less evident from the river.
The gorge and waterfall at the end of the trip deserve
exploration — on foot.
        There is a hand-painted gauge on the left abut-
ment of the Cass Mill Road bridge in South Alexandria. It is
possible to scratch down the river with a water level of
–0.5. Medium water is considered to give a reading of
 0.5; high water is 1.0.

977   NH-104 — Profile Gorge   8 mi [13 km]
        Flatwater, **Class III–IV**
        High or medium water: *April to mid-May*
        Forested, Town
            USGS: Cardigan 15, Holderness 15

        Access from Smith River Road: The best access is
off the old highway, now called Smith River Road,
although part of it may be snow-covered in early spring.
The upper end of it can be reached by turning off NH-104
at Murry Hill Road. To reach it at South Alexandria, turn off
at Cass Mill Road.

Below the NH-104 bridge is ¼ mile of class III ledges, including an old dam; then ¾ mile of smoothwater to the bridge on Murray Hill Road.

Below the Murray Hill Road bridge (1 mi) there is a short stretch of flatwater; then comes the first rapid in a L bend. This is the first of two brief class III rapids, each followed by quiet stretches. Next comes a class IV section, full of small rocks and cross-currents, that rushes past a picnic area on the R shore and down to the next bridge (1¾ mi) on Smith River Road. For those desiring a shorter and slightly easier run, this bridge is a possible put-in.

Below the second bridge there is 1 mile of continuous class III–IV rapids, where the pace is very fast in high water. At the end of this mile there is a short drop in a R turn — a large rock and hole sit in the center forcing boaters to one side or the other. The L side is preferable, although another rock upstream of the main hole must be avoided. Below this drop the river divides around an island just before the Cass Mill Road bridge. The R side contains the hardest rapid on the river, a tough class IV over large rocks and ledges, and it should be scouted before running. The L side is much more gradual in descent and much easier to navigate.

Below the Cass Mill Road bridge in South Alexandria (3 mi), the first ½ mile contains class III–IV rapids, and it is often run with the stretch above. A set of powerlines (3½ mi) can be used to spot the point where the rapids moderate. This powerline crossing can be reached from Smith River Road, which follows the L bank from South Alexandria.

Below the powerlines (3½ mi) there are 2 miles of class III rapids, then ½ mile in which the rapids diminish to mere current. At this point the bridge to Smith River Campground (6 mi) is passed. Then there are 2 miles of smoothwater to a broken dam (8 mi) which can be run on either the L or the R at certain water levels. **Caution!** It is best to take out above the dam, as the river below is more suitable for sightseeing than boating.

Shortly below the broken dam (8 mi), the Smith River foams through Profile Gorge, a 150-yard rock-walled stretch which can be viewed from a high cement bridge at the gorge entrance. A quarter mile of moderate rapids follows to a bad drop just above the NH-3A bridge. Beneath the bridge is the beginning of Profile Falls (8½ mi), where the Smith River slides over ledges for 100 yards before plunging down a 30-foot vertical drop. A road on the L bank leads to a parking area at the foot of the falls. The river from there to the Pemigewasset River (9 mi) is class II.

SOUCOOK RIVER NH

North of Loudon near Pearls Corner, Bumfagon Brook and
Gues Meadow Brook join to form the Soucook River,
which flows south to the Merrimack River below Concord.
It is a pleasant, winding stream with a good current and
largely undeveloped banks.

It is possible to begin ¾ mile upstream from
Pearls Corner at the second bridge on Pearls Corner Road,
but that section has class II rapids blocked by deadfalls.

The last 11 miles beginning at the US-4 bridge
east of Concord are especially recommended because
there are no carries. This lower portion of the Soucook is
more difficult at medium water levels, when there are
several class II rapids and innumerable riffles. At high flows
many of them are washed out, so there are only occasional
rapids. If there is not enough water to run the rock dam
just above the bridge, the river is too low for an enjoyable
trip below.

Pearls Corner — Merrimack River	22 miles

Flatwater, **Quickwater**, Class I–II 35½ km
High water: *April*
Forested, Rural, Town
    USGS: Gilmanton 15, Suncook, *Concord*
  Portages: 5 mi L **dam at Loudon** — 50 yds
               8½ mi R **Cascade Park** — 200 yds

Put in just below the confluence at a bridge on a
side road E of Pearls Corner. There are 2½ miles of good
current in a winding meadow stream to the first bridge,
then another 2½ miles to the dam in Loudon, half of which
is deadwater. Take out on the L and carry across the road.
The short, rocky class II rapids below can be lined if necessary. There follow 2½ miles of good current and occasional
rapids between wooded banks to the new NH-106 bridge.

Below the NH-106 bridge (7½ mi) there is a mile
of flatwater to a rocky class IV rapid which can only be run
under favorable conditions. Portage 200 yards on the R
through the Cascade Park picnic area to a pool below. It is
½ mile to the next side road bridge (9 mi), below which the
river forms the eastern boundary of the city of Concord.
In 2 miles there is a 1-foot dam at a gauging station just
above the US-4 bridge.

Below the US-4 bridge (11 mi) the river passes under an old truss bridge almost immediately, and just beyond is a class II rapid. Then there is more quickwater as the river winds between steep, wooded banks that are often a hundred feet high. Watch out for fallen trees, particularly at high flows when the current is strong. The river passes a covered bridge with a new bridge below it. After the NH-106 bridge (15¾ mi) class II rapids occur with more frequency, ending with a fast class II drop at a ledge ½ mile above the high US-3 bridge (18½ mi).

Two and a half miles below the US-3 bridge occasional easy rapids start. In ¾ mile is a swimming hole (21¾ mi) reached by a dirt road on the L bank from the Plausawa Country Club. Just beyond the old RR grade you reach the Merrimack River (22 mi).

The nearest take-out point on the Merrimack is ¾ mile upstream at Garvin's Falls, or 3 miles downstream where River Road is adjacent to the R bank.

SOUHEGAN RIVER   NH

The Souhegan River rises in the Pack Monadnock and more southerly ranges and flows north and east to the Merrimack River between Manchester and Nashua. The upper portion offers a good, intermediate whitewater trip, while lower down the river has a mixture of smoothwater and rapids. The river banks are usually unsettled except near towns.

Greenville — Milford,   12¾ miles

This portion of the river contains a short stretch of class III rapids, then a longer section of class II rapids, followed by more class III rapids above Wilton. Below Wilton there are more class II rapids. Roads are nearby in case difficulties are encountered.

XXXX

Greenville — Milford		12¾ mi [20½ km]

Quickwater, **Class II–III**
High water: *late March to mid-April*
Rural, Towns
    USGS: Peterborough 15, Milford
    Portages: 6¾ mi L **first dam at Wilton**
                7 mi   **more dams in Wilton** — ½ mi
           12¾ mi   **several dams in Milford** — ½ mi

Although it may be possible to canoe above Greenville, it is not recommended due to an impassable gorge above the old power station below town.

Put in at the site of the old hydroelectric plant on a short side road off NH-31 a mile N of Greenville and ¼ mile N of a RR overpass. The rapids exposed by the removal of this dam should not be attempted because the reinforcing rods used to build it are still in place in the bottom of the river.

The first mile to the NH-31 bridge consists of rocky class III rapids with several small ledges. From this bridge there are 3½ miles of tough class II rapids to a through girder bridge on a side road. The rocks are small, so these rapids tend to wash out at high water. Then there are 1¼ miles of fast current to the NH-101 bridge, where the rapids begin again.

The class III rapids beginning at the NH-101 bridge (5¾ mi) are more difficult than those below the old power station. The paddler must dodge large rocks in a very swift current. In ¾ mile there is a sharp class IV drop over a ledge which is best run on the L. A dirt road leading away from the river on the L can be used for scouting, carrying, or taking out.

After the second section of difficult rapids there is ¼ mile of fastwater to the first dam in Wilton (6¾ mi). Portage on the L and continue through ¼ mile of rocky class III rapids to a bridge and the mouth of Stony Brook on the L. The second dam is just below them.

At the second dam (7 mi) there are two options. You can carry for ½ mile along the road through Wilton to the bridge at the E end of town, and by so doing avoid more dams and a stretch of river which is often dry due to diversion of the water into a power canal which parallels the river. However, if there is water in the river, you can put in below the last dam. Follow a steep, dirt road over the RR tracks, and run ½ mile of class II rapids to the bridge mentioned above, near which the power canal rejoins the river.

From the bridge at the east end of Wilton, class II rapids continue for ¾ mile, ending just past the truss bridge at Jones Crossing. This marks the end of the rapids on the upper river, and it is the usual take-out point for paddlers interested primarily in whitewater.

From Jones Crossing (8¼ mi) there are 4½ miles of winding stream with a fast current and a few fallen trees to Milford (12¾ mi).

If you are continuing downstream, there are several dams in Milford to portage. To avoid them, it is recommended that you break your trip above the first one and begin again below town. Take out above the bridge in the center of town and begin again in ½ mile.

Milford — Merrimack **13 miles**

XXXX | Flatwater, Quickwater, Class I–II | 21 km
High water: *spring*
Rural, Towns
USGS: *Milford,* South Merrimack, *Nashua North*
Portages: 12 mi L **Wildcat Falls** — ¼ mi
13 mi **dam at Merrimack**

Put in by carrying down between the houses opposite the A & P on NH-101A. Except for a rocky class II rapid beneath the high NH-101 bridge, this section begins with 2 miles of quickwater.

Below the NH-122 bridge (2 mi) it is 5½ miles past two more bridges to a sharp R turn where there is a class II ledge. Then the river splits around two low islands, below which is Indian Ledge, a class III rapid which should be scouted. The best carry starts on the R above the islands, but you can also run the class II rapids on the L and then line the main drop down a side channel. Then there are 2¼ miles of smoothwater to the Turkey Hill bridge.

The Turkey Hill bridge (10 mi) is a recommended take-out point if you wish to avoid the portage at Wildcat Falls farther downstream.

Three-quarters of a mile below the Turkey Hill bridge there is an easy class II rapid, followed by 1¼ miles of slackwater to Wildcat Falls (12 mi). Take out on the L and carry ¼ mile around the falls which are doubly hazardous as they are likely to be jammed with debris. Then it is ¼ mile with two short class II rapids to the high Everett Turnpike bridge, under which there is a short class III rapid. One-half mile further is the dam and US-3 bridge at Merrimack (13 mi). Only ¼ mile of fastwater brings you to the Merrimack River (13¼ mi).

STONY BROOK NH

Stony Brook, a small stream west of Manchester and Nashua, is a tributary of the Souhegan River. Because of its size, it is less reliable and less frequently runnable than the Souhegan. When there is enough water, Stony Brook provides a short run comparable, in the last part, to the tougher stretches of the Souhegan.

1975   Class II–III   4¾ km
High water: *late March to early April*
Forested
     USGS: Peterborough 15, Milford
     Portage: 2¾ mi   L   **sawmill — 20 yds**

From the put-in at the NH-31 bridge just below South Lyndeboro, there are 1½ miles of class II rapids to the next NH-31 bridge. The river then turns L under a RR bridge and drops through some class III ledges which should be looked over from the highway nearby. The next mile has many more such ledges, all runnable at the right water levels, but necessitating caution.

The dam at the sawmill (2¾ mi) above Wilton can be portaged on the L. More rapids continue to Wilton (3 mi). Take out on the R where there is an artificial, stone embankment.

In the next 100 yards to the Souhegan River, there is a dam which necessitates a short, steep portage on either side. Most boaters will not want to make this portage.

SUDBURY and CONCORD RIVERS   MA

Beginning near Worcester in Westboro, the Assabet River flows northeastward to the town of Concord where it meets the Sudbury, which, also starting in Westboro, has flowed east and then north. From the confluence of these two rivers, the Concord River flows northward to join the Merrimack in Lowell.

The Indians called the Concord River "Musketaquid." They planted crops on its meadows, fished from its banks, hunted the animals of its valleys, migrated along it annually to and from the seacoast, and used it as a trade route. Thousands of specimens of implements and weapons have been found just in Concord.

The early settlers first used these rivers as the Indians had, soon adding small dams, mostly on the tributaries of the main rivers, to run grist mills and saw mills. After the completion of the Middlesex Canal in 1803, the rivers were used more for transportation. Bog iron dug in Sudbury was shipped by boat to the iron works in Chelmsford, and there was a lot of traffic between points along the rivers and Boston via the canal. That traffic ended in 1840 when the canal ceased being used, a victim of the newly-completed railroads.

The water in the Concord River and its tributaries has, at various times, been used to power mills and later factories, flood the Middlesex Canal, and, in the case of the Sudbury, supply water to Boston. Some of the dams have been washed out, the canal is dry and can be followed only on foot, and Metropolitan Boston depends primarily upon the Quabbin Reservoir west of Worcester for its water. A brief history of the river can be found in *Concord River,* Barre Publishers, Barre, MA 01005, 1964.

Most of the Sudbury and all of the Concord River above North Billerica are influenced by the dam at Talbot Mills. These rivers have wide, marshy flood plains, much of which is included in the Great Meadows National Wildlife Refuge. In the high water of early spring, these flood plains resemble long lakes more than rivers, so the wind direction is a more important concern than current. In fact, the size of the meadows makes travel against a headwind difficult in any season.

Framingham Center — Saxonville   3¼ miles
SUDBURY RIVER

Canoeing above Framingham Center is impractical due to the size of the stream and reservoir use restrictions. Impoundment at these reservoirs may make this section very low, but there is usually enough water to float a canoe. The river in the last part is pleasantly suburban.

1975 | Framingham Center — Saxonville   3¼ mi [5¼ km]
Flatwater, Class I
Passable at most water levels
Settled
    USGS: Framingham
    Portages: 1½ mi e **low dam** — 10 yds
                 3¼ mi R **dam at Saxonville** — 100 yds

The best put-in is at Main Street, which is just S of MA-9. The river is sluggish, and parts of it are broad. There are many bridges, including those of MA-9 and I-90 (the Massachusetts Turnpike). One and a half miles from Main Street there is a low but dangerous dam which is easily lifted over. The last mile to Saxonville is more pond-like than the part above. Portage the dam at Saxonville (3¼ mi) on the R.

Saxonville — Concord 16¾ miles
SUDBURY RIVER

The urban setting of Saxonville is soon left behind as you travel downstream through sparsely settled, suburban communities. High wooded banks give way to the wide meadows that characterize this river and the Concord River below. From Saxonville to North Billerica, there are 27½ miles of unobstructed flatwater.

977

Saxonville — Concord	16¾ mi [27 km]

Lake, **Flatwater**
Passable at all water levels
Forested
    USGS: Framingham, Natick, Maynard, Concord

Saxonville can be reached by following Central Street N from MA-9 in Framingham Center. It crosses the river at the dam.

For a short distance the stream is very shallow in low water, when it will float only a lightly laden craft. Below the dam the river turns sharply L, passing under a concrete road bridge and an older stone RR bridge. In 2½ miles, there are a road bridge and the remains of a stone bridge which was built in 1673 and later became known as Stone's Bridge. From here the river meanders through a wide marsh to Concord.

One and three quarters miles below Stone's Bridge (2½ mi) a small tributary on the L can be canoed in high water for 300 yards to Heard Pond in Wayland. This stream is sometimes hard to find. There are four more bridges before the MA-117 bridge (11¾ mi) which is ½ mile before the river enters Fairhaven Bay.

Fairhaven Bay (12½ mi) is a ½-mile-long lake on the border between Concord and Lincoln. At the head of the bay was the Baker Farm, immortalized by Emerson. Further down on the L are Conantum Cliffs, named by Thoreau from an old cellar that was once part of the Conant Farm. North of the bay is Fairhaven Hill where Thoreau frequently picked berries.

The river is wider as it leaves Fairhaven Bay. There is one bridge before MA-2 (15 mi). Just below a RR bridge is the Old South Bridge (15½ mi), originally built around 1660, with the South Bridge Boat House next to it on the L. Next comes the stone Elm Street bridge. Then the river turns sharply R, skirts the slopes of Nashawtuc Hill on the L, and passes under one more bridge. On the R was the studio of Walton Ricketson, an intimate of Thoreau and the Alcotts. After passing the site of an old RR bridge (16½ mi), the Assabet joins the Sudbury River to form the Concord River. There is a good picnic spot here on the L at Egg Rock. The next take-out is 200 yards down the Concord River at the Lowell Street bridge (16¾ mi).

Concord — North Billerica   10¾ miles
CONCORD RIVER

This portion of the river has many spots of historical interest which are mentioned below. Only the volume of motorboat traffic disturbs the placid quality of the Concord.

1975	Concord — North Billerica	10¾ mi [17¼ km]
	Flatwater	
	Passable at all water levels	
	Forested, Rural, Settled	
	USGS: Concord, Billerica	
	Portage: 10¾ mi R **dam at Talbot Mills** (difficult in high water)	

From the Lowell Road bridge (0 mi) in Concord, 200 yards below the confluence of the Assabet and Sudbury rivers, the Concord River flows NE. On the L is the hill on which the Minute Men formed to march to battle from the farmhouse of Major Buttrick. The house still stands behind the present Buttrick mansion. A tablet marks the mustering field. At the first sharp bend of the river is the Old Manse on the R. Here is the orchard of which Hawthorne wrote, and beyond in a field were traces of Indian camps mentioned by Thoreau. Then the river passes under the Old North Bridge replica where "the embattled farmers fired the shot heard 'round the world." The original bridge was built on an old ford in 1654 and removed in 1792. The Minute Man statue stands nearby on the L, and there are memorial tablets and graves of British soldiers on the R. This area is a part of Minute Man National Historical Park.

In another ¼ mile Monument Street bridge is passed, but it does not afford easy access. The river flows NE for 2 miles and then swings N, keeping Balls Hill on the L. In another 2 miles the MA-225 bridge (4½ mi) is passed. Mill Brook enters ¾ mile farther on the R. Its mouth is marked by large stones known as the Two Brothers. These markers were reputedly set to mark the division of lands between Governor Winthrop and Deputy Governor Thomas Dudley, in remembrance that they were brothers by their children's marriage.

The MA-4 bridge (6½ mi), also known as Hill's Bridge, was built by the people of Tyngsboro and Chelmsford after a riot and lawsuit with the people of Billerica who did not want it built for fear it would divert business from the center of that town, which was served by a bridge 2 miles further downstream. The river continues past the US-3 bridge (7½ mi), the MA-3A bridge (9¼ mi), and the North Billerica bridge (10¼ mi) to the dam at Talbot Mills (10¾ mi).

If you are continuing on to the Merrimack, the portage around this dam is difficult. There is no easy entry into the water below the dam due to industrial fencing. If possible, it is best to look this spot over and plan the portage before arriving at the dam. When the water is low, the canoe may be carried over the edge of the dam on the R.

North Billerica — Lowell   4½ miles
CONCORD RIVER

The last section of the Concord River is not recommended. The river itself is unattractive, and the water is polluted. Passage around the three dams is difficult, and a set of rapids is unusually nasty because of debris in the river.

Thoreau did not canoe on this part of the river in *A Week on the Concord and Merrimack River*. He took the canal from North Billerica to Lowell.

972 | North Billerica — Lowell | 4½ mi [7¼ km]
Flatwater, Class II
Passable at most water levels
Urban
    USGS: Billerica, Lowell
    Portages: 3 mi L **10-foot dam** (difficult)
                    4¼ mi R **20-foot dam** (difficult)

Once past the North Billerica dam, there is about a 3-mile flatwater paddle to a 10-foot dam. This dam and the rapids below can be portaged on the L up over a small concrete bank, then for 20 yards through rubble parallel to the river, and back over the bank through bushes to the water. After another ½ mile of flatwater there is a class II rapid that is especially difficult due to a number of jagged obstructions.

One-half mile beyond the end of the rapids there is another dam. This one, 20 feet high, can be portaged with difficulty down steep inclines on the R. One-quarter mile beyond, the Concord empties into the Merrimack River (4½ mi).

SUNCOOK RIVER   NH

The Suncook River flows from Crystal Lake in Gilmanton, through the two Suncook lakes, and then southwest to the Merrimack River at Suncook. Although there are four dams, there is some fine quickwater in the 29¼ miles described here. There is also a substantial amount of flat-water which can be run throughout all of the canoeing season.

Lower Suncook Lake — Pittsfield   7¾ miles

1975   Lakes, Quickwater, Class I–II   12½ km
                  High water: *needed for the rapids, April*
                  Forested, Towns
                       USGS: Gilmanton 15
                       Portages: 4¼ mi e **dam in Barnstead** — 50 yds
                                   7¾ mi R **dam in Pittsfield** — 300 yds

The river becomes canoeable below Lower Suncook Lake. Put in from a side road upstream of NH-28. There is ½ mile of class II water to the NH-28 bridge. From the bridge there are 1¼ miles of class I rapids that lead to an old damsite just above the first bridge in Center Barnstead (1¾ mi). There is a class II rapid for a short distance in the vicinity of that bridge. The current gradually eases off in the next ½ mile, and then there are 2 miles of flowage to the dam in Barnstead.

Below the dam (4¼ mi) there are some rapids for 1½ miles to a 2-mile backwater behind the Pittsfield dam (7¾ mi).

There is access to the river at several points above both dams from side roads.

Pittsfield — Epsom Circle   8¾ miles

1975   Quickwater, Class II–III   14 km
                  High water: *April*
                  Forested, Towns, Settled
                       USGS: Gilmanton 15, Gossville

Put in 200 yards downstream of the Pittsfield dam on the L. The river is small and fast, and there is evidence of beaver activity. It is an easy class II run for the first 2 miles to a sharp L turn at a ledge, below which the rapids become more difficult. Between the powerline and the bridge at Webster's Mills is the most difficult drop, a class III rapid best run on the R in high water.

Below the bridge (3 mi) the river becomes wider with big waves in high water, but in medium water the river is scratchy. Class II rapids continue for 1 mile before ending abruptly, to be followed by 1½ miles of quickwater to the bridge at North Chichester (5½ mi). Just below the bridge a low dam can be run under favorable conditions.

In the last 3¼ miles to Epsom Circle (8¾ mi), the river is easy and pleasant as it meanders through meadowland.

Epsom Circle — Short Falls   4 miles

975   Flatwater, Quickwater, Class II–IV   6½ km
       High water: *needed for rapids, April*
       Forested, Settled
           USGS: Gossville, Suncook
           Portage: 1¼ mi R **dams at Bear Island**

After ¼ mile the Little Suncook River comes in on the L. The river becomes ponded by a dam which is 1¼ miles below the bridge near Epsom Circle. This dam is located at the head of "Bear Island" on the topographic map.

The island is about a mile long. The channel on the L starts by going over a low dam, and it has a number of tricky class III and IV drops which local covered boaters find exciting. The R-hand channel requires a portage around the dam on the R. The rapids on this side of the island are class II.

The rapids end shortly below the island. Fast-water continues for about 1¾ miles to the bridge at Short Falls where there is a riffle just above the bridge (4 mi).

Short Falls — Suncook   8¾ miles

975   Flatwater   14 km
       Passable at all water levels
       Forested, Settled
           USGS: Suncook
           Portage: 4 mi e **dams at NH-28 bridge**

Below the bridge the water is ponded, and there are big estuaries at the mouth of all the tributaries. The L bank is mostly wild, but in many places on the R there are cottages and trailer parks.

In 4 miles a bridge on NH-28 is followed by an island with a dam on each side. Take out on either side of either dam. There is current for only a short distance before you reach a backwater which extends for the remainder of the 4½ miles to the US-3 bridge (8½ mi) in Suncook. Below the bridge there is a small pond and a high dam (8¾ mi).

From the dam the river drops nearly 100 feet in the first half of the remaining mile to the Merrimack River.

WARNER RIVER NH

The Warner River flows eastward from Bradford towards Concord. It empties into the Contoocook River a little below the town of Contoocook. The upper part contains thrilling rapids for covered boaters, the middle portion has easy rapids, and lower down the river meanders thru wild swamps. It passes under two covered bridges and runs down the median of I-89.

Bradford — Warner	**9 miles**

1975	Flatwater, **Quickwater, Class II–IV**	14½ km

High water: *necessary for upper part, March and April*
Medium water: *sufficient for lower part, April and May*
Forested, Towns, Settled
USGS: Mount Kearsarge 15
Portages: 5 mi R **dam**
8 mi L **dam in Waterloo**

Put in at the NH-114 bridge SE of Bradford. The broken milldam at Melvin Mills (3 mi) can be run. After leaving the pond below the mill, the river flows through continuous class III rapids where many quick decisions are required. The river is small, and there are many sharp turns. In about a mile — around a L turn — the river splits, and part of it goes into an old millrace on the extreme L. Immediately below is the first tough rapid — approximately ½ mile of continuous class IV drops which terminate in a chute between cement abutments directly above a small bridge which is easily visible from NH-103.

After that first difficult pitch the river eases up to class II for about ½ mile before entering the second and most difficult rapid — a series of five closely spaced class IV drops in a gorge beyond an old millsite which is adjacent to a small picnic area. There is an old tar road on the L which can be used to scout or portage. Below the second difficult rapid the river eases up. Soon there is a stretch of water behind some houses which turns out to be a millpond. Portage the small dam by the abandoned mill on the R.

Below the dam (5 mi) there is quickwater for a mile as the river meanders in a big loop, passing under NH-103 twice. At the second bridge another long section of class III–IV rapids starts. These are beautiful and continuous rapids with one-boat eddies. There are no pools for rescue, but there are no sharp drops either, except near the end where the river makes a sharp R turn and goes over a 3-foot ledge which is hard to diagnose from the boat and which is difficult to run without scraping. Directly below the ledge there is a bridge on a small dirt road (6½ mi).

Below the third difficult section the rapids quickly ease up from class II to quickwater. In 1½ miles, just below the covered bridge at Waterloo, there is a dam which is followed immediately by a short class IV drop. Take-out on the L and portage along the old RR as far down the rapids as you wish. It is another mile to the I-89 bridge (9 mi).

Warner — Contoocook River   10 miles

1977   Quickwater   16 km
High or medium water: *April thru May*
Forested, Towns
   USGS: Mount Kearsarge 15, Penacook 15, Hopkinton
   Portage: 7½ mi L **dam in Davisville** — ¼ mi

The river below here makes a very pleasant run with only a few fallen trees to present problems. Put in near exit 9 off I-89 at the junction with Stevens Brook.

There are a few riffles through Warner and several bridges in the following 3 miles. The interstate highway crosses twice, and the river flows for a while through the median. After flowing through a swamp for a couple of miles, it reaches the bridge at Davisville (7½ mi). Portage ¼ mile down a road on the L bank to an old road leading directly to the river. This by-passes an old, partially washed-out dam and the class IV rapid below it.

From the dam (7½ mi) it is a pleasant 2½ miles to the Contoocook River (10). Paddle down the latter for 1½ miles to the bridge at Tyler (11½ mi).

WINNIPESAUKEE RIVER   NH

The Winnipesaukee River is a river of intermittent rapids, some of which are long and difficult. The water is clear, although there is some debris and trash below Tilton. It flows through two milltowns, and at one time a 5-mile section of the river had ten dams. Four of them are gone completely, and three others are partially washed-out.

The river below Tilton is relatively isolated. Above Franklin it flows through a narrow, wooded valley where there are nearly continuous class III–IV rapids. Franklin itself is masked from the river in this section by the steepness of the valley and the roar of the rapids. Abandoned factories suggest an industrious past.

The flow in the Winnipesaukee River is controlled by Lochmere Dam, located between Winnisquam and Silver lakes. Each fall the Water Resources Board (603-271-1110) draws down the levels of Winnipesaukee and Winnisquam lakes about three feet — that is a lot of water! This release provides medium to high water levels for several weeks.

Route 140 — Franklin   6 miles

1977	Flatwater, **Class II–IV** 9¾ km

High water: *late March to early April*
Medium water: *late April to mid-May and fall*
Dam-controlled: *annual fall drawdown*

Forested, Settled, Town

USGS: Penacook 15

Portages: 2¼ mi L **1st dam at Tilton** — 20 yds
2¼+ mi **2nd dam at Tilton** (dangerous approach) — 30–100 yds
5¾ mi L **old dam above Franklin** — 20 yds

This description begins very close to exit 20 off I-93. There is a launching ramp on Shaker Road just E of the NH-140 bridge. It provides public access to Silver Lake, located upstream.

The first ½ mile headed downstream is flat. After passing under the I-93 bridges there is ½ mile of class II rapids, followed by more flatwater. Then there is a small chute under a RR bridge (1½ mi), with a washed-out dam next to US-3 just beyond. The clearest channel through the latter is on the R, but it is bony in medium water. There is another, easy chute under the second RR bridge, and a short class II drop just after the next highway bridge, with smoothwater continuing under adjacent highway and RR bridges (2 mi) to the dam in Tilton.

Carry the dam at Tilton (2¼ mi) on the L. Below, the rapids are class II. **Caution!** Check this area carefully. In medium water it is possible to run these rapids and pull out on the L to lift over an old, partially washed-out dam beside a factory on the L. If the water is too high, you may not be able to do this, and a more difficult carry on the R may be necessary. Immediately below this old dam the river divides into two channels between collapsing walls. The clearest passage is on the L, and it is the beginning of a 100-yard class II rapid with heavy waves; it gives a taste of things to come.

The rapids below Tilton end at a pool preceding a R turn (2½ mi). After some quickwater the river opens into a wide floodplain. There are 100 yards of rapids at another R turn (3¾ mi) that are class II in medium water, class I in high water. Then there is another ¾ mile section of flatwater before the heavy rapids above Franklin.

The difficult rapids begin at the Cross Road bridge (4½ mi) where the river enters a narrow, wooded valley. At first there are a series of rapids and pools as the river flows over runnable, washed-out dams and past ruined factories. There are many turns in the river, and the rapids get longer and harder, up to class IV, as you approach and pass under a covered RR bridge (5½ mi). Now be on the lookout for a brief section of easier, fast-moving water just above the remains of a dam which must be lifted around on the L. More class IV rapids continue, but they end abruptly at a millpond just below the US-3 bridge (6 mi) in Franklin.

The route through Franklin is tedious. The first dam should be portaged on the R, but the take-out is difficult. The river is smooth to the second dam. There is an easier take-out on the R, but it is in the middle of town, and the only practical way to get back to the river is to carry a short distance along US-3 and sneak down a steep bank behind some stores. Easy class II rapids below the second dam soon end, followed by smoothwater the remaining distance to the mouth of the Pemigewasset River where the Merrimack River begins (7 mi).

CHAPTER 12
PISCATAQUA
WATERSHED

Cocheco River   313
Exeter River   314
Great Works River   318
Isinglass River   319
Lamprey River   320
Little River   323
North River   324
Piscassic River   325
Salmon Falls River   326

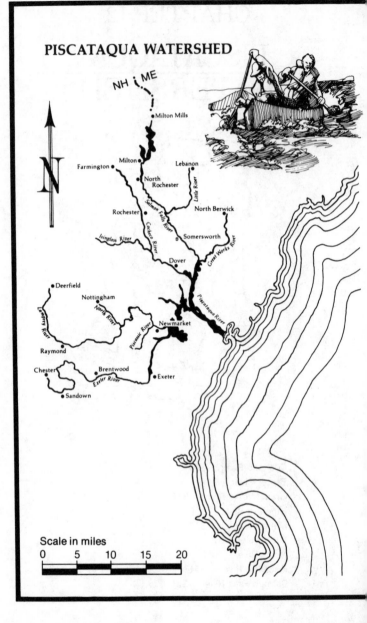

PISCATAQUA WATERSHED

N

NH | ME

Milton Mills

Farmington •   Milton   Lebanon

North
Rochester

Rochester   North Berwick

Somersworth

Isinglass River   Dover

• Deerfield

Nottingham

Raymond   Newmarket

Chester   Brentwood

• Exeter

Exeter River

• Sandown

Piscataqua River

Great Works River

Little River

Salmon Falls River

Cocheco River

Lamprey River

North River

Piscassic River

Scale in miles

0   5   10   15   20

INTRODUCTION

The Piscataqua Watershed is by-passed by many canoe-ists on their way north. The rivers are generally small and, rising from no snowy heights like the Saco to the north, they have a short run-off. During the peak three to six weeks, however, they offer excellent quickwater and class I–II rapids in channels that are narrower and more intimate than most paddlers are familiar with.

The North and Little rivers offer by far the best class II water in the spring, although portions of other rivers have shorter stretches of rapids worth exploring. The Cocheco from Farmington to Rochester and the last 5 miles on the Exeter to Fremont are the best of many quickwater stretches.

Summer canoeing is quite limited. Portions of the Exeter, Lamprey, Salmon Falls, and Great Works rivers offer flatwater in all but dry summers, but the tidewater portions of the Exeter and Salmon Falls, as well as the nearby York River in Maine, are of course always canoe-able. While not covered in this book, they are easily navi-gated with a topographic map and tide tables; add forty to fifty minutes to Boston tide times for each 5 miles from the open ocean.

The Piscataqua River itself is a tidal estuary formed by the confluence of the Cocheco and Salmon Falls rivers, continuing the line dividing Maine and New Hamp-shire previously marked by the Salmon Falls River. It drains both these rivers and several others which flow into Great Bay. The upper part is wide with little current. Below Dover Point, where Great Bay empties into the river, it is marked by one of the strongest tides on the eastern seaboard. It is only recommended for experienced tidewater canoeists — preferably with class II experience as well — because of the powerful currents.

COCHECO RIVER   NH

The Cocheco River rises above Farmington, becoming canoeable there as several smaller branches join forces. It is a pleasant paddle to Rochester.

Its course through Rochester to tidewater at Dover is marked by dams, waterfalls, dangerous gorges, and pollution. Therefore the lower section is not recommended.

1974   Flatwater, **Quickwater**, Class I   17 km
            High water: *late March thru early May*
            Rural, Urban
                 USGS: Alton 15, Berwick 15
                 Portage: 1½ mi   **culverts** — 50 yds

Put in at the bridge ½ mile SE of the center of
Farmington. A flood control and river grading project has
given the section near town an aseptic look. Soon the river
begins twisting and turning with a moderate current.
Watch out for fallen trees and overhanging bushes in this
area. In 1½ miles the river disappears into a pair of
culverts placed there by the Vickers Gravel Company.
Caution! If the river is high, these culverts may be entirely
underwater and hazardous because they create a strong
suction. Take out with care and portage.

The next 5 miles are ideal for the beginning
whitewater canoeist, as they offer many sharp turns with
a moderate current, plus a number of riffles and class I
rapids. The current slows down near a bridge (6½ mi) on a
back road connecting Chestnut Hill Road with NH-11. This
is the recommended take-out.

The remaining 4 miles are through a built-up
section of Rochester, and most are in the backwater of
the first dam. If continuing, be careful to take out at or
above the NH-11/US-202 bridge (10½ mi) as there is a
dangerous waterfall 40 yards beyond this bridge.

EXETER RIVER   NH

The Exeter River was known in early times as the Squamscott River, and it is still so-named on its lower, tidal section. It rises in Chester and flows 34 miles before reaching
tidewater at Exeter, a trip the proverbial crow would need
only 15 miles to make. Because it doubles back so much
on itself, it does not pick up many feeder streams, so it is
narrow for its entire length.

Chester — Sandown   4 miles

This is a section which is useful for building character.
It is recommended only for determined bushwackers and
explorers, especially those interested as well in running
narrow class III rapids.

Chester — Sandown   4 mi [6½ km]

Flatwater, Quickwater, Class I–III

High water: *late March to mid-April*

Forested

    USGS: Haverhill 15

    Portages:
¼ mi	**culvert** — 10 yds	
½ mi	**dam at end of swamp** — 10 yds	
1½ mi	**snowmobile bridge near powerline** — 10 yds	
2½ mi	L **unrunnable drop in last rapids** — 10 yds	

Put in at Wilson Brook on NH-121, 1¼ miles S of the junction with NH-121A in Chester. Within ¼ mile there is a culvert which must be portaged. Soon after, Wilson Brook joins the Exeter River in a swamp. Proceed straight ahead to a sharp point on the R where the course bears R. There is a dam to be portaged at the end of the swamp.

Below the dam at the end of the swamp (½ mi), there are 100 yards of class III rapids. One mile further, a snowmobile bridge near a powerline must be lifted over or portaged. The next mile to a bridge on a back road features frequent, narrow class II rapids and two 30-yard sections of class III rapids below old damsites.

Below the bridge (2½ mi) are another 40 yards of class II rapids with one unrunnable drop in the middle. Portage on the L. The remaining 1½ miles to Sandown are gently flowing river with some brush and blowdowns and a short, swampy area where the course may be hard to find.

Sandown — Fremont   12½ miles

Much of the first 7 miles below Sandown is through marshes where perseverance, a map, and a compass are all helpful. There are also a few snowmobile bridges which may have to be lifted over.

The last 5 miles to Fremont, and continuing for the following 4 miles to West Brentwood, are the finest on the river for scenery and absence of hazards. It is probably the best quickwater in the Piscataqua Watershed.

1976

Sandown — Fremont   12½ mi [20 km]
Flatwater, **Quickwater**, Class I
High water: *late March to late April*
Rural

    USGS: Haverhill 15, *Mount Pawtuckaway 15*

  Portages: 1 mi e **gorge at millsite**
                1¼ mi e **dam**
                1¾ mi e **millsite**
             12¼ mi R **Fremont Dam** — 10 yds

From Sandown, where the put-in is on NH-121A just N of town, the river flows gently ¼ mile to Lily Pond, which is ¼ mile long and easier to get through than the name implies. There is no dam at the outlet.

Below Lily Pond there are class I rapids for ½ mile to an old millsite (1 mi) and a gorge which probably is unrunnable. The gorge can be inspected in advance from the bridge just below.

After another ¼ mile a small backwater is formed by a dam which can be portaged on either side. Shortly below it there is another gorge at an old millsite with some interesting stonework remaining. There is another bridge just beyond.

Below the second bridge (1¾ mi) the river enters a large swamp where route-finding is difficult in high water, and even more difficult in low water. The old RR grade is used as a snowmobile trail, and the river is spanned at the crossings by sagging bridges. In the next 3 miles it flows under two more road bridges, followed by 3 miles more of brushy meadow.

After passing under the seventh bridge (7½ mi), the river becomes narrow and quick. There is some brush to be avoided and an occasional tree across the stream, but from here past three more bridges there are no impassable or dangerous sections. There is a short slackwater behind the dam at Fremont, which is about ¼ mile after the first houses appear on the L bank. Portage on the R. The remaining 500 yards to the center of Fremont is flatwater.

Fremont — Brentwood   5½ miles

There are mile-long millponds on either end of this run. The connecting 2½ miles of quickwater frequently are passable during the summer. The upper pond is undeveloped and offers many attractive picnic sites. The class II rapids, all between the West Brentwood dam and NH-125, are short but exciting in high water.

Fremont — Brentwood   5½ mi [8¾ km]
Flatwater, Quickwater, Class II
High water: *late March to early May*
Medium water: *moderate summer rainfall*
Forested, Towns
    USGS: Haverhill 15
    Portages: 1 mi R **2nd dam in Fremont** — 20 yds
               4½ mi R **West Brentwood Dam** — 20 yds
               5½ mi L **waterfall** — 150 yds

From the bridge next to the general store in Fremont, the river goes through 100 yards of class I rapids to a lake extending 1 mile to a dam. Portage on the R. The next 2½ miles are quickwater with one short, swampy section. Just below a campground on the R bank, there is a crude rock dam that is runnable in high water.

The last mile to West Brentwood is backwater from the dam (4½ mi) with many cottages on both banks. **Caution!** The dam is just *above* the second bridge in West Brentwood. Take out on the R. In high water you can continue immediately below the dam, putting into a 50-yard class II rapid. After a brief pause there is a second class II rapid at the site of a former dam, and ½ mile further is an easier class II rapid, also about 50 yards long.

Caution! Take out on the L above the NH-125 bridge, as a class III rapid begins directly under the bridge and leads immediately to a 10-foot waterfall under a second bridge 200 yards downstream.

Brentwood — Exeter   12 miles

The backwater from Pickpocket Dam dominates the middle of this section, both by slowing the flow of water and by making the course far from obvious. Above this, however, are 2 miles of pleasant quickwater through dense second-growth; and below the dam there are several challenging class II rapids that are runnable in high water.

Brentwood — Exeter   12 mi [19½ km]
Flatwater, Quickwater, Class I–II
High water: *late March to early May*
Medium water: *moderate summer rainfall*
Forested, Settled
    USGS: Haverhill 15, Exeter
    Portage: 5 mi R **Pickpocket Dam** (cross bridge, put in L)
                     — 50 yds

Put in at least 50 yards below the waterfall. The easiest access is from the L bank. The first 100 yards are class II, followed by quickwater and occasional class I rapids to a bridge 2 miles below. Most of the next 3 miles are in the backwater behind Pickpocket Dam (5 mi). The course is hard to follow here. **Caution!** Portage the dam *and* the chutes below it, because they are more dangerous than they may appear. Put in near the bridge below.

The first 150 yards past Pickpocket Dam are class II rapids which must be run in fairly high water. Then there are intermittent class I and II rapids to the NH-111 bridge (6 mi) a mile below the dam. One-quarter mile downstream, around a blind R turn, is a 75-yard class II rapid which is especially difficult in high water.

The remaining 6 miles to Exeter are flatwater with little current. The river passes under a RR bridge 1 mile below NH-111, a back road another mile further, and the NH-108 bridge ¾ mile beyond that. There has been recent beaver activity in this area; be ready to climb over some of their dams. The final 3 miles to Exeter contain many sharp meanders and confusing junctions with side channels. A careful observation of the current will get you through.

Caution! There is a 10-foot dam just below the first bridge in Exeter with no adequate access near it. Take out on the R 50 yards above the bridge, just when it is first visible; or ½ mile above the bridge at the public park on the L, adjacent to the Phillips Exeter Academy playing fields.

Below Exeter the river, called the Squamscott, is tidal. In 6 miles it enters Great Bay (18 mi).

GREAT WORKS RIVER   ME

This is an unassuming little river which claims the distinction of running the first water-powered mill in the United States in the section of South Berwick called Great Works. Mills continued there without a break for over three hundred years until the 1940's, when the few remaining ones fell into disuse.

North Berwick — South Berwick	11½ miles

1976	**Flatwater**, Quickwater, Class I	18½ km
	High water: *late March thru mid-May*	
	Passable at most water levels: *last 3½ miles*	
	Forested	
	USGS: Kennebunk 15, *York 15,* Dover 15	

The first 5 miles to Emerys Bridge on Hooper Sands Road are narrow and winding, and the river shallows out early in the season. The next 3 miles to Junction Bridge, at the W end of Emerys Bridge Road, hold water a little longer. Both sections are prone to blow-downs.

The final 3½-mile section from Junction Bridge to the village of Great Works is canoeable in all but a very dry summer, and it is entirely flatwater. Take out at the Brattle Street bridge (11½ mi) ¼ mile below the ME-236 bridge.

Caution! Below the Brattle Street bridge is a series of falls and rapids called Rocky Gorge. Stay well above it. It is not feasible to continue to the Salmon Falls River into which the Great Works River flows because this obstruction would necessitate a 1-mile portage.

There is a dam on the Great Works River at the confluence with the Salmon Falls River.

ISINGLASS RIVER   NH

The Isinglass River flows from Bow Lake in Strafford to the Cocheco River in Rochester. At one time it provided water power for several mills in Barrington, but all that remains today is the small dam above the US-202 bridge. The banks are mostly wooded, and there are only a few houses within sight of the river. The river itself is quite clean, and there is an attractive waterfall near the end.

The first 2 miles can be done only in very high water. Check the old mill sluice above the US-202 bridge. If there is enough water here, the rapids above, which are considerably easier, will be runnable. Very high water in the river downstream tends to make class I rapids easier and class II rapids harder.

 Route 126 — Cocheco River   **10½ miles**

976   Flatwater, **Quickwater**, Class I–II   17 km
High water: *late March thru April*
Forested, Rural
   USGS: Mount Pawtuckaway 15, Dover West, *Berwick 15*
   Portage: 8 mi R **waterfall** — 125 yds

There is a good current for about 1½ miles below the NH-126 bridge in Barrington. Then there are three short, easy class II pitches as the river parallels US-202. Stay to the L of the island. Just above the US-202 bridge there is a quiet pool behind an old dam. **Caution!** The sluiceway is runnable, but it must be scouted, for there are some sharp boulders to avoid. When the water is really high, there are powerful currents which make it difficult to control a boat in the narrow channel.

The river below the US-202 bridge (2 mi) is mostly quickwater for 2½ miles to a small iron bridge beside a house on the R. In this section there are two pairs of bridge abutments which predate the Revolution. Past the bridge the river is sluggish for ½ mile, below which there is another ½ mile of class I and II whitewater. Halfway down the rapids at a sharp R turn there is a ledge, passable on the L, which stretches almost all the way across the river. The rapids end 50 yards below the Berrys Hill bridge (5½ mi). The remaining 2 miles to NH-125 contain flatwater.

Below the NH-125 bridge (7½ mi) there is ½ mile of slack current to a 25-foot waterfall. **Caution!** At a stone abutment on the R, 20 yards above the first sign of rapids, take out on the R and carry 125 yards along an old road. This is a good picnic and rest spot, for the falls shoot out between massive rocks, and they make an impressive sight. The next ¼ mile is class II–III: difficult in very high water, scratchy in moderately high water, and impassable in anything else. The rapids end with an "S" turn between high banks followed by a rock garden likely to add a few scratches to your boat. The next 1½ miles to the Rochester Neck Road bridge is a pleasant run of quickwater over a sandy bottom; catfish are often visible here.

One-half mile below the Rochester Neck Road bridge (10 mi), the Isinglass empties into the Cocheco River (10½ mi). It is 1¼ miles down the Cocheco to the next crossing, a covered bridge on Country Farm Road (11¾ mi). This section is all flatwater except for the last 100 yards where there is an easy class II rapid.

LAMPREY RIVER   NH

The Lamprey is one of the longest rivers in the Piscataqua Watershed, and it is probably the flattest. The section above Raymond offers class I rapids for the spring canoeist, while below that town the river can be run most of the year because there are few rapids. Packers Falls, class II or III depending on the water level, is run well into the summer by kayakers and canoeists.

Deerfield — Raymond   **8 miles**

Three-quarters of a mile above Raymond, a tributary named Cider Ferry enters on the R. It flows from Onway Lake, and it got its name from the slipping and bursting of a barrel of cider being taken over the stream by the early settlers before there was a bridge. "But," as someone remarked, "as fish do not drink cider, no harm was done."

1975 Deerfield — Raymond   8 mi [13 km]
Flatwater, Quickwater, Class I–II
High water: *late March to early May*
Forested, Settled
    USGS: Mount Pawtuckaway 15

Put in 2 miles S of Deerfield Center at the junction of NH-43 and 107. The Lamprey at this point is a narrow trout stream, with class I–II rapids, shallow riffles, and quickwater. Beavers have made a strong resurgence on this part of the river, and several of their dams are sure to be encountered. One and a half miles below, before reaching the first bridge, there are two ledges. The first is runnable on the L in very high water; the second has to be lined or carried. From the first bridge to NH-101, it is 2½ miles: largely flatwater with a few class I rapids, including a 100-yarder that ends right at NH-101.

From the NH-101 bridge (4 mi) the next 1½ miles are flat and wide: follow a straight course here. Then there are more class I rapids in the next mile to the Langsford Road bridge (6½ mi) with a class II–III ledge just below. The rapids end in another ¼ mile, and the final 1¼ miles to Raymond (8 mi) are once again flat and wide.

Raymond — West Epping   **5 miles**

    USGS: Mount Pawtuckaway 15

This section is mostly flat, but note that there is an unrunnable gorge just before the Route 102 bridge that is very difficult to portage. Rapids continue below this bridge.

West Epping — Wadley Falls   **12 miles**

1976 **Quickwater**, Class II   19¼ km
High or medium water: *spring*
Forested, Town
    USGS: Mount Pawtuckaway 15
    Portages: 12 mi R **dam at Wadley Falls**

Below the dam in West Epping, there is a short pool. Class II ledges begin under the next bridge and continue for ½ mile, gradually becoming easier. A few rock dams are passed, and the final ledge is underneath the first bridge in Epping (3½ mi).

Below Epping (4 mi) there are 3 miles of meandering river to the NH-87 bridge. This is succeeded by a long, smooth stretch twisting through old pastures and woods for another 5 miles past the mouth of the North River (10¾ mi) to the Wadley Falls dam (12 mi).

Wadley Falls — Newmarket   10½ miles

For a quiet retreat into the woods, the first 4 miles are superb. Canoeists continuing below the bridge on Lee Hook Road may have a scratchy time in moderately high water as the rapid starting under the bridge, and another, shorter one a mile further, need rather high water to run well.

One feature of the lower stretch is Packers Falls; not actually a falls but rather one of the most challenging rapids in the Piscataqua Watershed. It is a roaring class III run in early spring, and it is often run well into the summer as a class II drop. There are well-developed portage trails for those who want to run it several times.

1975   Wadley Falls — Newmarket   10½ miles [17 km]
        Flatwater, Class I–III
        High water: *late March to early May*
        Medium water: *average summer rainfall*
        Forested
            USGS: *Mount Pawtuckaway 15,* Dover 15
            Portage: 7¼ mi L **Wiswall Falls Dam** — 50 yds

Below the dam at Wadley Falls, there is a brief rapid; then 4 miles of quiet paddling past densely forested banks of hemlocks and hardwoods to the Lee Hook Road bridge. Below the bridge are 200 yards of easy class II rapids with large combers in high water. At the end of the rapid, there is a broken dam running diagonally across the river; it can be run easily by following the current rather than the shore. A camp and trailer park extends for the next mile along the L bank to a short rapid on either side of an island (5 mi).

It is another 2¼ miles to the Wiswall Road bridge and Wiswall Falls Dam (7¼ mi). Below the dam is a 200-yard class II rapid which, if unrunnable, can be carried on the L. Another ¾ mile brings you to Packers Falls (8 mi).

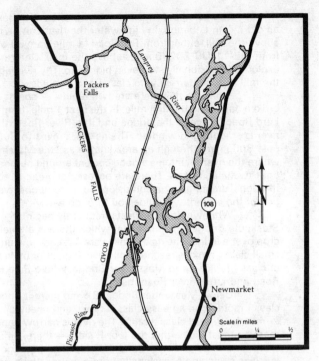

Caution! Take out on the L at least 20 yards above the bridge and scout Packers Falls (8 mi). This run is a difficult class III in high water, and a moderate class II with some scratching at the bottom in medium water. There are two more short class II rapids just below Packers Falls, then 2½ miles of flatwater to Newmarket. Follow the map. The Piscassic River (9¾ mi) enters on the R. Take out at Newmarket on the L just above the dam (10½ mi).

LITTLE RIVER   ME

The canoe season is short but exciting on the Little River. Canoe it early in the morning or on an overcast day, for it heads into the afternoon sun for most of its length.

Lebanon — Salmon Falls River	**11¼ miles**

1976	Flatwater, Quickwater, Class I–II 18¼ km
	High water: *late March to early May*
	Forested
	USGS: Berwick 15

The usual put-in is below the broken dam beside an old mill in Lebanon. In high water the river can be run above the mill, either from Fall Road (a mile upriver) or from ME-11/US-202 (3 miles above the mill). Determined explorers occasionally start even higher up. The river above the mill is quite narrow with class I and II rapids.

From the mill there are two rapids — one at a broken dam — in the first mile. In the next 1 mile, from the Lord Road bridge to the bridge on Little River Road, the river is smooth and winding. The next 4¼ miles to Stackpole Bridge are through an area known as "the Marshes," where the river maintains a good current around numerous tight twists and turns. There are occasional breakthroughs, creating some confusion, but careful observation of the current will guide you through easily.

Whitewater enthusiasts frequently begin at Stackpole Bridge (6¼ mi), under which there is a small drop over a ledge. The next 2 miles are flat and slow until a small class I rapid is reached, followed soon after by ¼ mile of class I rapids up to Messenger Bridge, where Pine Hill Road and Little River Road meet.

Below Messenger Bridge (8½ mi) there is another class I rapid, then an easy class II rapid, and finally a ¾-mile-long, hard class II rapid. The river is narrow enough that you must pick either the L or R side — there is no room for a middle route — and the only clear passage involves switching occasionally from a course down one side to a course down the other. Stop and scout frequently unless you like piling up onto ledges and into impassable rock gardens.

The long rapid ends with a small ledge on a sharp R turn, and the last ½ mile of it to a back road bridge (9½ mi) is very scratchy when the rapids above are marginally canoeable. Flatwater follows. One-half mile above the Hubbard Road bridge (11¼ mi), there is a broken dam at the end of a sharp "S" turn which can be run with extreme caution or lined from the R bank.

The Little River empties into the Salmon Falls River (11¼ mi) just below the Hubbard Road bridge. Somersworth is 5 miles downstream (16¼ mi).

NORTH RIVER   NH

The North River is a short tributary of the Lamprey River above Wadley Falls. Its canoeing season is brief, but it definitely offers the best whitewater run in the Piscataqua

Watershed with a 2½-mile, continuous class II run above NH-152.

In very high water it can be run from the back road bridge near the outlet to Pawtuckaway Pond or from NH-152 2½ miles north of Nottingham; both of these branches are somewhat overgrown but canoeable, and both have quickwater and class I rapids. The usual put-in is by the school in Nottingham.

Nottingham — Wadley Falls	8¾ miles

Flatwater, Quickwater, Class II   14 km
High water: *late March to late April*
Forested
     USGS: Mount Pawtuckaway 15
     Portage: 4 mi R **NH-152 bridge** — 30 yds

The first 1½ miles are flat with a fair current. About 100 yards above the Merellis Road bridge, class II rapids begin. Eighty yards below the bridge is the most difficult rapid. It is class II–III and must be taken in the center. Class II rapids continue with only brief pauses for 2½ miles to Harvey's Shingle Mill at the next bridge, NH-152.

Caution! Take out in the eddy on the R just above the NH-152 bridge (4 mi), because there is class IV rapid below it at the shingle mill. Put in on the L below the mill. The next mile to the Birch Hill Road bridge is swift running with class I rapids. Along this stretch there are some fine stands of sycamores — unusual for New Hampshire. In the next 1½ miles to the NH-125 bridge (6½ mi), the river flows with a moderate current past a sugarbush (maple sugar grove) on the L.

Below NH-125 there is 1 mile of flatwater to the Lamprey River (7½ mi), with another 1¼ miles down that stream to the dam at Wadley Falls (8¾ mi).

PISCASSIC RIVER   NH

The Piscassic River is a large brook that flows eastward from Fremont and Epping to the Lamprey River just above Newmarket. The section above NH-87 is extremely difficult, and it is not recommended unless you enjoy hacking your way through thick alder and vine tangles. Below NH-87 the river is more open, and it has many narrow, tight turns in quickwater.

1975   Flatwater, **Quickwater**, Class I–II   9¼ km
        High water only: *late March to mid-April*
        Rural
            USGS: Dover 15

Put in at the NH-87 bridge. Just below there is an old millsite with some steep, narrow class II rapids which can be run solo or carried 100 yards on the R. In ½ mile an old RR bridge is passed, and in another 1½ miles a bridge (2 mi) on a back road. The river is swift and meandering here, with many trees and bushes narrowing passages and challenging your steering.

Another mile of good running brings you to the bridge SE of Four Corners. One mile further there is another bridge (4 mi) where there is a class II rapid which sometimes is unrunnable. In 1 mile there is another sharp class II drop which can be carried 40 yards on the L. Shortly after that, the NH-152 bridge is reached, with ¾ mile remaining to the high dam (5¾ mi) just W of Newmarket.

If continuing, it is ¾ mile further to the Lamprey River and another ¾ mile to the dam at Lamprey River Falls (7¼ mi) in Newmarket.

SALMON FALLS RIVER   ME, NH

This river flows south from Great East Lake and forms the boundary between Maine and New Hampshire.

Three sections of the river are not recommended. Above Milton Mills it is a very small stream. It has shallow rapids that are seldom deep enough to run and a thick alder swamp where the channel is difficult to follow and frequently blocked by debris. Portions of the river immediately below Milton and from Berwick/Somersworth to South Berwick are also not recommended because of unrunnable rapids and dams.

1977   Lakes, Flatwater, Class II   14½ km
        High water: early spring
        Forested, Settled
            USGS: *Newfield 15*, Berwick 15
            Portages: 1 mi L **2nd dam in Milton Mills**
                        1¼ mi L **3rd dam in Milton Mills**

Below the first dam (about a mile N of town and just above a side road), the rapids, when runnable, are nearly continuous and very heavy. In ½ mile there is an old millsite with abutments and a short stretch of rapids before a second millsite; both of them should be lined, lifted over, or carried. The last ¼ mile is mostly backwater behind the second dam (1 mi). Take-out on the L immediately below the bridge. After this dam there is a short class II rapid; then flatwater to the third dam. Land on the L well above the bridge.

A canoe can be launched just below the third dam (1¼ mi). Paddle under the bridge and parts of the mill buildings. The first ¼ mile is an alder tangle, but canoeing improves as you proceed downstream. The river meanders extensively, and it is still somewhat impeded by fallen trees.

The river enters the extreme N end of Northeast Pond (4¾ mi), from which it is 2½ miles to the bridge (7¼ mi) between the lakes, and an additional ¾ mile to the SE end where there is a good take-out. From the bridge it is 1¾ miles to the dam at Milton (9 mi).

North Rochester — Somersworth   14½ miles

The heavy use of the river for water power in the 19th century is evident in dams, factory buildings and accumulated industrial detritus above the put-in, below the take-out, and halfway down when passing through East Rochester. The quickwater enthusiast will find a pleasant paddle above East Rochester, but he must be prepared to run over 50 yards of class II rapids entering town. The next 2 miles to Step Falls, like the first 4½ miles, are good only in high water. In contrast, the remaining 8 miles are flat and canoeable all summer.

976   North Rochester — Somersworth   14½ mi [23½ km]
Flatwater, Quickwater, Class I–III
High water: *late March thru early May*
Passable at all water levels: *below Little River*
Rural, Towns
    USGS: Berwick 15
    Portages: 4½ mi R **East Rochester** — 100 yds
           11½ mi   **dam**

Put in behind the Spaulding Paper Products plant just off NH-16. If your canoe makes it over the first riffles 10 yards below the put-in bridge, you will have easy going all the way to East Rochester, even though the river seems shallow.

The river meanders through sandy areas of marginal farms and suburban sprawl, but it has a beauty of its own. The rapids are small and minor until you reach East Rochester, where there is a class II rapid beginning 40 yards above an abandoned iron bridge. The most difficult section is directly beneath the bridge, and it should be scouted. The US-202 bridge is immediately below this rapid. **Caution!** There is a 10-foot dam 100 yards below the bridge. Portage on the R.

Below the dam in East Rochester (4½ mi), there are heavy class II rapids for 75 yards; then primarily quickwater until Step Falls (6½ mi), a series of ledges which are runnable under the proper conditions. Below this point the river is almost currentless for the remaining 8 miles to Berwick/Somersworth.

Five miles from East Rochester, the Little River enters on the L (9½ mi). A bridge on Hubbard Road 400 yards up this stream offers access to the Salmon Falls River, especially for summer paddling.

Two miles past the Little River is an 8-foot dam. You can take out here, at the Rochester Street bridge (13 mi), or at Parson's Park (14½ mi), ½ mile above the center of Berwick/Somersworth. **Caution!** There is no adequate take-out in town, and there is a dam 10 yards below the bridge connecting the twin towns of Berwick and Somersworth.

The next 5¼ miles are not recommended. First of all there is the dam ½ mile below the last take-out suggested above. Then there is a ¾-mile section of the river behind the General Electric plant in Somersworth which contains unrunnable rapids and dams. Determined canoeists can put in below this, but they have a 100-yard portage within the first mile. Below this, the river is pleasant for 3 miles to Salmon Falls (19¾ mi), a 15-foot drop just above a RR bridge. Another portage is necessary here, as there are 150 yards of unrunnable rapids below Salmon Falls. Finally, there is ½ mile of flatwater to the ME/NH-4 bridge (21¼ mi), immediately below which there is a 10-foot dam.

South Berwick — Cocheco River   3½ miles

This is an excellent section of the river for wildlife, whether it be the schools of alewives with striped bass in pursuit in the spring, or the great blue herons which usually nest here in the summer, or the ducks by the thousands stopping by the salt marshes for a brief respite on their way south each fall.

Near the confluence with the Great Works River is Hamilton House, a large and elegant mansion in Maine built in 1787 by Jonathan Hamilton, a prominent merchant in the early days of the Republic. The house is open in the summer as a museum, and the view from the lawn is unchanged from the days when the house was built. The State of Maine has acquired Vaughn Woods stretching one mile along the river, and the landowners on the New Hampshire side have left the river bank undeveloped in this area.

1976 South Berwick — Cocheco River 3½ mi [5¾ km]
Flatwater; **Tidal**
Passable at all water levels
Forested
    USGS: Dover 15

Put in on the Maine side of the river near the water treatment plant below the dam and the ME/NH-4 bridge. The river is narrow and winding for ¾ mile until it reaches the mouth of the Great Works River where it widens. At low tide there is a class I rapid here.

Below the Great Works River (¾ mi) salt marshes begin to predominate, broken only by Eliot Bridge 1½ miles below Hamilton House on the L. Midway between on the Maine bank is Cow Cove, where the first cows in New England are reputed to have been left off. You can take out at the Eliot Bridge (2½ mi) or at the confluence of the Cocheco River (3½ mi) where the Piscataqua River begins. Dover Point is 4 miles down the latter.

CHAPTER 13

SACO
WATERSHED

Saco River   333
Bearcamp River   340
Little Ossipee River   343
Ossipee River   346
Pine River   348
Swift River   350
West Branch   354

SACO WATERSHED

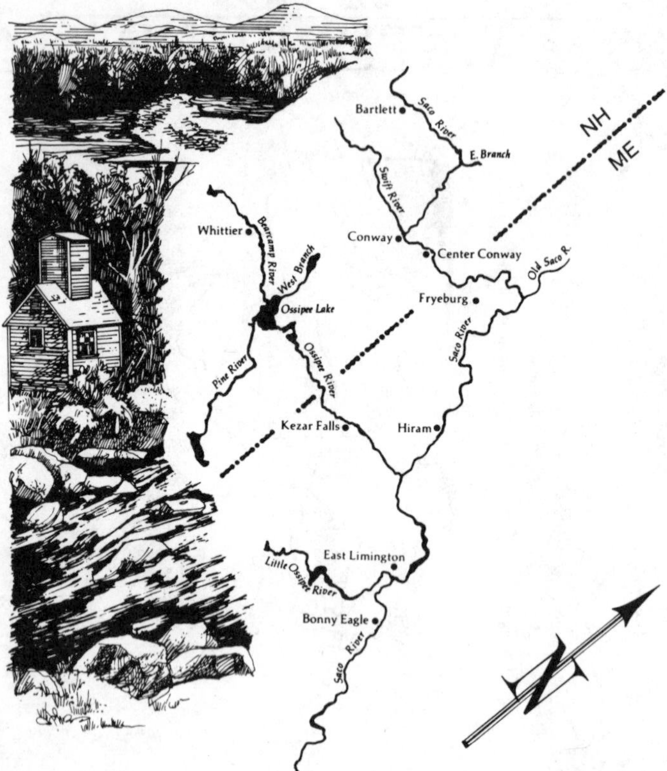

Bartlett

Saco River

E. Branch

NH

ME

Whittier

Bearcamp River

West Branch

Conway

Center Conway

Old Saco R.

Fryeburg

Ossipee Lake

Saco River

Pine River

Ossipee River

Kezar Falls

Hiram

East Limington

Little Ossipee River

Bonny Eagle

Saco River

Biddeford

Saco

Scale in miles

0   5   10   15   20   25   30

INTRODUCTION

The rivers of the Saco Watershed have always been clean, or nearly so. They offer many miles of boating for paddlers of varying abilities and interests.

For whitewater thrills the Upper Saco and the Swift rivers rate among the best and most difficult in New England. Nice runs with easier rapids can be found on parts of the Bearcamp and Ossipee rivers, and on the Saco below Bartlett.

The Little Ossipee is a good choice for an overnight canoe trip in the spring. The Pine River offers the most secluded setting, but it is not an easy run, being occasionally alder-choked and possibly blocked by fallen trees, with much of it impassable in low water. The Saco between Conway and Cornish is very popular for camping trips throughout the canoeing season. It is, in fact, too popular.

The Saco below Conway offers extensive canoeing in low water. Only the last few miles of the Bearcamp, Little Ossipee, and Pine rivers can be run in low water. However, two tributaries of Ossipee Lake, the Pine River and the West Branch, benefit from annual, fall drawdowns of the lakes from which they flow.

SACO RIVER   NH, ME

The Saco is one of New England's most popular rivers. Melting snow and spring rains provide for novice to expert whitewater boating near the headwaters, while below the Maine-New Hampshire border the river is mostly flat and passable at all water levels.

The river begins at Saco Lake just north of Crawford Notch. It drains the southern slopes of the Presidential Range and, in New Hampshire, flows through the Mount Washington Valley of tourist fame. From Conway it winds generally southeast to the ocean south of Portland, Maine.

Although settlement along the Saco began early in the 17th Century, few towns located right next to the river, so that it remains to this day a pastoral stream passing through only a few small settlements until it gets almost to the sea. State-supported protection is offered that portion of it in Maine by the Saco River Corridor Commission, which cooperates with local communities in matters relating to zoning and land-use planning.

The Saco River: A History and Canoeing Guide by Viola Sheehan, a book about the part of the river in Maine, is available from the Saco River Corridor Association, River Bend Farm, Simpson Road, Saco, Maine 04072. The price is $4.50. Add 25¢ for mailing and 23¢ sales tax if sent to a Maine address.

Davis Path — Bartlett   7¼ miles

This section, commonly known as the "Upper Saco," is one of the most exciting whitewater runs in central New England. In addition to the continuous rapids, the river passes through beautiful White Mountain scenery. Since the Saco drains the steep-sided Crawford Notch region, run-off takes place rapidly — warm, sunny days or spring rains can lead to a rapid rise in the level of the river.

1976   Davis Path — Bartlett   7¼ mi [11¾ km]
          Class III–IV
          High or medium water: *mid-April to mid-May*
          Forested
              USGS: Crawford Notch 15

From the Davis Path footbridge there is a short stretch of easy rapids leading to a very difficult class IV gorge at the mouth of Nancy Brook. The gorge is extremely narrow, less than a boat-length wide, with turbulence off the walls.

Since the portage around the gorge on the R is also very difficult, most groups prefer the steep and slippery put-in off US-302 about ¼ mile S of the Inn Unique at Notchland. Carry down the sandy bank just S of Nancy Brook, cross the RR tracks, and carry or line down to the picturesque pool below the gorge.

From the pool (½ mi) the rapids are continuous, generally class III, but some are class IV in high water. The first mile after the gorge is particularly shallow and twisty, with constant maneuvering except in very high water. Class III–IV rapids continue to the entrance of the Sawyer River (2¾ mi), where a small beach on the R makes a good lunch or resting spot. There is then another ¾ mile of rapids to a RR bridge (3½ mi), followed shortly by a class III drop in a sharp L turn. At this point US-302 is visible high on the R bank. In the next broad R turn lies a class IV stretch with large waves.

The difficulty diminishes again as the river approaches US-302 near Sawyer's Rock Picnic Area (4¼ mi). This is the start of a more suitable section for shorter runs with a less-than-expert party. There is ½ mile of class II rapids to another RR bridge (4¾ mi) with a wavy class III rapid underneath. The large hydraulics found there can be skirted on the L side. One hundred yards below the RR bridge is a R turn with large rocks on the outside — many inexperienced canoeists have left their boats on these rocks.

The last 2½ miles to the iron bridge in Bartlett have been bulldozed for flood control purposes. The result for canoeists is shallow riffles between bouldery banks. There is, however, one class III rapid about ¾ mile before the Bartlett bridge. From above this rapid the paddler can only see swift, shallow rapids to a blind L turn. Most boaters should scout the passage between large rocks in the turn and the ledge-and-wave combinations below. The Saco then passes through shallow riffles to the iron bridge in Bartlett (7¼ mi), where there is parking and access on the L bank.

BM 784 — Lower Bartlett 3 miles
EAST BRANCH

This small stream is recommended only for closed boats. Under the right conditions it can be run down to the Saco River near Humphrey's Ledge in late April or early May. The rapids are continuous, and many are class IV. They should be carefully looked over, for precise and quick maneuvering is necessary. Fallen trees may be unusually hazardous because it is hard to get out of the river once you have put in.

Scouting can be done on the north bank of the river from a paved road that leaves NH-16A in Lower Bartlett. The suggested put-in is at the first wooden bridge above the highway near BM 784 on the USGS North Conway 15 sheet.

Bartlett — Center Conway 22½ miles

The part from Bartlett to North Conway is a popular white-water run of medium difficulty. The current is swift and intermittent class II rapids, some of which have heavy waves in high water. The riverbed is wide most of the way, so that there are fine views of the surrounding mountains. There are only a few houses along the banks.

The lower part is somewhat more settled, particularly around Conway; but there are more good rapids below.

The current of the Saco is strong enough to undercut its sand and gravel banks and to topple the trees growing on them. Sometimes the water is high enough to remove the debris, but frequently it is not. Therefore, low-lying tree trunks are an ever-present hazard, especially at the outside of the turns where the main part of the current flows under them. There are always a few such obstacles to quench the enthusiasm and dampen the finesse of inexperienced and inattentive boaters.

| 1976 | Bartlett — Center Conway | 22½ mi [36¼ km] |

Quickwater, Class I–III
High water: *recommended, April to early May*
Medium water: *scratchy, late May*
Forested, Rural, Town
    USGS: Crawford Notch 15, North Conway 15, Ossipee Lake 15

In the first 8¼ miles to Humphrey's Ledge, the current is swift with frequent class I and II rapids. **Caution!** Be alert for fallen trees that block the main current at the outside of turns. After about ½ mile the river divides. The old, open channel goes to the R, and a new, narrower one continues straight into the forest. The latter was scoured out during the flood of July 1973, and it is more easily blocked by fallen trees than is the old route. There is a more difficult class II rapid which begins about ¼ mile above the US-302 bridge (4½ mi).

There are more rapids below US-302, with a class II rapid in ½ mile just above the Rocky Branch which enters on the L. Beyond the RR bridge (6 mi) easier inter-mittent rapids continue to the Ellis River which enters on the L just before a RR embankment. In ¾ mile the West Side Road follows along the R bank beneath Humphrey's Ledge. After 2 miles there is a short class II drop in the middle of an "S" turn beside a house on the R bank. Shallow rips continue for the next 9½ miles past the North Conway bridge (11¾ mi) and a RR bridge (16 mi) to the mouth of the Swift River, which is within sight of the covered bridge in Conway.

There is an easy class II rapid above the covered bridge (19¾ mi) and another one below the NH-16 bridge. In the last 2 miles to the US-302 bridge in Center Conway (22½ mi), there are three class II–III pitches with heavy waves, especially in high water.

Center Conway — Hiram   43¼ miles

This is the Sandy Saco, where low water during the summer months exposes miles and miles of beaches. It is a flatwater river in a wide valley of farms and forests. It flows alternately along the edges of fields and through stands of pines and swamp maples. There are a few small towns, but none of them infringe upon the river.

The setting is so peaceful, the water so clean, that the Saco attracts people: hundreds and hundreds of them on a nice summer weekend. Large numbers of them camp along the way, and by late afternoon many of the sandy beaches have been claimed for the night. This kind of high density usage can easily have an impact upon the water quality if human wastes are not disposed of properly. The place for them is in a shallow pit dug in the organic layer on the banks away from the river where vegetation and good soil can compost them. Anything buried in the sand bars will soon be in the river, either through leaching or because of erosion.

The river is clearest in the 17½ miles from Center Conway to the confluence with the Old Saco. The current is stronger, the river generally shallower, the banks more open, and the sand bars more numerous. As you approach and pass the Old Saco entering from the north, you will notice that the banks are more heavily forested and the water is darker.

You may park cars at Saco Bound on US-302 between Center Conway and the Maine border, at Swan's Falls (fee), at Canal Bridge on ME-5, at Walker's Bridge on US-302, at the Brownfield bridge on ME-160, and at Saco Valley Garage in Hiram (fee). There is also a public access at the south end of Lovewell Pond that is reached via a road which leaves ME-5/113 southeast of Fryeburg and north of a railroad crossing.

A good map of this portion of the river may be obtained from Saco Bound for 50¢. If you build a fire in Maine outside the established campgrounds listed below, you should obtain a permit. In Fryeburg, one can be obtained at Osgood Brothers or at Solari's Store.

---

77 Center Conway — Hiram   43¼ mi [70 km]
Flatwater, Quickwater, Class II
Passable at all water levels
Forested, Rural

USGS:	North Conway 15, Ossipee Lake 15, Fryeburg, Brownfield, Hiram

Portage:	10 mi	R	**Swan's Falls** — 50 yds
Campsites:	4¼ mi	R	**Sit 'n Bull** — commercial $ car
	10 mi	R	**Swan's Falls** — AMC $ car
	14 mi	R	**Canal Bridge** (ME-5) — commercial $ car
	23½ mi	L	**Walker's Falls** — AMC $
	29½ mi	R	**Woodland Acres** — commercial $ car

Just below the US-302 bridge near Center Conway, the river flows between the abutments of the old covered bridge and soon there are some class II rips that are bony in low water. The remaining 9 miles to Swan's Falls are mostly quickwater. The main highway approaches the river next to Saco Bound (3¼ mi), then there is Weston Bridge (6¾ mi), and finally Swan's Falls where there is a dam which should be approached cautiously in high water. Portage on the R.

After Swan's Falls (10 mi) flatwater and quickwater continue. About a mile past Canal Bridge (14 mi) the river swings to the N and a stream enters on the R. The latter can be followed upstream a hundred yards or so to Bog Pond, a small and secluded body of water. The next landmark is the Old Saco (17½ mi) which enters on the L.

The **Old Course of the Saco**, as the name implies, used to be the channel of the river. Above the confluence the Saco today follows a canal dug in 1817 for flood control. The western end of the Old Saco is silted in, but the eastern portion of it still drains Kezar Lake. There are 9¼ miles of flatwater paddling, with one dam, from the lake to the main river. See also the USGS Center Lovell sheet.

From the Old Saco (17½ mi) flatwater continues for 6 miles past Walker's Bridge, US-302 (21 mi), and the outlet to Pleasant Pond (23¼ mi) to Walker's Falls (23½ mi) where the short, easy rapids become flooded out at high water. Pleasant Pond is very close to the river, and from it there are good views of the mountains.

Two miles below Walker's Falls the outlet from Lovewell Pond enters on the R. Then the Saco winds somewhat, passing to the W of Brownfield Bog, a major nesting area for native ducks. Below the ME-160 bridge (29½ mi) there are more meanders for the next 13¾ miles to Hiram (43¼ mi).

Hiram — Bonny Eagle Dam (Route 35)   25¼ miles

This section is mostly flatwater, but there is a good current except at the end. There are occasional rapids, and one of them, Limington Rips, ranges from a nice class II run in low water to a difficult class III pitch with heavy waves at high water levels. There are a few cottages along the river, but most of them are confined to the area around East Limington.

This portion of the river receives much less use than does the section preceeding it. The water is not as clear as it is near Fryeburg, but the scenery is comparable. The occasional rapids are a feature not found on the section from Center Conway to Hiram.

In the spring when water levels are generally high, a very nice 20¾-mile run can be made by starting at Kezar Falls and running the Ossipee River to the Saco near Cornish, and then continuing down the Saco to the NH-25 bridge in East Limington.

Hiram — Bonny Eagle Dam (Route 35) 25¼ mi [40¾ km]
Lake, **Flatwater**, Quickwater, Class I–II
Passable at all water levels: *1 dangerous rapid in high water*
Forested, Rural, Towns

USGS:	Hiram, Cornish, Sebago Lake 15, Buxton 15	

Portages: 2¾ mi L **Great Falls Dam** — ¼ mi
14¾ mi L **Steep Falls** — 50 yds
25½ mi R **Bonny Eagle Dam** — 70 yds

Campsites: 14¾ mi L **Steep Falls** (at portage)
15 mi R **Steep Falls** (R turn below old dam)
19½ mi **Limington Rips** (island at top)

From Hiram there is flatwater for 2¾ miles to Great Falls Dam. **Caution!** In high water, go L of an island after a sweeping L turn. Land on the L above the dam and portage along a trail to a tar road which leads down to the river. There is a piped spring below a chain link fence to the L of the powerhouse.

Two-thirds of a mile below Great Falls Dam there is a class I rapid at a short L turn. Flatwater continues past the mouth of the Ossipee River (5¾ mi) to the ME-5/117 bridge in Cornish (6¼ mi).

There are riffles just past the Cornish bridge. After 2¾ miles you reach Old Bald Rapid, a short class II pitch with large waves in high water. There are some more riffles in the remaining 5½ miles to Steep Falls, but for most of the distance the river is flat.

Steep Falls (14¾ mi) is a dangerous 7-foot drop which must be portaged. You are apt to come upon it suddenly, especially in the fast-moving current of high water. Be alert for the sound of falling water, a glimpse of a house on the L bank, or the sighting of a green girder bridge below the falls. When you notice any of them, get quickly to the L bank where there is a short portage. After the falls there is ¼ mile of rapids, class II in low water, but rougher in high water. They continue under the bridge and past the remains of a dam.

Below Steep Falls, riffles continue intermittently

for a mile, followed by almost 3 miles of slackwater to
Parkers Rips, a short class II rapid near a house on the R
where the river swings L. In ¾ mile you reach Limington
Rips, a ½-mile set of class II rapids in medium water, but
class III with heavy waves in high water. Go L of the island,
for the other channel begins with an unrunnable drop.
The hardest section of this rapid is near the end, below the
ME-25 bridge (19¾ mi). You can carry around this rapid
using a tar road on the R bank.

Just past Limington Rips the Little Ossipee River
enters on the R (20 mi). A deadwater continues for the
remaining 5¼ miles to Bonny Eagle Dam (25¼ mi) just
below the ME-35 bridge. Take out on the R bank near the
powerhouse. If you are continuing down the river, portage
beyond the building about 50 yards to a set of steps which
lead down past a wellhouse to the river.

Bonny Eagle Dam (Route 35) — Biddeford   19 miles

xxxx   Lake, Flatwater   30½ km
        Passable at all water levels
        Forested, Rural, Towns
            USGS: Buxton 15, *Kennebunk 15*, Biddeford 15, *Portland 15*
            Portages: 1½ mi L **dam at West Buxton**
                        6¾ mi R **dam at Bar Mills**
                        10 mi R **Skelton Dam**

The following write-up is not current. More than
half of this section consists of deadwaters behind a
succession of dams. Near the ME-4A/117 bridge (8 mi) at
Salmon Falls (flooded out), you enter the third deadwater.
As the river opens into the wide lake behind Skelton Dam
at Union Falls (10 mi), head SE.

A couple of miles after the ME-5 bridge (14½ mi),
the flatwater is broken by a short rapid. Below the Maine
Turnpike (18¾ mi) there is a convenient take-out on the R
at Rotary Park (19 mi). There are dams in Biddeford and
Saco, below which the river is tidal.

BEARCAMP RIVER   NH

The Bearcamp River flows eastward into Ossipee Lake,
draining a large portion of the valley between the Sandwich and Ossipee ranges. Since much of the drainage area
is mountainous, the run-off from rain and melting snow
takes place quicky. The upper section is an easy paddle
through meadowlands, the middle section provides some
fine whitewater in the early spring, and the last 9 miles are
usually passable whenever the river is free of ice.

The countryside is relatively unsettled, and there are occasional views of the Sandwich Range to the north and the Ossipee Mountains to the south.

Bearcamp Pond — Bennett Corners   2¾ miles

This is the most scenic portion of the river. For much of the distance, the river flows through meadows. Watch out for fallen trees.

---

74 Bearcamp Pond — Bennett Corners   2¾ mi [4½ km]
Quickwater
High water: *April*
Forested, Rural
    USGS: Mount Chocorua 15

Bearcamp Pond Road leaves NH-25 on the N side 1.6 miles E of the NH-25/113 junction at Bennett Corners. In less than a mile it crosses the river just below the pond.

The Bearcamp winds through meadows for 1¾ miles to Cold River which enters on the L and about doubles the flow. After another mile of meanders between tree-lined banks, you reach the NH-113 bridge at Bennett Corners (2¾ mi).

Bennett Corners — Whittier   3¾ miles

This is the popular whitewater section. It offers a good training trip for intermediate paddlers if the water is not too high. Most of the hard rapids are visible from the road, so you can judge the difficulty before you begin. An aggressive party which scouts the bad drops during the car shuttle can make the run in an hour, while a large and poorly organized group can easily take all day.

---

74 Bennett Corners — Whittier   3¾ mi [6 km]
Flatwater, **Class II–III**
High water: *April*
Rural, Towns
    USGS: Mount Chocorua 15
    Portage: 1¾ mi L **old dam at South Tamworth** (difficult)
                — 20 yds

Below the NH-113 bridge at Bennett Corners, there is ½ mile of smoothwater with a slow current that ends at a rocky rapid, 100 yards long and class II–III. A wood road on the L bank can be used as a portage if necessary. Soon there are two shorter, easier class II rapids, followed by more smoothwater to South Tamworth. The road comes near the river (1 mi), and anyone who has experienced difficulties thus far should consider taking out.

A long rapid begins behind the post office, and ends below the next bridge (1½ mi) with a difficult ledge, class III–IV. One popular route is to hug the R bank above the bridge and then move quickly L underneath it, either running the ledge on the L or stopping in the eddy just past the bridge. There is a wood road on the L bank for those wishing to portage.

Caution! Just around the next corner to the R is Bearcamp Gorge, a narrow class III–IV chute which consists of 30 yards of turbulence between low ledges. It should be scouted. A large pool below it may cease to exist when the remainder of the dam downstream washes out.

The dam at South Tamworth can be inspected by walking upstream from a log yard off NH-25. It consists of a number of concrete piers supporting old timbers, and it is a definite hazard to boaters. Portage on the L. Below the dam the rapids are continuous, the next difficult pitch being a series of ledges just above the next bridge (2½ mi). There are more easy rapids, followed by a sharp class III rapid containing a moderate hydraulic. Easy rapids continue past the NH-113 bridge in Whittier (3¾ mi). In another ½ mile, just past a cemetery, there is a good place to take-out.

Whittier — Ossipee Lake   10½ miles

Except at the beginning, this section is passable for most of the canoeing season. The bottom is sandy for many miles as the Bearcamp winds through woods and farmlands.

There are many cottages and a large campground alongside the river in the 3 miles from NH-25 to NH-16, but the rest of it is isolated and very attractive.

	Whittier — Ossipee Lake	10½ mi [17 km]
1976	**Flatwater**, Quickwater, Class I	
	Passable at most water levels	
	Forested, Rural, Settled	
	USGS: Mount Chocorua 15, Ossipee Lake 15	

Below the NH-113 bridge in Whittier, class II rapids continue for ½ mile, after which there is about a mile of occasional riffles which are shallow in low water. These may be avoided by starting 1.3 miles E of Whittier on NH-25 where the road comes close to the river. After that there are only a few shallow sections, all of them short. Pass under a covered bridge (4¼ mi), NH-25

(5¼ mi), and NH-16 (8¼ mi). Under the latter, on the R, is a convenient take-out point.

If you continue onto the lake (10½ mi), paddle S to some cottages or N to a marina at Westward Shores off Nickols Road.

LITTLE OSSIPEE RIVER   ME

The Little Ossipee is a fairly popular trip in southwestern Maine. It flows west from Balch Pond, a small lake on the Maine-New Hampshire border, to the Saco River just downstream from the ME-25 bridge at East Limington.

In high water it is an easy two-day trip of 28¼ miles from Davis Brook near North Shapleigh to East Limington just above the confluence with the Saco River. The hardest rapids normally run are at Newfield, and they are class II. Those at Hardscrabble Falls below ME-117 are so difficult that all but the last hundred yards are usually portaged. The section below Ledgemere Dam is usually passable through the summer.

Davis Brook — Route 5   11¼ miles

The remotest part of the river is that section above New-field. Much of the area was burned in 1947, and today it is covered with scrub growth, predominately gray birch. In medium water all the rapids are shallow, so high water is recommended.

Just east of Newfield, ME-11 crosses Chellis Brook. If the depth of the water over the cement brookbed under the bridge is between 1¼ and 1½ feet, the Little Ossipee is probably at medium level. In that case, the recommended start is at Chellis Brook, which joins the main river in 100 yards. If the water under the bridge is less than 8 inches, this section will be scratchy in many places.

Davis Brook — Route 5   11¼ mi [18¼ km]
Flatwater, **Quickwater**, Class I–II
High water: *recommended, early spring*
Medium water: *rapids bony, late April to mid-May*
Wild, Forested, Towns
    USGS: Newfield 15

ME-11 crosses the Little Ossipee at the Newfield-Shapleigh town line. Just S of this point, follow Mann Road E for 0.9 miles to the double culvert over Davis Brook.

Davis Brook is a small stream that flows into the Little Ossipee ¼ mile from Mann Road. Then, in the next 4¼ miles, the main river is a mixture of flatwater and short, easy class I–II rapids. The river flows through some small meadows, and there is at least one beaver dam.

Approaching Newfield, there is a class II drop over some ledges. Then, beginning just above the bridge (4¾ mi), there is ¼ mile of hard class II rapids which must be lined in medium water. Most of the remaining 6¼ miles to ME-5 at Ossipee Mills is quickwater with no significant rapids. About halfway down you pass between the two old abutments of Clark's Bridge.

Route 5 — Ledgemere Dam   5¾ miles

The flashboards on Ledgemere Dam may not be in place, with the result that the level of the lake may be down a few feet. Ledgemere Flowage, renamed Lake Arrowhead by real estate developers peddling house lots, will then have some sections of shoals and extensive mud flats with exposed stumps. In some places sandy beaches will be exposed. Portions of the lake are attractive; other parts are not. There are a few houses, but most of the shoreline remains undeveloped.

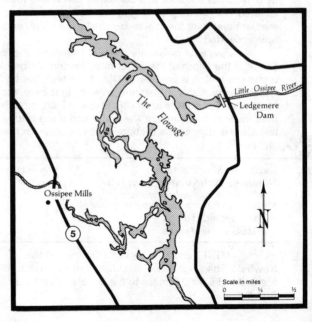

977 Route 5 — Ledgemere Dam   5¾ mi [9¼ km]
Lake
Forested
    USGS: Newfield 15, Buxton 15
    Portage: 5¾ mi R **Ledgemere Dam** — 100 yds

        The lake poses navigation problems. This map is
drawn from a topographic map which shows the normal
pool elevation, but the lake may not always be full. It may
be necessary to use it as a guide to the edge of the forest
surrounding the lake. If the water is low, you can detect a
current in some of the passages when there is no wind.

Ledgemere Dam — East Limington   **11¼ miles**
There is a lot of flatwater in this section and almost no
easily runnable rapids. The first of the two ledge drops,
Hardscrabble Falls, should be portaged, while the second
one is just after a logical take-out point near the end of
the river.
        The Little Ossipee is much larger below Ledge-
mere Flowage than it is above it. The banks are heavily
wooded all the way to East Limington, and near the end it
flows in a small, narrow valley with steep slopes close to
the riverbank.

977 Ledgemere Dam — East Limington   11¼ mi [18 km]
Flatwater, Quickwater, Class II
Passable at all water levels
Forested
    USGS: Buxton 15
    Portages: 4¼ mi R **Hardscrabble Falls** — ½ mi
               11¼ mi L **falls at East Limington** — 300 yds
    Campsite: 4¾ mi R **Hardscrabble Falls** (end of portage)

    Access at East Limington: The bridge above the
last portage is about a mile by road from the ME-25 bridge
over the Saco River. Heading E from the latter, take the
first L.
        The current is fast for a mile or so to a short
class I drop. Then it is slow past the ME-117 bridge
(1¾ mi) to the second bridge (4¼ mi) which is at the top
of Hardscrabble Falls. **Caution!** Stop on the R above
the bridge. The falls, which are ½ mile long, begin and
end with class II rapids, but the middle section consists of
a steep drop over a series of ledges that will not tempt
many canoeists. The portage follows a dirt road close to

the R bank, and it makes a sharp R turn after passing a field on the R.

From the end of Hardscrabble Falls (4¾ mi), the river is flat and winding for 6 miles to a short class II drop within sight of, and ½ mile above, the next bridge. **Caution!** This is the bridge at East Limington located just above the second dangerous pitch. Stop above this bridge (11¼ mi) on the L. The easiest take-out is just past it on the L, but you should look at the approach, particularly in high water.

If you are continuing the last ½ mile to the Saco, portage the falls at East Limington beginning along the road on the L. Another ¼ mile of flatwater brings you to the end of the Little Ossipee. Limington Rips is ¼ mile to the L, and Bonny Eagle Dam is 5¼ miles down the dead-water to the R.

OSSIPEE RIVER   NH, ME

The Ossipee River flows east 17½ miles from Lake Ossipee, across the Maine border, and into the Saco River near Cornish. It has a dependable flow in the spring, but by summer the water level is too low to run the lower section. It is primarily a whitewater river; the flatwater sections have little to recommend them.

Ossipee Lake — Kezar Falls   10¾ miles

Flatwater characterizes this section, although there is one very nice rapid just above the NH-153 bridge in Effingham Falls. There are several more short rapids before Kezar Falls, but for most of the distance the river is flat. There are vacation cottages along the banks near the beginning, and below East Freedom there are more cottages and houses, with a main highway close by on the left bank for much of the distance. Anyone seeking a paddle in remote surroundings will not find it here.

1976 | Ossipee Lake — Kezar Falls | 10¾ mi [17¼ km]

Flatwater, Class I–II
High and medium water: *spring*
Low water: *passable, some lining required at rapids*
Forested, Rural, Towns
    USGS: Ossipee Lake 15, Kezar Falls
    Portages: 10½ mi   **1st dam at Kezar Falls** (across island) — 30 yds
                10¾ mi R **2nd dam at Kezar Falls** — 30 yds

The dam at the outlet of Ossipee Lake is at the end of a side road 0.5 miles W of the junction of NH-25 and 153 in Effingham Falls. Put in below the gatehouse and run down the sluiceway to a pool of slackwater. Soon there begins ¼ mile of rapids that are class II or III depending on the water level. They are the hardest on the river, and they lead up to the NH-153 bridge (½ mi).

Then there are 1½ miles of flatwater past the NH-25 bridge (2 mi) to East Freedom, where ¼ mile of class II rapids leads under a bridge (4½ mi) to the Maine border. The remaining distance to Kezar Falls is mostly flatwater with two short class II rapids, one before and one after the ME-160 bridge in Porter (7¾ mi).

In Kezar Falls, go to the R of the island and take out at a small bridge (10½ mi). If you are continuing downstream, carry across the island to the foot of the main dam and continue ¼ mile through the town to the second dam (10¾ mi). Take out on the R, carry across the canal, and put in below the dam.

Kezar Falls — Saco River   6¾ miles

Below the second dam in Kezar Falls, the Ossipee River takes on a different character. It is a very scenic run past forests and farms almost all the way to the Saco River, with quickwater or rapids for the entire distance.

When the water level is up, the run from Kezar Falls to the ME-5/117 bridge over the Saco can be made in a little over an hour, but if you continue down the Saco for another 14 miles to the ME-25 bridge, you can make a long, scenic trip of mixed flatwater and rapids. Note, however, that Limington Rips, which begin just above the bridge, are very severe rapids in high water.

1976

Kezar Falls — Saco River   6¾ mi [11 km]
Quickwater, Class I–II
High water: *recommended, early spring*
Medium water: *late spring*
Forested, Rural
    USGS: Kezar Falls, Cornish

One-half mile E of the ME-25 bridge in Kezar Falls, turn N onto Garner Avenue and take the first R. Bear L at an old building to reach the dam, or turn R to reach the power station.

Below the dam there are nice class I and II rapids for 1 mile to Which Way Rips, where the river abruptly divides around an island. Go L. Quickwater and class I rapids continue to the first bridge (3½ mi), with more quickwater to the second (5½ mi). Below the second bridge and past a few cottages, there are some easy class II rapids that lead almost to the Saco River (6¾ mi) only ½ mile above the ME-5/117 bridge E of Cornish (7¼ mi).

PINE RIVER   NH

The Pine River is a small stream of moderate length which flows into Ossipee Lake from the south. Although it is crossed by two highways and three side roads, only short portions of them follow its secluded banks. For most of its length it flows either in narrow valleys, alder swamps, or wide meadows. Few streams in New Hampshire offer the river traveller such clean water and unspoiled scenery.

The river is narrow and occasionally choked with alders. When it flows through woodlands, it can be easily blocked by fallen trees. For years there were many such obstacles which made passage down the river difficult and frustrating. However, in the fall of 1976, all the obstructions except those exposed at low water were removed with the aid of a chain saw. Nonetheless, you should allow more time to run this river than experience on others might lead you to believe you will need.

Because of the gentle gradient and gravel bottom, parts of the Pine River provide year-round canoeing, and even the steepest sections are passable in medium water. Each fall the Water Resources Board (603-271-1110) draws down the level of Pine River Pond, and beginning usually in mid-October there is enough water in the whole river for one and a half weeks or more.

Pine River Pond — Granite Road   5 miles

The Pine River begins as a small stream confined between two low, glacial ridges. There are many places where alders choke the stream, and in other sections low limbs and overhanging trees are hazardous in the fast-moving current of high water. In less than medium water, some walking down will be required.

If the stream looks passable in the first few yards, there is sufficient water for the entire trip to Ossipee Lake. In the fall when the level of Pine River Pond is being drawn down, the effect will be less noticeable below Granite Road.

1977

Pine River Pond — Granite Road   5 mi [8 km]
Quickwater, Class II
High water: *April*
Medium water: *recommended, May and mid-fall*
Dam-controlled: *annual fall drawdown*
Forested
    USGS: Wolfboro 15

In Wakefield a road E from NH-16 near the Ossipee-Wakefield town line leads in about a mile to the Pine River just below the pond. For about a mile it flows through woods before it enters an alder swamp where there are several beaver dams. Then the current picks up again, and soon it flows past a gravel pit where there is a bridge. Just after a pumping station a short portage may be necessary where the river passes under a road in three culverts. Beyond a short distance is NH-16 (3 mi), near a RR crossing and the entrance to the gravel pit.

The section between the two NH-16 bridges begins with quickwater through some woods. Then the current slackens where the river is backed up by beaver dams in an alder swamp, but it picks up in the woods beyond.

From the second NH-16 bridge there is a good current as the river flows through another alder swamp and over some beaver dams. It flows through attractive woods for a short distance above the Granite Road bridge (5 mi).

Granite Road — Ossipee Lake   15 miles

Halfway between Granite Road and Elm Street there is a 2-mile section of quickwater where the river flows through a very attractive, wooded valley. Large pines and hemlocks grow along the banks between ridges which rise steeply from the flat bottomlands.

Below the Elm Street bridge the river is flat as it wanders through a wide valley of conifers and swamp maples. Occasionally there are places where people have camped in the past. From the mouth of the river at the south end of Ossipee Lake, there is a nice view of the Sandwich Range and the Moats.

1978 Granite Road — Ossipee Lake   15 mi [24 km]
Flatwater, Quickwater
High and medium water: *April, May and mid-fall*
Passable at most water levels: *below Elm Street*
Dam-controlled: *annual fall draw-down of Pine River Pond*
Wild, Forested
   USGS: Wolfboro 15, Ossipee Lake 15

Granite Road leads E from NH-16 at a cross-roads about 1½ miles S of the junction of NH-16/28 in Ossipee. In the first 3 miles the river wanders through an alder swamp where the flatwater is interrupted by an occasional beaver dam. Then there are 2 miles of quickwater, after which the river meanders through an open meadow where there are views of Green Mountain to the NE.

The river enters the woods again about ½ mile above the Elm Street bridge (8 mi). For the rest of the way the current is weaker. The river passes under NH-25 (14 mi), and a mile beyond it empties into the lake (15 mi).

A road from NH-25 a short distance E of NH-16 leads past the Pine River and along the SW shore of Ossipee Lake.

SWIFT RIVER   NH

The beautiful Swift River rises in the west end of Albany Intervale and flows eastward to meet the Saco River in Conway. Most of the river can be paddled, and there are many challenging rapids to be negotiated. From Rocky Gorge to Darby Field, the Swift is suitable only for covered boats, while elsewhere an open boat could find either pleasant flatwater or intermediate rapids.

Because of the large, high-altitude drainage, the Swift River tends to hold water fairly well — it is normally runnable from mid-April to the end of May. The Kancamagus Highway runs through the Swift River Valley, providing convenient access at many points.

Passaconaway Campground — Rocky Gorge 7 miles
The first half of this run is a pleasant quickwater paddle on a small, crystal-clear stream. The second half contains flatwater, but there is no easy take-out before the beginning of the rapids.

A gauge is located on the right, downstream abutment of the Bear Notch Road bridge. At a reading of 2.5 on this gauge the river is passable; 3.5 is medium water.

---

76 Passaconaway Campground — Rocky Gorge 7 mi [11¼ km]
Flatwater, Quickwater, Class III
High to medium water: *mid-April thru May*
Forested
    USGS: Mount Chocorua 15, Crawford Notch 15
    Portage: 7 mi R **Rocky Gorge** — 200 yds

A put-in can be made at the USFS Passaconaway Campground. Here the river is fast-flowing but smooth, with overhanging trees to be avoided. It is 3 miles to the Bear Notch Road bridge where the gauge is located. *This first paragraph is not current.*

From the Bear Notch Road bridge (3 mi) there are 2 miles of flatwater away from the Kancamagus Highway. Then the rapids begin abruptly and reach class III in difficulty. The toughest rapid is a double ledge in a R turn, where there are possible passages on both L and R. From here on, the highway can frequently be seen on the R bank.

Rocky Gorge, or Upper Falls, is ½ mile below the ledge drop, and boaters should be careful to pull out above it. Upper Falls is a vertical, 10-foot falls over ledges into a box canyon. The parking area on the R makes a convenient take-out.

Rocky Gorge — Lower Falls   **2½ miles**

This stretch is commonly referred to as the "Upper Swift." It contains continuous, difficult rapids to challenge paddlers seeking whitewater sport. Expert open boaters will be able to navigate this stretch, but it is usually undertaken only by closed boats.

---

977 Rocky Gorge — Lower Falls   2½ mi [4 km]
Class III–IV
High to medium water: *mid-April to mid-May*
Forested
    USGS: Crawford Notch 15, North Conway 15, Ossipee Lake 15
    Portage: 2½ mi R **Lower Falls** — 200 yds

A put-in is possible over a smooth ledge right by the wood bridge at Rocky Gorge (also known as Upper Falls). Class III rapids begin just below the gorge and continue for about a mile. Then there are a couple of more difficult rapids — first through some large boulders in a L bend and then two ledges after a R turn. These two ledges, sometimes known as the "Washboard," are right next to the Kancamagus Highway. Rapids continue at a class III pace, reaching class IV in a bouldery stretch just above Lower Falls.

Boaters should take out when they spot the recreation buildings on the R shore. Lower Falls is another 10-foot falls over ledges, though more gradual than Upper Falls. It has occasionally been run on the far L as a stunt, but it should generally be portaged. The picnic and parking areas enable boaters to take out or to put in for the stretch below.

Lower Falls — Darby Field   6 miles

This section of the Swift is one of the most difficult and continuous runs in all of New England. The stretch from the Gorge, 2 miles below Lower Falls, is often referred to as the "Lower Swift." It provides excellent sport for skilled boaters, but it is not a good run for inexperienced paddlers. When the water is up, a damaged boat and a long, unpleasant, and dangerous swim could result from any tip-over.

At the bottom of the Gorge, there is a hand-painted gauge on a rock on the R. A water level of 1.5 on this gauge is a medium, runnable level for this section.

1977   Lower Falls — Darby Field   6 mi [9¾ km]
         Class IV
         High to medium water: *mid-April thru May*
         Forested
             USGS: Ossipee Lake 15

The pool below Lower Falls makes a good put-in for this run. However, there is little chance for warm-up as the rapid below the falls is a rocky, turbulent class IV. Easier rapids, class III, follow to the covered bridge on Dugway Road (½ mi). Another 1½ miles of shallow class III rapids follow; this section can be very scratchy at medium water.

The next major rapids are at the Gorge (2 mi), where the river drops very steeply with the road high on the R bank. In order to recognize the Gorge, boaters should look for three cottages on the L bank and pull out above the next L turn in order to scout (best done from the road on the R). The sharp L turn and R turn dump the paddler into a short pool right above the Gorge. There are a variety of routes through the Gorge at different water levels, and the paddler who is new to the Swift should pick one from the shore, as the huge rocks in the Gorge make channel-choosing difficult.

Rapids continue below the Gorge, with a class IV drop ¼ mile further along. More class III–IV rapids continue to a L turn just above the Staircase (2¾ mi), where the boater should pull out and scout on the L. The Staircase is a short, steep, 50-yard drop over large boulders. It is class IV at medium levels, and class V in high water. For those who do not wish to run these rapids, it is possible to carry or line down to the L of a rock island on the L.

Below the Staircase (2¾ mi) difficult rapids continue for another ½ mile to the site of an annual slalom race (for details, contact Saco Bound, Box 113, Center Conway, NH 03813). The race course is set up in a class IV section were the Swift drops through and around many large boulders. More rapids follow, with class IV rapids and slightly easier rapids very close together. The last of the difficult rapids is at a spot where the Swift approaches the road, splits around a rock that is the size of a small house, and drops 2 feet into a hole (5½ mi). This last hole is formed by a V-shaped ledge whose apex extends upstream. This is the largest, widest hydraulic on the river, and it can easily hold a boat even at medium water.

The last ½ mile to the Darby Field Inn sign is class III with shallow rapids. The sign is painted differently every year; boaters can also recognize the spot by the river's sharp turn away from the road and a side road leaving the Kancamagus Highway. Take out on the R.

Darby Field — Conway   2¾ miles

This section of the Swift River is away from roads for much of the run. There is more hazard from fallen trees here than in the more difficult rapids above.

1977   Darby Field — Conway   2¾ mi [4½ km]
           Quickwater, Class II–III
           High to medium water: *mid-April thru May*
           Forested
               USGS: Ossipee Lake 15

From a put-in near the Darby Field sign, there are continuous rapids for about ¾ mile. These rapids are scratchy class III with many sharp turns required. The rapids moderate to class II and, later, to snaky quickwater. The river continues its twisting until a bridge on West Side Road and a covered bridge are reached, at which point there is another class II–III rapid (2½ mi). The Swift River enters the Saco River at a covered bridge over the latter in Conway, where there is another rapid.

Take out at the NH-16 bridge just below the covered bridge over the Saco (2¾ mi). Cars can reach the river by following a dirt road behind the shopping center.

WEST BRANCH   NH

The West Branch, also called the Silver River (although it does not appear so-named on maps) flows from Silver Lake in Madison to the north end of Ossipee Lake. It provides a secluded run of two to three hours in high water. It has a good flow in the spring and also in the fall when the level of Silver Lake is drawn down. Note, however, that this lake is not controlled by the Water Resources Board.

The first 2½ miles to Ossipee Lake Road are the most pleasant because the current is faster and the banks of the river are more open. The lower portion is entirely wooded, and there are a few trees blocking the stream.

Silver Lake — Ossipee Lake   6 miles

1976 **Flatwater, Quickwater**   9¾ km
High water: *recommended, spring and mid-fall*
Medium water: *some wading required, late spring and early summer*
Dam-controlled: *annual fall draw-down of Silver Lake*
Forested
  USGS: Ossipee Lake 15

The dam on Silver Lake is next to Silver Lake Road, which leaves NH-41 on the R just over 2 miles N of West Ossipee. A marina at Westward Shores on Ossipee Lake (W of the mouth of the river) can be reached by turning E off NH-16 onto Nichols Road 2 miles S of West Ossipee.

The quickwater at the beginning slackens somewhat as the stream enters a broad, open valley. Soon you reach the first of a score of beaver dams that dot the entire length of the river. Many of them can be run in high water. The banks become wooded again as you pass a sawmill on the R shortly before the Ossipee Lake Road bridge (2½ mi). In the remaining 3½ miles the river winds more, and there are a few obstructions.

Appendix

American Whitewater Safety Code

The following code was prepared by the American Whitewater Affiliation, Box 1584, San Bruno, CA 94066. Part V, "International Scale of River Difficulty," appears in the Introduction on page 16.

I. **PERSONAL PREPAREDNESS AND RESPONSIBILITY**

1. **Be a Competent Swimmer** with ability to handle yourself underwater.

2. **WEAR a Lifejacket.**

3. **Keep Your Craft Under Control.** Control must be good enough at all times to stop or reach shore before you reach any danger. Do not enter a rapid unless you are reasonably sure you can safely navigate it or swim the entire rapid in event of capsize.

4. **BE AWARE OF RIVER HAZARDS AND AVOID THEM. Following are the most frequent KILLERS.**

    A. **HIGH WATER.** The river's power and danger, and the difficulty of rescue increase tremendously as the flow rate increases. It is often misleading to judge river level at the put-in. Look at a narrow, critical passage. Could a *sudden* rise from sun on a snow pack, rain, or a dam release occur on your trip?

    B. **COLD.** Cold quickly robs one's strength, along with one's will and ability to save oneself. Dress to protect yourself from cold water and weather extremes. When the water temperature is less than 50 degrees F, a diver's wetsuit is essential for safety in event of an upset. Next best is wool clothing under a windproof outer garment such as a splash-proof nylon shell; in this case one should also carry matches and a complete change of clothes in a waterproof package. If, after prolonged exposure, a person experiences uncontrollable shaking or has difficulty talking and moving, he must be warmed immediately by whatever means available.

C. **STRAINERS**: Brush, fallen trees, bridge pilings, or anything else which allows river current to sweep through but pins boat and boater against the obstacle. The water pressure on anything trapped this way is overwhelming, and there may be little or no whitewater to warn of danger.

D. **WEIRS, REVERSALS, AND SOUSE HOLES**. The water drops over an obstacle, then curls back on itself in a stationary wave, as is often seen at weirs and dams. The surface water is actually going UPSTREAM, and this action will trap any floating object between the drop and the wave. Once trapped, a swimmer's only hope is to dive below the surface where current is flowing downstream, or try to swim out the end of the wave.

5. **Boating Alone** is not recommended. The preferred minimum is three craft.

6. **Have a Frank Knowledge of Your Boating Ability.** Don't attempt waters beyond this ability. Learn paddling skills and teamwork, if in a multiple-manned craft, to match the river you plan to boat.

7. **Be in Good Physical Condition** consistent with the difficulties that may be expected.

8. **Be Practiced in Escape** from an overturned craft, in self rescue, in rescue, and in **Artificial Respiration.** Know first aid.

9. **The Eskimo Roll** should be mastered by kayakers and canoers planning to run large rivers and/or rivers with continuous rapids where a swimmer would have trouble reaching shore.

10. **Wear a Crash Helmet** where an upset is likely. This is essential in a kayak or covered canoe.

11. **Be Suitably Equipped.** Wear shoes that will protect your feet during a bad swim or a walk for help, yet will not interfere with swimming (tennis shoes recommended). Carry a knife and waterproof matches. If you need eyeglasses, tie them on and carry a spare pair. Do not wear bulky clothing that will interfere with your swimming when water-logged.

II. BOAT AND EQUIPMENT PREPAREDNESS

1. **Test New and Unfamiliar Equipment** before relying on it for difficult runs.

2. **Be Sure Craft is in Good Repair** before starting a trip. Eliminate sharp projections that could cause injury during a swim.

3. Inflatable crafts should have **Multiple Air Chambers** and should be test inflated before starting a trip.

4. **Have Strong, Adequately Sized Paddles or Oars** for controlling the craft and carry sufficient spares for the length of the trip.

5. **Install Flotation Devices** in non-inflatable craft, securely fixed, and designed to displace as much water from the craft as possible.

6. **Be Certain There is Absolutely Nothing to Cause Entanglement** when coming free from an upset craft; i.e., a spray skirt that won't release or tangles around legs; life jacket buckles, or clothing that might snag; canoe seats that lock on shoe heels; foot braces that fail or allow feet to jam under them; flexible decks that collapse on boater's legs when a kayak is trapped by water pressure; baggage that dangles in an upset; loose rope in the craft, or badly secured bow/stern lines.

7. **Provide Ropes to Allow You to Hold Onto Your Craft** in case of upset, and so that it may be rescued. Following are the recommended methods:

   A. **Kayaks and Covered Canoes** should have 6 inch diameter grab loops of ¼ inch rope attached to bow and stern. A stern painter 7 or 8 feet long is optional and may be used if properly secured to prevent entanglement.

   B. **Open Canoes** should have bow and stern lines (painters) securely attached consisting of 8 to 10 feet of ¼ or ⅜ inch rope. These lines must be *secured* in a way that they will not come loose accidentally and entangle the boaters during a swim, yet they must be ready for immediate use during an emergency. Attached balls, floats, and knots are *not* recommended.

   C. **Rafts and Dories** should have taut perimeter grab lines threaded through the loops usually provided.

8. **Respect Rules for Craft Capacity** and know how these capacities should be reduced for whitewater use. (Life raft ratings must generally be halved.)

9. **Carry Appropriate Repair Materials:** tape (heating duct tape) for short trips, complete repair kit for wilderness trips.

10. **Car Top Racks Must Be Strong** and positively attached to the vehicle, and each boat must be tied to each rack. In addition, each end of each boat should be tied to car bumper. Suction cup racks are poor. The entire arrangement should be able to withstand all but the most violent vehicle accident.

III. LEADER'S PREPAREDNESS AND RESPONSIBILITY

1. **River Conditions.** Have a reasonable knowledge of the difficult parts of the run, or if an exploratory trip, examine maps to estimate the feasibility of the run. Be aware of possible rapid changes in river level, and how these changes can affect the difficulty of the run. If important, determine approximate flow rate or level. If trip involves important tidal currents, secure tide information.

2. **Participants.** Inform participants of expected river conditions and determine if the prospective boaters are qualified for the trip. All decisions should be based on group safety and comfort. Difficult decisions on the participation of marginal boaters must be based on total group strength.

3. **Equipment.** Plan so that all necessary group equipment is present on the trip: 50 to 100 foot throwing rope, first aid kit with fresh and adequate supplies, extra paddles, repair materials, and survival equipment if appropriate. Check equipment as necessary at the put-in, especially: life jackets, boat flotation, and any items that could prevent complete escape from the boat in case of an upset.

4. **Organization.** Remind each member of individual responsibility in keeping group compact and intact between leader and sweep (capable rear boater). If group is too large, divide into smaller groups, each of appropriate boating strength, and designate group leaders and sweeps.

5. **Float Plan.** If trip is into a wilderness area, or for an extended period, your plans should be filed with appropriate authorities, or left with someone who will contact them after a certain time. Establishment of checkpoints along the way at which civilization could be contacted if necessary should be considered. Knowing location of possible help could speed rescue in any case.

IV. IN CASE OF UPSET

1. **Evacuate Your Boat Immediately** if there is imminent danger of being trapped against logs, brush, or any other form of strainer.

2. **Recover With an Eskimo Roll if Possible.**

3. **If You Swim, Hold Onto Your Craft.** It has much flotation and is easy for rescuers to spot. Get to the upstream end so craft cannot crush you against obstacles.

4. **Release Your Craft if This Improves Your Safety.** If rescue is not imminent and water is numbing cold, or if worse rapids follow, then strike out for the nearest shore.

5. **Extend Your Feet Downstream** when swimming rapids to fend against rocks. **Look Ahead.** Avoid possible entrapment situations: rock wedges, fissures, strainers, brush, logs, weirs, reversals, and souse holes. Watch for eddies and slackwater so that you can be ready to use these when you approach. Use every opportunity to work your way toward shore.

6. If others spill, **Go After the Boaters.** Rescue boats and equipment only if this can be done safely.

Bibliography

Canoeing on the Connecticut River, Vermont State Division of Recreation, Montpelier, VT 05640, 1964

Charles River Canoe Guide, Charles River Watershed Association, 2391 Commonwealth Avenue, Auburndale, MA 02166, 1973

Connecticut River Guide, Connecticut River Watershed Council, 125 Combs Road, Easthampton, MA 01027, 1974

Farmington River and Watershed Guide, Farmington River Watershed Association, 195 West Main Street, Avon, CT 06001, 1974

Ray Gabler, *New England Whitewater River Guide,* Tobey Publishing Company, New Canaan, CT 06840, 1975 (detailed descriptions of selected rivers)

Walter Hard, *The Connecticut,* Holt, Rinehart, and Winston, 1947 (history)

Ralph Nading Hill, *The Winooski,* Holt, Rinehart, and Winston, 1949 (history)

Raymond P. Holden, *The Merrimack,* Holt, Rinehart, and Winston, 1958 (history)

Maps of Saco River Watershed, Saco Bound Canoe and Kayak, Box 113, Center Conway, NH 03813, 1974

New Hampshire Atlas and Gazetteer, David DeLorme and Company, Yarmouth, ME 04096 (detailed highway maps of New Hampshire; Maine edition also available)

Laurence Eaton Richardson, *Concord River,* Barre Publishers, Barre, MA 01005, 1964 (history)

Roioli F. Schweiker, *Canoe Camping, Vermont and New Hampshire Rivers,* New Hampshire Publishing Company, Somersworth, NH 03878, 1977 (guide to selected rivers)

Viola Sheehan, *The Saco River: A History and Canoeing Guide,* Saco River Corridor Association, Saco, ME 04072, 1976

Chard Powers Smith, *The Housatonic,* Holt Rinehart, and Winston, 1946 (history)

Arthur Bernon Tourtellot, *The Charles,* Holt, Rinehart and Winston, 1941 (history)

Wampanoag Commemorative Canoe Passage, Plymouth County Development Council, Box 1620, Pembroke, MA 02359, 1976 (brief guide)

Index

Agawam River   211

Ammonoosuc River   85

Ashuelot River   88

Ashuelot River, South
 Branch   92

Assabet Brook   260

Assabet River   258

Baker River   262

Bantam River   179

Barton River   32

Batten Kill   68

Bearcamp River   340

Beaver Brook   263

Black River, *Memphremagog
 Watershed*   33

Black River, *Upper Connecticut
 Watershed*   94

Blackledge River   159

Blackstone River   212

Blackwater River   265

Brookfield River   155

Canoe rentals   23

Charles River, *Central Coastal
 Watersheds*   235

Charles River, *Southeastern
 Watersheds*   223

Chicopee River   137

Chipuxet River   214

Clarendon River   62

Clyde River   34

Cocheco River   313

Cockermouth River   268

Coginchaug River   138

Cohas Brook   268

Cohasset Tidal Rips   214

Cold River, *Upper Connecticut
 Watershed*   96

Concord River   299

Connecticut River, *Lower
 Connecticut Watershed*   132

Connecticut River, *Upper
 Connecticut Watershed*   76

Contoocook River   269

Copicut River   215

Crooked River   245

Davis Brook   343

Dead Creek   40

Deerfield River   139

Deerfield River, North
 Branch   138

Deerfield River, Northwest
 Branch   139

Dog River   41

Drinkwater River   220

East River, *South Coastal
 Watersheds*   189

Eight Mile River   141

Exeter River   314

Fall River, *Southeastern
 Watersheds*   228

Falls River, *Lower Connecticut
 Watershed*   142

Farmington River   142

Five Mile River   193

French River   194

Gale River   97

Gale River, Ham Branch   99

Great Works River   318

Green River, *Housatonic River
 Watershed*   180

Green River, *Lower Connecticut
 Watershed*   149

Halls Stream   99

Hammonasset River   190

Hockomock River   215

Hoosic River   70

Hop River   195

Housatonic River   177

Huntington River   42

Indian Stream   101

Indian Head River 220
Ipswich River 242
Isinglass River 319
Israel River 102
Jeremy River 160
Konkapot River 181
Lamoille River 43
Lamprey River 320
Lemon Fair River 48
Lewis Creek 49
Little River, *Merrimack Watershed* 274
Little River, *Piscataqua Watershed* 323
Little Ossipee River 343
Little Sugar River 103
Little Suncook River 275
Mad River, *Champlain Watershed* 50
Mad River, *Merrimack Watershed* 275
Mascoma River 103
Matfield River 225
Mattapoisett River 217
Merrimack River 254
Metawee River 51
Mill River, *Central Coastal Watersheds* 237
Mill River, *Champlain Watershed* 51
Millers River 150
Missisquoi River 52
Moose River 107
Moosup River 196
Mount Hope River 197
Mousam River 244
Mystic River 241
Nash Stream 108
Nashua River 277
Natchaug River 198
Naugatuck River 182
Nemasket River 219
Neponset River 234
New Haven River 55
Newfound River 279
Nissitissit River 280

North River, *Lower Connecticut Watershed* 153
North River, *Piscataqua Watershed* 324
North River, *Southeastern Watersheds* 220
Norwalk River 189
Nulhegan River 108
Ompompanoosuc River 109
Ossipee River 346
Ottauquechee River 109
Otter Brook, *Upper Connecticut Watershed* 111
Otter Creek, *Champlain Watershed* 57
Otter River, *Lower Connecticut Watershed* 154
Parker River 243
Passumpsic River 113
Pawcatuck River 222
Pemigewasset River 280
Pemigewasset River, East Branch 281
Phillips Brook 114
Pine River 348
Piscassic River 325
Piscataqua River 313
Piscataquog River, North Branch 287
Piscataquog River, South Branch 288
Poor Meadow Brook 225
Powwow River 290
Poultney River 60
Quaboag River 154
Queens River 222
Quinebaug River 199
River Classification 16
Saco River 333
Safety code 355
Salmon Brook, *Merrimack Watershed* 290
Salmon River, *Lower Connecticut Watershed* 158
Salmon Falls River 326
Sandy Brook 162
Satucket River 225

Saugatuck River   189
Saxtons River   114
Seven Mile River   155
Shawsheen River   291
Shepaug River   182
Shetucket River   203
Single Island River   215
Smith River   292
Soucook River   295
Souhegan River   296
South Meadow Brook   228
Stony Brook   298
Stop River   237
Sudbury River   299
Sugar River   115
Suggested River Trips   26
Suncook River   304
Susquetonscut Brook   204
Swift River, *Lower Connecticut Watershed*   163
Swift River, *Saco Watershed*   350
Taunton River   226
Tenmile River   184
Thames River   193
Three Mile River   227
Tinmouth Channel   62
Town River   215
Tully River   164
United States Geological Survey   15
Upper Ammonoosuc River   116
Usquepaug River   222
Wading River   227

Waits River   117
Walloomsac River   71
Wampanoag Commemorative Canoe Passage   210
Wardsboro Brook   118
Ware River   165
Warner River   306
Water Resources Board (NH)   20
Wells River   119
West Branch, *Saco Watershed*   354
West River, *Upper Connecticut Watershed*   120
Westfield River   172
Westfield River, Middle Branch   171
Westfield River, North Branch   168
Westfield River, West Branch   171
Weweantic River   228
White River   121
White River, First Branch   124
White River, Second Branch   124
White River, Third Branch   125
Williams River   125
Willimantic River   204
Winhall River   127
Winnipesaukee River   307
Winooski River   62
Wood River   228
Yantic River   205